WINES OF THE RHÔNE

WINES OF THE
RHÔNE

MATT WALLS

infiniteideas

Matt Walls is a freelance wine writer and consultant based in London and Avignon. He is a contributing editor at *Decanter* and writes regular articles for magazines and websites such as *Foodism*, *Club Oenologique* and timatkin.com. He won the Best Newcomer award at the 2013 Fortnum & Mason Food and Drink Awards for *Drink Me*, his first book on wine, which has sold over 10,000 copies. He publishes a popular wine blog, www.mattwalls.co.uk, for which he won International Wine & Spirit Competition Blogger of the Year in 2015. When not writing,   ‘ he advises restaurants on wine lists, hosts tastings, judges food and wine competitions and develops wine apps. Matt is interested in all areas of wine, but specializes in the Rhône. He is Regional Chair for the Rhône at the Decanter World Wine Awards.

First published in 2021 by
Infinite Ideas Limited
www.infideas.com

A CIP catalogue record for this book is available from the British Library

ISBN 978–1–9996193–2–9

Maps: Darren Lingard

Printed in Great Britain

CONTENTS

Preface   ix

Acknowledgements   xi

Part 1: Background   1

1. A sense of place   3
2. Winemaking in the Rhône   15
3. Grape varieties   27
4. The appellation system   49

Part 2: The Southern Rhône   67

5. Around Avignon   69
6. The Ventabren massif   101
7. Dentelles terroir   119
8. Ventoux and Luberon   147
9. The Visan Valréas hills   157
10. Mountain fringes   171
11. Massif d'Uchaux and surrounding terraces   183
12. Upper west bank   199
13. Lower west bank   221
14. The Diois   241

Part 3: The Northern Rhône   249

15. Around Ampuis   251

16. Around Tain l'Hermitage   285

Appendix I: Ageing wines   335

Appendix II: The mysteries of Rayas by Simon Loftus   351

Glossary   355

Bibliography   357

Index   359

PREFACE

This book was born during turbulent times: the tortured machinations of Brexit on one side of the Channel, furious *gilets jaunes* on the other. How reassuring, I thought it would be, to immerse myself for a while in the timelessness of wine. But since I first put pen to paper (or finger to keyboard) two years ago so much has changed that I have needed to update many details and have come to realize just how quickly the wine scene evolves in the Rhône.

Most change is caused by the decisions and actions of individuals – a novel viticultural approach, a fresh philosophy, vineyards bought and sold. And when a new generation takes over a family estate, the wines are no longer the same. But it's no longer just men and women creating change; that fundamental element of terroir, climate, is also shifting.

There are some elements of a place, however, that remain the same, so I hope this book retains its usefulness for a little while. That was my aim: to write a book on the Rhône that is, above all, useful. But with so much information now freely available online, what can a book such as this possibly offer? Several things, I think. The internet is unbeatable for dispensing information on a given subject, but where it can fall down is comparison, context and a steady point of view from an independent outsider. So on top of supplying some background on the terroir of each appellation – why the wines taste as they do – I've tried to describe what to expect in the glass. Not just what a typical Côte-Rôtie tastes like, but how it compares to a Hermitage and a Cornas. And how the Côte-Rôties of Yves Gangloff compare to those of Stéphane Ogier. With more than 200 featured domaines getting their own entry (and more than twice as many recommendations) there isn't room to offer exhaustive information, but I do give a steer as to style and quality. The profiles serve as jumping-off points for further research and visits. Lists of recommended producers could never be comprehensive however, and no shortcomings are implied by omission.

During my travels I took many photos of the people and places that make the region unique. I have been able to include some of them in this book. You can see more on my website, www.mattwalls.co.uk: just search by appellation.

The book is organized by appellation, or more accurately by place, with each chapter covering one or more linked regions. For example, you will find a chapter entitled 'Massif d'Uchaux and surrounding terraces', not 'AOC Côtes-du-Rhône Villages Massif d'Uchaux'. Since people are most commonly presented with the wines of the Rhône by appellation this seemed the most logical approach if I wanted this work to be as easy to follow as possible. Some aspects of the appellation hierarchy are helpful, but we should not consider it immutable. And one truism throughout the world of wine is that when it comes to quality, there is no more reliable indicator than its producer.

I hope this guide helps to open up the Rhône – particularly the gallimaufry of the Southern Rhône – for those less familiar with it. The various types of appellation, their number, and the sheer scale of the terrain in the south can be off-putting, so I've divided it into ten zones, bite-sized chunks, each with its own personality. After all, I know how much there is to be gained from venturing further afield from the big names of Châteauneuf-du-Pape, Gigondas and Vacqueyras.

I've made space for all appellations, not just the big or celebrated ones: it can be difficult to find information elsewhere on the smallest ones, and small or rare doesn't mean insignificant. Some may be slight in stature now, but let's not forget that not so long ago Condrieu only amounted to 8 hectares. As I say, things change; the story of the Rhône is still being written.

ACKNOWLEDGEMENTS

Having the chance to deepen my understanding of the Rhône and share that knowledge is an incredible opportunity and a privilege. I would not be writing at all if it wasn't for the early encouragement and opportunities provided by Tim Atkin MW, Adam Lechmere, Justin Liddle, Chris Losh, Richard Siddle, Amy Wislocki and Guy Woodward – thanks for giving me a leg-up.

Every year the team at Inter Rhône provides invaluable support with organizing visits and tastings; I'm hugely appreciative of their responsiveness and professionalism. The Fédération des Syndicats de Producteurs de Châteauneuf-du-Pape is also incredibly helpful. Thanks as well to the Syndicat de Gigondas, the Syndicat de Vacqueyras, and indeed all the other *syndicats* around the Rhône which have assisted me with my research, as well as Intervins Sud-Est.

When people ask me what it is about the Rhône that I love so much, there's no need to reflect – it's the people. There are countless growers and winemakers who open their doors and cellars to me, some on a yearly basis, and I want to say thanks to all of them. Some names that spring to mind immediately are Denis and Jean-Etienne Alary, Xavier Anglès, Michèle Aubrey-Laurent, Vincent Avril, Elodie Balme, Philippe Barral, Louis Barruol, Vincent Baumet, Jacky Bernard, Bruno Boisson, Christian Bonfils, Julien and Laetitia Barrot, Emmanuel Bouchard, Vincent Boyer, Julien Brechet, Jérôme Bressy, Michel Chapoutier, Robert Charavin, Alex and Frédéric Chaudière, Jean-Louis and Erin Chave, Yann Chave, Pierre and Olivier Clape, Sébastien Clément and Lysiane Maggi, Daniel Coulon, Jean-Paul Daumen, Claire Darnaud, Rodolphe des Pins, Adrien Fabre, Francis Fabre, Philippe Faure, Bernard

Faurie, Serge and Frédéri Férigoule, Pierre Gaillard, Sabine Garagnon, Philippe Gimel, Jean Gonon, Fabrice Gripa, Philippe Guigal, Charles Helfenbein, Jean-Paul Jamet, Florent Lançon and Manon Stehelin, Fabien Lombard, Remi Niero, Gaël Petit, Eric Plumet, Raphaël Pommier, Emmanuel Reynaud, Guy Ricard, Vincent Rochette, Marc Sorrel, Anaïs Vallot, Christine Vernay and Paul Amsellem, Christian Voeux … I could go on for pages, but you know who you are! I'd also like to thank Philippe Cambie and Jean-Louis Grippat for their contributions to the book, and Danièle Raulet-Reynaud for her kindness and hospitality.

I wanted to highlight in particular my heartfelt thanks to the great Georges Truc, oenogeologist, for teaching me so much about the terroir of the Rhône.

From Infinite Ideas I'd like to thank Richard Burton, Rebecca Clare and Sarah Jane Evans MW for their belief and their patience.

I would never have got here without the love of my mum, dad and sister Julie – how lucky I am to have you. I mustn't forget my beautiful boys Jay and Buddy who make me smile every day. And last but not least my amazing wife Louisa, the ultimate partner in wine fun.

PART 1
BACKGROUND

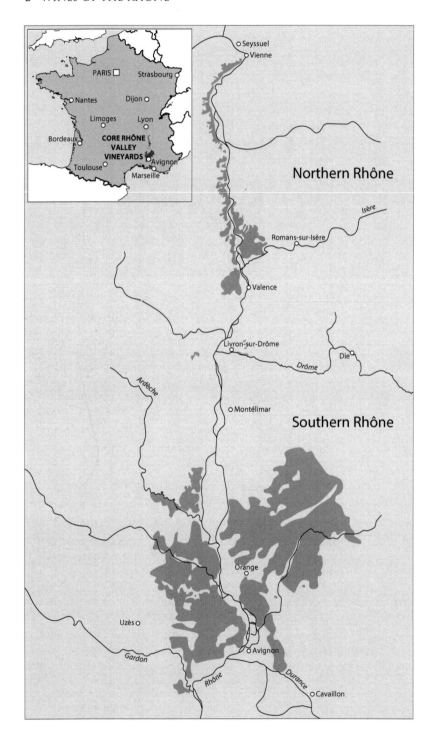

Map 1: The Rhône Valley

1

A SENSE OF PLACE

A BIRD'S EYE VIEW OF THE TERRAIN

If we could board a boat in the canton of Valais where the Rhône emerges from the Rhône Glacier in the Swiss Alps, we would glide down the river for three weeks or so before it emptied us out in the Mediterranean. In all, we would cover 813 kilometres of waterways. And what an idyllic trip it would be: by the time we reached Lyon we would have already passed through some fascinating wine regions, drinking Chasselas, Petite Arvine and Humagne Rouge along the way. But it's just south of Lyon that the wine region known as the Northern Rhône begins, and it's here that we pick up the story, following its twists and turns through the Southern Rhône as the river meanders its way to the sea.

The Northern Rhône runs from Vienne to Valence (or a little further south if you include the resurgent appellation of Brézème). Today, the river runs broadly north to south, following the eastern edge of the hulk of granitic and metamorphic rock known as the Massif Central. The vineyards don't stray far from the river; the majority are perched on the dramatic slopes of the west bank of the Rhône. The only two appellations on the east bank of this stretch of the river are Hermitage and Crozes-Hermitage. Although the Northern Rhône receives a lot of attention it makes up just 5 per cent of the wine produced by Rhône Valley vineyards.

The Northern and Southern Rhône are connected by a river and a few shared grape varieties but are otherwise distinctly different, not only

3

in soil type, but also in climate, flora and the typical character of its inhabitants. There is little in the way of vineyards in the 25 kilometres between the Northern Rhône and Montélimar, the town that marks the gateway to the Southern Rhône. As the river continues its journey south from here, the valley opens up and spreads wide. The Southern Rhône is less verdant, flatter, and the trees are notably different; suddenly there are olive groves, tall cypresses and Aleppo pines. Apart from fields of lavender, the landscape has more yellows and browns than the Northern Rhône, particularly in summer. The Southern Rhône growing area is vast; if you include the appellation of Duché d'Uzès, it covers more distance east to west than it does north to south. East of the river, the vineyards occupy as much land as they can before they hit the inhospitable Prealps. To the west, they stretch to the Cévennes. Follow the Rhône as it dog-legs south-west at Avignon, and you'll get to Costières de Nîmes and eventually the Mediterranean Sea. Skirt around the southern edge of Mont Ventoux instead and you'll enter the Luberon. All of this makes up the geologically diverse land that produces the remaining 95 per cent of Rhône Valley wines.

The Rhône, here not restricted by the Massif Central, has changed its snaking course over millennia, switching paths like channels of rain down a windowpane. Although only the fourth longest river in France, it is powerful and fast moving, bringing vast amounts of debris on its journey from the Alps, including the emblematic pale-brown stones known as *galets roulés* that have been rounded and polished over centuries by rivers and glaciers. I'll continue to use the French term *galet roulé* in this book as there is no direct translation in English; the closest approximation would be 'cobblestone' but this brings to mind something smaller and more uniform. *Galets roulés* vary in size, typically anything from a hen's egg to a human head, occasionally even larger, and they vary in colour from cream to brown to crimson. They are most commonly associated with Châteauneuf-du-Pape, but deposits from various sources are found all over the Southern Rhône.

The east bank is more extensive, with more varied terrain than that of the west bank, and three different types of growing area. Firstly, there are a number of raised terraces, typically at around 100–150 metres, of ancient alluvial deposits over clay, sand or gravels (or any combination), which tend to produce powerful and potent wines. Secondly, there are three rolling low massifs: Massif d'Uchaux (280 metres), Ventabren (390 metres) and the Visan Valréas Hills (500 metres), each with their own character. Thirdly, there is the mountainous terroir among the Dentelles de Montmirail, on the slopes of Ventoux and around the Montagne du Luberon.

Southern Rhône 'côtes' don't overlook the river Rhône as those in the Northern Rhône do. Instead they overlook the main tributaries of the Rhône that criss-cross the terrain, principally the Aigues, Ouvèze and Lez on the east bank, the Cèze, the Tave and the Ardèche on the west bank. Although there are plentiful rolling hills and plateaux on the west bank, the valleys of the Cèze and Tave are broader and the vineyard land tends to be lower and flatter – vineyards don't scale the slopes to the extent they do on the east bank. It is however just as diverse in terms of soils. A few domaines start to ascend the Cévennes to the far west, but there is no mountain terroir to speak of. There is a difference in character between the wines of the west bank and those of the east bank. The red wines of the west bank tend to be relatively lean and straight, with a savoury mineral edge (for a more in-depth look at this phenomenon, see Laudun, p. 200). Traditionally there have been larger volumes of white wine, pale red and rosé cultivated here. The red wines of the east bank are rounder and more generous and, for now at least, more varied in style, ageing for longer and reaching higher peaks of quality. Part of this distinction is down to the different types of soil typically found on each bank. There is more sand on the west bank, more clay on the east. Wines grown on the same soil type often share certain characteristics. Speaking about red wine:

- Granite: vibrant in colour, upright, serious, saline;
- Schist: perfumed, precise, airborne;
- *Galets roulés*: bold, high in alcohol, muscular, rounded;
- Clay: deeply coloured, thickly tannic and velvety, fruity, potent;
- Sand: pale in colour, elegant, fine tannins;
- Limestone: pale in colour, aromatically fresh, straight, lean, tense.

These are gross generalizations – needless to say these characteristics don't always appear – but they are observations made after years of in-depth tasting. We'll look at the terroir of each appellation as we address it.

A geological history of the Rhône Valley[1] by Georges Truc

Tracking down a concise geological history of the Rhône Valley isn't easy, so I asked Georges Truc, an expert in the vines and geology of the Rhône, to explain.

The North is easier to understand because the viticultural land is really stuck closely to the Rhône and its valley, it's extremely straight, without many vineyards spread further out. In the south, if you look at Luberon, Ventoux, Duché d'Uzès and Costières de Nîmes, it spreads enormously from the axis of the Rhône Valley, so things become much more complex. In the Northern Rhône, the main geographical feature is the Massif Central, dating back around 300 million years. It's derived from magma that cooled to produce granite. There is also metamorphic rock – sedimentary rock that, under high temperature and pressure, became the micaschist and gneiss that you find particularly around Côte-Rôtie. Although rarely discussed, the second crucial thing about the Northern Rhône is the tectonic plate that pushed against the Massif Central. The result is a number of faults that can be seen all along the viticultural border in the form of tributary river valleys. There are lots of these little valleys, and they're very important – the north-west facing slope is cold, but the southeast facing slope is favourable for planting vines. You can see them at Saint-Joseph, Château-Grillet, Condrieu, Côte-Rôtie.

In the Southern Rhône the movement of tectonic plates was also important, but here it created major regional fractures. The Nîmes Fault, for example, is responsible for the existence of the Gigondas–Beaumes de Venise massif. Although it was a major event it didn't have the same type of influence as in the North, as it didn't create the tributary river valleys of the Rhône. Another major effect of tectonic movement in the South was the creation of folds. These occur when the sedimentary covering of the earth is pushed together, moving upwards and downwards, like a sheet of fabric when you push it together. You can see it in the mountains of the Luberon, Apt, as far as the Diois, from when the southern plate was pushing towards the north.

To understand all of this properly we need to go back 230 million years, when the total growing area of the Rhône was underwater. We're at the bottom of the Thetys Sea, right at the start of the Triassic Period, which was characterized by great aridity. The water in this gulf gradually evaporated, and, similarly to how salt is harvested today, great deposits of salt and gypsum were laid down around Gigondas and Carpentras, and all the way to Nîmes. You can find colossal 7–8 metre deep deposits. This salt isn't used directly in

1   Edited from an interview conducted with Georges Truc, Cave de Visan, on 7 February 2020.

viticulture, but it plays a very important role later on. At the start of the Jurassic Period, the climate flipped, becoming tropical, humid, almost equatorial. The water teemed with ammonites, reptiles and coral. Our basin started to subside, gradually filling up with deposits. These became either marl – a mix of clay and limestone – or limestone. During the Jurassic and the Cretaceous, alternating layers of marl, then limestone were laid down. From 200 million to 65 million years ago, this basin gradually deepened and laid down more and more deposits. Oceanic life is partly responsible, because this limestone is made up of microscopic fragments of the skeletons of animals or traces of plants that lived in this oceanic body. The marls came from the Massif Central, which was covered in forests, and the rivers brought down small particles in the form of clay. These layers of limestone and marl were laid down to a depth of 11 kilometres around Carpentras – exceptionally deep! At the end of the Cretaceous – along with the death of the dinosaurs and some significant climatic events – the Tethys Sea disappeared. At the start of the Tertiary Period [66 million–2.6 million years ago], the African plate pushed against France, while the Iberian plate was also in play, and this resulted in the birth of the Pyrenees, 45 million years ago. Another east–west chain, like the Luberon, like the Alpilles, the Baronnies, the Diois – how did these folds form? Simply through the kilometres of marl and limestone sliding on the deposits of salt and gypsum of the Triassic. The salt and gypsum became viscous under the intense pressure of the deposits on top of them – becoming fluid, a bit like soap.

Around 30 million years ago there was a period of very great fracturing, creating the north-east to south-west fractures that we find in the Massif Central. The most important one in the Southern Rhône is the Nîmes Fault, which starts in Catalonia, goes through the Dentelles de Montmirail via Nîmes and ends in the sub-Alpine mountain chain. Triassic soils in the Dentelles, sitting on salt and gypsum, were pushed upwards along the length of the fault. With the marl here, and soils rich in magnesium and potassium, it became perfect for vine growing. That's how this dynamic event became an important part of the viticultural story. Before eventually settling down, this period of great fracturing did produce one other important event. Corsica and Sardinia pivoted down to take their current positions, and in the second half of the Tertiary Era the Gulf of Lion opened up. This in turn caused the entrance of the Mediterranean Sea into the Rhône Valley during the Miocene Period.

By this point the Alps had started to emerge, and between the Massif Central and the Alpine arc, a kind of corridor came into being. As the Alps rose up, the Rhône corridor deepened. The Mediterranean Sea rushed in and flooded this area – into the Luberon, Carpentras, to Rasteau, Cairanne, up to Hermitage, up to Savoie, up to Hungary. The young Alps were attacked by erosion: as they lifted up, rivers tore off material. The smaller particles – sand, clay – were washed away and deposited in this sea. In Provence, the term used is *safre* – sand that is often rich in sea-shell debris. Eventually this sea disappeared as sediment built up. Rivers continued to flow however, and lakes formed, sometimes linked by rivers. This is how the materials came together to make the hills of Saint-Pantaléon, Valréas, Visan, Saint-Maurice-sur-Aygues, Vinsobres, and on the other side Villedieu, Saint-Roman-de-Malegarde, Buisson, Cairanne, Rasteau, Roaix. These two great hill masses, consisting of lake and river deposits of 180–200 metres deep, have produced superb viticultural terroirs, because the marl–pebble mix is ideal. The pebbles give a permeability and water can be stored in the clay, the marl. Here we reach the end of the Miocene.

Suddenly the African plate started moving again, closing the Strait of Gibraltar. This meant that 5.92 million years ago the Mediterranean Sea was no longer being fed by the Atlantic, so it started to dry out, like an infernal cauldron, laying down salt and gypsum again. Because the coastline continued to drop, rivers that once fed into it, such as the Rhône, started to re-emerge, digging out their valleys once again at an extraordinary rate to re-establish their lost profiles.

Then, a miracle occurred. The two jaws of the Strait of Gibraltar opened once again. Water flowed into the Mediterranean at a rate of several kilometres cubed per second – per second! – and the canyons that the river had cut were once again filled by the sea, which came all the way up to just south of Lyon. This was during the Pliocene Period: it's characterized by deposits of marl but most of all sandy deposits.

Later on, right at the start of the Quaternary Period, this area was taken up by the river Rhône once more. At this time, it was engorged by contributions from the Rhine – because the Rhine Valley at that time, instead of flowing towards Alsace, flowed into the Saône, which itself runs into the Rhône. As such, it was capable of transporting large deposits, very big galets, which it scattered throughout the Rhône, laying down the first great Quaternary terrace of the Rhône, known as the Villafranchian terrace: the terrace of Châteauneuf, the terrace of Lirac and of Tavel, all the terrace of Costières de Nîmes, the terrace of Donzère in Grignan-les-Adhémar and down to Gadagne. The Rhône scattered all this material over the course of 200,000–300,000 years. The *galets roulés* that you find in Roaix and Rasteau came at the end of the Miocene. They have nothing to do with the Rhône. The Villafranchian terrace laid down by the Rhône brought materials from the heart of the Alps; the Aigues and the Ouvèze bring limestone from the Baronnies, the Diois, the Sub-Alpine chain. With Rhône deposits, you'll find enormous amounts of granite, gneiss and micaschist; you'll never find these types of rock around the Aigues and the Ouvèze.

What happened afterwards is no less interesting. The alluvial terraces of the Southern Rhône are not very rich in clay and made up of stones: big stones, some small stones, granular sands … Is this interesting for viticulture? Yes and no. It can be drying, draining – far from favourable for the vine. And yet weathering took place after the Villafranchian. It attacked the limestone on the terraces, and dissolved it, it drained into the soils and was subsequently washed away. The granite galets that came from the heart of the Alps, the gneiss and micaschist, were also attacked by this weathering. The minerals that were in these deposits, aluminium silicates, mica, were destroyed by this long and violent weathering. The minerals were broken down, into their fundamental constituents: silica, aluminium, iron, magnesium, potassium, etc. In a sense, the silica and aluminium were liberated. But Mother Nature is generous: she takes a molecule of silica and a molecule of aluminium, and she refabricates aluminium silicate. And this aluminium silicate is no longer a hard crystal of feldspar or mica, it's in the form of clay. This is the miracle of weathering – taking materials that weren't suitable for growing grapes, and turning them into materials that are. When you see the great terraces of galets of Châteauneuf-du-Pape, you wonder to yourself 'how can a vine live in that – it's impossible!' But dig down 20 centimetres or so and you'll find clay. After two or three metres you find clay mixed with stones, along with reserves of water and reserves of minerals that the vine can use. This terrace, which should never have been good for growing vines, has become suitable. In the Northern Rhône, the granite and the micaschist of the Massif Central were also broken down, just like the galets and the alluvions of the Rhône – well before the Villafranchian in fact. It's the same story: the granite was subject to weathering, the minerals were broken down and produced sandy clay. Later on, when winemakers decided to plant vineyards here, they built walls to stop erosion washing away this weathered surface. And it's weathering, not erosion; erosion is mechanical, whereas weathering is chemical and biochemical – there's no movement involved.

After the Villafranchian, the Rhône continued to lay down terraces. Next came the Quaternary Period, with alternating glacial and interglacial periods. During each period of glaciation, it laid down another terrace. For example, the terrace of the Plan de Dieu, the 'garrigues' terrace of Vacqueyras, the terrace to the west of Gigondas are all terraces that are more recent than the Villafranchian. Dating back between 700,000 and 450,000 years they were laid down either by tributaries of the Rhône or by the Rhône itself. Each one, after being laid down, also suffered weathering, but much less violent than that of the Villafranchian. Nonetheless, the vine benefits. The most important terrace in the Northern Rhône is that of Crozes-Hermitage. The recent terrace of the Isère river was laid down in the last glaciation of the Würm, 24,000 years ago.

So that's the undoubtedly complex geological history of the Rhône Valley. It continues its path today.

CLIMATE: SUN, HEAT, RAIN, WIND

Trying to generalize about the climate in the Rhône Valley isn't terribly helpful. Châteauneuf-du-Pape and Hermitage are separated by 110 kilometres, a huge distance. Ampuis, the heart of Côte-Rôtie, is equidistant between Châteauneuf-du-Pape and Beaune. It's rare that any given year will see identical weather patterns in the Southern and Northern Rhône.

The climate in the Northern Rhône is continental. Winters are cold and it enjoys 'summers whose effect on the grapes can be exaggerated by the steep slopes to which many of the better Northern Rhône vineyards cling,' as Jancis Robinson eloquently puts it. According to Météo France, between 1981 and 2010 the weather station at Lyon recorded an average minimum monthly temperature of 8.1°C and an average maximum monthly temperature of 16.9°C. The climate in the Southern Rhône is Mediterranean, with warmer temperatures in winter and summer, and less precipitation. The weather station at Orange confirms this:

1981–2010	Lyon	Orange
Average minimum monthly temperature (°C)	8.1	9.4
Average maximum monthly temperature (°C)	16.9	19.7
Total precipitation (mm)	831.9	709.1
Number of days with precipitation	104.1	66.0

By precipitation, we mean rain. Snow isn't common in the Northern Rhône, and even rarer in the Southern Rhône. In the two years I lived near Avignon, I only saw it snow once, in winter 2019. It was heavy, lasted about 30 minutes and covered the ground thickly. Children enjoyed it while they could; within 30 minutes, it was gone.

Hail is also more common in the north, and is increasingly unpredictable. On 17 April 2016 it hailed on Hermitage, badly affecting yields, an occurrence so rare that Jean-Louis Chave told me it was the first time he had ever experienced it. Later in the season Crozes-Hermitage was also hit. It was even more severe in Crozes in 2019. Some producers lost most of their crop – three quarters of Domaine de la Ville Rouge vineyards for example were stripped bare, with many other producers reporting similar devastation. Compared to other regions of France, frost is unusual, but does happen. In 2017, Château Pesquié in Ventoux lost 60 per cent of its crop as a result. 'It's the first time that's happened,' says co-owner Fred Chaudière. 'It's a new way to show that we're cooler than the rest – but not our favourite way!' It's not the only extreme weather phenomenon in the Southern Rhône in recent years. The 2019 vintage saw a heatwave which broke all previous meteorological records, with a high of 45.9°C in Gallargues-le-Montueux, 20 kilometres south-west of Nîmes. At the end of the growing season I saw sunburnt grapes that had dark, leathery patches where they faced the sun. Severe cold snaps are rarer still, but can have even more radical effects. The frost of 1956 was so intense it killed off many of the region's olive trees, making way for significant new plantings of vineyards and marking a turning point in Rhône viticultural history (see Chapter 2).

Many winemakers I have spoken to report the same thing – the climate is getting hotter, harvest dates are getting earlier, rain is becoming increasingly rare during summer. 'We had a stream that used to flow by the house', says Denis Alary of Domaine Alary in Cairanne. 'It doesn't flow any more. It stopped in 2003 … We have around the same amount of rain, but now there's often a period of two months in the summer when it doesn't rain at all.'

Changing climate, changing wines

As I write this chapter sitting in my home near Avignon, I have the windows flung open to enjoy the 22°C warmth. I should be enjoying it, but I feel uneasy. Mainly because it's 3 February in a region known for its cold winters and I'm sitting here in a T-shirt. What's more, I'm reading a recent study into climate change made by Cédric Hallereau for Groupe ICV, a nationwide French viticultural and oenological consultancy. It makes for sobering reading, backing up winemakers' anecdotal climatic observations with some scientific research. It shows that between 1980 and 2010, in the Southern Rhône (Orange) the average annual air temperature has risen steadily by 1.1°C. Figures for Châteauneuf-du-Pape show that the amount of annual rainfall is fairly constant, but rainfall is increasing in autumn and winter and decreasing in spring and summer. Average night-time temperatures there have increased by 0.7°C from 1988 to 2019. As a result, all stages of the growing cycle (budding, flowering, maturity) are starting increasingly early in the year, increasing the risk of spring frosts and coulure. Instances of hydric stress during the growing season have grown, which can increase the build-up of phenolics in the skins, but interrupt ripening when severe. Analysis of Grenache grapes in Châteauneuf-du-Pape on a given day each year shows that since the late 1980s, berries are gradually getting smaller and giving less juice, juice which is increasingly high in sugar and polyphenols and increasingly low in acidity. Average picking dates in Tavel and Châteauneuf-du-Pape are now around 15 days earlier on average than they were 60 years ago, and there is a widening gap between sugar ripeness and physiological ripeness, i.e. sugars are building up more quickly, but tannin ripeness isn't progressing at the same rate, which means having to pick either with unripe flavours or at high alcohol levels.

A penetrating wind

When we think about climate, the first things that come to mind are temperature, sunshine hours and rainfall but in the Rhône there's another major factor to consider, and that's the wind. While there are many local air currents that influence winegrowing throughout the region, the mistral is all-important, affecting both the Northern Rhône (where it's sometimes called *la bise*) and the South. It's a violent, chilly, dry north wind caused when there is high pressure in the Bay of Biscay and low pressure in the Gulf of Genoa, when the flow of air from high to low pressure zones brings cold air from the north. This is then funnelled down the Rhône Valley towards the Mediterranean where it can reach speeds of over 100 kilometres per hour.

It's said to blow on average one day in three (though personal experience suggests it's much less than this), and is particularly common in winter and spring. Blustery and maddening, it's the kind of wind that makes you pedal when cycling downhill into it. Even on hot summer days it's unpleasant – it's just too boisterous and invasive. In winter it's bitter, penetrating your clothes like skeletal fingers. Spare a thought for vignerons pruning the vines in January. It can cause damage to vines too, particularly Syrah and Viognier. The mistral does however have its benefits. It's particularly common after rain, so it quickly dries out wet vines, helping to keep diseases at bay. It also brings with it clear skies, meaning more sunshine. The night sky following the mistral glitters with stars.

Some of these changes might not be caused by a warming climate. Earlier ripening can also be attributed to an increase in trellising vines on wires over the past few decades, giving foliage and grapes more exposure to the sun. Jean-Paul Jamet suggests that a further reason for earlier picking times is the prevalence of the destemmer, meaning growers can pick earlier, not needing to worry about the ripeness of their stems. Vineyard practices such as debudding, leaf-plucking and green harvesting may also be partly to blame for earlier harvests and more concentrated juice. A push for greater phenolic ripeness among some vine growers is another factor. A reduction in herbicide use has led to more cover crops, which compete with the vine for available water, contributing to hydric stress.

Nevertheless, the climate is changing and winemakers need to adapt. Thankfully, Southern Rhône vineyards have plenty of varieties to play with, so planting later ripening ones that retain acidity and produce lower levels of alcohol is one possibility. 'The problem is this region has been planting too much Grenache for decades,' says Philippe Gimel of Saint Jean du Barroux in Ventoux. He believes looking into alternative varieties, perhaps from Spain, will be important in the future. Vincent Bouyer of Château Bizard in Grignan-les-Adhémar wonders if Tempranillo could work in his terroir. Other vignerons are planting late-ripening white varieties among their parcels of reds, and planting on cooler sites. Louis Chèze in northern Saint-Joseph is now planting white varieties on north-facing slopes. Pierre-Jean Villa in Condrieu advises that 'before changing varieties, we should think about rootstocks,' and has had some success by using once ill-advised alternatives such as rupestris du lot and gravesac. Using different clones and changing pruning methods back to *gobelet* could also help bring back balance, as could reducing planting densities. Irrigation could have numerous benefits, reducing hydric stress, helping to maintain yields, helping to preserve acidity and limiting alcohol levels – but there are downsides (see page 14).

Adapting their methods to account for climate change may help vignerons produce balanced wines for longer. But these are short-term fixes that do little to address the causes of our increasingly chaotic climate. I've heard precious little from wineries about renewable energy, carbon capture, bulk shipping or lighter weight bottles. It's not surprising therefore that some winemakers' attitudes are fatalistic. 'We're going back to the old ways,' says Thibaud Chaume of Domaine Chaume-Arnaud in Vinsobres, referring to polycultural farming. 'I'm planting lavender, fruit trees,' he says, as a way of hedging against climate change. Adrien Fabre of Domaine la Florane in Visan is doing the same. 'You can't irrigate the slopes,' he says with a shrug of resignation.

It's not bad news for every part of the Rhône. A warming climate has opened up areas such as Puyméras to more consistent, better quality wines. James King of Château Unang in Ventoux admits it's also been the key to making better wines in his cool microclimate: 'now nature is on our side,' he says. It might be at present: whether it still is in twenty years, time will tell.

Irrigation – cure or curse?

You see it more and more frequently in the Southern Rhône: snaking black hosepipes following rows of vines, dripping water onto the base of each plant. Growers can't open the taps whenever they wish; they need to wait for very dry conditions to be officially declared at the start of summer. That happens almost every year now.

But it's a contentious topic. Some growers argue that if it makes for a better wine, then why not? After all, it's not designed to be used to increase yields, just to ease blockages in the vine caused by water stress. This can lead to better ripeness, not to mention helping to maintain acidity and tempering alcohol levels. And parched summers are becoming increasingly common. 'If we want to continue making Grenache and Syrah we'll have to irrigate,' says Valentine Fesselet, winemaker at Domaine de Cristia in Châteauneuf-du-Pape. Others aren't so keen. 'Irrigation is the negation of an appellation. You kill the notion of terroir,' says Pierre Gaillard. He argues that the way the water is delivered to the plant is part of what gives the finished wine its character. He would rather see growers reduce yields or switch grape varieties. Jean-Luc Colombo also finds that it changes the nature of the wine, lessening the floral register and accentuating fruit flavours. Vincent Baumet in Rochegude is also against irrigation, primarily as he views it as an unnecessary waste of a precious resource.

Whether you are for or against irrigation, it is unlikely to be a long-term solution to the changing climate.

2

WINEMAKING IN THE RHÔNE

HISTORY OF WINEMAKING

Vitis vinifera arrives in Marseille

Based on tartaric acid residues found in household jars in the Zagros Mountains of Iran, making wine from grapes dates back at least as far as 5000 BC. It wasn't until around 600 BC, however, that viticulture reached the south of France, when *Vitis vinifera* vines arrived with the Greek settlers who founded what is now the city of Marseille. Granted, it's not strictly the Rhône, and it's likely that these new arrivals didn't plant vineyards far from their settlements to begin with due to hostile local tribes. The existence of commercial viticulture is only evident much later, in the second century BC, with the arrival of the Romans, who founded a colony in Narbonne in 118 BC. Viticulture spread from here, but was halted by the Roman emperor Domitian in 92 AD to ensure that land was reserved for producing wheat. This edict was eventually lifted by emperor Probus in 276 AD.

The river Rhône soon became a practical route for moving goods into mainland France and beyond, and countless fragments of wine amphorae have been found lining the banks and riverbeds of the Rhône and the Saône, with large findings in Chalon-sur-Saône, just south of Beaune. The Rhône wasn't just a corridor for transportation, it was also recognized for the wines grown on its banks as far as Vienne. The poet Martial praised 'Vitifera Vienna' at the end of the first century, and

Pliny the Elder celebrated the wines of the Allobroges, a Gallic tribe whose capital was at Vienne. The Allobroges even exported their wines as far as Britain. Roman artefacts have been found in Condrieu, and further south in Tain-l'Hermitage, known in Roman times as Tegna. The Romans had left by 476 AD but with their wines so highly prized, local people no doubt went on producing, although documentary evidence is scarce until the Middle Ages.

Thirsty popes

The Albigensian Crusade (1209–1229) instigated by Pope Innocent III against the Cathars took place in the Languedoc, but it indirectly influenced winemaking in the Rhône. Legend has it that on returning home injured from the campaign in 1224, a crusader named Henri Gaspard de Stérimberg came across the hill, built a retreat and planted vines there. The wine became so popular that two centuries later they called his wine 'vin de l'Hermitage', a name that has stuck with it ever since. The movement of the papal seat from Rome to Avignon in 1309 had far more wide-reaching consequences when Clement V encouraged the planting of vineyards, particularly to the north of Avignon. He fell ill, and died on 20 April 1314. After two years of infighting, the former bishop of Avignon, Jacques Duèse was elected as Pope John XXII, and it was he who was responsible for the building of the castle in the town now known as Châteauneuf-du-Pape, 12 kilometres north of Avignon. By the time the popes left Avignon on 13 September 1376, viticulture was well established on both sides of the Rhône. Shipments continued to be sent back to Rome; in 1561 for example, a sailor from Martigues in Provence transported 32 barrels of Châteauneuf and Laudun.

International trade and renown

The more widespread distribution of Rhône wines was hampered between the fourteenth and sixteenth centuries, when the duchy of Burgundy banned the transport of non-Burgundian wines north via the Saône. However, the opening of the Canal du Midi in 1681 made available trade routes to Bordeaux, Paris, the British Isles and beyond. By the seventeenth century, Rhône wines were held in increasingly high esteem. Louis XIV presented Charles II of England with 200 barrels of fine wine, made up of Champagne, Burgundy and Hermitage. A state decree issued in 1737 stated that wines coming from the west bank of the Rhône should be branded CDR (for Côte du Rhône – note the singular – since at this time it was the wines of the west bank that were lauded) in an early attempt to protect and guarantee the wine's origin. Without cooperatives or other large enterprises, there are few archives to explore regarding early exports of Rhône wines. However, records show that Paul Clair Martin of Domaine de la Solitude in Châteauneuf-du-Pape was exporting wine to Austria and England: 540 litres to the UK in 1826 and a further 1,620 litres in 1827.

A poisoned chalice

In 1862, a seemingly innocuous gift from an American friend to a M. Borty in what is today the appellation of Lirac put an end to this flourishing industry. In his excellent book *Phylloxera, How Wine was Saved for the World*, Christy Campbell recounts the story:

> *No plaque marks the house, in a narrow street at the edge of the sleepy town with its plane-shaded market square and Romanesque gothic church of Saint-Jean-l'Évangéliste. No D-Day-style route phylloxerique marks the invader's path. Only the very inquisitive come here. The little walled vineyard at the rear of no. 21 rue Longue disappeared long ago under garages and bungalows. But like the supposed crash site of some alien spacecraft, 'le Clos Borty' in Roquemaure was identified much later by investigators from the French Academy of Sciences as the place where the conflagration began.*

M. Borty's American friend Mr Carle paid him a visit in 1861. Noting that they both enjoyed growing grapevines, Mr Carle promised to send his French *ami* some cuttings of his own vines, just for interest. The following year, a package arrived unannounced, containing a case of rooted vines, each variety displaying a different name tag: Emily, Post-Oak, Clinton. M. Borty duly planted them in his garden. A vineyard in the neighbouring village of Pujaut was the first to show symptoms the following year. Leaves yellowed early, the edges reddened, and by August they had dropped off completely. The following year, M. Borty's Grenache and Alicante vines started to shrivel. Vines showed blackened, rotten, crumbling roots. In 1865 it crossed the Rhône; from there the plague spread far and wide.

The cause, well-known now, was identified as early as 1868 – an aphid that feeds on the roots of European grapevines – but a cure took longer to find. Eventually, two methods became apparent. Firstly, creating hybrids of European and American vine species was attempted, with some success. Early efforts proved hardy and resistant to fungal diseases, but the quality of the resulting wine was often disappointing. Secondly, grafting French vines onto American roots that were resistant to the insect was found to be effective, and this began in earnest in 1880. By this time, almost 2.5 million hectares of vineyards across France had been destroyed.

Establishing the modern industry

By 1890, the Rhône Valley's growers were deep in the work of replanting and restructuring their vineyards. This year also saw the birth of one of Châteauneuf-du-Pape's most famous sons, Baron Pierre Le Roy de Boiseaumarié, who went on to achieve so much for Châteauneuf-du-Pape and the Rhône in general (see Châteauneuf-du-Pape, page 72). He died in 1967, but not before he could unveil a sculpture and bust in Saint-Cécile celebrating his life, delivering the official speech himself.

February 1956 was the coldest month recorded in France since records began in 1900. Temperatures dropped to -20°C in Aix-en-Provence and Saint-Tropez saw 70 centimetres of snow. On top of this, the Rhône was hit by a ferocious mistral of up to 180 kilometres per hour. The day before the sudden drop was unseasonably warm, and legend has it the sap had begun to rise, only to be frozen in its tracks. The next day you could hear the olive groves 'screaming' as the frozen sap exploded and cracked branches and trunks. Olive groves throughout the Southern Rhône were decimated. Since olive trees take so long to produce good fruit, the land was often replanted with vines to secure a quicker return. At this stage, most estates in the Rhône were still polycultural, growing fruit, vegetables and cereals along with grapes: 1956 was the year that many estates started to concentrate on wine.

The period after the Second World War saw the establishment of co-operative wineries throughout the Southern Rhône (see page 25), and to a lesser extent, the Northern Rhône. Access to heavy machinery such as bulldozers brought previously inaccessible terrain into play, such as the plateau of Vallongue in Lirac and Tavel. The return of the Pieds-Noirs in the early 1960s following the Algerian War also helped develop large scale mechanized viticulture in appellations such as Lirac and Grignan-les-Adhémar.

The end of the 1970s and the early 1980s saw the first green shoots of organic viticulture, which really took hold at the start of the twenty-first century (see below). This movement towards environmentally sensitive and sustainable viticulture can only be a positive, but the extreme and unpredictable weather of the first twenty years of the twenty-first century suggest much more needs to be done. Perhaps the next twenty years will see different parts of the wine industry in the Rhône come together to address this. To date I have seen little evidence of this happening.

WINEMAKING IN THE RHÔNE – CURRENT ISSUES

Organic, biodynamic, natural

Denis Guthmuller is president of the cooperative Cave Cécilia in Sainte-Cécile-les-Vignes, and president of organic producer collective Sud-Est Vin Bio. He explains that the post-Second World War push to produce food and drink quickly and in large quantities led farmers to take up the new agrochemicals that had been developed around the same time. Though some long-established producers like Domaine Saladin (see Saint-Andéol) claim that synthetic products have never been used on their vineyards, such examples are rare.

Early adopters of organic viticulture include Château de Beaucastel in 1950, which progressed to biodynamics in 1974. Another pioneering estate is Domaine Gramenon (see Valréas, page 169), which has been organic since its birth in 1978, and was certified biodynamic in 2010. In the Northern Rhône, Michel Chapoutier was one of the first producers to use biodynamics on a large scale. But the biggest jump in organic production was in the early 2000s. Many of the early organic or biodynamic estates were driven by both green values and a quest for improved quality, but Guthmuller notes that many more recent converts have been convinced by economics. A disastrous vintage in 2002, coupled with overproduction in France, led to a price crash – he remembers Côtes-du-Rhône *en vrac* prices dropping in a few years from around 160€ per hectolitre down to 90€. To save money, growers started using fewer products and in lower quantities. In 2006–7, a market for organic wine *en vrac* developed, at around 200€ per hectolitre, encouraging more growers to give up using chemical products altogether.

Eventually the gap in price between conventional and organic wine narrowed, so some growers returned to using chemical products on their vines. Others were badly affected by black rot in 2013 or flavescence dorée in 2014 and 2015, which pushed them back to the consistency of crop and therefore financial security offered by agrochemicals. Organic and biodynamic viticulture in the Rhône Valley is now on the increase again, with organically produced wine representing 9 per cent of the 2018 harvest.

Some areas take it more seriously than others. In Châteauneuf-du-Pape over 25 per cent of the total harvest in 2018 was organic; Costières de Nîmes wasn't far behind, with 22 per cent. Despite a higher average bottle price, the northern *crus* produced just 6 per cent certified organic wine in 2018, whereas the southern *crus* managed more than double this at 13 per cent. Organic viticulture in the sloping, terraced vineyards of the damper Northern Rhône is particularly difficult, since all the work has to be done by hand. Weeding with a hoe in the sun is hot, back-breaking work; for domaines that would like to go organic, finding people prepared to do the work is a constant struggle. Making wine organically in the Southern Rhône is more straightforward, but still not an easy option. 'It's more expensive,' says Guthmuller, 'it takes longer, there's more tractor work, so more petrol used. Not to mention the real and serious risk of losing your harvest. It's really a question of conviction I think.'

Bush vines vs trellising

There are two main ways of training your Grenache vines in the Southern Rhône: trellised on wires (usually as cordon de Royat) or as self-supporting bush vines, locally called *gobelets* ('goblets'). Cédric Guillaume-Corbin of Domaine la Péquélette in Vinsobres has both on his estate and has no doubt which he prefers. 'The *gobelets* give better quality, better balanced wines, and the vines live longer,' he says. The sap has a longer course to follow with cordon de Royat and he finds that it doesn't flow in a uniform fashion through the plant.

As the benefits of bush vines become increasingly apparent, some estates, such as Domaine Santa Duc, are going back to planting with this in mind. Julie Paolucci of Domaine la Luminaille in Rasteau is planting both Grenache and Carignan this way. She says that *gobelets* give more protection from the sun, and that younger vines naturally give lower yields when grown this way; the resulting wines are more concentrated. The drawback is that all the work in the vineyard has to be done by hand. Planting in *gobelet* is certainly the traditional method in the Southern Rhône; in Châteauneuf-du-Pape, it's obligatory to grow

Grenache, Mourvèdre, Piquepoul Noir and Terret Noir this way. 'The wires came with the harvesting machines,' says Vincent Baumet, another voice in favour of *gobelets*. This is the primary benefit of wire trellises – they make mechanization much easier.

Mechanization has its benefits. You don't have to rely on finding enough pickers at the right moment, so you can decide exactly when to pick. This is particularly important with varieties like Viognier, which can build up sugar alarmingly quickly at the end of the season. It also means you can pick at night more easily, which can help preserve freshness. And trellising delivers more uniform ripeness. Its main benefit of course is that it helps to keep costs down, a benefit to growers and drinkers alike.

Attack of the clones

Grenache's biggest weakness? Building up large amounts of sugar, leading to high levels of alcohol, which can result in unbalanced wines. Yves Gras of Domaine Santa Duc in Gigondas explains that Grenache's natural propensity to generate sugar was made even more extreme through clonal selection in the late twentieth century when quantity was put before quality, favouring plants that produced generous yields and high alcohol. Propagating cuttings from pre-clonal old vines therefore is particularly important for Grenache – Gigondas now has a nursery (conservatory) of plants taken from old-vine material to this end.

Louis Barruol of Château de Saint-Cosme in Gigondas describes the widespread adoption of clones as 'catastrophic'. He once planted 1.5 hectares which he has since ripped out. He adds that these high-yielding clones have stems which struggle to ripen, making for green flavours in resulting wines, and it was this that eventually led to the introduction of the destemming machine in the 1970s. This has compounded the effect of high alcohol in Grenache, as using stems in ferments can reduce the final alcoholic degree.

Massal selection has its benefits, but some producers are happy with the status quo, particularly as massal selection means an added burden of paperwork. 'It's easier just to take a clone,' says Daniel Chaussy of Mas de Boislauzon in Châteauneuf-du-Pape, echoing the thoughts of most growers. Where clones aren't available however, massal selection is the only way. To ensure her vineyards were populated with Serine, an ancient local variant of Syrah, Agnès Levet of Domaine Levet in Côte-Rôtie had no choice but to propagate her plants by massal selection (see page 264).

The growth of stems

Before the invention of the destemming machine, almost all wines in the Rhône Valley were fermented as whole bunches – stalks and all. (All except some Châteauneuf-du-Pape and Hermitage, which were traditionally destemmed by hand.) The widespread adoption of the destemmer in the 1970s was no doubt welcome after some of the cooler, wetter vintages of the 1950s and 1960s. Using green, unripe stems can lead to vegetal flavours and harsh tannins. They also absorb colour, an unpopular effect in a region that values dark-coloured wines. The overall effect on quality was positive, and stalky wines were largely shunned by critics and journalists at the time as lacking finesse. Mechanical grape harvesters, introduced around the same time, knock berries from stalks as they pass through the vineyard, further cementing the destemmed style as the accepted norm. Thus, what was considered the *typicité* of the region began to change.

A minority of estates ignored these developments and continued to work with whole bunches, and this more traditional style is currently enjoying a renaissance. This reappraisal, along with an improved understanding of how to get the best from using stalks, has resulted in a growing trend, particularly in the Northern Rhône, for using at least a proportion of whole clusters. Some producers say they only use stems that have gone brown, but Jean-Paul Jamet in Côte-Rôtie says his stalks never go fully brown, and he uses them anyway. To begin with, the aromas can be vegetal, but they eventually turn floral. 'If you want to use stems, you need to harvest 8 to 10 days later,' he says, 'and you have to accept losing some of your grapes.'

Those working with whole bunches claim a range of benefits: increased freshness, deeper aromatic complexity, lower alcohol (partly by dilution as stems contain water, partly due to stem matter absorbing alcohol) and more textural relief in the finished wines. These benefits are becoming increasingly attractive as the climate warms. 'The stalks are part of terroir, part of the fruit, in the same way that pips are part of the fruit,' says Louis Barruol of Château de Saint-Cosme in Gigondas. 'Some people complain about having a vegetal element, so I say they should remove the pips as well. How far should we go with removing things? We can go too far.'

But not all winemakers (and indeed wine drinkers) agree, with some, such as Château de Vaudieu, using ever more precise destemmers to remove any non-fruit matter from their ferments in a quest to achieve their vision of purity and finesse. 'It's part of a complex model of viticulture,' admits Barruol. 'You can't for example cultivate productive clones with big green stems, big berries and yields then turn around tomorrow and say you are going to work with whole bunches because you like it, it's trendy, it wouldn't work. You can only do it in a certain context. Destalking with one vigneron can make an enormous amount of sense, with another it can be an error. You can't talk about techniques in an isolated manner.'

Carbonic maceration – a growing trend?

With destemming machines being a relatively recent import, using whole bunches was once typical in the Rhône Valley. There are variations on the way they can be used; bunches can still be squashed to release the juice before fermentation if desired, or whole bunches can be processed using carbonic maceration (when whole bunches are placed in a sealed tank filled with carbon dioxide and berries undergo intracellular fermentation). Carbonic maceration was once more commonly used for basic, fruity reds for early drinking, but the technique is being used to increasingly impressive effect. Though at the more basic end of their ranges, Domaine les Aphillanthes Côtes-du-Rhône 'Rouge Carmin' and Château du Mourre du Tendre Côtes-du-Rhône 'Cuvée Paul' are both delicious.

It's also occasionally seen for making top of the range terroir wines. Domaine Saladin in Saint-Andéol uses semi-carbonic fermentation for all its Grenache, Carignan and Cinsault. In this case, tanks aren't first filled with carbon dioxide, but instead the weight of the grapes causes some berries to split, and juice then ferments. The build-up of carbon dioxide from this classic fermentation kick-starts carbonic maceration in the remaining intact berries. At Domaine Saladin this technique is even used for the top cuvée, Haut Brissan, and the result is an ineffably pure, aerial expression of Grenache. Elisabeth Saladin suspects it remains rarely used as the results are pale and relatively delicate, in a land where power is more typically praised.

The other master of the art is Eric Pfifferling of Domaine l'Anglore in Tavel. He believes it is the key to the aromatic, floral notes in his wines. 'It's a lot of work, you have to do everything by hand, and you need impeccable hygiene,' he says, one reason it's still relatively rare in the region. But given that his wines are now arguably the best in the appellation – indeed some of the most fascinating in the Rhône as a whole – others will surely follow suit.

While it's more common in the Southern Rhône, the technique is occasionally employed in the Northern Rhône. Jean-Michel Stéphan in Côte-Rôtie uses carbonic maceration for some of his wines, which can be utterly spellbinding, and Lionel Faury in Saint-Joseph uses a combination of uncrushed whole bunch and lightly crushed destemmed fruit for his reds, which results in a combination of intracellular fermentation and classic fermentation. Carbonic maceration is still often associated with basic Beaujolais, but in the right hands it can create wines with stunning aromatic fireworks.

Pssst. You after any acid?

Considering the cagey manner in which many winemakers talk about acid adjustments in the winery, you'd think it was banned. But adding tartaric acid to must or wine is permitted, and increasingly widely practised in the Southern Rhône. 'In Châteauneuf everybody does it,' one winemaker told me – though in practice it's not every domaine. Due to warming temperatures and hydric stress during the growing season, levels of acidity in ripe grapes are gradually dropping, leading some winemakers to add acid. Other winemakers like to leave grapes on the vine for longer to build up colour and tannin, then rectify the acidity in the winery. Low acidities don't just affect a wine's flavour: they can make a wine less stable and prone to problems such as *Brettanomyces* infections (brett), they can reduce a wine's ability to age or lead it to fall outside the acceptable acid levels as stipulated in an appellation's *cahier des charges*. But given that the oenologues (consultant winemakers) often sell winemaking products such as tartaric acid, it's in their interest that winemakers use them.

Whatever the reason, it can be an effective procedure – tartaric acid occurs naturally in the grapes after all – discreetly bringing wines back into balance (it's practised with both red and white wines). Sometimes the acidity sticks out though, or feels at odds with the finished wine. If a wine's acidity can be kept in check through vineyard intervention, so much the better. Xavier Gérard in Côte-Rôtie for example passes through the vineyard twice when picking his Condrieu: an early pass to favour acidity, and again at a later date for fully ripe fruit. In the words of Louis Barruol of Château de Saint-Cosme in Gigondas, acidification 'doesn't change the nature of your grapes – you can't buy freshness.'

Cave cooperatives: still 'a beautiful project'?

Geologist Georges Truc, who will soon be entering his ninth decade, has a long view of viticulture in the Rhône and has no doubt about the importance of the cave cooperative (or cave co-op): 'The cooperative system saved French viticulture,' he says, 'it is a beautiful project.'

Throughout the nineteenth century, apart from some domaines in Châteauneuf-du-Pape, growers in the Southern Rhône didn't make their own wine. They sold their grapes to winemakers, who would then market the end product. Growers were paid by the ton, so their focus was on quantity, not quality. Other types of agricultural cooperatives came before wine, such as collective production of oil, butter and honey. The first viticultural cooperative in France was established in Damery in Champagne in 1891, but more influential for the Rhône would have been the cave co-op in Marussan in the Hérault, which opened in 1901. The first cave co-op to be opened in the Gard was in 1914. Grape growers were driven to set up co-ops by economic necessity. They were paid low prices for their crops by the winemakers, but had no other means of selling their grapes. Growers realized that if they could club together to fund collective wineries, they could make a better living. Truc explains: 'the cooperative system was brilliant as it allowed all these small and medium-sized producers to put in place – with the aid of the state, the chamber of agriculture and the banks – collective structures. A cooperative cellar – the buildings, everything – belongs to its members. It's a common good.' Twenty-seven were opened in Southern Rhône *départements* between 1925 and 1930, a golden age for co-ops. By 1946, 50 per cent of Côtes-du-Rhône wines were made by co-ops. By 1981 that figure had risen to 68 per cent, but by 2018 it had fallen to 62 per cent. The growth of co-ops is one of the reasons that viticulture became such an important industry in the Southern Rhône. Instead of having to invest in winery equipment or commercial expertise, growers could invest in more land to plant.

Not everybody believes that co-ops are such a positive phenomenon. Michèle Aubrey-Laurent of Domaine Gramenon says that they have had a standardizing effect on wines. 'They've created an idea of what wine should be that's hard to escape from,' she says. They may also have reinforced the idea among locals that they are fruit growers rather than winegrowers, which could be holding the region back in terms of diversity, quality and price. Denis Guthmuller, president of Cave Cécilia in

Sainte-Cécile, says that 'it's not an easy time for co-ops'. Members are leaving, retiring or setting up their own estates. Co-ops have certain fixed costs, so losing members (and the hectares of vines they represent) is problematic. Locals are drinking less wine and many co-ops are having to merge to survive. Some, such as Cave Cécilia, are pushing hard for better quality, and it's increasingly common to see *cru* bottlings, organic cuvées and wines with no added sulphites. 'These top-level wines are increasingly equalling the wines from private domaines,' says Truc, who considers this focus on quality to be vital to the ongoing health of cave cooperatives – which means the ongoing well-being of thousands of local grape growers. And let's not forget the important social aspect they play for many farming communities.

It's true that some very good wines are now being made by co-ops, but a large proportion of the more forgettable wines I encounter also originate from these structures. Even at the better co-ops, it's not unusual for ranges to be very mixed in quality and lacking in consistency from year to year. In the Southern Rhône, Les Vignerons d'Estézargues in Signargues deserves particular praise; the quality is every bit as good as (if not better than) most nearby domaines. In the Northern Rhône, Cave de Tain makes some excellent wines, being particularly strong in red Saint-Joseph and red and white Hermitage (of which the co-op owns significant holdings). For good quality, good value wines with a sense of local terroir, Marrenon in the Luberon, La Vinsobraise in Vinsobres and Rocca Maura in Lirac are also recommended. Other names to look out for are Maison Sinnae and Les Vignerons des 4 Chemins in Laudun, Les Vignerons de Valléon in Saint-Pantaléon-les-Vignes, Vignerons Créateurs in Costières de Nîmes, Cave Cécilia in Sainte-Cécile (also known as Chantecôtes), Cave de Visan, Cave des Coteaux Saint-Maurice, Cave de Cairanne, Gigondas La Cave and Clairmont in Crozes-Hermitage. Le Cellier des Dauphins is the biggest with 2,300 members and a total of 12,500 hectares but don't write it off on account of its size: the inexpensive wines are often well made with a good sense of place.

3

GRAPE VARIETIES

Since Burgundy can get by perfectly well with so few grape varieties, you might wonder why the Southern Rhône needs so many. In fact, for red wines it could function quite happily with just Grenache and Syrah, which make up 85 per cent of total plantings. But with a growing area as vast and varied as this, having so many permissible types brings real advantages to winemakers: some excel on limestone, others on clay; some ripen early, others late; some are prone to certain diseases, others resistant. Wherever they are based, and whatever the season throws at them, growers can adapt. True, there is a long tail of lesser-known varieties; but think of that tail as more peacock than rat. These varieties bring complexity to the finished wine, bestowing ineffable local character, and are increasingly valuable when it comes to finding ways to balance out Grenache's natural propensity to excess. The Rhône would be much less Rhône without them. To quote the American designer Charles Eames, 'the details are not the details; they make the product.'

The grape varieties below are allowed in AOC wines in the Rhône Valley. Varieties are listed from most to least prevalent in terms of hectares planted in 2020. The countless other varieties the Rhône is home to must be bottled under an IGP or Vin de France rather than an AOC.

RED GRAPES

Grenache Noir (37,368 hectares)

Grenache Noir (usually referred to simply as Grenache) is France's second most planted grape after Merlot. Across all Rhône Valley vineyards,

Grenache Noir makes up nearly 50 per cent of vines planted. It is particularly dominant in Châteauneuf-du-Pape, where it makes up nearly
80 per cent of plantings. Along with Syrah, it produces some of the
greatest bottles in the Rhône. It is also responsible for oceanic volumes
of ordinary, forgettable wines. Though well-adapted and well-suited
to the Southern Rhône, it would appear to originate elsewhere, probably Spain, and possibly Sardinia before that. It is the same variety as
Cannonau, which the Sardinians claim as their own, and is also known
there as Granaccia. Sardinia was ruled by the Spanish kingdom of Aragón
from 1297 to 1713, so it's possible Grenache originated in Sardinia then
found its way to Spain. What is now Roussillon was ruled by the kingdom of Aragón for four centuries, until 1659, so it's likely that it was imported into France during that period, before making its way east. It was
certainly established in the Southern Rhône before 1800, but probably
not long before that. That Grenache is not native to the Southern Rhône
makes its success here all the more surprising. But this is the northerly
limit of Grenache, and – like Syrah in Côte-Rôtie – when a grape variety
is on the edge of ripening it often gives its most virtuoso performance.

Here Grenache is traditionally grown as bush vines, but some vignerons also train it on wires (guyot, cordon de Royat) making mechanization easier. Bush vines have great longevity here, with centenarian vines
not uncommon. It helps that the vine has relatively good resistance to
trunk diseases like esca. It is however prone to coulure, downy mildew
and botrytis. Relatively early budding and late ripening, it needs a hot
climate like the Southern Rhône and is resistant to drought. It is prone
to build up very high sugar levels, leading to high levels of alcohol –
14.5–15% potential alcohol is fairly standard in the Rhône today before
the grape reaches physiological ripeness, and can be higher. High alcohol is nothing new with this variety – Georges Truc remembers picking
Grenache at over 17% abv in the 1950s. Blending with other grapes
such as Cinsault and Counoise can help bring the final level down.
Acidity however tends to be moderate at best.

Flavours when young vary from strawberry to damson via dark plum,
only rarely straying into black fruit flavours. You can also expect dried
herbs (sage, thyme), tobacco, occasionally rose and violet. The wines
have a full, flowing mouthfeel, generous, with ample glycerol and alcohol sweetness and viscosity of texture. Berries tend to be small, with fairly thick skins here, so wines can be somewhat tannic in youth, though
texturally speaking they tend to be more chewy and dense than upright

and angular like Syrah's. Grenache is prone to oxidation, so needs careful handling, and takes less well to small wooden barrels as a result. Grenache is used mostly for dry wine production in the Rhône, and also for sweet Vins Doux Naturels, particularly in Rasteau.

Syrah (23,031 hectares)

With Syrah's synonym Shiraz sharing a name with a city in Iran, it was long posited that Syrah had ancient Persian roots. But DNA analysis in 1998 showed that Syrah is a natural cross between Mondeuse Blanche (mother) and Dureza (father) which was likely to have taken place in the Rhône-Alpes region, probably Isère. There's been some renewed interest in Dureza as a result, with some curious vignerons such as Yves Cuilleron undertaking new plantings in the Northern Rhône.

Syrah is the only red grape that is permitted in the *crus* of the Northern Rhône. It can however be blended with a small amount of Marsanne and/or Roussanne in Saint-Joseph, Crozes-Hermitage and Hermitage (extremely rare in practice) and up to 20 per cent Viognier in Côte-Rôtie (much more common). Although it's a red grape, unusually the noun in French is feminine – *la Syrah*. Syrah didn't have far to travel to find its way to the Southern Rhône, where it is now the second most widely planted variety, amounting to just over a quarter of total plantings. It is however a relatively recent phenomenon; it was first planted in Châteauneuf in the early 1830s, but in the rest of the Southern Rhône it only started to be planted widely in the 1950s, when hybrids were cleared out to make way for 'improving varieties'.

Today Syrah is grown all over, in particularly high proportions in Vinsobres, Signargues, Grignan-les-Adhémar and Duché d'Uzès. It brings a welcome strictness of tannic structure to Grenache, and also contributes acidity, depth of colour (violet/purple) and complementary, higher-toned aromatics. In the North, classic aromas include just-ripe blackberry, occasionally raspberry and blackcurrant, violet, bacon, black olive and occasionally black pepper (see box on rotundone, page 30). It varies from fresh and light-bodied on cooler sites when cropped high, to full-bodied, dense and powerful in Hermitage and occasionally Cornas in warmer vintages. The wines have a less pliable structure in the mouth than Grenache, having a more precise, finely-sketched tannic frame with a certain coolness and crunch. Alcohols vary typically from 12.5% to 13.5% abv (with no lack of flavour ripeness or impact), and can push higher in hot vintages.

Rotundone

In the late 1990s, Australian winemakers started to move away from an intensely concentrated, fruit-driven style of Shiraz towards a more savoury, spicy style. In an effort to support them, the Australian Wine Research Institute started looking into the source of the spicy, peppery aromas often associated with Northern Rhône Syrah. They started the project in 1999, but it wasn't until 2005 that they finally cracked it, a chemical called rotundone.

Rotundone is a naturally occurring compound that's found in all plants that have a 'peppery' aroma, and it was first identified in a plant called nut grass weed (*Cyperus rotundus*). Concentrations vary considerably across different fruits, herbs and spices. White pepper contains approximately 2,025,000 nanograms per kilogram; black pepper contains 1,205,000; dried marjoram 208,000; rosemary 86,000 and 'peppery' smelling grapes just 190 nanograms per kilogram. The human sensory threshold is 8 nanograms per litre in water or 16 nanograms per litre in wine. A nanogram is one billionth (1/1,000,000,000) of a gram – the human nose is an acutely sensitive organ. Not everyone can detect it however: in tests, the AWRI noted that 20 per cent of panellists couldn't identify it at any concentration.

Rotundone is particularly prevalent in Syrah, but has also been found in other grape varieties, including Duras, Durif, Fer Servadou, Gamay, Graciano, Mondeuse, Négrette, Pineau d'Aunis, Pinot Noir, Prunelard, Schioppettino, Vespolina and even white grapes such as Grüner Veltliner and Riesling. Not all Syrahs contain rotundone. It tends to be more prevalent in cooler or higher elevation sites. Its presence and concentration also vary across vintages. Quite what causes high concentrations of rotundone remains unclear, but it appears to be a combination of factors, including length of time between veraison and harvest, clonal selection, fruit exposure to sunlight and vine age. Using stems and leaves in ferments could also be a factor, since the compound is found in green matter as well as the skins of the grapes – but not the pulp or pips.

In the South, Syrah gives a different expression. Varietal wines rarely, if ever, match the clarity and definition of aroma and textural finesse of the best reds of the Northern Rhône (though Ventoux can make some compelling examples) but it works well in a blend. Aromatically, you can expect ripe blackberry and chewy, blackberry-skin tannins. Liquorice is a common characteristic, as is tar; spice flavours trump herbal ones, and Szechuan pepper is more common than black pepper. Use of stems is an increasingly common trend, particularly in the Northern Rhône (see page 256).

The vigorous plants need careful trellising to protect them from the wind. In the Southern Rhône, training on wires is the most common technique. In the Northern Rhône, the use of wooden (or occasionally plastic or metal) stakes called *échalas* is traditional, a more practical option on steep terraces. Syrah only has a short window to be harvested in perfect ripeness, and berries can shrivel quickly once ripe. It's prone to chlorosis, botrytis, mites and Syrah decline (see box, page 197). Unlike Grenache, it's a reductive variety, so needs treating accordingly to mitigate unappealing aromas.

It takes well to oak barrels, and barrel ageing is common in both the south and the north. The fashion for new oak barriques is thankfully subsiding, with more and more producers opting for larger barrels and less new oak, resulting in wines with better balance, more naturalistic fruit tannins and a clearer expression of terroir. Overwhelming use of oak is however still a common problem, particularly in Côte-Rôtie. Syrah-based wines can be particularly long-lived, particularly in Hermitage, where wines typically start to show their best after 20 years in bottle. Though not unique to Syrah, wines do seem particularly prone to go through a 'dumb' or closed period between 4 and 8 years of age.

Carignan Noir (4,522 hectares)

Carignan is only found in any quantity in its dark-skinned guise for Côtes-du-Rhône and southern *cru* wines (Carignan Gris is not permitted, and regrettably Carignan Blanc is only permitted in restricted quantities in Tavel). Like Grenache, this grape is thought to have originated in Spain, most likely Cariñena in Aragón.

Carignan may only amount to 6 per cent of production, but it's the third most planted grape in the Rhône Valley, being planted a little all over, especially Cairanne and to a lesser extent Rasteau. Quantities in the blend are often restricted by appellation rules and it's not permitted at all in some big AOCs such as Gigondas and Châteauneuf-du-Pape. It was once widespread in the south of France, especially the Languedoc, but EU vine-pull schemes in the 1990s gave financial incentives to winegrowers to replace it with so-called 'improving' varieties such as Grenache, Syrah and Mourvèdre.

Carignan's global reputation has been rehabilitated slightly in recent years, partly thanks to the quality of some contemporary Chilean examples, but it still feels like something of a second-class grape. A hugely productive variety, it can yield up to 200 hectolitres per hectare if given half a chance, so strict conditions in the vineyard are required to contain it and are the key to good quality, as it is prone to bitterness at high crop loads. Vine age is also a distinct predictor of quality with Carignan. Late budding and late ripening, it craves a hot climate such as the Southern Rhône. It is prone to powdery mildew, downy mildew and grape moths. Bunches cling tightly to the vine, making mechanical harvesting a challenge.

The best results are impenetrably dark in colour, high in acidity with powerful tannins and intense, driving dark-fruit flavour – all things that make it a good blending partner for Grenache. Carbonic maceration can help bring out its floral aspect and red fruit character, and soften its tannins. Domaine la Luminaille in Rasteau uses this technique on its old Carignan bush vine blending component to good effect.

Late ripening and drought resistant, with zesty acidity, moderate alcohol levels and good tannic intensity, perhaps Carignan's use in the Southern Rhône is worth reappraisal. For those with access to old vines, quite possibly.

Mourvèdre (2,730 hectares)

While Carignan might currently be the third most planted grape in the Rhône Valley, it is surely only a matter of time before it's overtaken by Mourvèdre. After all, for many Southern Rhône blends, a proportion of Syrah and/or Mourvèdre is a mandatory supporting actor to superstar Grenache.

Another grape of Spanish origin, it was probably introduced to Provence from the Camp de Morvedre [sic] area of Valencia in the sixteenth century where it was originally known (and still is known) as Monastrell. Early plantings in the Southern Rhône were at Château de Beaucastel in Châteauneuf-du-Pape (shortly after the Second World War) from cuttings taken from the revered Domaine Tempier in Bandol, still the heartland of French Mourvèdre. Mourvèdre's adoption in the Southern Rhône outside Châteauneuf is more recent, arriving even later than Syrah, and to begin with it often struggled to fully ripen. They say that 'Mourvèdre likes it feet in the water and its head in the sun' – it likes a hot, sunny climate but it doesn't like overly dry conditions. The Southern Rhône now regularly delivers on the extended heat and sun that it needs, and on certain soils (such as clay) or favourable sites with water sources, it can offer adequate moisture too. It has been gradually creeping northwards in the Southern Rhône and now can be found all the way up to Grignan-les-Adhémar.

Mourvèdre gives low yields of compact bunches made up of small berries with thick skins. The dark wines have good acidity and dense, sometimes chewy or leathery tannins. Alcohol is fairly high but not as high as Grenache, and the aromatic profile is quite particular: black-berry, blueberry, violet, and sometimes a sweet, earthy character like a bag of peat. Prone to reduction, it needs regular racking to avoid off aromas and takes well to maturation in barrel. Pure Mourvèdres are rare but can be found (at Domaine du Joncier in Lirac for example), and the variety has good ageing abilities. The variety is gaining an enthusiastic following all across the Southern Rhône; expect to see more and more of it – where sites allow – in future.

Cinsault (2,359 hectares)

This is the only other grape with more than 2,000 hectares planted in the Rhône Valley, making up 3 per cent of plantings. Found in small quantities all over the Southern Rhône it is particularly prevalent in Tavel, where it makes up a fifth of the vineyard area (where it's used for rosé). Cinsault is a member of the Piquepoul ampelographic group, which all come from the Vaucluse or the Languedoc, suggesting it origi-nated in the south of France. It is first mentioned by Olivier de Serres in 1600 in his *Botanicum Monspeliense* under its old synonym Marroquin.

A fairly delicate variety with big bunches and large berries, it is well adapted to the Southern Rhône due to its drought resistance and affin-ity for hot conditions. Conversations with vignerons indicate that it's a well-liked variety, though whether this growing popularity will result in increased plantings remains to be seen. It makes gentle, amiable wines, often red-fruited with raspberry, strawberry and raspberry-leaf aromat-ics, and often a light, floral perfume. It has a lightness and fluidity on the palate, with gentle, very fine tannins like wet clay. Acidity is moder-ate, as are alcohol levels, and despite its aerial nature it ages well. It does however suffer badly from esca.

One downside for growers is that the wines are often pale in colour. Rhône vignerons, particularly of the older generation, still set a lot of store by dark colouring in a wine. It's understandable. Pale colouring can suggest dilution; Grenache loses its colour with high crop loads, so darker wines can be easier to sell to négociants. But if it discourages growers from working with excellent local varieties such as Cinsault and Counoise, then this preoccupation with colour would be better forgotten. After all, consumers don't seem to mind paler, transparent red wines; in fact, at the time of writing they are currently more fashionable than dark wines.

Cinsault is capable of real excellence; Rhône vignerons with any doubt only need look to the best of South Africa. A barrel tasting of the Cinsault component of Château de Fonsalette is an unforgettable experience. A more accessible example of how pure and drinkable it can be is Domaine le Sollier's 'Les 4 Chemins', albeit a blend of 60 per cent old-vine Cinsault with younger Syrah. I hope, and suspect, that in time we will see more of it.

Négociants

Most of the hill of Hermitage has now been acquired by négociants. It's testament to the commercial and financial might that these businesses wield. Négociants are effectively businesses that buy grapes, must or wine and bottle them for sale under their own labels. It's a common business model seen all over France, particularly in Burgundy, Bordeaux and the Rhône. At the time of writing there were around 50 négociants based in the Rhône.

Family-owned estates may excel at viticulture and vinification, but they don't always shine when it comes to sales and distribution. Négociants are often businessmen and businesswomen first and foremost, who excel at brand building, and export and sales, particularly to large structures such as supermarkets. Négociants can buy from numerous sources and create the kind of large-volume blends that smaller domaines can't provide. Large négociants can exert a powerful influence over whole communities of growers, even whole appellations. This can be a stylistic influence, or a more practical one, regarding yields or methods such as organics. When a massive négociant blend such as Jaboulet's Côtes-du-Rhône Parallèle 45 turns organic, if growers want to sell their crop, they must go organic too. These 'locomotives' can also be instrumental in promoting lesser-known appellations outside the region.

In the Rhône, négociants are often located close to the most renowned appellations. In Côte-Rôtie, noteworthy négociants include **Guigal** and **Les Vins de Vienne**. In Tain there are several: **Chapoutier**, **Jaboulet**, **Delas**, **Ferraton**, **Nicolas Perrin** and, a little further south, **J.L. Chave Sélections**. In the southern part of the Rhône, in Châteauneuf-du-Pape, there is **Ogier**, **Famille**

Perrin and **Alain Jaume**. Around Gigondas you'll find **Gabriel Meffre**, **Pierre Amadieu** and **Saint Cosme**. Elsewhere in the Southern Rhône, **Tardieu-Laurent**, **Dauvergne-Ranvier** and **La Ferme du Mont** are worthy of praise.

Not all négociants own any land, but it's becoming increasingly common for them to invest in their own vineyards. Conversely, more and more domaines are introducing a négociant side to their business. If a private domaine has unused capacity in the winery, it makes good financial sense to use this by buying grapes, particularly if it has demand it can't meet. In this way, a domaine can make and sell more wine without having to invest in vineyards. Some producers differentiate their offering by using a different name for their négociant wines: for example, **Château de Saint Cosme** for wines from owned vineyards, **Saint Cosme** for négociant wines. Others, such as **François Villard**, use the same name for both. Why would we want to know which wines are from domaine fruit and which wine are from négociant activity? Because a private domaine that grows its own grapes and make its own wine has more control over every stage of the process, and can take more care and pay more attention to detail as a result. Négociants would counter that they aren't tied to specific vineyards, and can buy different parcels according to quality each year. Many négociants have long-term partnerships with growers however, and can even dictate the growing methods, from yields to picking dates. According to Damien Brisset at Ferraton, 'it's all about human relationships, not just commercial ones.'

But it's not the same as owning your own vines. 'I have trouble with the idea of *grand vin* and terroir with a négociant,' explains one prominent Saint-Péray winemaker. 'For wines that tell a story, you need to be in the vines. To understand a vintage, you need to be in the vines. If you haven't worked the vines and observed the conditions of the vintage, and the crop just lands at the winery, how do you know what to do with it?' This isn't to say that négociant bottlings from bought grapes can't be as good as many domaine bottlings. But it's often the cuvées produced from a négociant's own vineyards that are the most impressive in their range.

Marselan (945 hectares)

Marselan is the most popular crossing on our list, produced in Montpellier in 1961 by Paul Truel by crossing Cabernet Sauvignon and Grenache Noir. It now makes up just over 1 per cent of vineyard area and is allowed to be used in some satellite Other Rhône Valley appellations and AOC Côtes-du-Rhône wines, but crossings can't make up more than 10 per cent of a producer's plantings. It was produced in an attempt to create a variety with large berries and generous yields, but the result actually has small berries and gives low yields. Quality however can be good, and the vine is resistant to powdery mildew, mites, botrytis and coulure, so has since been welcomed by many growers. The deeply-coloured grapes give dark wines with silky tannins and intense aromatic red and black berry fruits. Late ripening, and prone to green, herbal flavours if it doesn't ripen fully, it needs plentiful water. It's a grape variety that's attracting attention elsewhere in the world. Subject to final agreement by the INAO, it's likely to soon be added to the permitted list of grape varieties for AOC Bordeaux and AOC Bordeaux Supérieur. It's also seeing significant plantings in China, particularly in Ningxia.

Counoise (146 hectares)

Counoise is a minor but talented player. Although most common in Châteauneuf-du-Pape, it crops up here and there all over the Southern Rhône. It's part of the Piquepoul ampelographic group, originating in the south of France and was first mentioned in 1626 in Avignon. It grows well in hot, stony terrain and has big berries that ripen late. Counoise is particularly useful in Southern Rhône blends as it has good acidity and only moderate alcohol. Wines tend to be pale, with subtle tannins, and the aromatic profile is spicy and peppery with crunchy red berry fruit. Varietal Counoise is more common in the USA than in the Rhône, but Domaine de Piaugier in Sablet makes one, and Domaine Alary in Cairanne has done in the past. Counoise isn't a variety that delivers powerful aromatics or great structure, but it helps to rein in Grenache, adding freshness and brightness to a blend – not to mention bringing down overall alcohol levels. An undervalued variety.

Muscat à Petits Grains Noirs (116 hectares)

Only used for rosé and red Muscat de Beaumes de Venise (see chapter 7) and as a minor component for Clairette de Die rosé and Crémant de Die, this dark-skinned natural mutation of Muscat à Petits Grains Blancs is usually found co-planted among blocks of the white-skinned version. It is blended with Muscat à Petits Grains Blancs to make Muscat de Beaumes de Venise rosé. Muscat de Beaumes de Venise *rouge* must use exclusively Muscat à Petits Grains Noirs. It shares the white-skinned version's vibrantly floral and grapey aromas, often with some darker berry fruit flavours and gentle tannins.

Caladoc (33 hectares)

The second cross in the list of admissible red grapes, Caladoc was first produced by Paul Truel by crossing Grenache Noir and Malbec, in Montpellier in 1958, in a successful attempt to produce a variety resistant to coulure. It is also resistant to botrytis and fairly resistant to powdery mildew and its main advantages are consistency of crop level and resistance to drought. It was allowed for use in AOC Côtes-du-Rhône production from May 2019. It's admissible for AOC Côtes-du-Rhône wines only, not Côtes-du-Rhône Villages. Resulting wines are dark in colour, full-bodied, robustly tannic and can be very good.

Gamay Noir (22 hectares)

You might be surprised to see Gamay in this list, but all four of the most common Burgundy grapes are found in the Rhône. Like Pinot Noir, Gamay may only be used for Châtillon-en-Diois *rouge* and rosé, where it is the principal variety, making up at least 60 per cent of the blend. (It is also permitted as a minor component of Clairette de Die rosé.) Still Diois Gamay tends to be bright and crunchy with a certain depth of fruit, colour and tannic density that marks it out from Beaujolais. Though not allowed in AOC wines in the Northern Rhône, it is still possible to find small parcels of Gamay, which can make for delicious wines.

Muscardin (15 hectares)

Though permitted throughout the Southern Rhône, Muscardin is one of the rarest red grapes in the Rhône. It would appear to originate in Châteauneuf-du-Pape, which is home to 11 of the 15 hectares found across the region. Rather like Counoise, it tends to be pale in colour, with relatively low alcohol and high acidity. It ripens early, and has a floral perfume that can bring lift and freshness to a blend.

Piquepoul Noir (14 hectares)

Piquepoul comes in three berry colours, *blanc*, *gris* and *noir*. They are all possibilities in AOC Rhône wines, though Piquepoul Gris is only permitted in Châteauneuf-du-Pape, and even here it is vanishingly rare. Piquepouls Blanc and Noir are only found in tiny quantities, but are permitted in Other Rhône AOC wines too. Of the region's 14 hectares of Piquepoul Noir, 4 are located in Tavel. It likes dry, unfertile soils and ripens fairly late. Like most minor players, the wines it produces are relatively pale. Acidity is high, which can be useful in a blend; alcohol levels also tend to be high.

Vaccarèse (12 hectares)

Vaccarèse would appear to originate in the Southern Rhône, where it was first mentioned in 1538. Its official name is Brun Argenté, but I've never heard a vigneron in the Rhône use this synonym. It's also known as Camarèse, which I have only heard in Chusclan, where it was once commonly used to make Chusclan rosé. Of the 12 hectares in production across the Southern Rhône, half are in Châteauneuf-du-Pape; considering so few vignerons grow Vaccarèse, it's surprising it has so many names. Vaccarèse ripens late and likes plentiful sun. Its large bunches of fat berries are prone to botrytis. It gives fresh, floral wines with low alcohol – François Perrin of Château de Beaucastel compares it to Cinsault. Château des Fines Roches in Châteauneuf-du-Pape makes a pure varietal example called Forget Me Not.

Pinot Noir (11 hectares)

The only AOC permitted to grow Pinot Noir is in the Diois, for Châtillon-en-Diois. Pinot Noir can be used for Châtillon-en-Diois *rouge* and rosé, to a maximum of 25 per cent, where it adds a little lithe finesse to the Gamay and/or Syrah.

Terret Noir (3 hectares)

One of the rarest of all Rhône grape varieties, almost all of which is found in Châteauneuf-du-Pape. I'm yet to find a winemaker with anything terribly positive to say about it, which might explain its rarity. Like Piquepoul, Terret comes in three berry colours, Blanc, Gris and Noir. Only the dark-skinned mutation is permitted in Rhône appellations. This late ripening, vigorous variety from the Languedoc was originally planted due to its ability to produce massive yields. Wines tend to be pale in colour, with good acidity and moderate alcohol, giving them a certain value in a blend.

Couston (2 hectares)

Couston was added to the list of admissible varieties in May 2019 at the same time as Caladoc. Similarly, it is only allowed for AOC Côtes-du-Rhône wines, not AOC Côtes-du-Rhône Villages and crossings can't make up more than 10 per cent of a producer's total plantings. This natural crossing of Grenache and local grape Aubun was discovered by Julien Couston in the early 1970s. Wines are full-bodied and tannic, with very high alcohol and deep colour. Like Caladoc, a major advantage is its resistance to coulure, but it needs plenty of water. Prone to green flavours if picked unripe, it can take on sugar alarmingly quickly as it ripens.

Calitor (no data)

Once common in Provence, particularly Bandol, Calitor is now nearly extinct. In the Rhône it is only used in Tavel, and a producer's total plantings are restricted to a maximum of 10 per cent. The big bunches of fat berries yield pale wines that are low in alcohol and acidity.

WHITE AND PINK GRAPES

Grenache Blanc (1,958 hectares)

Grenache Blanc makes up 20 per cent of white and pink grape plantings (representing just 2 per cent of total plantings). The white-skinned version of Grenache Noir is only found in any quantity in the Southern Rhône, where it is found everywhere, even in appellations that don't make white wine (the only AOC without any to speak of is Gigondas). It buds and ripens a little earlier than the dark-skinned version, and is marginally less sensitive to coulure, though this remains a recurrent problem. It can be rather plain; some might even say bland. It gives full-bodied wines, fat and oily with plenty of glycerol and alcohol on the palate. It can be uncomfortably high in alcohol in fact, and its lack of acidity does nothing to hide this, though it can communicate a sense of minerality, which helps bring balance. Aromatically the grape is subtle; gentle red apple or pear notes, perhaps a streak of apricot, sometimes gently floral.

Grenache Blanc works in some ways like a canvas for local vignerons. Many other Southern Rhône grape varieties can be either too weak or too strong by themselves, but when used as a palette of colours on a background of Grenache Blanc they can produce something beautiful. It is, therefore, almost always used in a blend, as it gains much from the more aromatic and acidic grapes that might be a little too intense by themselves. Outside Spain and Roussillon, Châteauneuf-du-Pape is where it creates most interest. For a pure varietal example that might convert you to its discreet charms, try Château de Vaudieu Châteauneuf-du-Pape *blanc* Clos du Belvédère; grown on limestone, it has a mineral tension that brings it to life.

Muscat à Petits Grains Blancs (1,617 hectares)

The huge amount of Muscat à Petits Grains Blancs might come as a surprise, but the vast majority is for sparkling wine, mostly Clairette de Die (where it makes up a minimum of 75 per cent of the blend) and Crémant de Die (maximum 10 per cent). The other wine it is used for is Muscat de Beaumes de Venise (100 per cent Muscat à Petits Grains Blancs for white and blended with Muscat à Petits Grains Noirs for rosé). Dozens of different grape varieties include the name Muscat, and Muscat à Petits Grains Blancs is considered among the highest quality. It has smaller berries than other types and is susceptible to botrytis, but this is avoided in Muscat de Beaumes de Venise. Still dry wines using Muscat do exist in the Rhône, some very good (such as Domaine des Bernardins), but must be bottled under IGP or Vin de France.

Viognier (1,423 hectares)

Considering that it's not permitted in Châteauneuf-du-Pape, and only allowed in two appellations for whites in the Northern Rhône, Viognier is remarkably prevalent today in the Rhône Valley, making up 15 per cent of white and pink plantings (but accounting for less than 2 per cent of total plantings).

It originates from the Northern Rhône, probably from Condrieu or Côte-Rôtie, and was first mentioned in 1781. In their peerless reference book *Wine Grapes* (to which this chapter owes a great debt), Jancis Robinson, Julia Harding and Jose Vouillamoz point out that Viognier is either a sibling or grandparent of Syrah, and is also related to Nebbiolo. An early-budding variety, it can be susceptible to frost, and with a dislike of windy sites it is often grown on wires. Viognier ripens early, and can rapidly build up sugar as it approaches ripeness, with a corresponding dip in acidity so choosing the date of picking wisely is particularly crucial with this variety. It has reasonable resistance to botrytis.

There is a plethora of options when it comes to winemaking (see Condrieu, page 272). In the Northern Rhône it's used pure in

Condrieu for dry wines (and, very rarely, sweet wines such as Guigal's Luminescence). In the South its use is widespread; varietal wines are in the minority but can be very good (such as Domaine de Grangeneuve's Grignan-les-Adhémar Cuvée V) but are more commonly blended. A cap on the percentage of Viognier permitted in southern appellations is common, as it can quickly dominate a blend. The question of ageability is often raised. The short answer is that Viognier is best drunk young, apart from the best Condrieu, which can develop and gain interest and complexity for 20 years or more. I do not believe this is a matter of taste. Like great white Burgundy, great Condrieu, though comparatively rare, is exquisite in age as it is in youth.

Considering there is so much now planted in the Rhône Valley, it's surprising that in 1965 there were only 8 hectares in existence. Its renaissance, thanks in large part to the work of Georges Vernay (see page 274), has been swift, and it's now planted all over the world. The Viogniers of Condrieu however are yet to find an equal elsewhere, and despite the exuberance of the grape variety, Condrieu is now unquestionably among the greatest of all white wines.

Clairette Blanche (1,322 hectares)

Clairette Blanche (usually referred to simply as Clairette) is one of the most characterful and quintessentially Southern Rhône of all the white grapes grown here. Aside from a couple of tiny parcels, it is only grown in the Southern Rhône, and makes up 14 per cent of total Rhône Valley white and pink plantings. It's the most popular white grape in Tavel and all the Southern Rhône *crus* that produce white wines – apart from Châteauneuf-du-Pape and Lirac, where it comes a close second to Grenache Blanc. There are even 13 hectares in Gigondas, which is a lot considering AOC Gigondas doesn't make white wine – yet (see box on white Gigondas, page 127). The Southern Rhône even has two appellations dedicated wholly to this grape variety – Clairette de Bellegarde in the deep south and Coteaux de Die in the Diois. It's the only white grape in the Southern Rhône that gets the spotlight for an appellation solo.

One of the oldest grape varieties in the south of France, Clairette is now thoroughly at home in the Rhône, though it possibly originates in the Hérault *département* of the Languedoc. The name may refer to the tiny white hairs on the underside of the leaves which reflect the light. The vigorous plants grow upright and withstand the wind. It is not prone to powdery mildew or botrytis and is very late to ripen. Local vignerons often refer to the grape's characteristic freshness, but the acidity is never terribly marked; on the contrary it can be quite flabby, often requiring some additional pep from spikier varieties. Its freshness is more a gentle aerial aromatic lift, somewhere between flowers and freshly laundered linen. It gives wines that are full-bodied, generous on the palate, silky and flowing. Its use in the Diois is mostly for sparkling wines. Crémant de Die must contain at least 55 per cent, and Clairette de Die (some-what contrarily, considering the name) is limited to a maximum of 25 per cent Clairette Blanche, Clairette Rose or a combination.

Blending

Are some varieties better than others? It doesn't really work like that. It's true that if you could only plant one variety to make white wine for example, it probably wouldn't be Bourboulenc, which can feel a little hollow on the mid-palate and lacking in generosity of fruit. But the acidity and salinity it can bring to, say, Grenache Blanc can make it invaluable in a blend. 'The idea of blend-ing is one plus one equals three,' says Ralph Garcin of Château de Nalys. With so few varieties permitted in the Northern Rhône, blending is much more common in the South, where it's intrinsic to winemaking culture. Though the occasional varietal wine can be found (especially pure Grenache wines in Châteauneuf), they are rare. Blending can start in the vineyards with co-planting, or take place in the winery, either during or after fermentation.

Before phylloxera, field blends were common, but since then it has become traditional to plant in blocks of single varieties. It's an eminently reasonable and sensible approach; varieties can be matched to the right soils; plants ripen at the same time so can be picked together. There is however a nascent trend to re-turn to field blends, with producers such as Domaine la Péquélette in Vinsobres and Domaine Santa Duc in Gigondas moving in this direction (at least for cer-tain vineyards) and finding more complexity and character in the final wines. Others, such as Domaine de la Vieille Julienne, have done this for decades.

Those who grow varieties separately can either decide to co-ferment or fer-ment separately then blend afterwards. For those with many different varieties, often the only practical option is to dedicate some tanks to single varieties and co-ferment others. Even when a viable option, only a minority choose to co-ferment since blending before bottling offers more control. But some winemakers believe that co-fermenting brings more harmony to the finished wines than fermenting each variety separately. Blending is a key moment for almost all Southern Rhône wineries, and often takes hours or days of intense tasting and discussion before the final decision is made.

The singular lens of a lone variety, whether it be Syrah in the Northern Rhône or Pinot Noir in Burgundy, does offer a certain clarity when it comes to identifying specific terroirs or winemaking decisions in the final wine. The proliferation of grape varieties (not to mention the particular treatment of each one), and the infinite different possible blends thereof makes Southern Rhône winemaking less obvious from tasting the wines alone. Blending is a creative act, which brings an added layer of human intervention to the final product. It is perhaps surprising therefore that so many estates in the Southern Rhône are christened after local features of the terroir, whereas estates in the Northern Rhône are more commonly named after the winemaker.

Roussanne (1,016 hectares)

Genetically and stylistically similar to Marsanne, Roussanne is rich, broad and full-bodied wherever in the Rhône it is grown. Along with Marsanne, it was first mentioned in a manuscript dating back to 1781 referring to its use in Hermitage. Its name in all likelihood refers to the *roux* or russet colour of the grapes as they ripen. Like Marsanne, it does well on poor, stony soils but is susceptible to powdery mildew, botrytis and mites. It is harder to grow than Marsanne and more subject to fungal diseases. It also tends to brown quicker once in bottle. It would appear to have made its journey south earlier than Marsanne, since unlike Marsanne it is permitted in Châteauneuf-du-Pape. It's certainly better adapted to life in the Southern Rhône; it seems to handle the hotter, drier conditions better, and is therefore planted more widely and in greater volumes, particularly in Lirac and Vacqueyras.

In terms of weight and shape on the palate, Northern Rhône Roussanne is similar to Marsanne: full and rounded with deep-set acidity and typically higher alcohol than many other white grapes. Texturally it can be a little grainy (think pear flesh) and is often thicker and creamier than Marsanne. Aromatically more straightforward than Marsanne, it presents more pear on the nose, along with quince and white flowers. In the Southern Rhône it is most often used in a blend, offering the weight and breadth of Grenache Blanc but with more aromatic interest. Unblended, it gives particularly full-bodied, unctuous and generous wines, especially when fermented and/or aged in oak barrels. Roussanne does have a particular affinity with oak, and the results can be extravagantly, sometimes outrageously, rich, such as Château de Beaucastel Châteauneuf-du-Pape *blanc* Roussanne Vieilles Vignes, Domaine Raymond Usseglio Châteauneuf-du-Pape *blanc* Pure Roussanne and Domaine Grand Veneur Châteauneuf-du-Pape *blanc* La Fontaine. Like Marsanne, it is used mostly for still wines, but can also appear with or without Marsanne in sparkling Saint-Péray. It can also be used for sweet Hermitage Vin de Paille.

Marsanne (816 hectares)

Indigenous to the Northern Rhône, Marsanne probably takes its name from the commune of Marsanne, to the north-east of Montélimar. José Vouillamoz's work on grape DNA strongly suggests a parent–offspring relationship with Roussanne. Now by far the most common white grape in the Northern Rhône, it is used either solo or blended with Roussanne in all its white-producing appellations (apart from Condrieu and Château-Grillet, which must be pure Viognier). In the Southern Rhône it is always used in blends, usually in AOC Côtes-du-Rhône and AOC Côtes-du-Rhône Villages. Roussanne is much more popular in the South than Marsanne. Though rarely seen outside France, the heights of quality that the grape can achieve are not in question. Michel Chapoutier uses the grape exclusively for his array of white Hermitage wines, which are among the most extraordinary white wines in the world.

With large bunches of small berries Marsanne is very productive, so needs strict control in the vineyard. It produces bold, rich whites with plenty of body and weight, matched with an adequate, if never high, acidity. Aromatically it can be very broad depending on where it is grown. Fruits can range from mango and apricot through to quince and pear, occasionally with a slight vegetal streak like rhubarb. It often gives floral honeysuckle-like notes, taking on flavours of honey, and nuts like hazelnut and almond, as it ages. Though mostly used for still wines, it's also used for dry sparkling wines in Saint-Péray. Sweet Marsanne can be found in the form of the rare Hermitage Vin de Paille.

Ugni Blanc (556 hectares)

Ugni Blanc's use is restricted in the Southern Rhône, where it is often allowed (though rarely used) as a minor player in red *crus*. It is permitted in Lirac *blanc* and rosé to a maximum of 20 per cent, but not allowed in Tavel, Cairanne *blanc*, Vacqueyras *blanc* or Châteauneuf-du-Pape *blanc*.

It is allowed in AOC Côtes-du-Rhône and AOC Côtes-du-Rhône Villages and some satellite Other Rhône Valley appellations, but only as a minor component. However, it can be used up to 50 per cent in the Luberon. Ugni Blanc is a Tuscan import, locally known as Trebbiano Toscano. It's not a new arrival, however; it was brought to France in the fourteenth century, and is mentioned as 'uniers' in 1514 in Vaucluse. High yielding and adaptable to different soils but sensitive to strong winds, its main benefit is its usefully high acidity, though the wines age quickly. It can a contribute a fresh, gently floral character but is otherwise of minor interest.

Vermentino (525 hectares)

The star grape of the Luberon, where it is now as widely planted as Grenache Blanc, Vermentino is not permitted elsewhere in the Rhône, except in restricted amounts in the white wines of Other Rhône Valley appellations of Ventoux, Duché d'Uzès and Costières de Nîmes. The local name for it is Rolle, but most winemakers here call it Vermentino. A very old variety, native to Italy, and still found around northern Italy, it is now more commonly planted in southern France. Not the easiest grape to work with, it crops high one year and low the next and suffers from powdery mildew and trunk diseases such as esca, so old vines are rare. Despite this, it is popular with winemakers for the character of its wines.

Vermentino has a very different character to most other Rhône varieties. Typically light- to medium-bodied, with zesty acidity and a pithy, citrusy note that brings refreshment, it often displays a certain pleasing bitterness on the finish. Nonetheless it marries well with other Rhône varieties grown in the Luberon, and provides the aperitif style of white that the Rhône has previously been lacking.

Bourboulenc (231 hectares)

It may be relatively rare with just 2 per cent of white and pink plantings, but in the Southern Rhône Bourboulenc is an important white grape that brings a lot to the blend. It's dotted all over the Southern Rhône, and originates from Vaucluse; its name is likely to come from Barbolenquiera, the ancient name for a small vineyard in Aubignan, near Beaumes de Venise. The only Bourboulenc I'm aware of being grown outside the Rhône or the Languedoc is at Tablas Creek in Paso Robles, USA.

Bourboulenc has thick skins, loose bunches and ripens late but retains its acidity well whilst keeping alcohol levels moderate – and therein lies its usefulness. I've never encountered a finished wine made with pure Bourboulenc, but tasting a varietal Bourboulenc before blending also reveals a zesty citrus aroma and a certain salinity. It lacks a little fruit on the mid-palate however, which it can easily find in a blend from Grenache Blanc, Clairette or Roussanne. Domaine Pierre André's Châteauneuf-du-Pape *blanc*, a 50–50 blend of Bourboulenc and Clairette, delivers a complete and delicious wine.

Clairette Rose (103 hectares)

Clairette Rose (not Rosé) is the pink-skinned mutation of Clairette. Small plantings are found dotted all over the Southern Rhône but particularly on the west bank, in Lirac, Tavel, Laudun and Chusclan. It is also popular in Ventoux and Châteauneuf-du-Pape. Pierre Charnay is damning in his *Vignobles et Vins des Côtes du Rhône*, saying it's 'devoid of any aromatic originality' and only occasionally chosen instead of Clairette Blanche as it gives higher levels of alcohol. This seems unfair. Though varietal examples are extremely rare, La Bastide Saint Dominique makes a Châteauneuf-du-Pape *blanc* consisting of a third each Clairette Rose, Grenache Blanc and Roussanne, which always jumps out of a line-up for its gentle floral perfume, which I can only attribute to the Clairette Rose component. Isabel Ferrando of Domaine Saint-Préfert in Châteauneuf bottles some pure from time to time, and says it smells of white lilacs. It's permitted in Clairette de Die in small quantities but not Crémant de Die, which can only contain Clairette Blanche.

Grenache Gris (35 hectares)

The pink-skinned version of Grenache Noir, with which it shares many viticultural characteristics, is permitted widely throughout the Southern Rhône but usually just for inclusion in red wines. This is a shame, as it can produce excellent, characterful whites with real tension. Domaine Alary in Cairanne is currently planting more with this in mind. Mostly used for dry wines, it is also permitted in all colours of Rasteau Vin Doux Naturel. Along with Grenache Blanc, it's the only other permitted grape in Rasteau Vin Doux Naturel *blanc*.

Piquepoul Blanc (31 hectares)

An 'accessory' white grape variety, along with Ugni Blanc, for AOC Côtes-du-Rhône and AOC Côtes-du-Rhône Villages, Piquepoul Blanc can only be used as a minor component in the blend. There is even less

Piquepoul Blanc planted than Ugni Blanc, even though its use is more widely permitted in Southern *crus*. Nonetheless, it's still the most widely planted of the three colours of Piquepoul. It is highly adapted to the Southern Rhône insofar as it grows well in hot climates, ripening late but retaining its acidity.

Chardonnay (29 hectares)

Chardonnay needs little introduction but has very limited application in the AOC wines of the Rhône. It's only used in the Diois, for Châtillon-en-Diois *blanc*. Wines can be pure Chardonnay or a blend with Aligoté.

Aligoté (27 hectares)

The second most planted white grape in Burgundy, Aligoté, like Chardonnay, is only permitted in the Diois. It is mostly used for Châtillon-en-Diois *blanc*, in which wines can be pure Aligoté or blended with Chardonnay. It's also a minor grape in Crémant de Die.

Carignan Blanc (4 hectares)

Only permitted in Tavel (where it must not exceed 10 per cent of a producer's plantings), Carignan Blanc is the white-skinned mutation of Carignan Noir. It is late ripening, with moderate alcohol and lively acidity, which makes it useful in the blend with Grenache.

Macabeu (3 hectares)

Macabeu is only allowed in Costières de Nîmes, where it could theoretically make up as much as 50 per cent of whites and 20 per cent of rosés. Likely to have been imported from Spain, via Roussillon, it ripens late and does well in dry conditions, but can be easily wind-damaged. Large, compact bunches of spherical grapes give lightly floral wines that are high in alcohol and low in acidity.

Piquepoul Gris (3 hectares)

The pink-berried version of the Piquepoul family (see Piquepoul Blanc and Piquepoul Noir) is only allowed in Châteauneuf-du-Pape, and exceedingly rare. The only estates I have encountered that grow any are Domaine de Beaurenard and Domaine Gourt de Mautens near Rasteau (whose wines are bottled under IGP Vaucluse). Daniel Coulon of Domaine de Beaurenard is fascinated with old local grape varieties and keeps a conservatory taken from old vines of the estate. In terms of flavour, he says Piquepoul Gris is similar to Piquepoul Blanc but fresher, and is 'very finely tannic, but no more than Bourboulenc'.

Picardan (1 hectare)

This ancient variety indigenous to the south of France was popular in the nineteenth century. Picardan is now practically extinct except for a tiny amount scattered around Châteauneuf-du-Pape, the only appellation in the Rhône where it's permitted, and practically the only one where you'll find it. The few estates that own some vines include Domaine Roger Perrin and Domaine l'Or de Line; Château de Vaudieu and Clos des Papes have more than most. It has big bunches and berries, likes hot, dry sites and its major attractions are its fairly high acidity and highly aromatic nature. Laurent Brechet of Château de Vaudieu says 'it's fantastic – like a white version of Cinsault.'

Other grape varieties in the Northern Rhône

There are only four grape varieties in the Northern Rhône: Syrah for reds, Marsanne, Roussanne and Viognier for whites. Or are there?

For the eight *crus* that's correct, but let's not forget AOC Côtes-du-Rhône, IGP Collines Rhodaniennes and Vin de France. Here are some examples of wines from Northern Rhône terroirs made with different varieties:

- Cave Julien Cecillon makes a Gamay from a 2 hectare planting in Ardoix in the Ardèche.
- Domaine Romaneaux-Destezet also makes some old-vine Gamay on this side of the river.
- Domaine de Monteillet grows Cugnette (the local name for Jacquère) on the east bank of the Rhône, and Clairette near the winery.
- Domaine des Amphores in Chavanay grows a little Clairette.
- Domaine Gonon makes a Chasselas.
- Domaine Jamet grows a little Grenache Blanc to blend into the Marsanne, Roussanne and Viognier for a Côtes-du-Rhône *blanc*.
- Domaine Catherine & Pascal Jamet makes a little Merlot and Cabernet Sauvignon.
- Cave Yves Cuilleron has planted Dureza, Durif, Persan and Chatus.

4

THE APPELLATION SYSTEM

> ## Top line Rhône Valley statistics (2019)
>
> - Second largest French AOC wine area after Bordeaux.
>
> - Vineyards in the following French *départements*: Ardèche, Drôme, Gard, Rhône/Loire/Isère, Vaucluse
>
> - Total production of AOC wines from all Rhône Valley vineyards: 2,796,392 hectolitres
>
> - 75 per cent red, 15 per cent rosé, 10 per cent white
>
> - 1,727 independent wineries
>
> - 91 cooperative wineries
>
> - Bottles sold: 355 million
>
> - Amount exported: 33 per cent (117 million bottles)
>
> - Top three markets by volume: USA (17 per cent), UK (16 per cent), Germany (16 per cent)

The French *appellation d'origine contrôlée* (AOC) system (effectively synonymous with the broader European *appellation d'origine protégée* or AOP) was first developed by Baron Le Roy in Châteauneuf-du-Pape in the 1920s and '30s and it remains deeply entrenched today. There are five different levels:

- Other Rhône Valley appellations (e.g. AOC Luberon)
- AOC Côtes-du-Rhône

- AOC Côtes-du-Rhône Villages
- AOC Côtes-du-Rhône Villages with a geographical designation (e.g. AOC Côtes-du-Rhône Villages Sablet)
- *Crus* – villages or areas that have their own appellation (e.g. AOC Gigondas or AOC Lirac)

Until recently it been presented as a quality pyramid, with Other Rhône Valley appellations at the bottom, and *crus* at the top. This isn't really fair, as the Other Rhône Valley appellations are something of a law unto themselves and quality can be very high. Nevertheless, let's look at the five levels in turn.

OTHER RHÔNE VALLEY APPELLATIONS

There are eight: Costières de Nîmes, Clairette de Bellegarde, Duché d'Uzès, Côtes du Vivarais, Grignan-le-Adhémar, Ventoux, Luberon and the Diois (which actually contains four discrete appellations). These appellations surround the main Southern Côtes-du-Rhône growing area, and despite the large volumes of wine they produce, it's more helpful to consider them as separate Rhône-like satellites rather than as the base of a quality pyramid. The wines made in each use largely the same grapes as AOC Côtes-du-Rhône, and are often allied to the Rhône in terms of style (except the Diois, the most recently affiliated 'other' appellation, which is something of an outlier in style and location). They range in size from a single commune (Clairette de Bellegarde) to some of the largest appellations in France (Ventoux, Luberon), and each has its own specific *cahier des charges* rulebook.

All together, they make just over half the volume produced by AOC Côtes-du-Rhône. Traditionally, these appellations have been the source of oceans of cheap, dull wines pumped out by co-ops and négociants, and it's still easy to find plenty of forgettable wines within their boundaries. Land prices are therefore relatively low. This makes them attractive to outsiders, and they are becoming hotbeds of experimentation; rules are fairly relaxed, there is little consumer expectation and there are pockets of interesting terroir to uncover. Because of this they are now home to an increasing number of the most exciting and characterful estates in the Rhône, and can be a source of excellent value wine.

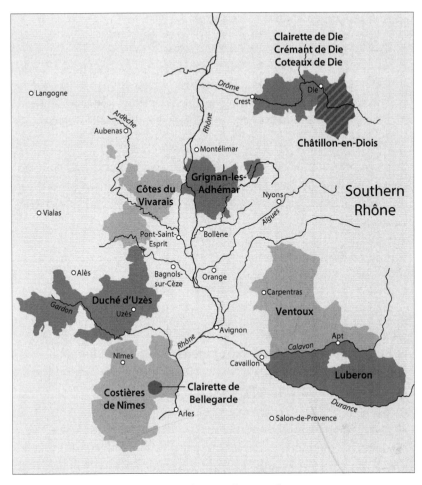

Map 2: Other Rhône Valley appellations

AOC CÔTES-DU-RHÔNE

The generic AOC Côtes-du-Rhône growing area stretches from Avignon to Vienne, a distance of around 180 kilometres. The vast majority is produced between Avignon and Montélimar, which is closer to 70 kilometres north to south, and the growing area stretches 50 kilometres west to east. It covers 171 communes, and vineyards cover nearly 50,000 hectares. Of the wines produced in 2019, 86 per cent were red, 8 per cent rosé and 6 per cent white. In the *cahier des charges* there are pages upon pages of stipulations regarding exactly what you can grow, where, and how, but here are the key points.

Permitted grape varieties for red and rosé wines

* Principal varieties: Grenache, Mourvèdre, Syrah
* Accessory varieties: Bourboulenc, Caladoc, Carignan, Cinsault, Clairette, Clairette Rose, Counoise, Couston, Grenache Blanc, Grenache Gris, Marsanne, Marselan, Muscardin, Piquepoul Blanc, Piquepoul Noir, Roussanne, Terret Noir, Ugni Blanc, Vaccarèse and Viognier.

Reds and rosés must be a blend of at least two principal varieties and must include Grenache (or at least one principal variety if north of Montélimar) and principal varieties must make up at least 60 per cent of the blend.

Permitted grape varieties for white wines

* Principal varieties: Bourboulenc, Clairette, Grenache Blanc, Marsanne, Roussanne, Viognier
* Accessory varieties: Piquepoul Blanc, Ugni Blanc.

Whites must contain a majority of principal varieties. Minimum alcohol content for all wines is 11.5% abv (or 10.5% north of Montélimar). Maximum yield is 51 hectolitres per hectare.

Perhaps unsurprisingly, there is a huge variety of styles and quality levels. Generally speaking, these are inexpensive, straightforward weekday wines. But there are some Côtes-du-Rhône wines which punch well above their weight and offer exceptional value for money. There are several reasons for this. Within this huge expanse of land, there are pockets of exceptional terroir unrecognized by the system. Mistakes have been made when drawing up appellation boundaries, leaving out exceptional vineyards; there are exceptional white wines made in appellations that only allow reds; and some producers decide to declassify their wines. Examples of big-hitting AOC Côtes-du-Rhône wines include the red and white wines of Domaine des Tours, Château de Fonsalette, Domaine la Réméjeanne, Domaine Cros de la Mure, Domaine Gramenon, Domaine Clape, Domaine Alain Voge and Domaine Jamet; and the white wines of Domaine Chaume-Arnaud, Domaine Vallot – Le Coriançon and Domaine la Luminaille.

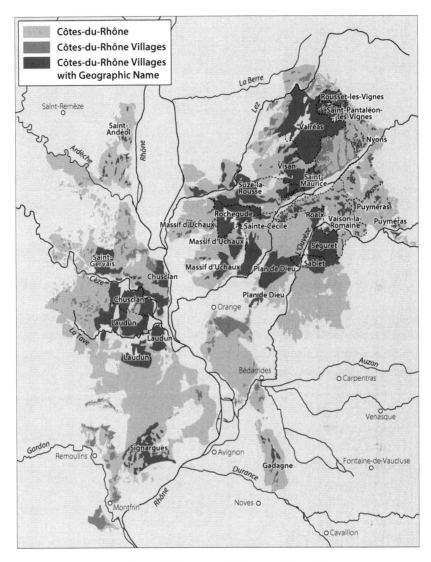

Map 3: Côtes-du-Rhône and Côtes-du-Rhône Villages

AOC CÔTES-DU-RHÔNE VILLAGES

This level is similar to the previous one, just a bit more stringent. The growing area for AOC Côtes-du-Rhône Villages is tighter than that of AOC Côtes-du-Rhône – just 95 communes instead of 171. Grape varieties are the same as AOC Côtes-du-Rhône, but crossings aren't permitted – so no Couston, Caladoc or Marselan. Blending rules are the same as AOC Côtes-du-Rhône for whites; reds must contain at least two principal varieties (one must be Grenache) and these must make up at least 66 per cent of the blend. Minimum alcohol content for all wines is higher, at 12% abv. Yields are lower at 44 hectolitres per hectare.

Compared to the 30,281 hectares dedicated to AOC Côtes-du-Rhône in 2019, only 2,923 hectares were dedicated to AOC Côtes-du-Rhône Villages, while 6,229 hectares were used for AOC Côtes-du-Rhône Villages with geographic designation. In theory this appellation layer should guarantee a step up in quality, but my experience is that this is often not the case. I would therefore question the validity or interest in this level of the appellation structure.

AOC CÔTES-DU-RHÔNE VILLAGES WITH GEOGRAPHIC NAME

This is where things start to get interesting. Selected villages are permitted to append AOC Côtes-du-Rhône Villages with their name. At the time of writing, there were 22 of these, and they can make red, white and rosé except where noted:

Chusclan (red and rosé only)
Gadagne (red only)
Laudun
Massif d'Uchaux (red only)
Nyons (red only)
Plan de Dieu (red only)
Puyméras (red only)
Roaix
Rochegude
Rousset-les-Vignes
Sablet

Saint-Andéol (red only)
Saint-Gervais
Saint-Maurice
Saint-Pantaléon-les-Vignes
Sainte-Cécile (red only)
Séguret
Signargues (red only)
Suze-la-Rousse (red only)
Vaison-la-Romaine (red only)
Valréas
Visan

They largely follow the same rulebooks as standard AOC Côtes-du-Rhône Villages; grape varieties are the same, as are blending stipulations. Minimum alcohol content for all whites and rosés is still 12% abv, but the minimum for reds is up to 12.5% abv. Yields are lower still at just 41 hectolitres per hectare.

Gradually more and more names get added to this list as villages put together working groups of local vignerons called *syndicats* in order to lobby the INAO to be promoted. Each *syndicat* collates a dossier of information (historical information, terroir studies, etc.) to prove its worth, which typically takes around 10 years to get passed if successful. If and when a village is eventually promoted to a *cru*, it will be selected from this list. The last was Cairanne, which was promoted from AOC Côtes-du-Rhône Villages Cairanne to AOC Cairanne in 2016. In theory, like each *cru*, each name on this list will have its own character and *typicité* discernible in the wines. In practice, some are more distinctive than others. This is the appellation band in which some of the best value wines in the Rhône are to be found: groups of producers who are striving to improve quality and define their terroir, but don't belong to a *cru*, so can't yet charge *cru* prices.

One gripe about this particular appellation bracket, however, is its name. Historically, it has been specific villages that have been promoted to this level (or, to be more precise, specific communes). More recently, instead of whole communes being promoted, *syndicats* have clubbed together to elevate explicit terroirs, usually defined along soil boundaries rather than arbitrary communal boundaries. For example, AOC Côtes-du-Rhône Villages Plan de Dieu, minted in 2005, isn't named after a village or commune but after a raised terrace of alluvial deposits that covers part of four different communes. This is sensible. The problem is what to call this appellation bracket. 'AOC Côtes-du-Rhône Villages with geographic name' doesn't exactly trip off the tongue. Conversationally they have long been referred to as 'Named Villages', but since the names no longer refer to villages as such, this is no longer strictly correct. But until somebody comes up with a better alternative, 'Named Villages' is likely to stay the colloquial English term, and the one that I'll use in this book.

CRUS

This is the top level of the appellation structure. There are currently eight *crus* in the Northern Rhône and nine in the Southern Rhône.

Northern Rhône

Château-Grillet	Côte-Rôtie	Saint-Joseph
Condrieu	Crozes-Hermitage	Saint-Péray
Cornas	Hermitage	

Southern Rhône

Beaumes-de-Venise	Gigondas	Tavel
Cairanne	Lirac	Vacqueyras
Châteauneuf-du-Pape	Rasteau	Vinsobres

Each *cru* has its own dedicated *cahier des charges*, though in practice they are often quite similar. Some, such as Châteauneuf-du-Pape, are very broad in what they allow; more recently elevated *crus* tend to have tighter restrictions. Though they each have their own character, similarly to Named Villages, some are stronger than others.

THE TEN SECTIONS OF THE SOUTHERN RHÔNE

With tasting, the differences between Hermitage and Côte-Rôtie become clear. The more dedicated among us can distinguish a northern village Saint-Joseph from a southern village Saint-Joseph. But how many wine lovers can pick out a Saint-Gervais from a Saint-Maurice, a Vinsobres from a Ventoux – or even a Cairanne from a Rasteau? It's more difficult to get under the skin of the Southern Rhône than the North.

There are many reasons for this. In the Southern Rhône, the volumes of wine are immense, the terrain is vast and complex, there are over 40 appellations to get to know, dozens of grape varieties – and that's before you include IGPs. And quality is highly variable. Trying to understand the Southern Rhône would be easier if it were split up into separate zones. The question that has preoccupied me throughout writing this book is the most helpful way in which to do this. Wine never fits neatly into categories. Nonetheless I've tried to define roughly a number of different areas that have some similarities in terroir, wine style or both. Since soil types are a major influence on wine style, I considered dividing up the book on this basis, but it didn't work. Soils change frequently within a small area; winemakers more often work within appellations, blending soil types within AOC boundaries; and wines grown in close proximity on different soil types often have more in common than those grown far away but on the same soils.

The result is ten different zones. This is more than I would ideally have liked, but fewer would have meant lumping together distinct zones that really belong apart. The number wasn't arbitrarily chosen, it is simply the sum of the different zones that appeared organically. These ten zones aren't the only way the growing area can be divided up, and there is a degree of subjectivity involved. I don't suggest these boundaries should be permanent; appellations evolve, winemakers come and go, as do trends – and the climate is changing too. But I believe that it is the most helpful way – at least for now.

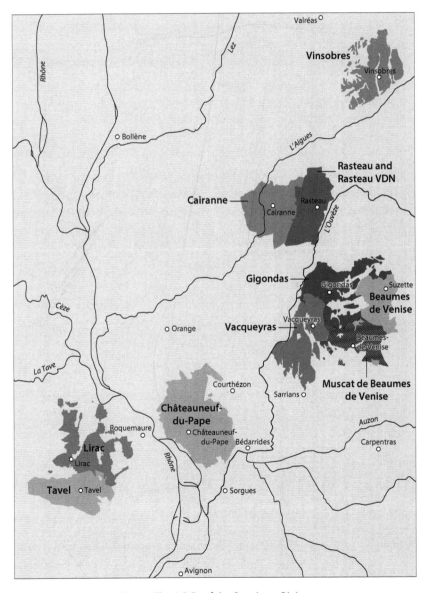

Map 4: The AOCs of the Southern Rhône

Tiny appellations – a case for demotion?

With five appellation levels in the Rhône Valley, and over 50 appellations in total, would it make life easier for wine lovers if some of this hierarchy was stripped out and simplified? Of course it would. And it seems obvious where to start – the ever-growing list of Named Villages. Some of these have been around for over 50 years and still haven't been promoted to *cru*. They've had their chance and the market wasn't interested. Who's even seen a Rousset-les-Vignes, let alone tasted one? At least this was my thinking before I set off around the Rhône to visit them.

What I came to realize is that some of the smallest appellations contain some of the most characterful wines. Saint-Maurice and Saint-Gervais may only have a few producers each, but the wines have a distinct character – and they're delicious, not to mention great value. Roaix is another Named Village that deserves to be better known. 'The problem is that we only have 130 hectares, we don't have the means to communicate, so we've always remained quite marginal,' says Franck Molénat, president of the cave cooperative Les Vignerons de Roaix Séguret. To get Roaix better recognized 'we need a new generation,' he says, 'and more people making their own wine'. Elodie Balme of Rasteau also makes a Roaix, but 'it's easier to sell a generic Côtes-du-Rhône,' she says. One issue is that there are so few on the market, meaning there is no consumer recognition. Négociants buy up good Named Village grapes or wines but then use them for their generic Côtes-du-Rhône blends. Another problem is that there is no longer a cooperative based in the village that would serve as a way of attracting people to the village itself – a problem shared with Saint-Gervais. But she still believes in the Roaix appellation: 'We want to protect what makes us special,' she says.

They might be small today, but these tiny appellations serve as a reminder that there is buried treasure in some of these micro terroirs. Hopefully they will act as a beacon to newcomers, who might in time help to re-establish them.

THE TWO SECTIONS OF THE NORTHERN RHÔNE

'Here we're closer to Burgundy than to Châteauneuf,' says Jean-Louis Grippat. In the Southern Rhône you'll find all five layers of the appellation system. In the Northern Rhône, essentially there are only *crus*

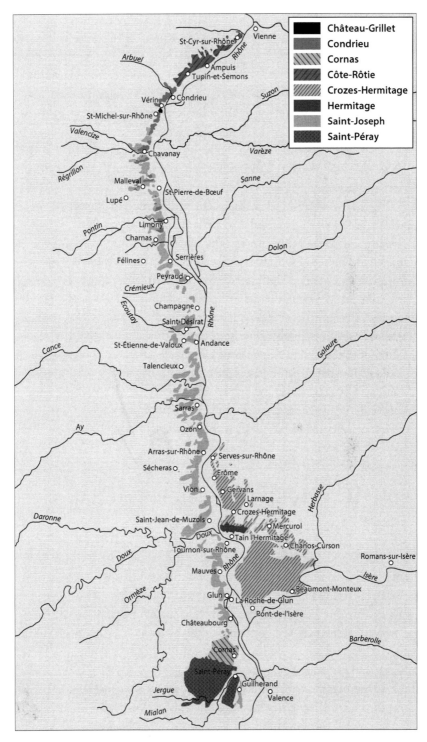

	Château-Grillet
	Condrieu
	Cornas
	Côte-Rôtie
	Crozes-Hermitage
	Hermitage
	Saint-Joseph
	Saint-Péray

Map 5: The AOCs of the Northern Rhône

– eight in total – and some IGP Collines Rhodaniennes, which is almost always used here instead of AOC Côtes-du-Rhône. It's a relatively homogeneous growing region compared to the Southern Rhône, but there are some differences between the northern end around Ampuis and the southern part, closer to Tain. The red wines of this cooler northern end, whether Côte-Rôties or northern Saint-Josephs, are typically light- to medium-bodied and have a distinct florality and spice to their aromatic profile. Viognier is only found in the northern reaches, producing the whites of Condrieu and Château-Grillet, and is blended with Syrah in many Côte-Rôties.

The reds of Hermitage, Cornas and southern Saint-Joseph all share a density that rarely feels quite so natural further north. This is mostly down to latitude – Tain is nearly 50 kilometres south of Ampuis, with a correspondingly warmer climate. Each of these appellations has its own particular character; if Hermitage is leonine, Cornas is lupine and southern Saint-Josephs combine the sleek finesse, sinew and precision of birds of prey. Though the white Saint-Josephs of the northern end contain Marsanne and Roussanne, the southern end is the heartland of these white varieties, used in Saint-Péray, Crozes-Hermitage and Hermitage.

Many Northern Rhône producers make wine over several appellations, so it's not always obvious which appellation to file them under (especially négociants). I've either placed them in the appellation chapter where they are located, or filed them under the appellation that they are most commonly associated with.

INDICATION GÉOGRAPHIQUE PROTÉGÉE (IGP)

Most of the wines of the Rhône Valley are released under one AOC (Appellation d'Origine Contrôlée) or another, but a significant proportion is bottled under IGP (Indication Géographique Protégée), the quality category positioned between AOC and Vin de France. IGP was previously known as Vin de Pays, but this term was updated in 2009 to align with broader European Union quality categories (though Vin de Pays is still often used conversationally). Like AOCs, IGPs have a *cahier des charges* to adhere to, but the geographical area is considerably larger and the rules are less strict. Maximum yields are much bigger, and there is a longer list of permissible grape varieties, often including the highly obscure. One commercial benefit of bottling wines under an IGP is that they can be made from a single variety and labelled as such.

At the time of writing, in France there were 363 AOCs for wine, and 74 IGPs. Most IGPs are very large, and cover a plethora of different terroirs, so compared with AOC wines it's not always easy to generalize about the style of wine you're likely to find in the bottle. In theory they should at least deliver a broad sense of origin, and an acceptable level of quality. IGPs can be divided into three types: regional, departmental and zonal. Some are allowed to be further delimited with 'territorial references', such as 'IGP Méditerranée – Comté de Grignan'. A number of them overlap the AOC growing areas of the Rhône, and many producers will bottle some AOC wines and some IGP.

The two regional IGPs

IGP Méditerranée

This huge territory, covering 9,000 hectares of vineyards across 10 *départements*, spreads from the Rhône river all the way to Italy, extending further north than the Diois, and even including Corsica. It covers all of the Southern Rhône vineyards (except for those in the Gard *département*), and all of the Northern Rhône. It is not terribly popular among Rhône winemakers however, as it's more commonly associated with Provence rosé (70 per cent of IGP Méditerranée production is pink). The most popular red varieties are Grenache, Syrah, Merlot, Cabernet Sauvignon and Cinsault. The most common white varieties are Roussanne, Marsanne, Viognier, Chardonnay and Vermentino. Wines produced in the general vicinity of Grignan can use the supplementary territorial reference Comté de Grignan, and those close to Montélimar can state Coteaux de Montélimar.

IGP Comtés Rhodaniens

Another large territory, stretching north where IGP Méditerranée ends, this covers seven *départements*. It is one of the six regional IGPs of France, but is little used, bottling less than one tenth as much wine as IGP Méditerranée, half of which is rosé.

The four departmental IGPs

IGP Ardèche

The Ardèche is a large *département* stretching along the west bank of the Rhône from Pont-Saint-Esprit in the Southern Rhône as far as Limony in the Northern Rhône. It covers 339 communes in total, of which 150 in the southern Ardèche can use the further territorial reference Coteaux de l'Ardèche. Most of the production of this departmental IGP is red, with Merlot, Syrah, Cabernet Sauvignon and Gamay being popular varieties; Viognier, Chardonnay and Sauvignon Blanc are common for whites. There are several strong references, such as Matthieu Barret Sélections Black Flag Syrah from vineyards in Villeneuve de Berg, and the Domaine Vincent Paris Granit Blanc, a blend of Roussanne and Viognier grown on a north-facing slope within the boundaries of AOC Cornas (an appellation reserved for red wines).

Increasing numbers of small estates are popping up around the southern Ardèche – often organic, biodynamic or natural – as the potential for quality here is gradually being understood and realized. Soils are varied, but there are large deposits of limestone, granite and some basalt outcrops that are highly favourable for viticulture. Domaine Arsac, Domaine Salel & Renaud and Terre des Amoureuses all make interesting examples. This is a dynamic area within the Rhône Valley, and I predict we'll see an increasing number of exciting wines produced here.

IGP Drôme

This is the IGP for the Drôme, a largely mountainous *département* whose western border is the Rhône and whose eastern border skirts along the Prealps. It covers much of the northernmost part of the Southern Rhône, including Vinsobres and most of Grignan-les-Adhémar, Brézème and the vineyards of the Diois, and also includes Hermitage and Crozes-Hermitage further north. Two-thirds of IGP Drôme production is red, with Syrah a popular choice. The climate is slightly cooler than the Gard and the Vaucluse, so the wines typically show a little less generosity and more freshness as a result. As with IGP Méditerranée, wines produced in the vicinity of Grignan can use the territorial reference Comté de Grignan, and those close to Montélimar can use Coteaux de Montélimar.

IGP Vaucluse

Vaucluse is the heartland of the Southern Rhône, a *département* surrounded by rivers and mountains. The Rhône is its western border, the Durance its southern border; it shares a border with the Drôme to the north and includes Ventoux and the Luberon. Most IGP wines are grown outside AOC boundaries, perhaps on lower-lying land or on soil types outside

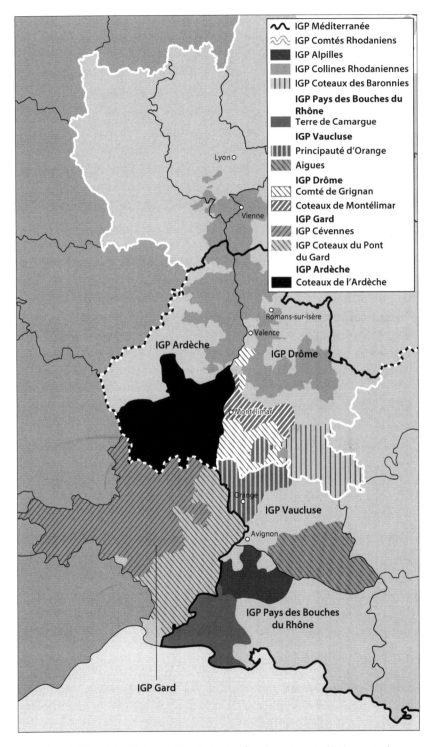

	IGP Méditerranée
	IGP Comtés Rhodaniens
	IGP Alpilles
	IGP Collines Rhodaniennes
	IGP Coteaux des Baronnies
	IGP Pays des Bouches du Rhône
	Terre de Camargue
	IGP Vaucluse
	Principauté d'Orange
	Aigues
	IGP Drôme
	Comté de Grignan
	Coteaux de Montélimar
	IGP Gard
	IGP Cévennes
	IGP Coteaux du Pont du Gard
	IGP Ardèche
	Coteaux de l'Ardèche

Map 6: IGPs of the Rhône Valley. Note, the five departmental IGPs cover the whole of their respective departments

of what is permitted. It also gives producers some leeway if they want to use blends or single varieties that don't conform to appellation rules. This IGP may include the territorial reference Aigues for those made in the far south in 59 named communes around the Luberon, and Principauté d'Orange for those made in 36 specific communes further north.

Several of the most interesting wines of the Southern Rhône are IGP Vaucluse in fact: some of the wines from the Reynaud stable of wines such as Domaine des Tours and occasionally Château des Tours are bottled as IGP Vaucluse. Jérôme Bressy of Domaine Gourt de Mautens had to drop out of AOC Rasteau when it was promoted to *cru* as his vineyards contained too high a proportion of 'accessory' grapes such as Counoise, Vaccarèse and Piquepoul Gris. Most of the wines of Chêne Bleu use IGP Vaucluse instead of AOC Ventoux, and Ad Fines in the Luberon have to use IGP Vaucluse as their wines contain Cabernet Sauvignon, a grape not permitted in the Luberon *cahier des charges*. Around two-thirds of production is red, using typical Southern Rhône varieties as well as Merlot, Cabernet Sauvignon, and crossings such as Marselan.

IGP Gard

The Rhône is the eastern boundary of this *département*, so all of the west-bank appellations of the Southern Rhône sit inside it (except for AOC Côtes du Vivarais and AOC Côtes-du-Rhône Villages Saint-Andéol, just over the border in the Ardèche *département*). The *département* stretches much further west than the most westerly Rhône Valley vineyards however, up into the Cevennes, sharing a border with the Hérault *département*.

The four zonal IGPs

IGP Collines Rhodaniennes

This is a fairly small but important IGP, and roughly follows the *crus* of the Northern Rhône. Soils are predominantly granitic and it's the only IGP that reliably produces wine in a Northern Rhône style. The list of available grapes is considerably shorter than for most other Rhône IGPs, and at 80 hectolitres per hectare the yields are relatively low too. Most of the production is red, and most of that is Syrah, with Gamay and Merlot playing an important supporting role. Whites are usually Viognier, along with smaller amounts of Marsanne and Roussanne. It only produces a tiny amount of rosé. IGP Collines Rhodaniennes has been embraced by Northern Rhône winemakers, and is much more commonly used here than AOC Côtes-du-Rhône. Winemakers in

Côte-Rôtie and Condrieu often make some IGP Viognier and IGP Syrah in order to extend their range. Some examples, such as Domaine Georges Vernay 'Le Pied de Samson' Viognier and Domaine Stéphane Ogier 'La Rosine' Syrah are outstanding wines that can easily be mistaken for grander appellations, so for those looking for value in the Northern Rhône, this is the best place to start.

IGP Coteaux des Baronnies

This small zonal IGP sits within the northern IGP Drôme, and is reserved for high-altitude vineyards among the Baronnies mountain range, a pre-alpine chain between the Diois and Mont Ventoux. This sparsely populated, captivatingly pretty terroir usually makes fairly light wine, around two-thirds of which is red. Cabernet Sauvignon plays an important part, and for whites, Chardonnay is common.

IGP Cévennes

Producers within a demarcated area towards the northern end of IGP Gard can use the IGP Cévennes, designating a largely calcareous, mountainous terrain that enjoys a moderated Mediterranean climate – summer days are hot but nights are cool. Rhône varieties such as Carignan, Grenache and Cinsault are joined by international ones such as Merlot and Cabernet Sauvignon. Common whites are Chardonnay, Sauvignon Blanc and Viognier. Domaine le Sollier in Monoblet make a range of IGP Cévennes, majoring in grapes such as Cinsault, Alicante Bouschet and Merlot, which show the IGP – and the concept of IGPs – to good effect.

IGP Coteaux du Pont du Gard

This zonal IGP represents the southern and eastern portions of the IGP Gard, which more closely shadow the west bank Southern Rhône AOCs. Terroir is more calcareous in the eastern portion, with endless banks of *galets roulés* to the south. Château Mourgues du Grès for example makes an IGP Coteaux du Pont du Gard – Terre d'Argence contains a little Petit Manseng, a grape not permitted in the AOC Costières de Nîmes *cahier des charges*.

There are two other IGPs nearby, to the south of the main Southern Rhône growing area: IGP Pays des Bouches du Rhône and the small IGP Alpilles. These are more commonly associated with the wines of Côtes de Provence rather than the Rhône.

Opting out

The French vineyard classification system has been copied the world over. It was designed to help protect a local speciality from fraud and the whims of fashion, while acting as a guarantee to the consumer. But with so many rules and restrictions, some producers opt out of the AOC and IGP system and bottle their wines as Vin de France. Some find so many stipulations stifle their creativity, and that they can make better wines outside the system. Others simply don't believe that the system is fit for purpose, or that it effectively guarantees anything. It's a viewpoint particularly common among natural wine producers.

However, the classification system does act as a useful framework for those wishing to understand the region as a whole. The problem with those that drop out of the system is that it can make them less visible outside of their local area and immediate clientele. Although this book is divided up by appellation, I've occasionally included exceptional producers that make wines within that appellation (or close to it) even if they bottle their wines under IGP or Vin de France.

PART 2
THE SOUTHERN RHÔNE

5

AROUND AVIGNON

CHÂTEAUNEUF-DU-PAPE

Like any big personality, Châteauneuf-du-Pape incites strong opinions. It's the loud diner laughing heartily in the restaurant; does its garrulous nature add to the convivial atmosphere? Or do you cast disapproving looks over your shoulder? Its larger-than-life character – and glamorous connections – has for centuries drawn interest from around the world.

A rich history

Traces of Roman civilization have been found throughout the Rhône Valley, and Châteauneuf is no different. The first written reference to the town, however, dates back to 1094; it was originally based around what is now its oldest monument, the chapel of Saint-Théodoric, before the settlement spread up the hillside nearby. Before the fourteenth century documentation is rare, and Châteauneuf is referred to variously as Castrum Novum, Castro Novo and, from 1213, variations upon Châteauneuf Calcernier, which remained its official name until as recently as 1893. The name *calcernier* refers to lime kilns and the production of lime for construction, which, along with making tiles, was once an important part of the town's economy.

The first written references to wine date back to 1157, but viticulture is likely to pre-date this significantly, for sacramental purposes, local consumption and commerce. However, with the arrival of the popes winemaking in Châteauneuf took on a greater significance. Clément V, archbishop of Bordeaux, was elected pope in 1305, and instead of taking a seat in Rome, in 1309 he chose Avignon instead. This marked the start of the Avignon Papacy, during which seven successive popes took up residence in the city (it was part of the Comtat Venaissin at the time, and thus belonged to the Holy Roman Empire). Clément V visited Châteauneuf in 1312, 1313 and 1314, the year of his death. His successor, Jean XXII, first visited the village in 1316, and in 1317 he started the construction of his own *château neuf* (new castle), which took 16 years to complete.

In 1344, there were approximately 2,000 inhabitants; not far off the total living there now. Many of the family names that feature on the census that year can still be found among its citizens today. Jean-Claude Portes, in his invaluable *Châteauneuf-du-Pape: Première AOC de France*, calculates that there were between 286 and 572 hectares under vine at that time. Today, there are over 3,000 hectares. In 1560, the Tulle de Villefranche family bought the building and farmland that was to become Château la Nerthe, marking the start of the establishment of large private estates in the region. The château itself was built in several stages from 1694 to 1760, and it was around 1730 that the wines began to be sold commercially, to wide acclaim. La Nerthe understood the value of local links to the papacy, and by the end of the century the name Châteauneuf-du-Pape was being widely used. Before the end of the century the Tulle de Villefranche family was exporting wine around Europe and to the United States, and the name Châteauneuf-du-Pape began to be recognized internationally.

Between 1716 and 1800, plantings increased from 162 to 668 hectares, and as the wine of Châteauneuf-du-Pape gained a following, more and more large private estates came into being. Some, such as Coteau-Brûlé (established 1816), have long since disappeared. Others, such as Domaine Condorcet (established 1826), are still with us; one of its major contributions was to introduce Syrah to Châteauneuf in the early 1830s. Domaine de la Solitude (established 1809) is another historically important estate, which, along with La Nerthe, was one of the first estates to export wine and to use private labels on its bottles.

The arrival of the railways in the mid-1800s opened up the domestic market and reduced shipping costs, bringing down prices. This period also saw the growth of négociants; Châteauneuf became particularly popular with those of Burgundy, who used the more powerful wines to bolster their Pinot Noirs. The village became prosperous. Life was good. It didn't last. The effects of phylloxera were first observed here in 1866, and it took hold definitively the following year. By 1869, Châteauneuf had lost nearly 40 per cent of its vineyards. By 1880, only 200 hectares were left. Many citizens abandoned the village; those who lost their vines often replaced them with fruit trees. Even the Tulle de Villefranche family lost hope, selling La Nerthe to Joseph Ducos in 1877. From 1883, the Hérault *département* started grafting to American rootstocks to combat the infestation, but the adoption of this method in Châteauneuf was largely more gradual and cautious. Ducos, however, was an early adopter, rapidly replanting the entire domaine. By 1899, Châteauneuf was recovering and La Nerthe was on its way to reclaiming its former glory.

Phylloxera was a catastrophe for countless families and businesses, but due to the economic importance of the wine industry in France, it also represented a financial crisis for individual *départements* and the wider French economy. France had to start importing wine to meet domestic demand. Fraud became a problem: winemakers were using dried grapes as well as fresh, adding sugar, adding water, adding alcohol. Plantings of low-quality, high-yielding grapes such as Aramon and hybrid varieties exploded. Vineyard practices that favoured high yields were employed to meet demands. By 1900 there was a domestic oversupply and prices crashed, leading to angry demonstrations, some ending in tragedy, such as the revolt of Languedoc winemakers in 1907. The result was new laws to regulate the wine industry and the birth of the controlled appellations (*appellations d'origine contrôlées*).

Appellation: AOC Châteauneuf-du-Pape
Birth of the appellation: 1936
Communes: Bédarrides, Châteauneuf-du-Pape, Courthézon, Orange, Sorgues
Total surface area sold under the AOC in 2019: 3146 hectares
Average yield in 2019: 30 hectolitres per hectare
Colours permitted: red and white only
Production in 2019: 92 per cent red, 8 per cent white
Grape varieties permitted: Reds and whites can be made from Bourboulenc, Cinsault, Clairette, Clairette Rose, Counoise, Grenache Blanc, Grenache Gris, Grenache Noir, Mourvèdre, Muscardin, Picardan, Piquepoul Blanc, Piquepoul Gris, Piquepoul Noir, Roussanne, Syrah, Terret Noir and Vaccarèse.

The first appellation

When it came to protecting its intellectual property and promoting its wines, Châteauneuf was ahead of the curve. In 1893, the mayor successfully submitted a request to change the official name of the commune from Châteauneuf-Calcernier to Châteauneuf-du-Pape, the name of its wine. The year before, the commune had successfully had the castle listed as a historic monument. Between 1890 and 1892, Joseph Ducos created the first winemaker *syndicat* in Châteauneuf, with the intention of protecting the reputation of Châteauneuf-du-Pape by guaranteeing the genuine local provenance of its members' wines. This first *syndicat* didn't last long, but it was succeeded by another in 1904; this also struggled to define an official growing area, and disbanded.

It wasn't until the involvement of Baron Pierre Le Roy de Boiseaumarié (1890–1967) that the appellation and its broader rules were set in stone. Baron Le Roy, as he became known, was born in Franche-Comté and trained as a lawyer, but returned to the family wine estate in the Languedoc after the death of his father in 1912. During the First World War he excelled as a fighter pilot and was awarded the Légion d'Honneur. After the war he married Edmée Bernard Le Saint, daughter of the owner of Château Fortia in Châteauneuf-du-Pape. Baron Le Roy was a towering presence in French wine for the first half of the twentieth century, with countless achievements to his name: in 1935 he co-founded the Institut National des Appellations (INAO); he held the presidency of the Organisation Internationale de la Vigne et du Vin (OIV); and he helped to create the Comité Interprofessionel des Vins des Côtes-du-Rhône.

His most notable achievement, certainly for his adopted village, was spearheading the establishment of Châteauneuf-du-Pape as one of the first *appellations d'origine contrôlées* in France. In 1923, he was asked by local winemakers to create a new, third, *syndicat* to defend the reputation of the local wines and stamp out fraud, and he accepted. The committee's first actions were to delimit the growing area, stipulate permitted soil types and grape varieties, ban habitual irrigation and set a minimum alcohol limit of 12.5% abv. Needless to say, this was not an easy process, and they faced many opposing voices. But after ten years of legal wrangling, internal disputes and further hammering out of viticultural and vinification minutiae, the rules were passed in a final tribunal in 1933. It wasn't until 1936 that the first AOCs were officially named in law: Châteauneuf-du-Pape, Arbois, Tavel, Cognac, Cassis and Monbazillac. To honour the example set by Baron Le Roy and the Châteauneuf *syndicat*, its official decree was published one day before the others, on 14 May 1936. They would go on to serve as a model for the *appellation d'origine protégée* laws used throughout Europe today. We'll consider the modern history of Châteauneuf and its contemporary issues a little later.

How many grapes?

The work of Baron Le Roy paved the way for other French appellations to defend and promote their wines in the same way, and despite some revisions in 1966, 1992 and 2008 the Châteauneuf-du-Pape official *cahier des charges* hasn't changed greatly since it was ratified. The most basic stipulations are that, despite the existence of sweet and sparkling examples in the past, contemporary Châteauneuf-du-Pape must be a still, dry wine, either red or white. The appellation is well known for the multitude of grape varieties permitted; 13 is the number often stated, but this doesn't take into account the colour declinations of certain varieties, such as Grenache Gris and Grenache Blanc. The actual number is 18 if you include them all, and if you speak to some vignerons they'll privately admit to the existence of a few more dotted around, such as Alicante Bouschet. Interestingly, unlike most other Rhône appellations, there are no further rules regarding blending. As long as a wine's final colour remains either red or white, you can put red grapes in white wines, white grapes in red wines, make a wine from a single variety or include all 18.

Among red varieties, Grenache makes up the vast majority of plantings (77 per cent), with relatively small proportions of Syrah (12 per cent), Mourvèdre (7 per cent) and Cinsault (3 per cent); all others amount to just 1 per cent.[2] White wines only make up 7 per cent of the total volume of Châteauneuf produced, and plantings of white and pink grapes are more even: mostly Grenache Blanc (35 per cent), followed by Clairette (32 per cent), Roussanne (16 per cent), Bourboulenc (15 per cent) then all others (2 per cent). Mourvèdre is growing in popularity, and several vignerons, such as Thierry Sabon at Clos du Mont-Olivet, intend to plant more Counoise and Vaccarèse as they ripen at 13.5% abv, which helps to bring balance to Grenache-based blends. Maximum yields weren't stipulated in the original *cahier des charges*, but they have since been set to 35 hectolitres per hectare, though the ten-year average (2009–2018) is just 29 hectolitres per hectare.

2 Data taken from most recent survey 2012/2013.

White Châteauneuf: an overlooked classic

Thanks to its cachet and broad consumer recognition, many retailers and restaurants consider red Châteauneuf-du-Pape a must-list wine. White Châteauneuf, by contrast, is comparatively rare. It's much more than a local curio however, having a long history of production in the area (it was historically used as sacramental wine), and is taken seriously by winemakers. Stylistically it shares the opulence of the reds, often accentuated by barrel fermentation and maturation, sometimes using new oak, especially for Roussanne components. This richness can be pushed further by lees stirring. The naturally low acidity and high glycerol of its most common white grape varieties is another factor, as is malolactic fermentation (usually completed, though occasionally blocked). All of this can lead to wines that feel overly fat and gloopy.

Winemakers who balance this natural richness with acidity, aromatic freshness, noble bitterness, textural grip or minerality – or a combination of these – can make compellingly delicious wines of great wealth and complexity. Though delicious young, the best can gain interest for 20, even 30 years or more. Whites are liable to go into a dumb phase after their first drinking window, when they can appear oxidized. This can pass however, as the wine transitions into a second phase, swapping ripe stone fruits for orchard flavours of apple compote, quince, nuts and honey. Among the great white wines of the world, white Châteauneuf is often erroneously overlooked.

It's not easy to describe a typical Châteauneuf: it is a diverse style of wine. This isn't just due to the easy-going approach to grape varieties, but also the range of terroir; it's a huge tract of land that includes several very different types of soil. But what usually marks out a Châteauneuf, in both colours, is its size. It is wider, taller, deeper – altogether grander, more generous and fatter than other Rhône wines. It is more imposing, with greater resonance. This applies to both colours.

Situation and soils

The growing area itself, 12 kilometres to the north of Avignon, is spread across five communes; most of the wine is made in the commune of Châteauneuf-du-Pape. The other four surround it, with Orange to the north, Courthézon north-east, Bédarrides east and Sorgues south-east. The west and south of Châteauneuf is surrounded by a curving section of the Rhône, and its proximity to the river has been a benefit through-out its history, helping to move wines within France and to other markets further afield.

Since it covers such a large growing area, it's hardly surprising that the soils are so varied. Much of the appellation, particularly to the west, sits over a limestone bedrock. White shards proliferate on the surface in some vineyards, and it's not commonly considered the best terroir for reds. Much of the western section was added later in an amendment to the appellation. There are also significant deposits of sand and sandstone, particularly to the north-east. A dark red sandstone known as *grès rouge* is also fairly common, giving an elegant, tight style of wine. The famous *galets roulés* and clay were laid down over the bedrock much later, during a succession of ice ages and warmer interglacial periods. The Würmian deposits to the south of the appellation towards Sorgues are the youngest, at around 100,000 years old; the Villafranchian deposits further north are considerably older and also higher in altitude, up to 128 metres at *lieu-dit* Pied Long. These higher sites have long been considered superior terroirs.

The soils change frequently from one place to the next, with some *lieux-dits* containing one prevailing soil type, others containing several. Julien Barrot of Domaine la Barroche says, 'I don't know the soil of Châteauneuf, no one can say they know Châteauneuf … it's 600 years we've been farming here and I'm just starting to understand it.' Though not certified, he works organically, like a growing number of his neighbours. Over a quarter of the Châteauneuf growing area is now organic.

There are dozens of *lieux-dits* in this rolling, almost monocultural landscape that help us to position ourselves on the map. The question of whether to divide this enormous appellation into different *crus* raises its head from time to time, and the most obvious way would be to use these boundaries. But in practice they are not ideal; rather than following soil types, in Châteauneuf the *lieux-dits* tend to follow roads and the limits of old vineyards. And some of the best areas, such as La Crau to the east of the village, are spread across several *lieux-dits*. The problem with classifications is that elevating certain parcels or estates necessarily devalues others; they are essentially divisive. It is hardly surprising therefore, that one has never been ratified by the *syndicat*, whose role is to defend the appellation and unite its winemakers – despite the wishes of Baron Le Roy, who wanted some kind of classification put in place.

Châteauneuf-du-Pape

Modern Châteauneuf

In recent decades, winemakers have ushered in a type of homegrown classification however with the advent of the *cuvée spéciale*. The tradition in Châteauneuf has long been to own various parcels around the appellation and blend them to produce one red cuvée (and perhaps one white). Many estates, such as Clos des Papes and Le Vieux Donjon still do this. But 1989 saw the birth of several new special bottlings: Clos du Mont-Olivet Cuvée du Papet, Château de Beaucastel Hommage à Jacques Perrin, Domaine les Cailloux Cuvée Centenaire and Domaine de Marcoux Vieilles Vignes. (Arguably the first *cuvée spéciale* was a white – Château de Beaucastel Roussanne Vieilles Vignes, the first vintage of which was 1986.) Since then, it has become common practice to produce a *cuvée classique,* referred to in Châteauneuf as a *tradition* bottling (usually with no specific cuvée name) alongside one, or perhaps several, higher-priced *cuvées spéciales* each with its own particular title.

The *cuvée spéciale* in Châteauneuf-du-Pape: an entirely positive development?

'Vignerons always knew that some parcels were more interesting than others, old vines that were better,' says consultant winemaker Philippe Cambie, 'but now they identify them and make the most of them.' Châteauneuf is a sprawling appellation with a variety of different expressions; with no official classification of parcels or properties in place, individual estates gradually and spontaneously took it upon themselves to illustrate this variety by branching out from the traditional single red bottling (and perhaps single white bottling) to a range of different *cuvées spéciales*.

The first of these either selected plots of old vines or particularly high-quality small parcels or single vineyards. Since this is not an official term however, other estates have made *cuvées spéciales* from single grape varieties, barrel selections or extended élevage – in a spirit in keeping with the creative freedom of the appellation, domaines can do as they wish. This development has largely been a positive one for Châteauneuf. It has encouraged individual vignerons to get to know their parcels more intimately and brought more attention to just how good top Châteauneuf can be. Special cuvées have attracted the interest of journalists and critics, bringing high scores and enabling producers to increase prices. 'It's very good for sales,' says Fabien Brunel of Domaine les Cailloux, 'and we can't pay our taxes with poetry.' Initially it injected some much-needed cash into the region, allowing producers to invest. Throughout the 1990s, many more estates began to create their own special bottlings, but the quality wasn't always necessarily better than their *tradition*. Often, the elements that were accentuated in a wine were those components that were already present in ample quantity. And when everything is turned up to 11 it doesn't produce harmony, it creates a cacophony. 'At the end of the 1990s and 2000s, we went too far into maturity, extraction, power and concentration,' says Claire Fabre of Le Vieux Donjon, 'we forgot finesse and drinkability. But that's coming back. There's virtually no more new oak, people are picking earlier. Sometimes the alcohol can still be high, but we're moving towards balance again.' The other main complaint about special cuvées is that they remove the best parts of the main *cuvée tradition*, leaving it all the poorer.

Although the *cuvée spéciale* phenomenon has given birth to some mutant caricatures, it has also introduced some phenomenal wines to the Châteauneuf pantheon. Most often this has happened when sensitive vignerons have simply put the spotlight on their most prized parcels of vines, without artifice or embellishment. After all, if there's one appellation that doesn't need exaggeration, it's Châteauneuf. In the words of Ralph Garcin of Château de Nalys, 'You can create concentration – but you can't create finesse.'

The birth of the *cuvée spéciale* coincided with (and is likely to have been a product of) a growing interest in the wines of Châteauneuf from critics in the United States (Robert Parker first published his *The Wines of the Rhône Valley and Provence* in 1987). In the 1980s, the wines of Châteauneuf, and the Rhône more broadly, were still underappreciated outside France. And inside their own country for that matter; Fabrice Brunel of Domaine les Cailloux says that in Paris at that time they were considered 'rustic and unrefined'. Until the 1980s, selling wines in bottle was still unusual for many producers, and the use of generic Châteauneuf-du-Pape labels without a domaine name was widespread. Parker was instrumental in opening up the United States, marking a new period of growth and prosperity for Châteauneuf. One winemaker I spoke to went so far as to assert 'Parker created Châteauneuf'. His influence on sales and prices during the 1990s and early 2000s is hard to overstate. When he published a 100-point score for Clos Saint Jean Deus Ex Machina 2005, Vincent Maurel recalled 'we had faxes all night, calls all night … I was shaking.' Baptiste Grangeon of Domaine de Cristia says that at the end of the 1990s and early 2000s 'Parker made good weather for us', and that high-scoring cuvées would sell out over a weekend. Many winemakers are happy to admit they courted the tastes of American critics during this time to help sell their wines. It encouraged many domaines to up their game and modernize equipment, throwing out bretty old barrels in favour of new ones. Looking back, this 'modern' period is often considered something of an aberration: too much concentration, too much alcohol, too much sweetness, too much oak. Wines became heavy and hard to drink, and many haven't aged well.

Critics aren't the only ones who have had an influence over wine styles in Châteauneuf; consultant winemakers (*oenologues-conseil*) have too. Very few estates are large enough to have their own laboratories to carry out the legally required analyses, so working with an oenologist on some level is compulsory. Some estates however opt for a more in-depth relationship, seeking detailed consultancy on their viticulture and winemaking. This has become increasingly common in the last decade, and top consultants can work with dozens of different estates. Making wine can be a lonely job, and a sounding board like this can be a useful source of ideas, advice and succour. But some winemakers believe that their widespread use has led to standardization within the appellation.

Some estates persist with 'modern' style Châteauneuf; there is still a market for such wines, and they still attract high scores, making them easy to sell. But today the excesses of modern Châteauneuf are largely recognized as such, and many domaines are swinging back to a more traditional, less exaggerated style that they personally prefer to drink. Speaking in 2017, Jean-Paul Daumen of Domaine de la Vieille Julienne said 'Ten years ago, many producers picked the grapes late, overripe, powerful, strong, rich and coloured but without enough balance. It was a kind of fashion, to seduce. But it was too much. Today, because customers are looking for more drinkable wines, more accessible wines … now there is less maturity, less overripeness.' François Perrin of Château de Beaucastel agrees, saying, 'We are no longer in the era of extraction, we're in the era of elegance – but the elegance of *chez nous*.' Trying to pedal back from this style is not being helped by a warming climate. But climate change has had less of an impact on the wines than some might believe. Châteauneuf-du-Pape has always been a powerful, high-alcohol wine.

Despite a slight swing back towards balance, Châteauneuf-du-Pape takes a degree of flak from the fine wine community. It is often criticized for being too alcoholic, too powerful, too overbearing on the dinner table. One of the weaknesses of the appellation is its size: the growing area is huge and diverse, with 300 producers, many of whom make multiple cuvées. The reality is that a lot of these wines simply aren't terribly interesting or well balanced, and many of them sell on the strength of the Châteauneuf brand alone. Among the appellations of the Southern Rhône, Châteauneuf-du-Pape comes bottom when it comes to value for money. On the global fine wine stage, however, the opposite is true: if you know what to buy, £60 (about US$75) goes a long way in Châteauneuf, especially when you compare it to the other great wines of France and Italy.

Another weakness of Châteauneuf is, perversely, that it's delicious young. Great Châteauneuf only fully unveils its majesty when fully mature, between 10 and 20 years old, but far too much is drunk much younger than this. 'To know it, you have to age it,' says Daniel Brunier of Domaine du Vieux Télégraphe. 'The problem is that it's good at three years old.' This isn't unique to Châteauneuf of course; it is true of all the greatest Grenache-based wine, both within and outside the Rhône.

So what makes Châteauneuf-du-Pape the greatest wine of the Rhône? And is it, really? In the context of the Southern Rhône, there is nothing especially remarkable or distinctive about its terroir to the naked eye; its soils are not unique to the appellation. It doesn't enjoy any strongly characteristic elevation or exposure; the climate is comparable with neighbouring well-exposed, fairly flat appellations. It is particularly open, well exposed to the sun and wind, but again, this is not uncommon in the Vaucluse. Practices in the vineyard and cellar are largely analogous with its neighbours. One particular characteristic of the wine, however, is its ability to travel: that is to say, to age. Historically it was this attribute that enabled Châteauneuf to build its brand throughout France and overseas before many others. It lasts longer in bottle than surrounding appellations, and benefits more from it. But today, we no longer need a wine to be robust enough to withstand arduous journeys. To the detriment of Châteauneuf, the current fashion is for lighter styles of wine. But fashions change.

One of the reasons Châteauneuf is so exalted is its historical tie to the popes; its name tells its story. This connection is one reason we have more documentation about Châteauneuf than other Southern Rhône appellations, so we know its history in more depth, giving it a greater sense of import. Its early fame has drawn more ambitious and talented winemakers to it over the years. Its early wealth led to more investment, and greater self-confidence. But are its wines truly that much greater than those of its neighbours? They were. But the likes of Gigondas, Rasteau and Cairanne are catching up now in terms of quality, and frequently offer more satisfying drinking. It is hard to argue, however, that the very greatest, most majestic and complex wines of the Southern Rhône are to be found more frequently in any other appellation than Châteauneuf. Like any bold and uncompromising style of wine, Châteauneuf doesn't please everyone; nor should it try. 'They have their qualities and their faults,' says François Perrin, 'but they're ours!'

Key producers

Domaine du Banneret

Châteauneuf-du-Pape

www.domaine-banneret.fr

Affable Jean-Claude Vidal was an architect in Toulouse when he inherited the tiny 1.5-hectare family Châteauneuf estate. He made his first two vintages, 1989 and 1990, under the guidance of Henri Bonneau. The estate has since grown to 4 hectares and is managed by his daughter Audrey. They have always favoured a traditional approach: a single red cuvée, all 13 varieties co-planted, no destemming and a two-year maturation in large old barrels. The red is typically made up of 60 per cent Grenache, 10 per cent Mourvèdre and 10 per cent Syrah, with the remaining 20 per cent made up of lesser-known varieties.

Since the 2015 vintage, they have made a highly promising white cuvée, Le Secret du Banneret. It's a fine, tense blend of 40 per cent Grenache Blanc, 40 per cent Clairette, 10 per cent Picardan, 5 per cent Roussanne and 5 per cent Bourboulenc, from old vines grown on the limestone and *galets roulés* soils of *lieu-dit* Terres Blanches, aged mostly in stainless steel.

This is not a famous estate with a large international presence but I don't hesitate to include it among the most notable of the appellation. Their red is a fresh, robustly structured but drinkable style that ages with interest and complexity. I suspect the white will too: I look forward to finding out.

Château de Beaucastel
Châteauneuf-du-Pape
www.beaucastel.com

Château de Beaucastel is the emblematic, exemplary, classic Châteauneuf estate by which all others can be measured. This does not mean their wines are necessarily the best (though a case could be made). But its wines today have achieved a consistency of style and quality that is uncommon; grand, architectural Châteauneufs that rarely fail to satisfy. 'The definition of a great wine is one that brings emotion,' says François Perrin, whose family has owned Beaucastel for over a century. And Beaucastel can do that.

Beaucastel cellars

The estate dates back to 1549, when Pierre de Beaucastel bought a plot of land and a barn in the *lieu-dit* Coudoulet, in the far northeast of the appellation. His family became one of the most important in the region, and in 1687, Pierre de Beaucastel was made Captain of the town of Courthézon by Louis XIV – the family still has the letter, signed by the king himself. The estate was bought by Pierre Tramier in 1909 with the original intention of planting olive trees as most of the vines had been destroyed by phylloxera. Tramier passed it down to his son-in-law Pierre Perrin, who then passed it to his son Jacques Perrin, who changed the name from Domaine de Beaucastel to Château de Beaucastel in 1976. Today the estate is run by fourth generation brothers François and Jean-Pierre, and the fifth generation, Marc, Thomas, Pierre, Cécile, Matthieu and César. Today the estate covers 130 hectares, 100 hectares of which are planted with vines. Seventy hectares are in AOC Châteauneuf-du-Pape, with the remaining 30 hectares just outside the appellation in AOC Côtes-du-Rhône. It's practically one single block around the property, classic *galets roulés* and clay soils over a sandstone bedrock. The Perrins were early adopters of organic viticulture, starting in 1950, and biodynamics too, since 1974.

The range is straightforward: two reds and two whites. All 13 red grapes are used in the blend for the classic red Châteauneuf, including a high proportion of Mourvèdre (30 per cent), not to mention 10 per cent Counoise. The white also employs all six grapes, majoring on Roussanne (85 per cent). These two might 'only' be their *tradition* bottlings, but they are regularly among the best in the appellation. Occasionally I hear their reds accused of excess brett; this may be true of certain vintages in the 1980s and 1990s, but that's not the case anymore.

The *cuvées spéciales* are less classic and both quite fascinating. Hommage à Jacques Perrin is an expression of the estate's Courrieux vineyard, planted with Mourvèdre in 1909 (now representing around 80 per cent of the blend), softened by their best Grenache, Counoise and Syrah. It is destemmed and fermented with natural yeasts, then aged in small second- and third-use foudres. The result is an endlessly complex, almost baroque Châteauneuf that ages for decades. The first vintage was 1989, and though some vintages (1994, 1995, 1999, 2003) have been less exciting, since 2005, only the 2011 has been anything less than excellent. The white Roussanne Vieilles Vignes comes from a plot of Roussanne planted in 1901. It's picked a little overripe, and the resulting wine, though dry, is unbelievably opulent. Use of oak isn't excessive, with around a third going into new and recently-used barriques. It's an unforgettable wine. The Coudoulet de Beaucastel red and white Côtes-du-Rhônes from land adjacent to the Châteauneuf vineyards are made with the same care, and are better than many a Châteauneuf.

Château de Beaucastel is the jewel in the crown of the Perrin empire, but the range of wines is extensive. They also own the excellent Domaine du Clos des Tourelles in Gigondas, have a number of *sélections parcellaires* including the brilliant Gigondas L'Argnée and Vinsobres Les Hauts de Julien. Their range of négociant Rhône bottlings is reliable, and they also make the wines for Miraval, the Provençale property of actors Brad Pitt and Angelina Jolie, one of the few celebrity wines of any real quality.

Domaine de Beaurenard

Châteauneuf-du-Pape

www.beaurenard.fr

With 32 hectares of widely-dispersed plots in Châteauneuf, 25 hectares in Rasteau and 6 hectares in Côtes-du-Rhône 'you have to be organised!' says Daniel Coulon. Even more so considering it's all farmed biodynamically. Thankfully there are plenty of hands on deck: brothers Daniel and Frédéric took over from their parents Paul and Régine, and now Daniel's son Victor has joined the estate, representing the eighth generation in the business.

They use all available varieties in all their colour mutations for their red and white Châteauneufs. Daniel is particularly interested in lesser-known local varieties and for over 20 years has been cultivating a conservatory populated with cuttings of old vines from their estate. A new cuvée Gran Partita, only made so far in 2012 and 2015, has been developed to explore them. Freshness, purity and transparency are words I often find myself using for the red and white *tradition* bottlings. These characteristics are accentuated in the red and white Boisrenard cuvées, which are rarely less than excellent, wines of great depth and intricacy. They embrace the natural wealth of Châteauneuf, and manage to walk the fine line between richness and excess like few others.

Domaine Henri Bonneau

Châteauneuf-du-Pape

In the Rhône, I often find that the size of the sign outside the estate is in inverse proportion to the greatness of the wines. This is certainly true of Henri Bonneau. There is no outward clue as to what lies beneath his modest terraced family home near the church. Rickety steps at the back of the house lead down into a labyrinthine series of passageways, rooms and chambers, with over 100 barrels of various sizes dimly lit by dangling bare bulbs. The walls are wet, the moulds varied in colour and form, the smell is dank but fragrant. The ruby wines drawn out of these ancient casks however are limpid and luminous. Henri, who died in 2016, was no less characterful: a chuckling, mischievous presence in worn overalls, all grins and eyebrows, never short of a joke and a story.

Henri, born in 1938, was the twelfth generation of winemaking Bonneaus. The estate amounts to just 6.5 hectares, around half of which is in La Crau. The rest is dotted around the east and south of the village including Bois de la Ville, Le Pointu and Grand Pierre. The estate today is almost entirely made up of Grenache, with a little Mourvèdre on La Crau. Contrarily, Henri was no fan of old plant material, favouring vines under 50 years old. He harvested late, didn't destem the berries, fermented in concrete vats, never used new oak barrels and bottled without filtration.

There are four Châteauneufs in the range, and the decision as to which will be made in any particular vintage is made at the end of the élevage – which could be up to seven years in barrel. The *tradition* bottling bears his name, Marie Beurrier is a step up in quality, Réserve des Célestins is effectively his top-quality bottling, made only in the best vintages. These are deep, soulful, sprawling expressions of Châteauneuf.

In 1990 and 1998 he also made a wine called Cuvée Spéciale, an unusual, very ripe, almost Port-like wine with some residual sweetness. Vin de France Les Rouliers, made from 80 per cent Grenache, 20 per cent Cinsault from vineyards in the Gard, is usually a blend of two different vintages. Since Henri's death, the estate has been largely administered by his commercial partner, Daniel Combin.

Domaine Charvin

Orange

T.: +33 (0) 4 90 34 41 10

Laurent Charvin has a mischievous side that reminds me of the late Henri Bonneau; he has the same cheeky chuckle. Laurent is also resolutely traditional in his approach. The estate was established in 1851; Laurent joined his father Gerard in 1990. Gerard sent the crop to the cooperative, but Laurent started estate bottling as soon as he arrived. You can see why – the domaine, now certified organic, has some terrific old vines in the north-west of the appellation, grown on *galets roulés* and limestone in *lieux-dits* Cabrières, Maucoil and l'Arnesque. There is just one red Châteauneuf. There's no destemming, and the wine is fermented and aged for 18 months in concrete with only light extraction, before the wines are bottled, unfiltered. No oak, no nonsense. It can take time to come together, and can appear quite gawky early on, but takes on impressive complexity with age. Since the 2016 vintage Laurent has made a white Châteauneuf based on Clairette Rose with a little Bourboulenc, which balances richness, softness and precision. Canny collectors squirrel away good vintages of his Côtes-du-Rhônes too.

Le Clos du Caillou

Courthézon

www.closducaillou.com

Originally a wooded hunting estate, this domaine was established by Elie Dussaud in 1895. In 1936, officials came to assess the terroir to see whether it should be included in the nascent appellation, but they were turned away by armed gamekeepers. The *lieu-dit* Le Cailloux is excluded from the AOC to this day. Bad news for the owners, good news for wine lovers: grapes grown there are only permitted to be bottled as AOC Côtes-du-Rhône, which makes for some great value wines. The estate's 9 hectares of Châteauneuf parcels are grown on mostly sandy soils in the neighbouring *lieux-dits* of Les Bédines, La Guigasse and Pignan. They produce poised and silky wines of supreme finesse.

The Pouizin family bought the estate in 1955. Current owner Sylvie Vacheron (née Pouizin) married Jean-Dennis Vacheron of the winemaking family in Sancerre, and they lived in the Loire until they returned to Châteauneuf to take over the estate in 1996. Sadly Jean-Dennis passed away in 2002, at which point Bruno Gaspard joined the estate as winemaker. The estate was certified organic in 2010, and now half of it is farmed using biodynamic principles. The old-vine cuvée La Réserve is worthy of particular praise. Equal parts Grenache and Mourvèdre are destemmed (like all their reds) and co-fermented before being aged for 18 months in demi-muids and a small proportion of terracotta amphorae. The result is a spellbinding and utterly seductive Châteauneuf.

Clos du Mont-Olivet

Châteauneuf-du-Pape

www.clos-montolivet.com

One way of reading the history of Châteauneuf-du-Pape is through tracing a handful of families that have played an important role. The Sabon family is one of them. At the beginning of the twentieth century, Séraphin Sabon married Marie Jausset, whose father Romain Jausset owned holdings in Châteauneuf. Séraphin and Marie inherited these vineyards, to which they added more. In 1932, they established Clos du Mont-Olivet, which they passed on to their eldest son, Joseph, in 1952. Today the estate is managed by Joseph's children, David, Céline and Thierry Sabon.

This 27-hectare estate is made up of many small vineyards around the appellation but the largest is a 10.4-hectare chunk of *lieu-dit* Montalivet near *lieu-dit* La Crau. They don't farm organically, but avoid insecticides. Such a variety of parcels gives them plenty of soil types to play with, and the Sabons use all the primary 13 grape varieties, helping them to achieve a particularly well-balanced, nuanced and restrained style of wine. La Cuvée du Papet, introduced in 1989, was one of the original *cuvées spéciales*. To begin with, it wasn't destemmed, but like all of their wines there is no strict recipe. Generally speaking, it comes from very old Grenache (some over 100 years old) from *lieux-dits* Montalivet, La Crau, Bois Dauphin and Pied de Baud, backed up with smaller proportions of Mourvèdre, and sometimes Syrah. It favours elegance and balance over oak and power, and lasts for decades; the 1989 was still fantastic in 2019.

Their white, which doesn't undergo malolactic fermentation, is particularly measured and precise, with no excess oak. While rightly known for the quality of their Châteauneufs, their Lirac cuvées are also well worth discovering, being among the best in the appellation.

Clos des Papes

Châteauneuf-du-Pape

www.clos-des-papes.fr

Grenache may be known as 'the Pinot of the South', but there aren't many Châteauneufs that could ever be described as Burgundian. There is one estate, however, where I find myself using the term, and that is Clos des Papes. Not all producers would appreciate such a comparison, but owner and winemaker Vincent Avril wouldn't mind: he, his father Paul and his vineyard manager Jean-Luc Lancelot all studied in Burgundy, and the estate has long been appreciated for its sublime finesse. Vincent cuts an imposing figure, but his large frame belies a certain sensitivity. He talks freely, but he listens too; he makes Châteauneuf, but drinks wine from all over the world.

One thing about Clos des Papes that may surprise is that it's not a walled vineyard as the name suggests – the *clos* is just one of its parcels near the ruined Château. This name was trademarked in 1902 by Vincent's great-grandfather Paul-Eugène, and it has been allowed to stand. The Pythonesque labels were designed in the same era. Their history goes back much further, as the Avril family has been making Châteauneuf since 1600. Today the estate is made up of 23 plots in total, amounting to 35 hectares, which is farmed organically. Vincent makes just one red Châteauneuf and one white. 'First of all, winemakers must make wines that they like to drink … our wines are to go with food, and it's for that reason we don't make *cuvées spéciales*. We never have and we never will.' His red cuvée is typically a destemmed, co-fermented blend of 65 per cent Grenache, 20 per cent Mourvèdre, 10 per cent Syrah and 5 per cent co-planted Counoise, Vaccarèse, Muscardin, Terret Noir, Cinsault and Piquepoul Noir. He keeps yields low, never more than 25 hectolitres per hectare. His white contains the same percentage each of Grenache Blanc, Roussanne, Clairette, Bourboulenc, Piquepoul and Picardan and doesn't go through malolactic fermentation. Vincent likes to use the full 'orchestra' of grape varieties. Reds are aged in large old foudres, whites in stainless steel – there is no new oak or small barrels. Both wines are exceptional, and age beautifully.

Domaine de la Janasse

Courthézon

www.lajanasse.com

Domaine de la Janasse is the story of another branch of the Sabon family. When Aimé Sabon returned from military service in 1967 he took the vines of his father, who had previously taken his crop to the nearby Cellier des Princes co-op. By 1973, he had finished building a cellar and started estate bottling, naming the domaine after one of his parcels, in *lieu-dit* La Jannasse, in the far north of the appellation. The domaine also has significant holdings in La Crau. The 15-hectare estate is today managed by Aimé's son Christophe and daughter Isabelle.

The reds are solid, dense and structured, despite the fact that they are mostly destemmed. Their 'Cuvée Chaupin' is 100 per cent Grenache from sandy soils, mostly *lieu-dit* Chapouin, with vines dating back to 1912. Their other red cuvées contain Syrah and Mourvèdre; Vieilles Vignes is from a number of plots, but the body of the blend comes from vines planted in 1920 and 1965. The very expensive Cuvée XXL has so far only been made in 2007 and 2016. White wines are very rich. There aren't many AOC Côtes-du-Rhône Villages (without village name) reds that spring to mind for their quality, but the two cuvées by La Janasse overperform.

Domaine de Marcoux

Orange

www.domainedemarcoux.fr

One of the first estates in Châteauneuf to follow biodynamic viticulture, Domaine de Marcoux has been farming this way since 1991. The methodology was established by Philippe Armenier before he left to consult to wineries in California. His sisters, Catherine and Sophie Armenier, stayed to run the estate. Sophie's son Vincent Estevenin joined in 2014; Catherine retired in 2019. The family is deeply rooted in the village, demonstrated by documents mentioning their family dating back to 1344.

The red and white *tradition* bottlings are both reliable options, wines with vibrancy, precision and real drinkability. Reds are destemmed and aged in concrete and large old foudres. Vieilles Vignes is a marriage of two plots of old vines: *lieux-dits* Charbonnières (planted in 1900) and Les Esqueirons. It's practically pure Grenache except for a few heads of Mourvèdre. The first vintage was in 1989: 'We only do it if the *tradition* is fantastic by itself,' says Sophie, 'and we only make 3,500 bottles.' It is well worth seeking out, an exemplary *cuvée spéciale* that works on depth, energy and longevity. There are now 18 hectares in the appellation; outside Châteauneuf, their organic Lirac *rouge*, Lorentine, is particularly impressive.

Château la Nerthe

www.chateaulanerthe.fr

Châteauneuf-du-Pape

One of Châteauneuf's oldest, largest and most picturesque estates, La Nerthe is one to visit if you're in the area. The property itself is grander than most and is one of the most historically important wine estates of the south of France. Positioned in parkland between the Route de

Sorgues and the Route de Bédarrides, it is surrounded by a 60-hectare block of vineyards, with a further 32 hectares on *lieu-dit* La Crau to the east – all of which are farmed organically. The estate was bought by the Tulle de Villefranche family on 25 November 1560, and already had vineyards planted by that time. By the end of the eighteenth century it was exporting wines to Russia, America, England, Germany, Italy and Spain, and it was one of the first Châteauneuf estates to ship its wine in bottle, at least as early as 1782. In 1877, after the estate was ravaged by phylloxera, it was acquired by Joseph Ducos, another great name in the history of Châteauneuf who re-established the estate and achieved much for the town and the appellation. La Nerthe was acquired by the wealthy Richard family in 1985.

The rolling estate covers all the major Châteauneuf soil types and benefits from two natural springs. These contribute a key aspect of the terroir here, and allow the planting of large quantities of white varieties and a particularly large block of Mourvèdre. Plantings of Grenache are relatively low, making up just 55 per cent. The classic red bottling tends towards freshness and elegance, and the recent reduction of new oak for their Syrah-heavy Cuvée des Cadettes has lifted the quality of this old vine cuvée even higher. The new 100 per cent Grenache cuvée Les Clavelles, which comes from La Crau, looks promising.

With 12 per cent of their vineyards planted with white varieties, they claim to be the largest producer by volume of Châteauneuf *blanc*. It's a style at which they have long excelled, both in their *tradition* and their Roussanne-based Clos du Beauvenir. This *cuvée spéciale* sees one-third aged in new oak barriques, but retains its freshness and mineral edge.

Domaine du Pégau

Châteauneuf-du-Pape

pegau.com

A *pégau* is a type of wine jug that was used to serve wine in the Middle Ages. The Feraud family's winemaking roots go back to the seventeenth century, but the domaine only took on its present name and started bottling in commercial quantities when, following her studies, the ir-repressible Laurence Feraud returned to the family domaine in 1987 to join her father Paul. They now have 23 hectares of Châteauneuf, and in 2012 they bought a 41-hectare estate in Sorgues, renaming it Château Pégau, where they produce Côtes-du-Rhône Villages, Côtes-du-Rhône and Vin de France.

Their approach to Châteauneuf is resolutely traditional and the reds call for some time in bottle. The Ferauds use all available grape varieties and most of their non-Grenache vineyards are co-planted. Their *tradition* bottling, Cuvée Réservée, is not destemmed, fermentation is in concrete using natural yeasts, followed by two years in old oak foudres. Cuvée Laurence is the same wine, but with four years' élevage. Cuvée da Capo is made in the same spirit, but is a parcel selection of 100-year-old vines planted in sandy parts of La Crau. So far only a handful of vintages have been released: 1998, 2003, 2007, 2010, 2015 and 2016. It's one of the more measured *cuvées spéciales*, and is all the better for it. Whites are controlled and orderly but not overly tinkered with. Their Cuvée à Tempo, a third each of Clairette, Roussanne and Grenache Blanc, smells more like a meadow than an oak forest.

Château Rayas
Châteauneuf-du-Pape

chateaurayas.fr

My favourite story about Louis Reynaud, a former owner of Château Rayas, takes place one day in 1979 when he is due a visit from Simon Loftus of English wine merchant Adnams. Loftus had been trying in vain to set up a meeting, so eventually sent Reynaud a letter telling him he would meet him at the winery at 3pm on a particular day in May. On arrival, Loftus found the winery empty, shutters firmly closed. Driving away, he glanced back only to see the furtive figure of Reynaud climbing out of the ditch in which he had been hiding. Loftus called out to him, asking if it was possible to visit the chais and taste his wine but received a firm 'Non'. No further explanation was given. Louis' son Jacques was equally eccentric (for more on the Reynauds see Appendix II, page 351).

Louis Reynaud was not the founder; it was established in 1880 by his father Albert Reynaud, a notary, who purchased the estate after going deaf at the age of 45. In 1920 it was handed down to Louis, who went on to purchase Château des Tours (see page 132) and Château de Fonsalette (see page 187). Louis passed Rayas and Fonsalette to his younger son Jacques; his older son Bertrand received Château des Tours. When Jacques died in 1997, all three domaines were passed on to Bertrand's son Emmanuel. Though by no means as eccentric as his uncle, you're unlikely to encounter him pouring wine from behind a table at a tasting. Neither is the winery geared up for tourism. The only sign is well away from the main road, down a dirt track, hiding under an overgrown shrub. The winery itself appears abandoned from the outside, as it does from the inside. It has never really been finished, but it does its job: making and maturing the most individual and extraordinary of all Châteauneuf-du-Pape wines.

Château Rayas takes its name from the *lieu-dit* in which most of the vines are situated, a very sandy and noticeably cooler site towards the north-east of the appellation (the estate has more woodland than vineyards). The vines are well-spaced goblets of Grenache for the red wine, with equal amounts of Grenache Blanc and Clairette for the white. Emmanuel always waits for rain before picking; reds are not destemmed and are fermented in concrete. They are then aged in ancient 450-litre, 600-litre and 33-hectolitre barrels or foudres before being bottled unfiltered. After Château Rayas, the estate's other red Châteauneuf is 'Pignan', which comes from a 2-hectare plot of Grenache from the eponymous *lieu-dit*, and is processed the same way. It's stylistically similar, and is often close to Rayas in quality. Emmanuel also makes Château de Fonsalette at this site and any barrels that don't make the final blend for their respective wines go into Côtes-du-Rhône *rouge* 'La Pialade', a blend of Grenache, Cinsault and Syrah.

The wines of the Rayas stable taste like no others in Châteauneuf. The reds are particularly pale in colour, they have plenty of glycerol fat and are often fairly low in tannin. Aromatically they are unique, and highly distinctive. They combine red fruit with orange peel and display a floral dimension like pot-pourri and dried rose, along with dried herbs including thyme and peppermint. With time they become achingly fragrant, adding leather, spices like sandalwood and leaf mulch. Despite their delicacy, the wines age very well in good vintages. Where this peculiar character comes from is not entirely clear. It can't just be terroir; the wines from all three estates, made in two different wineries, all carry the same signature (though it's true that all three share predominantly sandy soils and north-facing parcels). Some commentators have suggested it's the ancient greying barrels in the Rayas barrel room, but again it can't be down to this alone as there are two different chais. Emmanuel says this distinctive style comes from harvesting fully ripe grapes, extracting very gently with no *pigeage*, and adding nothing along the way. 'Winemaking work is respecting the fruit,' he says. Rayas guards its secrets, and its mysteries endure.

Domaine Roger Sabon

Châteauneuf-du-Pape

www.domainerogersabon.com

Séraphin Sabon had three children: Joseph, Noël and Roger. Joseph took over Clos du Mont-Olivet, Noël married into Domaine Chante Cigale, and, in 1956, Roger established the estate that bears his name. It was handed down to Roger's three sons, Jean-Jacques, Denis and Gilbert in 1976. Jean-Jacques' raffish son-in-law Didier Negron has been in charge of winemaking since 2001.

Today the estate has 18 hectares of Châteauneuf vineyards across 14 different plots, producing four red cuvées: Les Olivets (Grenache, Syrah, Cinsault), Réserve (Grenache, Syrah, Mourvèdre), Prestige (Grenache, Syrah, Mourvèdre, Counoise, Vaccarèse) and the top cuvée Le Secret des Sabon (very old Grenache). Didier opts for a long maceration with gentle extraction, followed by a long élevage, typically in foudres, large tronconic wooden vats and demi-muids. Les Olivets is approachable, whereas Réserve and Prestige are both powerful, burly, very classic expressions that can offer a lot of rambunctious pleasure. Le Secret however is very different in style, and is the only cuvée to retain some of its stems. The result is an extraordinarily deep, pure expression that reminds you why old-vine Châteauneuf-du-Pape Grenache is so special. Lovers of white Châteauneuf should seek out the refined Renaissance.

Domaine Saint-Préfert

Châteauneuf-du-Pape

www.st-prefert.com

When a wine-loving pharmacist from Avignon, a Monsieur Serre, discovered there was a *lieu-dit* in Châteauneuf that shared his name – Les Serres – he couldn't resist investigating further. In 1932, he bought some land and planted a vineyard, eventually building a winery some time later. With no successors to take on the estate, it was sold in 2002 to Isabel Ferrando. Born in Carpentras, she worked in banking but had always wanted to make wine; with the birth of her daughter, she decided to take the plunge. Almost literally, when the sale coincided with the biblical floods of that catastrophic vintage. Her first wine was the 2003.

The estate was 12 hectares, but she has since expanded it to 24 hectares of Châteauneuf and 8 hectares of Côtes-du-Rhône. The original vineyards surrounded the property in *lieu-dit* Grandes Serres, and she bought in *lieux-dits* Colombis, Rayas and Pied Long. They have been organic since 2013 and certified biodynamic since 2019. In the hot, dry and draining *galets roulés* of Grandes Serres, she has recently introduced some drip irrigation. She says she had no choice: 'my vines were dying'.

On top of her reliable classic red and white cuvées, she makes a number of *cuvées spéciales*. Réserve Auguste Favier is a silky blend of 85 per cent old-vine Grenache and 15 per cent Cinsault, part destemmed. Collection Charles Giraud is a robust, non-destemmed blend of 60 per cent old-vine Grenache and 40 per cent old-vine Mourvèdre which she likens to a bull. Colombis is a juicy and elegant pure Grenache. A new cuvée, first vintage 2018, is F601, a pure Cinsault from the parcel of the same designation planted in 1928 near the winery. She also makes a special white from old white and pink Clairette, aged in demi-muid and bottled in magnums, called Cuvée Spéciale Vieilles Clairettes. The wines here have a touch of modern polish, but a great vibrancy and purity that makes them hard to resist.

Rotem & Mounir Saouma

Beaune

www.lucienlemoine.com

The Châteauneufs of this Burgundy-based Rhône producer, the husband-and-wife team Mounir and Rotem Saouma, are, perhaps unsurprisingly, a little different. The Saoumas followed similar paths: Rotem studied agriculture and wine in Dijon, while Mounir pursued viticulture and winemaking in Montpellier, then they both separately worked in various vineyards around the world. In 1999 they joined forces to create Lucien Le Moine, their négociant house based in Beaune, where they produce only Côte d'Or *premiers* and *grands crus*. When they decided it was time to buy land, instead of Burgundy, they looked to the Rhône. Mounir sees a kinship between Pinot Noir and Grenache; both exist in three colours, have white juice, and arc relatively neutral vessels that can fluently express and communicate their terroir. They now own 8.4 hectares of Châteauneuf in *lieux-dits* Pignan, Les Esqueirons, Le Pointu, Pied Redon and La Bigote, not to mention a further 9 hectares of Côtes-du-Rhône Villages in Orange.

Fascinated by antique winemaking methods, Mounir's winemaking and maturing techniques are highly individual. Following a long, cold maceration (two weeks), fermentation is long and slow. He puts the wines through a long élevage on the full lees with regular stirring, and he never racks. He uses minimal sulphur dioxide and neither pumps his wines nor fines or filters them. Unusually, he opts for a continuous press for both colours; for his whites, he works with very cloudy juice that he browns before fermentation in order to reduce the final phenolic content of the wine.

The results are highly idiosyncratic expressions of Châteauneuf. Reds are tight and savoury, almost austere, accentuating the salt and stone that gives Châteauneuf its longevity. The cherry-juice fruit is lean and fluid; they are not fat or fruity, though they have solid frames. In red, Omnia is a blend of different parcels, whereas Arioso is pure old-vine Grenache from *lieu-dit* Pignan. Experimental red cuvées include the Amph range of five whole-cluster fermented wines matured in unwaxed amphorae, and Le Petit Livre de A.M Bach, an iteration of Arioso that only uses free run juice and is matured for five years in barrel instead of three. The white Magis is, if anything, even more outlying, with precious few of the classic Châteauneuf stylistic markers. Focused, saline and reductive, it has the size of Châteauneuf without the over-generosity of fruit that some display. It is a compellingly original illustration of what white Châteauneuf can be.

In line with their quality, the wines are now among the most expensive in Châteauneuf, but for a great value introduction to the style, seek out their Inopia red and white Côtes-du-Rhône Villages.

Domaine de la Vieille Julienne

Orange

www.vieillejulienne.com

Since taking over the family estate at the northern limit of the appellation in 1990, the tall, twinkly-eyed Jean-Paul Daumen has gradually converted it to biodynamics. He has 22 hectares of land, two-thirds of which are in AOC Châteauneuf-du-Pape, with the rest just outside the boundary and bottled as very good value white and red Côtes-du-Rhônes. Vineyards are co-planted and spread over seven largely north-facing terraces, making this a relatively austere terroir. The top terraces are predominantly limestone and produce Les Hauts Lieux, powerful, long-lived and linear. The lower banks have a higher proportion of sand, producing a finer, more immediately approachable wine called Les Trois Sources. The Réservé, produced only in the best years, is particularly rich; in the past it has verged on the excessive but the 2018 suggests the style is being gently dialled back. Yields are kept low, grapes are destemmed, and Daumen never adds tartaric acid. The northerly siting and aspect of the vineyards was once a handicap; now it's an advantage.

Le Vieux Donjon

Châteauneuf-du-Pape

www.levieuxdonjon.fr

'Not modern, not fashionable; just always unchanging.' Claire Fabre's modest description of her family's house style is fitting but it doesn't do justice to the quality. From their 15-hectare estate close to the village, she and her brother François make a single red and single white cuvée as, according to Claire, they find that 'the blend of all is even better than the quality of the best parcels.' The family has had vineyards for six generations and estate bottled the wines since 1966.

They don't fully destem their red, and it makes for a textural, assertive style. It's also one reason that wines can appear hard, even disjointed or apparently rustic in youth. It's a very traditional style that requires significant ageing, but it comes together and delivers real complexity and enduring freshness in time. The white, which is half Clairette, half Roussanne (no oak, no malo), is similarly dry, structured and sincere.

Domaine du Vieux Télégraphe

Bédarrides

www.vieux-telegraphe.fr

I asked current co-owner Daniel Brunier what three things people need to know about Domaine du Vieux Télégraphe. 'La Crau, La Crau, La Crau!' was his reply. Henri Brunier bought the original parcel on this high plateau in 1891 to give to his son Hippolyte. 'Why did he buy it? We don't know,' says Daniel, 'it wasn't even vines, it was woods.' Not for long – with viticulture already established in the area, Hippolyte planted vineyards. Their *cuvée classique* is drawn entirely from their 50 hectares of this exceptional zone, from vines with an average age of 70 years, and some as old as 100. They have a long history of making whites too, and about 10 per cent of their Vieux Télégraphe Châteauneuf is white, also from La Crau.

Daniel manages the estate together with his brother Frédéric. Their sons, Edouard and Nicolas, both joined in the mid-2010s. The family is fiercely independent, and does not work with consulting winemakers. Their holdings are extensive, and now the 100-hectare estate is farmed organically, though not certified. For Daniel, however, avoiding irrigation is even more important in terms of quality – he wonders why there's no certification for that. One of the biggest jobs for them is dealing with natural grapevine mortality – they need to replant the equivalent of 3.5 hectares every year.

They do not and will not make a Vieux Télégraphe *cuvée spéciale* (their bottles state 'La Crau' on the label, but this is not a cuvée name as such). They do however make many other wines, including other Châteauneufs. Piedlong is a blend of 75-year-old Grenache from *lieu-dit* Pied Long with 10 per cent 50-year-old Mourvèdre from *lieu-dit* Pignan. Clos la Roquète is a particularly fine and mineral white Châteauneuf from *lieu-dit* La Roquète, a blend of a third each Roussanne, Clairette and Grenache Blanc. Télégramme is a destemmed red cuvée from younger vines and other parcels. (There is also Cuvée Hippolyte – an experimental wine, different each year, but not sold commercially.) Their extensive range also covers Gigondas (Domaine Les Pallières), Ventoux (Mégaphone), IGP Vaucluse (Le Pigeoulet) and even Lebanon's Beqaa Valley (Massaya).

Through their winemaking decisions they try to achieve two main things: flavours in the wine that come from the terroir, not the cellar; and supreme tannic finesse. They make an elegant, balanced, refined style of Châteauneuf that is eminently classic. Though delicious in youth, the wines only really blossom after a decade or two in bottle.

Other good examples

With nearly 300 producers making a Châteauneuf-du-Pape, there are dozens of notable estates. Of those producing a more measured, subtle style, I would include **Domaine de Bois de Boursan**, **Domaine de Ferrand**, **Domaine de Villeneuve**, **Domaine Duseigneur**, **Domaine Pierre André**, **Domaine de la Biscarelle** and **Domaine Mas Saint-Louis** – all with different approaches, but each making savoury and highly drinkable wines.

Producers fashioning excellent contemporary Châteauneufs that combine freshness, elegance and power are **Domaine la Barroche**, **La Bastide Saint Dominique** and **Guillaume Gonnet**.

Very good examples of a classic, bold style can be found from **Domaine de la Charbonnière**, **Domaine Raymond Usseglio**, **Mas de Boislauzon**, **Domaine les Cailloux**, **Domaine de la Solitude**, **Domaine Grand Veneur**, **Domaine André Mathieu**, **Vignobles Mayard**, **Domaine Font de Michelle** and **Domaine du Cristia**.

Examples of popular modern Châteauneufs include **Château de la Gardine, Château de Vaudieu, Domaine de la Mordorée, Domaine Pierre Usseglio, Domaine Giraud, Domaine des Bosquets des Papes** and **Clos Saint Jean.**

It doesn't stop there of course; the following are less well known and often represent good value for money: **Domaine Chante Cigale, Domaine Croze Granier, Domaine Durieu, Domaine Eddie Féraud, Domaine la Fagotière, Domaine l'Abbé Dîne, Domaine Jérôme Gradassi, Domaine Patrice Magni, Domaine Roger Perrin, Château Beauchêne, Domaine Porte Rouge, Le Bois Pointu, Domaine Juliette Avril, Domaine de Saint Siffrein, Domaine des Sénéchaux, Château de la Font du Loup, Château Mont-Thabor, Domaine l'Or de Line, Domaine Georges-Lombrière** and **Cuvée du Vatican.**

Guigal (see Côte-Rôtie) bought Domaine de Nalys in 2017 and promptly renamed it **Château de Nalys.** They went on to acquire **Domaine les Clefs d'Or** in 2020. Both are currently seeing significant investment and restructuring, which will no doubt bear fruit in coming vintages. Of the other négociants bottling, **Chapoutier**'s La Bernadine is a reliable contemporary option in both colours. **La Ferme du Mont** makes three excellent examples: Vendange (red and white) and Capelan (red). **Ogier**, based in Châteauneuf itself, makes Châteauneuf under its Clos de l'Oratoire des Papes label, the white of which is particularly good.

GADAGNE

There are two important villages in the Southern Rhône whose name contains Châteauneuf: Châteauneuf-du-Pape and its less famous neighbour, 15 kilometres to its south-east, Châteauneuf-de-Gadagne. (There is also a Châteauneuf-du-Rhône in Grignan-les-Adhémar and Châteauneuf-sur-Isère in Crozes-Hermitage, amongst others.) Given that it means 'new castle' in English, and all castles were new at one stage, it's not surprising the name is so common. Between Châteauneuf-du-Pape and Châteauneuf-de-Gadagne, whose castle came first? Châteauneuf-de-Gadagne would argue that theirs did. So it smarts a little that they can only use AOC Côtes-du-Rhône Villages Gadagne on their labels and not the full name of the village.

Xavier Anglès of Domaine de Bois de Saint-Jean led the Châteauneuf-de-Gadagne *syndicat* in its quest for promotion to Named Village status.

After compiling the necessary documents and handing them over to the INAO their application was suspended at the eleventh hour due to a complaint raised by AOC Châteauneuf-du-Pape, which wasn't keen on another appellation just down the road using the hallowed name of Châteauneuf. Anglès battled against the powers that be, but eventually capitulated against an adversary with far greater means. 'At least it's short and easy to pronounce,' he says. 'But it's not pretty. It's a compromise.' Goliath won. Full name or not, the promotion is still a source of pride for local winemakers. Sébastien Clément of Domaine des Garriguettes explains 'I'm no longer drowning among other Côtes-du-Rhône wines – now I'm selling my place, my village.' He's less bothered about the naming debacle. Referring to AOC Châteauneuf-du-Pape, he says 'I understand their position. And anyway, I don't want customers to confuse my wine with a Châteauneuf-du-Pape.'

Although similar in name they differ significantly in size. Châteauneuf-du-Pape covers 3,200 hectares, whereas Châteauneuf-de-Gadagne is closer to 180 hectares – a mere 6 per cent the size of its neighbour. But the popes of Avignon recognized the potential of both terroirs, and you can still find several *bornes papales* – post-box-sized territorial stone markers that displayed their ownership. The wines have been appreciated for centuries, and were exported as early as 1804.

In a sense, Gadagne is a continuation of Châteauneuf-du-Pape terroir – a kind of solar flare of *galets roulés* ejected south-east that skirts around the eastern edge of Avignon as far as the river Durance. 'It's the same terroir,' agrees Anglès. 'It doesn't just look the same, the soil analyses are the same,' he continues, and points out that a local shrub, the *bruyère à Balaï*, is unique to these two appellations. The official growing area was drawn up exclusively around this thin, intermittent bank of galets as it gallops through five successive communes. Of the five, Châteauneuf-de-Gadagne holds the most vineyard area, but it's not just famous for wine. This ancient village is also the birthplace of the Félibrige, the association founded on 21 May 1854 by Frédéric Mistral (1830–1914) and six other local poets, with the aim of codifying and preserving the Provençal language. It was brought into being at the Château de Fontségugne, which today represents one of the five private domaines making AOC Côtes-du-Rhône Villages Gadagne.

That there are so few producers making Gadagne (six including local co-op Demazet) means there is little collective means to promote the appellation. It also makes it difficult to define the style of Gadagne. They are unmistakably Southern Rhône, but there is no obvious stylistic trait that marks them out from many other Côtes-du-Rhône Villages wines. They are however typically broad shouldered and voluminous, with the breadth – and often high alcohol – you would expect from Grenache-based wines grown on *galets roulés*. They do tend to have a particularly dark fruit profile however, and although I don't always find the piquant spice that producers describe, I frequently find herbs such as thyme and sage. The major difference between an average Châteauneuf-du-Pape and a top Gadagne wine is that Gadagne is a third of the price.

Appellation: AOC Côtes-du-Rhône Villages Gadagne
Birth of the appellation: 2012
Communes: Caumont-sur-Durance, Châteauneuf-de-Gadagne, Morières-lès-Avignon, Saint-Saturnin-lès-Avignon, Vedène
Total surface area sold under the AOC in 2019: 97 hectares
Average yield in 2019: 33 hectolitres per hectare
Colours permitted: red only
Grape varieties permitted: As per communal Côtes-du-Rhône Villages regulations (see page 54)

Key producers

Domaine du Bois de Saint-Jean

Jonquerettes

www.domaineduboisdesaintjean.fr

There's a glint in Xavier Anglès' eye that suggests he might have some unprintable stories to tell over the course of an evening's drinking. He's achieved plenty of things that we can openly list here, however, not least of which was pushing through Named Village status for Gadagne during his stint as president of the local *syndicat*. He runs the family estate with his brother Vincent. Though based in Jonquerettes (where the family has lived since 1650 and grown grapes since 1910), holdings now include Vacqueyras and a little Châteauneuf-du-Pape. The Côtes-du-Rhône *rouge* 'L'Intrepide' frequently overdelivers, and the Côtes-du-Rhône *blanc* 'Madame d'Ust' is one of the most successful Viognier-based wines in the Southern Rhône.

Domaine de la Chapelle

Châteauneuf-de-Gadagne

www.domainedelachapelle.net

Follow the high plateau of *galets roulés* north of the village of Châteauneuf-de-Gadagne and eventually you'll get to Domaine de la Chapelle. Built by Jesuit monks in the seventeenth century, it's one of the oldest domaines in unbroken production in the Vaucluse. Purchased by Sylvain Boussier's grandfather in 1953, the estate covers just 8 hectares of vines, all within the Gadagne appellation. 'I want it to stay small,' says Boussier, whose other part-time job is teaching IT at Avignon University. Their white and rosé Côtes-du-Rhônes are refreshing and precise, but their Gadagne Réserve is arguably the best in the appellation, which is impressive considering the modest cellar. Complex and concentrated, in a good vintage it has the regal character you might expect from the other Châteauneuf.

Domaine des Garriguettes

Châteauneuf-de-Gadagne

T.: +33 (0) 4 90 22 50 10

Along with Clos des Saumanes, Domaine des Garriguettes is the other organic estate in Gadagne. Sébastien Clément recently took over from his father after *stages* in the Northern Rhône, Australia and Portugal. On his return he felt compelled to make some changes. 'I was fed up with my wines, bored of them,' he says. His first vintage of conversion to biodynamics was 2019 and Sébastien has felt an immediate change in the health of his vineyards and his relationship with them. The increased vibrancy and freshness in the wines is apparent. There is potential here, and a desire to meet that potential. In time, this could be the domaine that finally puts Gadagne on the map.

Other good examples

The organic **Le Clos des Saumanes** is less consistent, but the Gadagne Vieilles Vignes can be good. **Château de Fontségugne** make an easygoing, fruity expression.

6

THE VENTABREN MASSIF

RASTEAU

With a unified style of wine springing from a clearly defined terroir it's surprising it took so long for the dry wines of Rasteau to be granted full *cru* status. On visiting, and on tasting, the case is clear. Its vineyards inhabit the eastern half of the southern face of the Ventabren massif, a colossal hummock of pebbly yellow, grey and blue marls 22 kilometres north-east of Châteauneuf-du-Pape. This *montagnette* sits between two tributaries of the Rhône, the Aigues and Ouvèze, and rises up to 350 metres altitude behind the village of Rasteau. It's the key to understanding the consistency of these wines: vines are exposed to unhindered sun and sheltered from the mistral so achieving ripeness is rarely problematic; on the other hand, in hot, dry vintages its water-retaining marls help avoid blockages in maturity. Its elevation contributes a point of acidity and a welcome touch of aromatic freshness.

The hot terroir displays Grenache in all its opulent glory: intense purity of expression, smoothness of tannin, *sucrosité* of fruit and silkiness of texture. The wines can occasionally lack structure and focus, however, and are particularly susceptible to building up uncomfortable levels of alcohol. Two appellations coexist here, though they don't cover exactly the same terrain: AOC Rasteau for dry red wines, and AOC Rasteau Vin Doux Naturel for sweet wines across red, rosé and white (see below).

There are three subzones to Rasteau terroir, giving wines with slightly different characteristics. The lowest-altitude, most southerly subzone (covering around 20 per cent of the appellation surface) is an annexed section of the Plan de Dieu, referred to locally as Le Plan. The middle section doesn't have a commonly used name, so let's call it the Centre. The Montagne is the highest-altitude subzone of Rasteau, mostly to the north of the village. Le Plan sits at around 110 metres altitude, is fairly flat, and is made up largely of pebbly alluviums with a covering of red clay. The style of wine here tends to be very ripe, with deep black fruits, sometimes towards compote or fruit jam. The wines are often tannic and structured, and can make an excellent base for the more structured, long-lived style of Vin Doux Naturel. It's rarely a source of the most elegant dry wines. As you move north towards the Centre, the land begins to fold and rise. This is the most soulful terroir of Rasteau, its emblematic blue marls. These soils are actually pale grey, but take on a bluish sheen when wet. Wines from these soils tend to be a little paler in colour, with bright red fruit flavour and very fine tannins. The Montagne is the highest land, to the north of the village. Soils are much older, still deep with yellow and blue marl, but also littered in colluvial gravels and stones. It's bisected by a deep ravine that runs from the top of the Montagne to the village, and there are half a dozen other small valleys scratched into the hillside. Robert Charavin of Domaine des Coteaux des Travers explains that this is the origin of the name Rasteau – this series of small channels that cut down towards the village are shaped like a *rateau* – a rake. These sloping gullies provide different exposures to the hillside vineyards, which, along with the added height here, can bring freshness, tension and stylistic variety to the wines.

Dry wines

Appellation: AOC Rasteau

Birth of the appellation: 2010

Communes: Rasteau

Total surface area sold under the AOC in 2019: 951 hectares

Average yield in 2019: 34 hectolitres per hectare

Colours permitted: red only

Grape varieties permitted: The main red grape used must be Grenache, and wines must also contain Syrah or Mourvèdre (or both). Other minor permitted grapes are Bourboulenc, Carignan, Cinsault, Clairette, Clairette Rose, Counoise, Grenache Blanc, Grenache Gris, Marsanne, Muscardin, Piquepoul Blanc, Piquepoul Noir, Roussanne, Terret Noir, Ugni Blanc, Vaccarèse and Viognier.

Though Grenache is the heart and soul of Rasteau, there are also significant amounts of Syrah, followed by some Mourvèdre and Carignan, along with a squeeze of Cinsault. Syrah can provide the structure sometimes missing from pure Grenache, but some feel it's not suited to this hot microclimate. Charavin stopped planting Syrah around 2004 due to rising temperatures, and now opts for Mourvèdre instead. Laurent Robert of Domaine Combe Julière doesn't grow any Syrah at all, as it can build up very high potential alcohol levels and develop drying tannins. After Grenache, Robert favours Carignan, which is gaining a renewed following here after being largely ripped out in the 1990s. Julie Paolucci from Domaine la Luminaille believes in it, particularly when yields are kept low, as it's better adapted to drought.

Rasteau is a muscular and charismatic appellation, but can lack elegance and is sometimes unaware of its own strength. Thankfully, with more gentle extraction and handling, a new generation of winemakers is finding ways to cool its brow and help it lighten up. Rasteau is naturally bold and generous, but increasingly you can find an elegant side to this lovable brute.

Though the other sweet wine of the Southern Rhône, Muscat de Beaumes de Venise, has been made for nearly two thousand years, I've found no evidence to suggest that the wines of Rasteau were sweet before 1932. Robert Charavin of Domaine des Coteaux des Travers says it was introduced by a winemaker at a local cave cooperative who had experience of working in Rivesaltes, a town near the border with Spain with a long history of making sweet Grenache. On arriving in Rasteau he saw the potential for the local crop to be processed in the same fashion, and it quickly gained a following. Rasteau was given the appellation for Vin Doux Naturel in 1944, well before the appellation for dry wines; it was only given Named Village status for dry wines in 1999 and elevated to *cru* in 2010.

Rasteau Vin Doux Naturel (VDN) is largely grown in Rasteau, but there are also demarcated areas within Cairanne and Sablet that can produce it. Grapes are hand-picked, and yields can't surpass 30 hectolitres per hectare. The grapes are left to ripen longer on the vine until they reach a minimum natural sugar component of 252 grams per litre.

Fermentation starts as normal, but like all VDNs, grape spirit of 96% abv is added to stop the fermentation and raise the overall alcohol level to a minimum of 15% abv. The volume of spirit must equate to between

5 and 10 per cent of the finished wine. This process is called *mutage* – literally to mute or silence the noisily fizzing fermentation. It leaves natural grape sugars in the finished wine, making it sweet.

Sweet wines

Appellation: AOC Rasteau Vin Doux Naturel
Birth of the appellation: 1944
Communes: Cairanne, Rasteau, Sablet
Total surface area sold under the AOC in 2019: 15 hectares
Average yield in 2019: 26 hectolitres per hectare
Colours permitted: red, rosé and white
Production in 2019: 68 per cent red, 30 per cent rosé, 2 per cent white
Grape varieties permitted: For reds, those described as Grenat or Tuilé – grapes from the Grenache family must make up 90 per cent of the blend (at least 75 per cent of Grenache Noir). Minor permitted varieties are Bourboulenc, Carignan, Cinsault, Clairette, Clairette Rose, Counoise, Marsanne, Mourvèdre, Muscardin, Piquepoul Blanc, Piquepoul Noir, Roussanne, Syrah, Terret Noir, Ugni Blanc, Vaccarèse and Viognier. For rosé and white grapes from the Grenache family must make up 90 per cent of the blend. Minor varieties as for reds.

The wine can be white, rosé or red, and the red version is locally referred to as *grenat*, the French word for garnet. On top of this, extended ageing of any colour brings further categories into play: *ambré* for a white or rosé VDN with a further 30 months' oxidative ageing; *tuilé* for a red VDN with a further 30 months' oxidative ageing. *Ambré* and *tuilé* styles with a minimum of 60 months' oxidative ageing can use the term *hors d'age*. There is a final category, *rancio*, for *hors d'age* wines that have taken on a green rim and a distinctive nutty aroma.

Rasteau VDN is a curious category of wine. The young wines can be deliciously vibrant, but can lack length and complexity. The older styles can become highly complex, but can swerve into rusticity or unbearable levels of volatile acidity (VA). It's a style that producers find hard to sell, and it now makes up just 2 per cent of Rasteau's total output. It tends to be an enjoyable curiosity, rather than a life-changing bottle of wine. But it would be a shame to lose it.

Rasteau Vin Doux Naturel styles in a nutshell

Rasteau VDN Blanc: Reductive handling, bottled early, drink young. Classically pear and citrus peel flavours.

Rasteau VDN Ambré: Colour changes to a more copper gold colour, flavours take on more gingerbread and pear, with subtle nut flavours or honey and caramel. Often exhibits high VA and oxidative notes akin to amontillado sherry.

Rasteau VDN Rosé: Saignée method, reductive handling, bottled early, drink young. Pear, melon, citrus and red berry flavours. Can also be called Ambré with 30 months' oxidative ageing.

Rasteau VDN Grenat: Reductive handling, bottled early, drink young but should last 10 years. Typically black cherry, black fruits, spices, more or less tannic. Similar to a Ruby Port, but less alcoholic and less tannic; doesn't last as long.

Rasteau VDN Tuilé: *Tuilé* means the original red colour develops a colour like a roof tile. Flavours take on more prune, spice, tobacco, date, caramel, VA and oloroso sherry flavours.

Rasteau VDN Hors d'Age: Colour evolves further, flavour becomes more intense, concentrated and oxidative with huge impact.

Rasteau VDN Rancio: A *rancio* is defined not only by the length of oxidative ageing, but also by it taking on a green rim and a nutty, maderized flavour. It appears that this style is no longer in production.

Key producers

Domaine Elodie Balme

Rasteau

domaineelodiebalme.com

Petite and full of energy, Elodie Balme is one of the rising stars of Rasteau. Her parents previously delivered the estate's grapes to the co-op, but since 2006 Elodie has been bottling most of their production under her own label. For her, the most important quality factors are the terroir, the rootstock and the age of the vines – in that order. She opts for very little extraction, just some occasional rack and return and infusing the cap, and 10 to 12 days' maceration. The result is a full-bodied and juicy but very drinkable style she describes as 'fruity and immediate'. Her Vin Doux Naturel is in a similar style, picked early to preserve freshness and acidity, with *mutage* to the full 10 per cent. She also makes one of the most exciting wines in neighbouring Roaix.

Domaine Mikaël Boutin

Rasteau

domainemikaelboutinrasteau.over-blog.com

Mikaël has a hands-off, minimum intervention approach. He's been making wine since 2001, and his estate has been organic since 2011. There's just one cuvée here, MB, a blend of Grenache, Syrah, Carignan, Cinsault and Mourvèdre from his 2 hectares of Rasteau, spread across 7 separate parcels. Yields are low, and vines are planted in *gobelet* apart from the Cinsault. He does everything himself, by hand, and it pays off – his wine is undoubtedly one of the best in the appellation, in a deeply savoury and complex style.

Domaine la Collière

Rasteau

domainelacolliere.com

Georges Perrot was new to winemaking when he started working with his father-in-law in 1993 in Rasteau. By 2000 he had rented some vineyards and struck out on his own, and in 2002 he started making his own wine in the old cellar of André Roméro. He named his domaine after la Collière, a stream that runs through one of his parcels. All three of his Rasteau cuvées are fermented and matured in concrete and are usually destemmed. La Fontaine is particularly elegant, a blend of 95 per cent Grenache and 5 per cent Syrah all grown on blue marl, and his Vin Doux Naturel Grenat displays all the depth, concentration and purity of fruit of his dry wines.

Domaine Gourt de Mautens

Rasteau

www.gourtdemautens.com

I've met few winemakers as single-minded as Jérôme Bressy. He took over the family vineyards around Rasteau in 1996, and instead of delivering the crop to the local co-op, started bottling his own. Taking advice from friends and mentors such as Henri Bonneau and Domaine de Marcoux, he increased his plantings of well-adapted local varieties such as Vaccarèse and Piquepoul Noir and converted to biodynamics. The turning point came in 2010 when Rasteau was promoted from a Named Village to *cru*. Production rules were tightened and the authorities specified that the total of what they consider 'lesser' varieties – such as Vaccarèse – could only make up 15 per cent of an estate's total plantings. His contained 40 per cent. Instead of changing his wine, he dropped out of the appellation and bottles his wines to this day under IGP Vaucluse.

His vines are co-planted and pruned in *gobelets*. They naturally yield just 8–15 hectolitres per hectare, and he makes no adjustments to the juice except adding low levels of sulphites. Ferments can take over a year to complete. His professed ambition is to create not only a great Rhône wine but 'a great Mediterranean wine'. And within 20 years, he's achieved it.

Domaine la Luminaille

Rasteau

www.domainelaluminaille.com

When her father died unexpectedly in 2014, Julie Paolucci quit her job as sommelier to return home and take on the family domaine. She represents the fifth generation, and farms the estate organically with her partner Nicolas Brès. They own 9 hectares in *lieu-dit* La Luminaille, a sacred clearing on a succession of hillsides just north of the village. They've added 3 hectares higher up, in *lieu-dit* Les Gelegrières, and rent a further 5 hectares. They make two Rasteau cuvées from their minuscule winery: Luminaris and Garance (named after their daughter). Both contain Grenache, Syrah and Carignan and are partially destemmed; Luminaris contains a little Mourvèdre, Garance is a selection of 90-year-old vines and is particularly deep and expressive. Both are particularly well balanced, precise and elegant for the appellation. The exceptional white wines, grown in Rasteau terroir but necessarily bottled as Côtes-du-Rhône, prove that Rasteau can make white wines every bit as good as Cairanne. The Vin Doux Natural Grenat is fruity and elegant.

Domaine la Soumade

Rasteau

www.domainelasoumade.fr

It's a rare Rasteau tasting that doesn't have Domaine la Soumade amongst the top bottles. André Roméro, who set up the estate in 1979, was joined by his son Frédéric in 1996. Their style is easily recognizable: transparent, svelte and elegant with polished red fruits and superfine tannins. They attribute this in part to working with Bordeaux consultant Stéphane Derenoncourt, who they appointed in 2002. Including their unnamed *cuvée classique*, there are four Rasteau cuvées. Prestige, Confiance and Fleur de Confiance are all excellent, but the last of these three – low-yielding, old-vine Grenache grown predominantly on blue marl – is a compelling-ly pure expression of Rasteau. Their Gigondas is cut from the same cloth.

Other good examples

Domaine Rabasse Charavin, **Domaine Beau Mistral** and **Domaine Combe Julière** also come highly recommended. **Domaine de Beaurenard** (see page 83) made its first Rasteau in 1980, and now farms 25 hectares here biodynamically with excellent results. **Domaine les Aphillanthes** (see page 195) makes a brilliant old-vine bottling called 1921, which is often among the best in the appellation. **Domaine Wilfried** is an old estate with a new name that makes some excellent cuvées, especially a pure Grenache, Septentrion. **Villa Safranier** and **Domaine les Girasols** and especially **Domaine Gramiller** make fine, lighter styles; **Domaine des Coteaux des Travers**, **Domaine Brusset**, **Domaine Pique-Basse**, **Domaine Trapadis** and **Domaine des Escaravailles** make heartier ex-amples. **Domaine de l'Espigouette**, **Domaine les Grands Bois** and **Domaine de Verquière** all make very good Rasteau cuvées, as does local cooperative **Ortas Cave de Rasteau**, particularly their Domaine de Pisan.

CAIRANNE

Appellation: AOC Cairanne

Birth of the appellation: 2015

Communes: Cairanne

Total surface area sold under the AOC in 2019: 865 hectares

Average yield in 2019: 35 hectolitres per hectare

Colours permitted: red and white

Production in 2019: 95 per cent red, 5 per cent white

Grape varieties permitted: Reds must contain 40 per cent Grenache plus Syrah or Mourvèdre (or both). May also contain Bourboulenc, Carignan, Cinsault, Clairette, Clairette Rose, Counoise, Grenache Blanc, Grenache Gris, Marsanne, Muscardin, Piquepoul Blanc, Piquepoul Noir, Roussanne, Terret Noir, Vaccarèse, Viognier.

Whites must contain at least two of the following: Clairette, Grenache Blanc, Roussanne (and at least 20 per cent of any that are used). May also contain Bourboulenc, Marsanne, Piquepoul Blanc or Viognier, but no more than 10 per cent of any one, and no more than 30 per cent of these accessory varieties in total.

Whereas Rasteau has staked its claim over the eastern side of Ventabren's southern face, Cairanne has claimed the west. They share the same hill, a similar climate and general exposure, not to mention a central border. But some aspects of the terroir differ. Rasteau is more hilly and rugged, Cairanne a little flatter and gentler. Cairanne's terroir is less dramatic than Rasteau's; the wines are often more subtle too, less deep-voiced and bombastic.

There are three subzones. Like Rasteau, there is the Montagne, the hilly land that climbs up behind the village. At the foot of the hill, the appellation has also annexed a section of the Plan de Dieu (though in Cairanne it's referred to as the Garrigues). The third section, the Terrasses de l'Aigues, is cut off from the rest, lying on the other side of the Aigues river. The marls on this side of the massif are more typically grey than blue, with large outcrops of galets. Like Rasteau, it rises to 350 metres at its highest point, but there is less land at altitude, and it's more open to the mistral as the land slopes down gradually westwards to the Aigues. There are various exposures, but it's mostly south facing, and there is a more gradual tapering between the foot of the Montagne and the start of the Garrigue.

According to Bruno Boisson of Domaine Boisson, the Garrigues soils are less diverse than those of the Montagne, mostly deep brown and red soils with large pebbles, up to 50 metres deep. 'Winemakers were happy to have Syrah on the Garrigues 20 years ago,' he says, but now it's mostly Grenache, Mourvèdre and Carignan, and no longer any whites. The hot, dry terroir tends to be picked the earliest, and is the source of Cairanne's most powerful reds. To reach the Terrasses de l'Aigues, you need to cross the river. Boisson explains that the soil here comprises clay, sand and stones 'but [is] more gravelly than rocky'. These are lighter soils, giving fruity wines with some finesse, usually planted with Grenache and Syrah. Marcel Richaud of Domaine Richaud suggests that most of this third section has more in common with neighbouring Sainte-Cécile than Cairanne. Boisson took me to one further tiny but distinct area which is essentially a subsection of Ventabren in the extreme north-west of the appellation, a quarter called Les Sablières. A sandy patch of decomposed Helvetian sandstone of around 50 hectares, it gives pale coloured reds 'with the depth but not the tannins,' says Boisson, 'I love the spirit of these wines.'

Cairanne has long been home to a roster of overperforming producers, so it's surprising it took them so long to push for *cru* status. On application, there were three factors that the local winemakers decided to stipulate in their *cahier des charges* as unique to Cairanne. Firstly, machine harvesting was outlawed. Secondly, sulphite levels were restricted (total sulphites in reds must be equal to or less than 100 milligrams per litre; in whites, equal to or less than 150 milligrams per litre). Thirdly, they greatly reduced the amount of herbicides used in the vineyards. Romain Roche of Domaine Roche says that quality hasn't vastly improved since passing into *cru*. 'The quality was already there,' he says, and Cairanne had deserved *cru* status for a long time. He does however praise the 'positive energy' that came from working together to make it happen. Loïc Massart of Domaine les Chemins de Sève says since passing into *cru*, it's 'easier to spot the originality of the appellation' and what marks these wines out as unique. One of the more concrete benefits to local landowners of achieving *cru* status is that the price of vineyard land usually increases soon after. Roche confirms this to be the case in Cairanne, and also that prices of wine *en vrac* have increased, though prices of bottled wines haven't enjoyed the same uptick.

In terms of stylistic trends, Roche says, 'bit by bit, we're going back to elegance.' This was always a stylistic marker for Cairanne, and is ever more the case. The red wines have a natural concentration without heaviness, a silkiness of texture and general sense of harmony and balance that makes for a particularly drinkable style of Southern Rhône. It is arguably the most reliably classic Southern Rhône *cru*, inhabiting a stylistic middle ground between its neighbours: it has gentler tannins and more integrated acidity than Vinsobres; it's less four-square and more supple than Plan de Dieu; it's less powerful and potent than Rasteau.

Cairanne's talents don't stop at red wines. There are currently only four Southern Rhône *crus* that make white wine, and it borrows the best elements of each – as rich in body and fruit as you'd expect from this part of the world, but with a sense of balance and drinkability. With Vinsobres and Gigondas both pushing to include white wines in their respective *cahier des charges*, Cairanne may soon have strong competition. But for now, no appellation in the Southern Rhône makes more reliable and consistent white wines than Cairanne.

In the context of the Southern Rhône, Cairanne is an appellation without any obvious drawbacks. And considering the quality of both red and white wines, these are among the best value wines in the Rhône.

Key producers

Domaine Alary

Cairanne

www.domaine-alary.fr

Denis Alary has long been a leading light of the appellation and was instrumental in the programme to promote Cairanne to *cru*. The house style has evolved over time, but more recently has been one of less extraction and greater finesse. This has been accentuated since his son Jean-Etienne took the reins, following winemaking *stages* at Domaine Confuron-Cotetidot in Vosne-Romanée, Domaine Seresin in Marlborough (New Zealand) and Henschke in Eden Valley (Australia). He is extracting less, picking earlier, and planting Piquepoul Noir, Piquepoul Blanc and Grenache Gris. All the different cuvées are worth trying, but the Cairanne *rouge* L'Estevanas is aromatically thrilling, containing 50 per cent Syrah from what they claim is the first block of this variety planted in the Southern Rhône (outside of Châteauneuf) in 1959. The old-vine Cairanne Le Jean de Verde is the very essence of Cairanne Grenache. The whites are similarly excellent. The roots of this winemaking family go back to 1692; today it is one of the most contemporary and exciting estates in the Rhône.

Domaine des Amadieu

Cairanne

www.domainedesamadieu.com

Yves Jean Houser bought this 7-hectare estate in 2007, changing country and profession in doing so, and converting the estate immediately to organic viticulture. Since 2012 biodynamic methods have been embraced. They are regularly among the best in the appellation – look out for their Cairanne Vieilles Vignes which hits a particularly sweet spot between balance, typicity and value.

Domaine Brusset

Cairanne

www.domainebrusset.fr

In the context of the Rhône, this estate is relatively young. It was established in 1947 by André Brusset, who passed it on to his son Daniel, who in turn passed it on to his son Laurent, who manages it today. In this time the Brussets have built up an impressive 70 hectares around the Southern Rhône, including Cairanne, Rasteau, Ventoux, Côtes-du-Rhône, and some particularly fine parcels in Gigondas. Laurent makes wines in a ripe and polished style that makes for accessible and understandably popular wines – he exports 70 per cent of his 250,000-bottle annual production to 22 different countries. Currently all output is from estate fruit, with nothing bought in. An impressive operation, and I've no doubt Laurent will continue to build on his successes to date.

Domaine Oratoire St Martin

Cairanne

www.oratoiresaintmartin.fr

Approximately 30 per cent of Cairanne vineyards are farmed organically, but Oratoire St Martin is one of the few to be worked biodynamically. Run until recently by brothers Frédéric and François Alary, it is undoubtedly one of the flagship domaines of Cairanne. The reds are pure and elegant, and the white wines deserve particular praise as some of the best in the Southern Rhône. Most of their holdings are high on the Montagne close to the Rasteau border. In red Cairanne, from Réserve des Seigneurs, to Haut-Coustias up to Les Douyes, the average vine age increases, as does the focus on Mourvèdre. Whites are based around Roussanne and Grenache Blanc: Réserve des Seigneurs *blanc* includes a little Clairette, Haut-Coutias *blanc* contains 40 per cent Marsanne, and is sourced from very old vines. The Alary brothers share the same family roots as Domaine Alary, and can therefore trace their own family winemaking history back just as far. They sold the estate in 2020 to Château Mont-Redon in Châteauneuf-du-Pape; let's hope the new owners manage to uphold the same exemplary standard.

Domaine Richaud

Cairanne

T.: +33 (0) 4 90 30 85 25

After 45 years of making wine, Marcel Richaud is gradually passing over winemaking duties to his children but is still very much the figurehead of this extraordinary domaine. A charismatic and talkative man with piercing blue eyes, Marcel always seems to be on the move. He has built the estate up to 50 hectares in his time and it's been organic for twenty years: 'balance is first of all in the vineyard,' he explains. These are effectively natural wines: he uses indigenous yeasts, doesn't fine or filter his red wines and employs very small amounts of sulphites and only at bottling. He finds that a small dose of sulphites gives the wines 'straightness' and helps them stay on track as they age and develop. For him, what makes a good wine is 'vine age, low yields and respecting the terroir'. Being a bold, gifted and purposeful winemaker also helps. His entire range of bright, dynamic, textural wines is worth exploring, including his Côtes-du-Rhône and Vin de France wines. His red Cairannes however are exceptional, particularly his single-vineyard L'Ebrescade from near the Rasteau border.

Other good examples

Domaine les Hautes Cances has long been one of the best estates in Cairanne but it was sold to négociant Pierre Amadieu in 2019; let's hope they keep up the same high standard. There are plenty of other estates making very good Cairanne, such as **Domaine Boisson, Domaine Saint-Andéol, Domaine Rabasse Charavin** and **Domaine Roche** (don't miss his cuvée La Bousquette), all of which make very good, fairly muscular styles. **La Bastide Saint Dominique, Domaine le Renard** and **Domaine l'Ameillaud** make wines with finesse. Newcomer Loïc Massart of **Domaine les Chemins de Sève** is showing great promise in both red and white Cairanne considering the domaine was established as recently as 2013 – definitely one to watch. The recently rejuvenated **Cave Cooperative de Cairanne** offers some excellent value options.

ROAIX

If you approach the Ventabren massif from the south, you'll see Rasteau sitting east of centre. Keep travelling past Rasteau towards the Baronnies and you'll take a winding road pinched between the base of the *montagne* and the Ouvèze river. This takes you to the little village of Roaix and its vineyards; the appellation covers the south-east-facing slope of the Ventabren massif. Viticulture here was established by the Knights Templar, who built an outpost in 1137 in the *lieu-dit* Les Crottes (meaning 'the turds'; whatever it was like then, I assure you it's nicer now).

Rather like Rasteau and Cairanne, Roaix has some terrain on the slopes of Ventabren, and some on the plains at its base. Unlike its two famous neighbours, however, the land on the plain isn't gravelly, alluvial *garrigues* soils, it's a large patch of sand. It's these sandy soils, along with Roaix's exposure (east, south-east and south), that differentiate the terroir from that of Rasteau. Excluding a low-lying portion of IGP land close to the river, the whole commune can produce AOC Côtes-du-Rhône Villages Roaix.

Apart from the village itself and the occasional olive grove, vineyards carpet the rolling hillsides almost entirely. It's a particularly pretty corner of the Rhône Valley, with spectacular views north to the Massif de la Lance, east to the Baronnies, south-east to Séguret and south to the Dentelles de Montmirail. Its position reminds you just how mountainous this corner of France really is. As you begin to climb the Ventabren from the sands on the plain, the soils get heavier, with brown clay and marl. As you climb, the marls fade to yellow, and the ground gets increasingly pebbly. The highest vineyards, at just over 350 metres, are often covered in deep *galets roulés*.

Almost all production is red. These are dry wines – there is no appellation for Vin Doux Naturel here. Some are almost indistinguishable from Rasteau: big, bold, generous, with an inner *sucrosité* (a sense of sweetness despite the lack of detectable residual sugars). But thanks to its different exposure and sandy soils, most are slightly toned down – not quite so concentrated or structured, a little more red-fruited, and less likely to show unbalanced levels of alcohol.

The view east over Roaix

So why is Roaix so little known compared to Rasteau? There are a number of reasons. 'It's not a question of lesser quality of terroir,' says Elodie Balme. President of the Cave Cooperative de Roaix Séguret, Franck Molénat believes that the problem is principally one of scale: Roaix is a third the size of Rasteau. That so little wine is produced here means that 'we don't have the means to communicate, so we've always remained quite a marginal appellation.' Balme adds that there is no cave cooperative in the village itself, and that there are very few private domaines bottling under the appellation (only five within the commune, eleven including those based outside). Balme's Roaix is ample proof of the quality of this terroir. But while Cairanne has recognizable figureheads such as Denis Alary and Marcel Richaud, Roaix is currently lacking a charismatic trailblazer to draw people to the village and lead the way on the international stage. Some very good wines are being made here, but for the time being Roaix is a kingdom in search of a king.

Appellation: AOC Côtes-du-Rhône Villages Roaix

Birth of the appellation: 1967

Communes: Roaix

Total surface area sold under the AOC in 2019: 121 hectares

Average yield in 2019: 36 hectolitres per hectare

Colours permitted: red, rosé, white

Production in 2019: 96 per cent red, 2 per cent rosé, 2 per cent white

Grape varieties permitted: As per communal Côtes-du-Rhône Villages regulations (see page 54)

Key producers

Domaine du Bramadou

Roaix

www.domainedubramadou.fr

Damien Chave is not one to wax poetical about his wines. The estate was established in 2005 when they started bottling a proportion of their crop; they now vinify 10 of their 60 hectares themselves, the rest being delivered to two different cooperative cellars. Chave works in *agriculture raisonnée* and makes Roaix in all three colours – he's one of the few making a Roaix rosé. His reds are strong, towards Rasteau in style. Le

Serre Rouge is from a *lieu-dit* of the same name, an authentic old-vine blend of Grenache, Syrah and Mourvèdre. La Montagne de Mars, pure 50-year-old Syrah aged in barrique and demi-muid, is also worth trying. Fittingly, Domaine du Bramadou is named after a *lieu-dit* at the top of the appellation. Their wines also reach the top of what is being produced in Roaix today.

Other good examples

Domaine Elodie Balme's Champs Libres is an excellent example (see page 105). The potent, ripe red Roaix cuvées of **Domaine des Escaravailles** and **Domaine Pique-Basse** can be very good, as can Domaine Pique-Basse's zesty white cuvée L'Atout du Pique. Newcomer **Maison Plantevin** is making highly drinkable lighter styles using carbonic maceration.

VAISON-LA-ROMAINE

If the Ventabren massif's south-facing slopes are dominated by Cairanne and Rasteau, then what's on its north facing slopes? Vaison-la-Romaine, that's what. Well, part of it; the largest bit of the appellation is actually around the historic town of Vaison-la-Romaine, a hilly hinterland a few kilometres east of Roaix, just before the terrain gets increasingly mountainous up into the Baronnies.

Minted in 2016, this new appellation appears not terribly well thought through. For a start, the two parts of this quite rambling appellation are quite different in terms of terroir; grey marl to the west, sandstone and limestone to the east. And despite the quality of the whites in this fairly fresh part of the Rhône, it's an appellation for red wine only. To make matters worse, according to local winemakers many superior vineyards were incomprehensibly left out of the demarcated area. But whatever the eccentricities of the official documentation, it is home to some quality-minded estates.

There are five communes in the appellation. Just two of them, Saint-Roman-de-Malegarde and Buisson, occupy the north-facing side of the Ventabren massif as it slopes down towards the Aigues, overlooking Visan and Saint-Maurice on the opposite bank. This part of Vaison shares the same stony colluvial marls as Cairanne and Rasteau, but receives less sun and more mistral, combined with the cold pontias air current that whistles in from Nyons at night. There is one producer in each commune, Domaine Fond-Croze in Saint-Romain-de-Malegarde and Domaine Roche-Audran in Buisson, and both are strong domaines. As you travel east, the commune of Villeneuve shares most of these attributes, but enjoys an outcrop of blue marl. Again, there are precious few producers here, but look out for La Ferme des Arnaud. The two remaining communes, Vaison-la-Romaine and Saint-Marcellin-lès-Vaison, are located to the south-east of these three, further from the Aigues and close to the northern edge of the Dentelles de Montmirail. This is still a hilly terroir, not exclusively north-facing, and the soils are Miocene sandstone, with more limestone close to the town of Vaison.

There are too few producers to say with certainty that these five communes should or should not be lumped together into one appellation, but logic suggests it might one day be divided in two. For now, this hilly, northerly terrain expresses itself in a juicy, acidulated, red-fruited style that doesn't display the same depth as its more illustrious Ventabren neighbours, but engenders a sense of freshness and drinkability in the wines. The story of this appellation is more one of individual domaines than unified expression of terroir, but it's early days.

Appellation: AOC Côtes-du-Rhône Villages Vaison-la-Romaine
Birth of the appellation: 2016
Communes: Buisson, Saint-Marcellin-lès-Vaison, Saint-Roman-de-Malegarde, Vaison-la-Romaine, Villedieu
Total surface area sold under the AOC in 2019: 213 hectares
Average yield in 2019: 37 hectolitres per hectare
Colours permitted: red only
Grape varieties permitted: As per communal Côtes-du-Rhône Villages regulations (see page 54)

Key producers
Domaine Roche-Audran
Buisson
www.roche-audran.com

Along with a little Visan and Châteauneuf-du-Pape, the main part of Vincent Rochette's estate is in Vaison-la-Romaine, on the north-facing slope of the Ventabren massif. He built the winery in 1998 and converted to biodynamics in 2007. Since then, he's noticed the wines are richer, finer, more complex and better balanced. His Vaison-La-Romaine César is exuberantly fruity, filled with shiny raspberry and strawberry fruit, and his no-added-sulphites cuvée is highly successful. He's a strong advocate for whites to be accepted into the appellation, particularly the 'extraordinary Grenache Blancs' found locally. His gently aromatic, silky white Côtes-du-Rhône César would surely be one of the best in AOC Vaison-la-Romaine – if whites were permitted.

Other good examples

Domaine Fond-Croze, La Ferme des Arnaud and **Domaine Gros Pata** all come highly recommended, and **Domaine des Roches Fortes** is also worth checking out.

7

DENTELLES TERROIR

GIGONDAS

If you only ever visit one appellation in the Southern Rhône, let it be Gigondas, a Provençal jewel nestled amongst oaks and Aleppo pines on a western slope of the Dentelles de Montmirail. It's only a 5-minute drive up from the D977 but suddenly you feel the altitude, a faint alpine whisper. It won't take you long to wander around the lanes of densely-packed, slender houses or to scale the stone steps to the church at the top of the village, but it's not something you could ever tire of. And it supplies some vital physical activity between lunch and dinner; you can eat, rest, and of course drink very well here.

The Dentelles massif provides some excellent hiking and wildlife spotting all amongst some of the most striking countryside. The appellation most commonly associated with the Dentelles is Gigondas, but there are a number of others that have land here – the red wine vineyards of Beaumes de Venise, the Named Villages of Sablet and Séguret (not to mention some of the most northerly villages of AOC Ventoux). I'd long assumed that the word *Dentelles* has the same root as the English word *dental*: these giant slabs of limestone that jut out from earth resemble craggy teeth carved from tombstones that gnaw at the clouds. But *dentelles* actually translates as 'lacework'. They still look like teeth to me.

This little nook has long been attractive to humans. Relics from the Bronze Age have been unearthed, and we know there was a settlement of Roman veteran soldiers here since they left so many artefacts behind. It's not certain, but the origin of the name Gigondas may come from the Latin word *jucundus*, meaning 'joyful'. Vines have certainly been cultivated at least since Roman times: Château de Saint-Cosme is home to preserved Roman wine vats hewn from stone. In his section on the history of Gigondas in the book *Gigondas: Its wines, its land, its people*, Jean-Baptiste Amadieu lists some of the medals won by Gigondas in wine competitions of the late nineteenth and early twentieth centuries. Its status as one of the best Rhône terroirs is long established.

Gigondas' first attempt to gain *cru* status dates back to 1948, but requests were continually turned down. The head of the INAO at the time was Baron Le Roy of Châteauneuf-du-Pape, and he was considered by locals to be a bitter opponent to its promotion. When Baron Le Roy died in 1967, Gigondas submitted another attempt, and was successful, becoming the fourth *cru* of the Southern Rhône in 1971 after Châteauneuf-du-Pape, Tavel and Lirac.

Appellation: AOC Gigondas

Birth of the appellation: 1971

Communes: Gigondas

Total surface area sold under the AOC in 2019: 1,199 hectares

Average yield in 2019: 30 hectolitres per hectare

Colours permitted: red and rosé only

Production in 2019: 99 per cent red, 1 per cent rosé

Grape varieties permitted: Reds and rosés must be at least 50 per cent Grenache, and must include some Syrah or Mourvèdre (or both), even if less than 1 per cent. Can include no more than 10 per cent of the following grapes, alone or blended: Bourboulenc, Cinsault, Clairette, Clairette Rose, Counoise, Grenache Blanc, Grenache Gris, Marsanne, Muscardin, Piquepoul Blanc, Piquepoul Noir, Roussanne, Terret Noir, Ugni Blanc, Vaccarèse, Viognier. No Carignan allowed.

A combination of factors contribute to this superb terroir, but the most important, and most complex, element is its soils. The most basic way to make sense of the terroir of Gigondas is to divide it into three parts: the cone, the sands, and the Dentelles. The cone (effectively the sloping terrace at the bottom of the village, known locally as Le Cône de la Font des Papes) is the largest part of the appellation. It begins at the foot of the village at around 250 metres altitude and fans out downhill to the north-west towards the Ouvèze river. It covers an area of roughly

3 square kilometres and consists of sandy clay rich in colluvial limestone scree eroded from the Dentelles and gradually transported towards the river by streams. Closer to the river is the old alluvial terrace of the Ouvèze, containing more galets, gravels and silt. These well-draining soils enjoy the sunshine all day long, and are best planted to Grenache and Mourvèdre. They give intense, deeply fruited wines that are occasionally prone to tip into jamminess and excessive potency.

Around the foot of the mountain, between the cone and the Dentelles is a belt of Miocene marine sands and sandstone. The *lieu-dit* Les Bosquets features this kind of soil, and Julien Brechet of Domaine des Bosquets explains that the resulting wines have particularly good acidity – not because of the soil per se, but because this terroir is shaded for much of the day by the Dentelles. This fine, free-draining sand produces wines with good finesse, gentle tannins and a surprising potential to age. The dramatic Dentelles terroir behind the village is geologically extraordinary (some excellent videos explaining it are available at www.gigondas-vin.com/mediatheque). In the Triassic Period this was a sea, which gradually deposited deep layers of salt and gypsum. The Jurassic Period saw layer after layer of limestone and marl laid down to a depth of 8 kilometres. The Tertiary Period bore witness to extreme tectonic activity and the Nîmes Fault helped to push these layers from the horizontal up to the vertical, resulting in the resurfacing of these ancient marls and limestone soils and the upright limestone teeth we see today. These soils encourage deep root systems, help retain water, and supply abundant trace elements for healthy plant growth. They bestow a certain structure, tension and salinity to the Grenache grown here, which is accentuated by the altitude (up to 500 metres) and their typically shady north-west-facing exposure.

Although Gigondas is often spoken about in the same breath as Châteauneuf-du-Pape, the two have precious little in common when it comes to terroir. They may use broadly similar grape varieties but Châteauneuf tends to have a more natural upswell of power, fullness and tannic density, whereas Gigondas has a little more vibrancy and pep, in both aroma and texture. In the broader context of the Southern Rhône, Gigondas wines tend to be full-bodied, deeply generous, flowing wines with a fruit profile ranging from strawberry and raspberry through to damson, and occasionally darker fruits, depending on the blend. The style of the wines is tightly defined, with few stylistic outliers; you could argue the wines are too homogeneous, in fact. But the growing fashion for single-vineyard wines is helping to increase diversity. In terms of quality, Gigondas is the most consistent *cru* in the Southern Rhône.

Since they are based around Grenache, wines are usually approachable on release, lacking any major tannic resistance that you find in, say, young Cabernet Sauvignon or Nebbiolo. The flip side of this however is that the vast majority of Gigondas is drunk too young. The best wines tend to hit their stride 10–15 years after vintage, and continue to improve for some time. They seem to possess a natural vigour that helps them stay the course.

Gigondas

Although 99 per cent of production is red, Gigondas does have the right to make rosé. It's considerably less interesting than red Gigondas. Most of the wines I've tasted are excessively full in body and lack refreshment and drinkability. The best I've encountered are from Clos du Joncuas, and particularly Domaine des Bosquets, who take theirs particularly seriously. White wines are currently not permitted, but soon may be (see box, page 127).

Gigondas still sits in the shadow of Châteauneuf in the minds of many consumers, but is rapidly building a reputation for quality thanks to a combination of factors: distinctive terroir, reliable quality, over 100 private domaines (meaning large availability and distribution), a well-funded *syndicat* and a dynamic leader in Louis Barruol. The latest project by the *syndicat* has been to plant a vineyard containing 380 genetically unique plants, all massal selection Grenache from well-adapted, virus-free, old-vine Gigondas plant material. It's the biggest Grenache conservatory in the world, and local vignerons will be allowed to take cuttings to propagate their vineyards. This will benefit the appellation for generations to come. Gigondas has come a long way fast, and with its naturally fresh terroir, is well placed to continue this upward trajectory.

Key producers

Domaine des Bosquets

Gigondas

domainedesbosquets.wordpress.com

Sometimes you can get a little insight into a vigneron's winemaking style from his house, his clothes – or even the car he drives. When we took a tour of his Gigondas estate, Julien Brechet picked me up in a Audi 4x4 with spotless leather interior. He only returned to the family domaine in 2009 to design their website, he tells me, but then got hooked on the wine. Only just turned 40, he's achieved a great deal. The wines may be modern but the estate, established in 1644, is ancient. It's located in the sandy *lieu-dit* of Les Bosquets, with vineyards principally around the winery. Brechet's concentration on single-vineyard cuvées has attracted a lot of attention. The first was Le Lieu Dit, from *lieu-dit* Les Bosquets. It has since been joined by La Colline, from a 5-hectare vineyard of Grenache on blue marl and limestone, Le Plateau, from a small parcel of Mourvèdre planted on clay, blue marl and limestone in 1922, and Les Routes, from Syrah planted in 1992 on the cone near the *lieu-dit* Les Hauts Garrigues, with original cuttings taken from Château de Fonsalette. All are polished, vibrant, highly expressive wines, but certain cuvées have been prone to exaggeration in early vintages. When balanced, they can be brilliant, highly characterful wines of huge impact. The 2020 vintage should be the first certified organic; biodynamic farming is next.

Clos du Joncuas

Gigondas

www.closdujoncuas.fr

Clos du Joncuas is run by two sisters, Dani and Carole Chastan, who took over from their parents who established the estate in the 1950s. This was one of the first in Gigondas to convert to organics (in 1980), when they observed the collapse of a colony of bees after it was accidentally sprayed by neighbouring winemakers who were treating their vines. 'Organics is working with respect,' says Dani, 'respect for yourself, for others, for the vines, for the vegetation, for wildlife.' They have since incorporated some biodynamic practices into the way they farm. They now have 29 hectares, including their Gigondas vineyards, their Vacqueyras estate La Font de Papier and their Séguret estate Domaine la Garancière. They don't destem their Gigondas, age it in concrete and bottle without fining or filtration. The Clos du Joncuas itself faces west in the southern part of Gigondas on Oligocene marls. There is a stream next to it: a *jonc* is a bulrush. The style is classic, but distinctly harmonious and fresh, and the wines age well. Their top cuvée Esprit de Grenache is an exceptionally fine expression of what Carole calls 'the king of the grape varieties of our terroir'.

Domaine du Grapillon d'Or

Gigondas

www.domainedugrapillondor.com/en

Though the estate was created in 1806, the Chauvet family have lived in this part of the Rhône for even longer. The estate is now in the hands of Céline Chauvet, who manages to make the wines and run the business side as well. She owns 14 hectares of vineyards dotted around the appel-lation at between 150 metres and 500 metres altitude. She makes two cuvées. Aged in Old Oak Barrels is a blend of Grenache and Syrah aged in, yes, old oak barrels in order to round out the tannins, so it tends to be relatively early-drinking. Excellence is an old-vine cuvée containing 40 per cent Syrah, planted by her grandfather in the 1960s, that has su-perb ageing potential. This is a bright, polished, pure style of Gigondas.

Moulin de la Gardette

Gigondas

www.moulindelagardette.com

The wines of Château de Saint-Cosme attract plenty of praise and col-umn inches thanks to their bombastic bravado. Perhaps due to its al-together more gentle, restrained style, Moulin de la Gardette is less well known, but the wines deserve to be praised just as highly. Jean Baptiste Meunier took over the family winery in 1990 and has since converted their 25 parcels to organic viticulture. High altitudes, low yields and a light touch in the winery make for wines with all the rich, flowing fruits of traditional Gigondas, but immediately recognizable for their excep-tional balance, drinkability and breezy floral aromas. Meunier makes three cuvées: Petite Gardette from 10-year-old vines, Tradition from 40-year-old vines, and Ventabren from 80- to 100-year-old vines. All are lovely, but his Ventabren is frequently among the best wines of the appellation, an elegant, unforced and surprisingly ageworthy expression of this picturesque mountain village.

Domaine Raspail-Ay

Gigondas

T.: +33 (0) 4 90 65 83 01

This historic property is currently managed by fifth-generation owner Dominique Ay and his children Anne-Sophie and Christophe. It comprises a single block of 19 hectares around the family home and winery just beneath the village. The grapes are destemmed and fermented in concrete then aged for 18 to 24 months in large old oak foudres. They only make one cuvée, a blend of 75 per cent Grenache topped up with Syrah and Mourvèdre, and it's a totally classic expression of Gigondas, harmonious and pure with an inner *sucrosité*. Regularly among the best wines of the vintage.

Château de Saint-Cosme

Gigondas

www.saintcosme.com

Since he took over the family estate in 1992, Louis Barruol has transformed Château de Saint-Cosme, and with it the appellation of Gigondas. Before his tenure, the estate sold its wine to négociants, but on his arrival he started bottling, and established a small négociant business of his own. The estate dates back to 1490 and was built on the site of Roman ruins. Its heart and soul is the 15 hectares of Gigondas vineyards that surround the property, which feed into the three single-vineyard wines that have brought it such attention since their launch in the mid-2000s: Le Poste, Le Claux and Hominis Fides. There was a fourth, Valbelle, an old-vine cuvée, but its final vintage was 2015. A further unnamed Gigondas cuvée often represents good value, though it's far from cheap. A vertical tasting at the domaine of 2017 back to 2009 proved the ability of the wines to age; they only really start coming into their own after 10 years. It also confirms the fact that when young they do appear oaky, but in time they achieve balance (unusually Barruol uses around a quarter new oak barriques for the wines). His Clairette grown on Gigondas terroir is also superb, and his négociant bottlings from the Northern Rhône often impress. His purchase of the Château de Rouanne in Vinsobres in 2019 is another string to his bow. Barruol has been president of the Gigondas *syndicat* since 2013, and the appellation is lucky to have such a dynamic, eloquent and effective leader.

Domaine Santa Duc

Gigondas

www.santaduc.fr/en

Yves Gras and his son Benjamin are very different characters. Yves has the air of a retired East End enforcer but Benjamin is bookish and jovial. Benjamin represents the sixth generation of winemakers in his family, and he joined the estate in 2016 after *stages* at Domaine de la Romanée Conti and Vega Sicilia. Yves began working on the family estate in 1985 and promptly converted to organics – when Benjamin started, he progressed to biodynamics. Increasingly they are co-planting varieties in their vineyards, always using massal selection. Yves believes clones are poorly adapted to the terroir as they were originally selected for high yield and high potential sugars, and finds they don't age as well. Most of the estate is planted in *gobelet*, and the intention is to convert all the vineyards back to this style of viticulture.

Their entry level Gigondas cuvée Aux Lieux Dits is a blend of eight different terroirs. Les Hauts Garrigues is 50:50 Grenache–Mourvèdre from the eponymous *lieu-dit*, where their winery is located. Clos Derrière Vieille is a particularly fine north-west facing vineyard behind the village at 350 metres, bought in 1984. Wines are vinified in stainless steel, usually with a proportion of stems, with fairly short macerations followed by ageing in 36-hectolitre foudres and some terracotta amphorae. Stylistically the wines are classic, deeply fruited, vinous, fairly strict and textural, with very good ageing potential. They also make wines in Rasteau, Roaix, Vacqueyras and Séguret. Their four Châteauneuf-du-Pape cuvées are highly impressive.

Other good examples

With over 100 independent wineries producing a Gigondas cuvée, there are many more producers making excellent wine. **Domaine Brusset** is one of the very best Gigondas producers, see page 111. Other names that would deserve an entry of their own include the generous **Domaine la Bouïssière**, the elegant **Domaine de Montvac**, the vibrant **Domaine d'Ouréa**, the traditional **Domaine du Cayron** and **Domaine Font-Sane**, and newcomer **Domaine les Sibu** (see page 141). Don't miss the two top Gigondas cuvées of **Famille Perrin**, Domaine du Clos des Tourelles and their exquisite old-vine cuvée L'Argnée.

Other very good Gigondas wines can be found at **Domaine du Terme, Domaine les Pallières, Domaine Saint Gayan, Château la Croix des Pins, Domaine les Goubert, Domaine les Semelles du Vent, Domaine Bertrand Stehelin, Domaine la Roubine, Domaine du Grand Montmirail**, and **Gabriel Meffre** (particularly their Domaine du Longue Toque bottlings). Other reliable négociant wines can be found from **Pierre Amadieu, Dauvergne-Ranvier, La Ferme du Mont, Ogier** and **Chapoutier**. For value, **Domaine de Fontavin** and **Domaine le Clos des Cazaux** are often good calls. For a particularly elegant style, take a look at **Domaine la Soumade**. For something intriguingly different, try the long-élevage cuvées of **Domaine du Pourra**.

White Gigondas

Despite only having the appellation for reds and rosés, the village of Gigondas also has a history of white wine production. Château de Saint-Cosme has been making Clairette on Gigondas soils for over 100 years, and Pierre Amadieu has also been making white wine here for decades. The winemakers' *syndicat* has submitted a dossier to the INAO in order to update the *cahier des charges* to include white wines. If it's passed unamended, white Gigondas will contain 70–100 per cent Clairette, with 30 per cent of other classic Rhône varieties, and a maximum 5 per cent Viognier.

'Clairette doesn't have a home, it's a bit all over the place', says Louis Barruol of Château de Saint-Cosme, president of the appellation committee. 'Everywhere and nowhere. There's not one single place where it's dominant, powerful, with a very defined expression … I'd like Gigondas to become the home of Clairette.' It's well-adapted to the Mediterranean climate, but benefits from the altitude and northerly exposure in Gigondas, and performs well on the limestone soils. It can age well despite its low acidity, retaining a sense of freshness, florality and light pithiness.

Barruol's wines are 100 per cent Clairette, but he says there have also been some exciting experiments within the appellation with Roussanne grown at altitude. Julien Brechet of Domaine des Bosquets plans to plant some white varieties, including Clairette and Bourboulenc. Barruol hopes the first vintage will be 2021, but 2022 is perhaps more likely.

VACQUEYRAS

Appellation: AOC Vacqueyras

Birth of the appellation: 1990

Communes: Sarrians, Vacqueyras

Total surface area sold under the AOC in 2019: 1440 hectares

Average yield in 2019: 32 hectolitres per hectare

Colours permitted: red, rosé, white

Production in 2019: 94 per cent red, 1 per cent rosé, 5 per cent white

Grape varieties permitted: Reds must be majority Grenache, and must include some Syrah or Mourvèdre (or both), even if less than 1 per cent. Can include the following 'accessory grapes': Bourboulenc, Carignan, Cinsault, Clairette, Clairette Rose, Counoise, Grenache Blanc, Grenache Gris, Marsanne, Muscardin, Piquepoul Noir, Roussanne, Terret Noir, Vaccarèse, Viognier.

For rosés the main grapes are Cinsault, Grenache, Mourvèdre and Syrah; they can include the same 'accessory grapes' as reds.

Whites must contain at least two of the following: Bourboulenc, Clairette, Grenache Blanc, Marsanne, Roussanne, Viognier.

Does the appellation of Vacqueyras belong in a chapter entitled 'Dentelles terroir'? On reflection, yes it does. But it's tenuous. Most of the wine that comes from Vacqueyras originates from the vast Plateau des Garrigues (or just Garrigues) that lies adjacent to, rather than within, the Dentelles de Montmirail. A hillside near the village proudly displays a Hollywood-style sign heralding 'Vacqueyras et ses Vins', but the spirit of Vacqueyras inhabits the flat, not the slope. Vacqueyras shares a border with Gigondas, but while Gigondas reaches back into the mountain and inhales its breezes, Vacqueyras lounges in the sun to the south-west, merely propping its head on the hillside. Jacky Bernard, president of the appellation and owner of Domaine la Ligière, describes Vacqueyras as 'a microclimate influenced by, but not lying within, the Dentelles'.

Perhaps the ancient name Vallis Quadreria (valley of stones), from which the name Vacqueyras comes, referred to this stony plateau. The first written records of winemaking in Vacqueyras date back to 1414, and winemaking here gradually expanded both in surface area and number of producers from one century to the next until it was devastated by phylloxera in the late 1800s. It bounced back quickly, and between the early 1900s and the early 2000s expansion was rapid. In 1990 it was promoted to *cru*.

The Garrigues is the ancient alluvial riverbed of the Ouvèze, since overlaid with clay limestone and small, irregular *galets roulés*. From its north-western edge you can look sharply down to the current course of the Ouvèze resulting in a sensation of altitude, but its central point is little more than 100 metres above sea level. It's a sector entirely open to the Mediterranean sun and the mistral, and was once very arid. Cultivation of fruit and vegetables was made easier after the laying down of small, open irrigation channels, fed by the river Durance, that still criss-cross the plateau. Today it's a monocultural landscape, vineyards broken up by the odd rank of pines or cypresses, the occasional farm and plot of olive trees. The road that bisects the centre of the plateau, from Château des Roques in the east to the edge of the village of Jonquières in the west, acts as something of a boundary between the northern and southern Garrigues. Guy Ricard of Domaine le Couroulou explains that in his father's time people grew fruit and vegetables to the south, whereas trees and vines were more customary to the north. 'There's the Garrigues near the village of Vacqueyras, that's black clay with a few galets, but not that many,' he says. 'It gives austere wines, with heavy, thick tannins, and less expressive aromas. Below that, near Les Amouriers, it's red clay that's full of *galets roulés*. It's clay that holds water and gives it back very slowly. These are the best terroirs of Vacqueyras I think, the most expressive. Then more white clay [to the south] which is good soil, but underneath there's very deep gravels, up to 30 metres deep, that don't hold water at all, very draining and prone to drought. It used to be melons, tomatoes here [to the south of the road] – above it was vines, almonds, olives.' That's not to say the southern Garrigues are inferior: 'it's a good terroir, you just need to work it differently'. Irrigation is not uncommon in the drier zones to the south and west, particularly for young vines.

Aside from the Garrigues, there are three other terroirs. I say terroirs rather than subzones, since the sandy soils, which produce more gentle red wines, don't inhabit one particular area; they skirt around the length of the western, eastern and ruffled southern fringe of the Garrigues and sweep around the village of Vacqueyras. Another distinct terroir lies to the north of the village where the appellation abuts on Gigondas and shares some of its cone, mostly sandy clay with colluvial limestone pebbles. The final terroir at last breaches the Dentelles: a valley consisting of grey marl and limestone pebbles to the east of the village of Vacqueyras that sits between Beauregard (the hill with the Hollywood-style sign on it) and the edge of the Dentelles massif. The vineyards on the Dentelles side of the valley rise to 200 metres altitude around Le Clos de Caveau. This area is still heavily wooded. The vines for Domaine la Ligière's Vacqueyras *rouge* Furmitarde are grown here, and Jacky Bernard says the grapes mature more gradually, resulting in a more complex wine.

Vacqueyras is the only *cru* on the east bank of the Rhône permitted to make red, white and rosé (the only other Southern *cru* that can do this is Lirac on the west bank). Production has long been almost exclusively red but demand for white wine is growing as quality improves; quality is still mixed, but several are excellent, particularly those by Roucas Toumba, Domaine la Monardière and Domaine le Sang des Cailloux. I'm yet to be bowled over by a rosé Vacqueyras, though Domaine la Monardière proves that it's possible.

So what characterizes a classic red Vacqueyras? The personalities of the other Southern Rhône *crus* are relatively clear, but Vacqueyras is less distinct. It is an appellation that is particularly varied in both style and quality. This is likely to be down to a number of factors. It would appear that not all the terroir is equal in quality, and the different sorts of terroir are very varied. Another reason could be the lack of frontrunning estates with strong international brands. That said, compared to a typical red AOC Côtes-du-Rhône, you can expect red Vacqueyras to be a bigger wine, broader on the palate, with more concentration and weight. The best manage to combine power and finesse, and display dense if relatively soft tannic textures. They are rarely wines of great tension, but they can be wines of real charm and satisfaction. It may not be easy to pin down what defines a classic red Vacqueyras, but one thing is certain – there are plenty of estates in Vacqueyras making outstanding wine.

Key producers

Domaine le Couroulou

Vacqueyras

www.facebook.com/domainelecouroulu

The English name for the *couroulou* is the curlew – a large bird with a long, downward-curving slender beak. It gave its name to the Vacqueyras *lieu-dit* of Le Couroulou when it was populated with green oaks, and curlews waded among the ponds. Current owner Guy Ricard's grandfather was a local farmer growing melons, tomatoes and strawberries, and he gradually bought up parcels of land here, pulling out the trees and planting vines, eventually building up a vineyard of 21 hectares. He split the estate in two to share between his two sons; Pierre (Guy's father) was given one half, which retained the name Le Couroulou and Jean received the other half, which was renamed Le Sang des Cailloux (see below).

Guy makes Vacqueyras in all three colours. His reds are destemmed then fermented and aged in concrete for 18 months, producing a generous, expressive, muscular style. His Classique is very good; his Vieilles Vignes, which contains a higher proportion of Syrah, often comes top in the appellation in blind tastings.

Domaine la Monardière

Vacqueyras

www.monardiere.com

Martine and Christian Vache gathered together their old-vine family vineyards in 1987 to create the relatively new estate Domaine la Monardière. Their Grenache was planted in 1945 and 1965, and their Syrah and Mourvèdre in the 1990s. Today, any new plantings favour local 'accessory' grapes in order to help decrease alcohol levels and increase acidity; their vineyards feature 15 different varieties. Their son Damien joined them in 2007, the same year that the 21-hectare estate gained organic certification. Most of the vineyards are planted on the sandy soils to the north of the village of Vacqueyras. Grapes are harvested by hand and vinified without additions of any kind except low doses of sulphites. The style here is very drinkable and vibrant. They make all three colours of Vacqueyras, all of which are highly recommended. The top cuvées, Vieilles Vignes in red (65-year-old bush vines on average, one-third whole bunch) and Galéjade in white (20 per cent new oak), are exceptional expressions of Vacqueyras in their respective colours and both age remarkably well.

Roucas Toumba

Vacqueyras

www.roucastoumba.com

Roucas Toumba ('fallen rock' in the local Provençal language) 'had a very difficult beginning,' according to owner Eric Bouletin. His father died when he was 14, so Eric had to leave school at 16 to help on the estate. His neighbour Christian Vache of Domaine la Monardière could see he was struggling and offered to help. Today he has 16 hectares of organically farmed vineyards across various plots, and tries to do as much as he can on the estate himself: planting trees, repairing stone walls, making jams out of wild fruits. 'It's peasant life, quite simply,' he says. 'I go to bed with the sun and get up with the birds.' His plans for the estate? To plant some olive trees, install some beehives and perhaps teach his son who is beginning to show an interest. Like Bouletin, these wines are rooted in Vacqueyras, but they're not loud, they don't demand your attention, and that's one of the reasons they are so deserving of it. He makes authentic, pastoral Vacqueyras wines, both reds and whites, that gradually unfurl in the glass and satisfy deeply.

Domaine le Sang des Cailloux

Sarrians

sangdescailloux.com

Serge Férigoule, proud owner of the greatest moustache in the Rhône, worked for Jean Ricard at Le Sang des Cailloux for ten years, eventually purchasing the estate in 1990. He promptly converted the estate to organic viticulture, and has expanded it to 17 hectares. In 2003, Serge was joined by his son Frédéri, who gained organic certification for the estate and is now taking it towards biodynamics. Their wines are undoubtedly amongst the best in Vacqueyras, recognizable by their remarkable finesse. They make three red Vacqueyras: a *cuvée classique* that each year takes the name of one of his daughters, Floureto, Doucinello or Azalaïs; an old-vine cuvée called Lopy and a very-old-vine Grenache plot selection called Oumage, which is only made in the best vintages. Yields are very low. The grapes are hand-harvested, fermented in cement tanks and aged for a year in large old oak barrels. Their white Vacqueyras Un Sang Blanc, a blend of all five permitted varieties, which goes through malo, is equally worth seeking out.

Château des Tours

Sarrians

chateaurayas.fr

The third of three Southern Rhône properties owned by Emmanuel Reynaud of Château Rayas, Château des Tours is located right on the western edge of the appellation, on predominantly sandy soils. It was purchased by Emmanuel's grandfather Louis in 1935. Emmanuel was managing this property before he took over Rayas and Château de Fonsalette on the death of his uncle Jacques. At this property they produce Parisy (a Vin de Table rosé); Domaine des Tours (red and white

IGP Vaucluse and a rare varietal Merlot); and Château des Tours (red and white Côtes-du-Rhône, and a red AOC Vacqueyras). The wines are released when they are considered ready to drink, which can be anything from a few years to over a decade. The red wines are very much in the Rayas house style; whole bunch, pale in colour, light in tannin and full of red berry and pot-pourri floral character. Very little white is produced, but the Château des Tours (100 per cent Grenache Blanc) and particularly the Domaine des Tours (100 per cent Clairette) are unusual and fascinating. The Vacqueyras is particularly fine, more structured than the other cuvées produced here, and without question one of the best in the appellation. Not quite as eccentric as the Côtes-du-Rhônes and IGPs, it ages 20 years or more in good vintages.

Other good examples

Other good examples can be found from the following: **Domaine la Ligière, Domaine Montirius, Domaine de l'Espigouette, Domaine la Garrigue, Domaine de la Charbonnière, Domaine d'Ouréa, Domaine Fontaine du Clos, Le Clos du Caveau, Clos du Joncuas, Domaine les Amouriers, Mas de Restanques, Domaine de la Verde, Domaine les Ondines, Domaine Saint-Pierre, Domaine de la Pigeade, Domaine de Montvac, Domaine la Fourmone, Ferme des Arnauds, Domaine le Clos des Cazaux** and **Vignobles Alain Ignace.** Newcomer **Demoiselle Suzette** shows promise.

With the exception of the occasional cuvée by **Arnoux,** and **Gabriel Meffre**'s **Domaine de Longue Toque,** for whatever reason I have rarely found interesting Vacqueyras made by négociants or co-ops.

MUSCAT DE BEAUMES DE VENISE AND BEAUMES DE VENISE

Having a famous brother or sister can be a mixed blessing. On the one hand you benefit from a star-studded surname that can open doors. On the other, cynics may question the depth of your true talent, and it's hard to escape the shadow of your sibling. So it is with Beaumes de Venise. Most wine lovers have heard of its Muscats, but not so many are familiar with its reds. Both are worthy of your attention.

Beaumes de Venise is one of the three *crus* that approach and scale the Dentelles de Montmirail. Gigondas and Vacqueyras make among the best reds of the Rhône – so what's with all the Muscat in Beaumes de Venise? The fact is that although both appellations share the village name of Beaumes de Venise, the two styles are grown in different terroirs. The name Beaumes comes from *balma*, the Provençal word for cave. The village of Beaumes is close to the southern foot of the Dentelles, and the surrounding vineyards and hills are made of compacted sandstone so soft that it crumbles between your fingers. You can still find some caves that have been dug out of the village hillsides, now used as hangouts for the local kids to drink and smoke. Venise simply signifies that it was part of the Comtat Venaissin, a territory once owned by the pope. Clement V planted 70 hectares of Muscat in the fourteenth century, but its viticultural history goes back further than this – Pliny the Elder appears to mention it in his *Natural History* of AD 77.

Muscat adores the deep, sandy soils found around the village. It also loves hot conditions. Beaumes de Venise faces due south and is protected from the mistral, producing a hot microclimate ideal for growing Muscat à Petits Grains Blancs and the less common, dark-skinned mutation Muscat à Petits Grains Noirs which is responsible for the colour in the rarer rosé and red cuvées. It also brings a little structure to a blend, and is more rot resistant than the white-skinned version.

Making Muscat de Beaumes de Venise is labour-intensive and yields are low. The best producers make several passes through the vineyard to hand-pick grapes at their optimum ripeness, and the resulting juice must have a sugar content above 252 grams per litre before fermentation. Muscat de Beaumes de Venise is Vin Doux Naturel, meaning it has a small amount of pure alcohol added during fermentation (a process called *mutage*). This arrests the fermentation and leaves some natural grape sweetness in the finished wine. The finished product must contain at least 100 grams per litre residual sugar and a minimum of 15% abv. It's the only still, sweet white made in the Rhône Valley, except for minuscule amounts of Rasteau Vin Doux Naturel, Hermitage Vin de Paille and sweet Condrieu.

Some producers, such as the excellent Domaine des Bernardins, have experimented with making sweet Muscats without *mutage*, with mixed results. They've made wines up to 17% abv this way but owner and winemaker Romain Hall says adding alcohol to stop the fermentation gives them more control over the final balance of the wine, and is preferable to using sulphur. Picking early and adding alcohol to stop the fermentation helps them retain acidity, and wines with *mutage* stay fresher for longer and age in a more predictable manner.

Sweet wines

Appellation: AOC Muscat de Beaumes de Venise
Birth of the appellation: 1945
Communes: Aubignan, Beaumes-de-Venise
Total surface area sold under the AOC in 2019: 332 hectares
Average yield in 2019: 17 hectolitres per hectare
Colours permitted: red, rosé, white
Production in 2019: 2 per cent red, 13 per cent rosé, 85 per cent white
Grape varieties permitted: Wines can only be made from Muscat à Petits Grains Blancs and Muscat à Petits Grains Noirs; reds must be made exclusively from Muscat à Petits Grains Noirs.

Dry reds

Appellation: AOC Beaumes de Venise
Birth of the appellation: 2005
Communes: Beaumes-de-Venise, Lafare, La Roque-Alric, Suzette
Total surface area sold under the AOC in 2019: 675 hectares
Average yield in 2019: 32 hectolitres per hectare
Colours permitted: red only
Grape varieties permitted: Wines must contain Grenache and Syrah, which together must constitute the largest component of the blend; may also contain Bourboulenc, Carignan, Cinsault, Clairette, Clairette Rose, Counoise, Grenache Blanc, Grenache Gris, Marsanne, Muscardin, Piquepoul Blanc, Piquepoul Noir, Roussanne, Terret Noir, Ugni Blanc, Vaccarèse and Viognier.

The Muscat de Beaumes de Venise produced by Domaine des Bernardins is a good example of the traditional style – full-bodied, with rich flavours such as apricot, quince, honey and nuts. Generally speaking, it's a style of wine that's best drunk as young as possible, but theirs ages remarkably well. A 1987 tasted at the domaine in 2019 was a brilliant wine, with complex orange marmalade, brown sugar, lanolin and a lifted lemon verbena note, long in flavour and still well-balanced, with bitter orange on the finish, that was just starting to reveal a little spirit.

In recent years a more modern style has been developed by some producers. Domaine de Coyeux make some traditional styles such as their Vintage, but also some more contemporary styles such as the medium-bodied, gently tropical Muscat Rosé Enigmae, and the elegant, violet-tinged Alégrio. It's worth noting that these are two of the best producers: a lot of the more inexpensive Muscat de Beaumes de Venise that finds its way on to the market can be pleasantly fruity but otherwise forgettable.

Both traditional and modern styles are enjoyable simply drunk by themselves. The traditional style works well with desserts of pastry, nuts and orchard fruits, or hard cheeses. The modern style tends to be a little more drinkable, so works better as a sweet aperitif or with lighter, fruitier desserts, particularly with tropical fruits and sorbets or soft or fresh goats' cheeses. The wine's fortunes have waxed and waned. In the mid-1960s there was under 115 hectares left in production. It became popular again in the UK and US market in the 1970s, and by the early 1980s plantings had doubled. It had reached 330 hectares by the early 1990s, but as fashions have more recently swung towards dry wines, the area of Muscat under vine is beginning to shink once again.

Plantings of dry, red Beaumes de Venise however are on the up. Despite some overlap around the village with AOC Muscat de Beaumes de Venise, the vineyards for dry red wines tend to be planted at higher altitude, among the rolling hills, valleys and woodland of the Dentelles. As you ascend, the earth becomes less sandy yellow. There are Jurassic soils around the village of Lafare, composed of black marls, silt, clay and sand. Further up there are outcrops of red Trias soils, pushed up from deep beneath the surface by the emergence of the limestone Dentelles. There is also some white clay-limestone around La Roque-Alric, a pretty village perched around a lone pillar of rock.

The village of Suzette is at 425 metres, and vines continue to climb up to 600 metres, the highest in the Southern Rhône. The altitude, variety of exposures and woodland (which is protected by law and can't be cut down to plant vines) all help give a little more freshness to the terroir. Grenache and Syrah dominate the blend, and although there's a further 18 'accessory' grapes that can add a little seasoning, it's usually Cinsault, Mourvèdre or Carignan. Up to 10 per cent of the finished blend can be made up of white grapes (usually Viognier, Grenache Blanc, Marsanne or Roussanne), which can add a little juice and levity. Some good dry Muscat is produced here, but it currently has to be bottled under IGP. There is some talk of changing the appellation laws to include dry Muscat, but there are no immediate changes in the offing.

At its highest point the appellation borders Gigondas, but rather than the polished, flowing red fruits of its neighbour, stylistically it's closer to a musclebound Vacqueyras in need of a shave. It can be a little gruff, with domineering tannins and punchy levels of alcohol. Even the lightest styles tend to be fairly robust, and the most powerful examples can be overwhelming, especially when very young. It's rarely the most elegant of the Southern Rhône *crus*, but can be enjoyably dramatic and full of impact. Where producers have found ways of achieving balanced wines by mastering this terroir, the results can be delicious, and quality is improving year on year.

Key producers

Domaine des Bernardins

Beaumes-de-Venise

www.domaine-des-bernardins.com

This property has winemaking roots back to the 1500s. The current cus-todians bought it in 1820, and current winemaker Romain Hall repre-sents the seventh generation. His great-grandfather Louis Castaud was instrumental in securing the AOC for Muscat de Beaumes de Venise in 1945 – not long after Châteauneuf-du-Pape. Domaine des Bernardins is best known for its long-lived Muscat de Beaumes de Venise; there is a vintage wine every year, and a non-vintage blend of older wines called Hommage. Their Beaumes de Venise *rouge* however is excellent, and in good vintages it represents one of the best value reds in the Southern Rhône. Peppery and herbal, generous in fruit but by no means a big wine, it ages well – a 2005 tasted in 2019 was fully mature and in great shape. Early picking, no destemming, short (15-day) macerations in raw concrete and ageing in stainless steel rather than barrel add up to a fresh, chiselled, textural and balanced style.

Domaine de Coyeux

Beaumes-de-Venise

www.domainedecoyeux.com

Domaine de Coyeux is unique in a number of ways. For a start, rather than being dispersed over a number of plots, the sprawling 65 hectares of vineyards surround the winery in an extensive 112-hectare estate on the Montagne de Coyeux that looks down over Beaumes de Venise. Its current owner is Hugues de Feraudy, a local businessman not previously involved in wine production. He bought it in 2013 after the previous owner, Yves Nativelle, lost the business over a consignment of corked wine. Along with the vineyards and winery, de Feraudy inherited a large amount of wine in tank and stocks of bottled Muscat running back to the early 1980s. As such, he can offer wines that are mature and ready to drink. The estate makes a range of Muscats in different styles, and two red Beaumes de Venise – the rounded, highly drinkable Thetys for early drinking and the more structured Les Cavares from 35- to 65-year-old vines, which can age 10 years or more in good vintages. There is also a very good Gigondas called Imperis and a variety of sparklings and IGPs. With a recently completed building housing a cellar door, bar and events space, it's well worth a visit if you're in the area (check times on their website).

Domaine de Fenouillet

Beaumes-de-Venise

www.domaine-fenouillet.fr

This organic domaine is currently in the hands of brothers Patrick and Vincent Soard, the fourth generation of winemakers here: two of their children have just joined, representing the fifth. They make Muscat de Beaumes de Venise in all three colours, and their old-vine Sélection Ancestrale is undoubtedly one of the best wines of the appellation, in a traditional style. Of their collection of Beaumes de Venise dry reds, their Terres Blanches is particularly fine and elegant.

Domaine de la Ferme Saint Martin

Suzette

www.fermesaintmartin.com

Thomas Jullien is the third generation to make the wine at this organic estate in Suzette, with vines from 200–600 metres altitude. Fifteen hectares are devoted to Beaumes de Venise *rouge*, mostly grown on Trias soils, and it's farmed as naturally as possible. All three cuvées are very good: Les Terres Jaunes (80 per cent Grenache, 20 per cent Syrah) is structured and powerful; Costancia (50 per cent Grenache, 50 per cent Syrah) is elegant and fluid and Saint-Martin (85 per cent very-old-vine Grenache, 15 per cent Syrah) is the deepest, most intense and tannic of the three. They also make very good Ventoux and Côtes-du-Rhône.

Domaine Saint Amant

Suzette

www.domainesaintamant.com

Domaine Saint Amant offers a suite of polished, bright and well-made wines in a crowd-pleasing style that's hard not to like. The estate comprises 13 hectares made up of 20 plots at high altitude around Suzette – in fact it claims to be the highest domaine in the Rhône Valley. Established in 1992 by former tech entrepreneur Jacques Wallut, it is farmed without recourse to herbicides or pesticides. About a third of production is Grangeneuve, a juicy black-cherry scented Beaumes de Venise *rouge*. Their delicious Viognier-based whites, La Borry and particularly La Tabardonne, demonstrate the high potential for white wines on cooler sites within AOC Beaumes de Venise.

Other good examples

Château Redortier make austere, elemental reds. **Domaine Martinelle** and **Domaine la Ligière** make very good reds in a juicy, fresh style. **Domaine de Pigeade** and **Domaine de Durban** both make brisk and bright Muscat de Beaumes de Venise, and **Vignoble Alain Ignace** is particularly worth seeking out for fans of the style.

SABLET

Appellation: AOC Côtes-du-Rhône Villages Sablet

Birth of the appellation: 1974

Communes: Sablet

Total surface area sold under the AOC in 2019: 358 hectares

Average yield in 2019: 36 hectolitres per hectare

Colours permitted: red, rosé, white

Production in 2019: 90 per cent red, 2 per cent rosé, 8 per cent white

Grape varieties permitted: As per communal Côtes-du-Rhône Villages regulations (see page 54)

When I visited Sablet in May 2019 the local *syndicat* was busy compiling a dossier of information to present to the INAO in the hope of being promoted from Named Village to *cru*. To do this, they need to demonstrate that the wines have a distinct style as a result of their unique terroir. On this basis, they have a good case.

Sablet is a small appellation sandwiched between two more powerful ones: Gigondas to the south and Séguret to the north. Like most Dentelles terroirs it has several different terroir subzones. Around the village of Sablet there are three large outcrops of sand, which together make up the most emblematic part of Sablet terroir (the French word for sand is *sable*). It's this sandy soil, derived from the old marine sandstone underneath, that produces the lighter-bodied, pale red wines for which Sablet is best known. As the land starts to rise to the east of the village into the Dentelles there is a second section of more mountainous terroir known as Cheval Long, which has more clay and jagged colluvial limestone pebbles. It's west-facing, so it doesn't feel the sun until late in the morning, offering some valuable shade to the sandy village terroirs. It rises to 428 metres altitude, and the tree-lined vineyards up high impart a freshness and crisp structure to the fruit. The rounded section known as Les Briguières that buts up against AOC Gigondas has some particularly choice plots of old vines. The final subzone, to the west of the village, is cut off by the Ouvèze river. They've effectively annexed a small triangle of Plan de Dieu. This free-draining, flat, pebbly terroir doesn't feel like it belongs to Sablet in spirit, but it's useful in the blend, bringing body, volume and concentration to what can otherwise be a light wine. Thibaut Chamfort of Domaine de Verquière appreciates this part as much as the other two, describing it as "warm and sunny, made for Mourvèdre".

The reds often show their best when winemakers embrace their natural propensity for lightness. Occasionally you encounter estates pushing for more powerful cuvées but these tend to feel unnaturally bulky and forced. 'The great advantage we have is elegance', says Christian Bonfils, president of the appellation. Those who work in harmony with Sablet's natural light-heartedness produce wines with a floral, aerial demeanour which sets them apart from their neighbours.

Sablet makes a relatively large proportion of white wines, which offer similar finesse to the reds. Don't expect the same bombast as white Châteauneuf, or the same complexity. The best have a good sense of tension and occasionally a whiff of *garrigue* herbs and hot sand (this may be down to the power of suggestion, I'm still undecided!). A very small amount of Sablet rosé is produced, but it's rarely as interesting as the reds or whites.

A number of new estates have cropped up in recent years, bringing new energy to the appellation and raising overall quality. Domaine Fontaine des Fées, Domaine de Crève Coeur, and Château Cohola, all working either organically or biodynamically, are making some brilliant examples that are well worth exploring. Like many of the wines of Sablet, they offer excellent value for money. As global tastes move beyond the concentrated styles of the 1990s and 2000s, there is more demand for finer, more subtle styles. This is good news for Sablet. And although there are many good quality wines it still feels like this appellation has the potential to improve. Perhaps the process of seeking promotion from Named Village to *cru* will provide the focus and energy to propel them even further.

Key producers

Domaine les Goubert

Gigondas

www.lesgoubert.fr

In 2017 Florence Cartier took over this old family domaine in Gigondas from her father Jean-Pierre. Making two full-bodied Gigondas cuvées, she clearly feels she has nothing to prove when it comes to the Sablets: both red and white cuvées are fine, unforced, light-bodied examples with delicacy, drinkability and a beautiful sense of place.

Domaine les Sibu

Sablet

www.domainelessibu.com

Domaine les Sibu only bottled their first wine in 2015, but already their red and white Sablets are among the most impressive in the appellation. The vineyard is well established; fourth generation Loïc Alazard did a series of *stages* in France and New Zealand before returning to set up the winery back home. He now farms 21 hectares, mostly in Sablet, along with a little Gigondas. One to watch.

Domaine Bertrand Stehelin

Gigondas

www.vinstehelin.fr

Bertrand Stehelin previously made the wine at his parents' estate, Domaine Paillère & Pied-Gû in Gigondas, before striking out on his own in 2004. He began with 4 hectares of vines and gradually grew his property from there. He's better known for his Gigondas, but his Sablet *rouge* 'Cheval Long' has all the finesse and freshness you'd hope for from this appellation.

Domaine de Verquière

Sablet

www.domaine-de-verquiere.fr

The word *verquière* means walled vineyard in old French, and the sandy *clos* is situated next to the winery in the heart of the village. The laidback Thibaut Chamfort is the fourth generation to lead this family domaine, which now extends across 40 hectares in half a dozen appellations. After spending some time working in California and South Africa, Thibaut returned to the estate and converted it to organic viticulture. He likes to work at a steady pace: 3–4 days cold settling before fermentation, 30- to 35-day cuvaisons in concrete tanks, 2–4 years maturation before release. He makes measured, unshowy wines with a strong sense of place.

Other good examples

As mentioned above, **Domaine Fontaine des Fées**, **Domaine de Crève Coeur** and in particular **Château Cohola** are all very promising new estates. The reds of **Château la Thébaïde**, **Domaine Saint Gayan** and **Domaine de Cabasse** are elegant and classically styled. **Domaine de Piaugier** has also done a lot to put Sablet on the map, and its white wines in particular are among the best in the appellation.

SÉGURET

Appellation: AOC Côtes-du-Rhône Villages Séguret

Birth of the appellation: 1967

Communes: Séguret

Total surface area sold under the AOC in 2019: 489 hectares

Average yield in 2019: 36 hectolitres per hectare

Colours permitted: red, rosé, white

Production in 2019: 90 per cent red, 5 per cent rosé, 5 per cent white

Grape varieties permitted: As per communal Côtes-du-Rhône Villages regulations (see page 54)

Look north from Sablet and you'll spot the village of Séguret. From a distance it appears to be a village pretending to be a mountain – or is it a mountain disguised as a village? – the two seem almost merged into one. Get a bit closer and you realize it's one of those ornately pretty villages

that could only have come into existence by accident, after many bliss-
ful centuries without town-planning, building control or cars to think
about. The growing area that surrounds it is bigger than Sablet's and
takes up much of the northerly part of the Dentelles de Montmirail and
the land between the Dentelles and the Ouvèze river.

Stony limestone terroir with the Dentelles in the background

Most of the production is red wine based on Grenache and Syrah,
and there are three different growing zones, all with slightly different
characteristics. Below the village on the plain there is the Première
Terrasse (140 metres altitude). It's a jumble of soils, mostly clay limestone and sand with scatterings of pebbles. The wines here tend to be
vibrantly fruity. It's proving to be a happy home for Mourvèdre, which
is growing in popularity here. 'It wasn't adapted to the old climate,' says
Christian Voeux of Domaine de l'Amauve, 'but it is adapted to the new
one,' he adds, forebodingly. Picking dates are getting earlier and earlier
here, as they are throughout the Rhône.

The ascent toward the village is gentle, and the vines here on the Coteau (200 metres) share the clay limestone soils along with out-crops of sand and sandstone. These wines tend to be a little paler in colour, and finer in style. The roads get steeper as you pass the village and climb to the Montagne (400 metres) and hills beyond, develop-ing into the sprawling Dentelles scenery of green oaks, Mediterranean pines and *garrigue*, with outcrops of white limestone scree. The wines here are more concentrated and tannic and the land is harder to work. The soil is less rich so produces lower yields, the slopes are challenging to work with machines, and vineyards are prone to erosion. Sébastien Magnouac, winemaker at Domaine de Mourchon, says there is three weeks' difference between the earliest vines on the Première Terrasse and the highest, latest-ripening ones on the Montagne.

Much of the terroir is west-facing and at altitude, and this imbues the wines with a certain freshness and brisk drinkability despite their concentration and dark colouring. Rosés are among the best on the east bank of the Rhône, and fall into two camps, with good examples in each. The first is very pale in colour with precise, if subtle, fruit flavours. The second has more depth of colour and more generous red fruits. White wines are particularly worth seeking out: medium- rather than full-bodied, weighty but refreshing and with a good sense of tension.

Local co-op Les Vignerons de Roaix Séguret is still the dominant force, accounting for half of the appellation's output. Today it's com-plemented by three smaller co-ops and 31 independent wineries, many of whom are moving towards organic viticulture. Despite only occa-sionally hitting the kind of quality you'd hope to see in a *cru*, Séguret represents one of the strongest of the Named Villages in the Côtes-du-Rhône, making consistently good wines in all three colours. It's an ap-pellation on the up.

Key producers

Domaine de l'Amauve
Séguret

www.domainedelamauve.fr

Christian Voeux has a long Châteauneuf-du-Pape winemaking career, mostly at Château Mont-Redon and Château la Nerthe. When his par-ents retired in 2005, he took on the family property and now concen-trates his energies on developing the estate. It's made up of 11 hectares in total, with 8 hectares in Séguret, 2 hectares of which are planted to white varieties (Grenache Blanc, Clairette, Ugni Blanc and Viognier). His 26 parcels are dotted around the village, principally on the Première Terrasse. 'Precision' is his watchword. He takes great care to control yields in the vineyard by debudding and grassing between alternate rows; he harvests by hand and should be certified organic by 2021. His reds are lush and juicy; the white and rosé are focused and refreshing.

Domaine Jean David

Séguret

www.domaine-jean-david.com

Certified since 1987, this domaine is a pioneer in organic viticulture in the Rhône. Jean is now retired, and the estate is run by his daughter and her husband Jean-Luc. Theirs is a distinctly traditional approach, with no technology to speak of, not even temperature control. Some of their range might benefit from a more modern approach, as wines can occasionally verge on the uncomfortably rustic. Other cuvées however, like the Séguret *rouge* Les Levants, are thrilling and memorable wines, deeply authentic and true to terroir.

Domaine Eyguestre

Séguret

www.domaine-eyguestre.com

Deep in the hills you'll find the pretty, ramshackle farmhouse of Domaine Eyguestre. Laurent Bellion's great-grandfather established a polyculture farmstead here 100 years ago, but Laurent now concentrates on viticulture. He makes three Ségurets, one of each colour. His white and rosé have great energy and purity, his red is juicy, concentrated and generous.

Domaine Malmont

Séguret

malmont.fr

Nicolas Haeni is the son of the previous owners of nearby Domaine de Cabasse. This project is based much higher up compared to his previous family estate, in the hills above Séguret near Domaine de Mourchon. The first vintage was 2013. He makes three cuvées – a red, a white and a rosé – all of which are wines of real elegance, restraint and balance.

Domaine de Mourchon
Séguret

www.domainedemourchon.com

After selling his previous business, Englishman Walter McKinlay searched the south of France for two years to find a vineyard to call his own. Eventually he found Domaine de Mourchon, with fantastic high-altitude vineyards in Séguret, but no winery. Undeterred, he built one and has developed the estate from 17 hectares to 32 hectares. His first vintage was 1998, and since then the name has become established as one of the best in the appellation. Talented winemaker Sébastien Magnouac constantly experiments: using stems, no-added-sulphite cuvées, barrel-aged rosé, sweet wines, and more. The entire range of robust, muscular red wines is worth exploring, as is the pale rosé.

Other good examples
Château la Diffre makes some bold whites and reds; **Domaine de Cabasse** produces some juicy and characterful red and rosé Ségurets. **Domaine Clos du Palay** makes some eye-catching reds, and **Domaine de l'Amandine** can also be a source of good Ségurets in three colours.

8

VENTOUX AND LUBERON

VENTOUX

Ventoux is one of France's most territorially extensive appellations, but until 1973 it didn't contain a single private domaine – all the grapes went to one of the many co-ops or to négocians. Up until the early 2000s I remember people commonly referring to it as an appellation for bulk wines, thin and tart but reliably cheap. And broadly they were right. Today, however, it's home to some 150 private domaines, including some of the most exciting names in the Rhône Valley. There has been a revolution.

You can spy Mont Ventoux from almost everywhere in the Southern Rhône; peaking at 1,912 metres it's the dominant feature of the landscape. The growing area is in two sections. The larger part is effectively a large bowl that surrounds the town of Carpentras, enclosed by mountains on three sides: the Dentelles de Montmirail to the north, Mont Ventoux itself to the east and the Monts de Vaucluse to the south. The smaller second segment is found in the Luberon valley between the southern edge of Mont Ventoux and the Calavon river. There are fewer exciting domaines in this part and the terroir appears to have little to do with the appellation's more northerly flank. Intuitively this smaller tract feels more a part of AOC Luberon.

Ventoux is an extensive and varied appellation encompassing mountains and plains, so vineyards cover a range of altitudes and aspects. The soils are broadly clay-limestone with plentiful colluvial limestone gravels, and most of the best terroir of the northern section is found in the mountain foothills, right up into the fringes of the Dentelles de

Montmirail. Heat builds during the day, but cold air descends from Mont Ventoux at night, cooling the vines and contributing to the freshness and acidity found in the wines, an important part of their DNA. Cooling influences and marked acidity may be advantages today, but this wasn't always the case. Thirty years ago, full ripeness wasn't always guaranteed in many of the more mountainous vineyards, particularly when carrying heavy crops, and this was the source of Ventoux's unenviable reputation for insipid wines. But as the climate warms, they are revealing their potential to those prepared to treat them with love and care – just as longer established but hotter zones such as Plan de Dieu and perhaps even Châteauneuf-du-Pape are beginning to feel less bankable.

Not all of the appellation's 6,000-odd hectares have the same promise of course, but among them there are some exceptional plots that rival the best of Vacqueyras and Gigondas. It was this potential, coupled with the low price of land, which attracted so many newcomers in the early 2000s. James and Joanna King at Château Unang are Scottish, Even Bakke at Clos des Trias is Norwegian, Graham Short at Domaine Vintur is English. Philippe Gimel at St Jean du Barroux was a pharmacist in Lorraine before he devoted himself to wine. 'Sometimes it's only when you come from outside that you realize how great somewhere can be,' he says. These outsiders have come with fresh eyes, modern methods, belief in themselves and ambition, and they have turned Ventoux into a hotbed for experimentation.

Southern Rhône Syrah rarely produces wines that can rival those of the Northern Rhône, but it's particularly at home in the cooler parts of Ventoux, producing wines with sleek lines and finesse. The co-ops pump out plenty of rosé to meet demand, and Ventoux is one of the best sources for inexpensive pink in the Rhône. Whites are still fairly uncommon, but can be excellent; if demand for white Rhône continues to grow, this is an obvious appellation for growers to explore. I've also had delicious sweet wines and surprising sparkling wines from Ventoux.

Could Ventoux ever be promoted to a Southern Rhône *cru*? In theory it would have to journey through the subsequent layers of Côtes-du-Rhône appellations first, and be subject to grinding scrutiny at the hands of the INAO that could take decades. Soil analyses of such a massive and mountainous region would be incredibly time consuming. It's the kind of excruciating and largely thankless task that few local players have the appetite for. It would also prove divisive. Estates would likely be better off working together to promote Ventoux in other ways.

Appellation: AOC Ventoux

Birth of the appellation: 1973

Communes: Apt, Aubignan, Le Barroux, Le Beaucet, Beaumettes, Beaumont-du-Ventoux, Bédoin, Blauvac, Bonnieux, Cabrières-d'Avignon, Caromb, Carpentras, Caseneuve, Crestet, Crillon-le-Brave, Entrechaux, Flassan, Fontaine-de-Vaucluse, Gargas, Gignac, Gordes, Goult, Joucas, Lagnes, Lioux, Loriol-du-Comtat, Malaucène, Malemort-du-Comtat, Maubec, Mazan, Méthamis, Modène, Mormoiron, Murs, Pernes, Robion, La Roque-sur-Pernes, Roussillon, Rustrel, Saignon, Saint-Didier, Saint-Hippolyte-le-Graveron, Saint-Martin-de Castillon, Saint-Pantaléon, Saint-Pierre-de-Vassols, Saint-Saturnin-d'Apt, Saumane, Venasque, Viens, Villars, Villes-sur-Auzon

Total surface area sold under the AOC in 2019: 5,691 hectares

Average yield in 2019: 44 hectolitres per hectare

Colours permitted: red, rosé, white

Production in 2019: 54 per cent red, 40 per cent rosé, 6 per cent white

Grape varieties permitted: Reds must be a blend of at least two varieties; the majority of the blend must contain Carignan, Cinsault, Grenache, Mourvèdre and/or Syrah. May also contain Bourboulenc, Clairette, Counoise, Grenache Blanc, Marsanne, Marselan, Piquepoul Noir, Roussanne, Vermentino and Viognier.

  Rosés: as for reds.

  Whites must be a blend of at least two varieties; the majority of the blend must contain Bourboulenc, Clairette, Grenache Blanc and/or Roussanne. May also contain Marsanne, Vermentino and Viognier.

In my mind, Ventoux represents a kind of honorary *cru*. The best Ventoux wines are among the best in the Rhône – and often much cheaper than those from, say, Gigondas or Châteauneuf-du-Pape. In the meantime, it's not an appellation you can rely on as such – for every excellent domaine, there are many average ones. For now, it's a case of getting to know the individual ones that excel. This is something of a challenge, but an enjoyable one – there is an ever-growing list of exciting new names to explore.

Key producers

Domaine des Anges

Mormoiron

www.domainedesanges.com

The history of outsiders transforming the winemaking landscape in Ventoux goes back to the very first private domaine. The appellation was established in 1973, at which time all local producers delivered their grapes to one of the local co-ops. This was the year that Englishman Malcolm Swan bought a small domaine on a hilltop near Mormoiron, with the intention of bottling his own. To begin with he was threatened by other local vignerons for his flagrant breach of local traditions, but he continued unbowed, and soon gained recognition. Swan died in 2017. The appellation has much to thank him for. The current owner and wine-maker is Florent Chave (no relation to any Northern Rhône winemakers), and the estate continues to make attractive wines at very good prices.

Chêne Bleu

Crestet

www.chenebleu.com

Most of the appellations that share the Dentelles de Montmirail skirt along its southern and western reaches. There is however one estate in the north-eastern sector at 550 metres altitude: Domaine de la Verrière, whose wines go by the name of Chêne Bleu. The estate, which had lain derelict for many years, was a former priory. Its history goes back centuries, however. In 1427 a local craftsman by the name of Aliot de Montvin was given the rights to blow glass here, clearing woodland to power his furnace, and inadvertently clearing land that could be planted with vines. It was bought in 1993 by Xavier Rolet, former CEO of the London Stock Exchange, whose family owns vineyards in Jura.

The wreck has been beautifully renovated and now boasts impressive accommodation, catering and wine courses. Xavier's wife Nicole Rolet manages the estate, and has boundless energy and ideas, recently set-ting up the ARENI, 'a global research and action institute for the future of fine wine', not to mention countless sustainability projects. Xavier's brother-in-law, Jean-Louis Gallucci, makes the wine, and Xavier's daughter Danielle is also closely involved.

That the estate lies outside of any major appellation is a bone of contention; some of the wines are labelled AOC Ventoux, others IGP

Vaucluse. The quality, however, is as good as many a fine Gigondas. The first vintage was 2006, and the wines were to begin with quite demonstrative and international; the style however is moving towards more freshness and precision as they discover how best to express what is clearly a very special terroir.

Clos de Trias

Le Barroux

closdetrias.eu

High in the hills near the ancient fortified village of Le Barroux, the vibe at Even Bakke's Clos de Trias is two parts Provence to one part Mad Max. Born in Norway but raised in the US, Bakke worked in various Californian wineries before buying this Ventoux estate in 2007. His parcellated organic vineyards are grown on ancient Triassic soils and scale the mountainside to heights of 500 metres. Once vinified, he ages them in old barrels for up to 6 years before release. He describes himself as a 'post-industrial winemaker', working as simply as possible to create idiosyncratic wines that are as vital as they are challenging, exploring umami, salt and acidity to electrifying effect.

Domaine de Fondrèche

Mazan

fondreche.com

In the early 1990s, Sébastien Vincenti worked at Domaine les Cailloux in Châteauneuf-du-Pape. He dreamed of establishing his own domaine, but vineyards in Châteauneuf were prohibitively expensive so he was forced to look further afield. In 1995, when he was offered Domaine de Fondrèche at the foot of Mont Ventoux, he didn't hesitate. Today he makes some of the best pale rosés in the Rhône, but it's his reds that really impress – sleek, polished, precise expressions of Ventoux terroir. Though prices have been rising of late, the red, white and rosé in his Persia range all still offer impressive bang for your buck.

Château Pesquié

Mormoiron

www.chateaupesquie.com

Affable brothers Frédéric and Alex Chaudière are the third generation to run Château Pesquié, a sizeable traditional Provençale *bastide* property at the foot of the mountain. Their parents were pioneers of the Ventoux revolution, leaving the local co-op in 1990 to make their own wines. Back then there were fewer than 10 independent wineries; now there are over 100. At over 100 hectares, Pesquié is the largest, and is now certified organic. The highly differentiated range of bold, intense, attention-grabbing wines expresses the various aspects of the high-altitude terroir. The opulent whites and ageworthy reds are among the most impressive in Ventoux.

St Jean du Barroux

Malaucène

T.: +33 (0) 4 90 70 84 74

'If you study geology, you can find great terroirs that are still unknown', says Philippe Gimel. In 2003, after *stages* at Domaine de la Janasse and Château de Beaucastel in Châteauneuf-du-Pape, his search led him to Le Barroux. He's divided his vineyards into 99 plots, and can take a month to hand-pick at perfect ripeness since they've never yet been affected by rot. The largest bunches go into his early-drinking cuvée; the smaller, more concentrated bunches go into his bottlings designed to age. These get more stems in the ferments, but even these he sorts for quality. Gimel fizzes with excitement when he talks about his terroir. When you taste the wines, you see why. He creates thrillingly fluent and precise expressions of this fresh, wild, windswept terroir.

Other good examples

It seems that with every week that passes, I drink another lovely wine from Ventoux, from an estate that's entirely new to me. If there were room for more in the list above, it would certainly contain **Domaine du Tix**, **Château Unang**, **Les Terrasses d'Eole**, **Domaine Vintur**, **Domaine de Piéblanc**, **Château Juvenal** and **Domaine Martinelle**. Other estates producing interesting Ventoux wines include **Aureto**, **Domaine du Bon Remède**, **Domaine Mur-mur-ium**, **Mas Oncle Ernest**, **Domaine de la Gasqui**, **Domaine de la Ferme Saint Martin**, **Vindemio** and **Domaine Alloïs**. Most Rhône negociants produce a Ventoux, of which **Delas** and **La Ferme du Mont** are particularly reliable. Of the 16 co-ops that operate in Ventoux, **Marrenon** and **TerraVentoux** are consistently good.

LUBERON

The Luberon appellation, which lies within the boundaries of the Luberon Regional Nature Park, isn't just a sea of vines like some appellations further north. Cherry trees, olive trees, oaks and lavender give nuance and variety to what is already one of the most picturesque corners of the region. The diversity of crops grown also points toward the fact that prices for wine here are still low, amongst the lowest in the Rhône.

This extensive appellation, which occupies the south-eastern corner of the Rhône Valley vineyards, is shaped like a flat oblong stretching from Cavaillon in the west to Manosque in the east. Along the middle runs the Montagne du Luberon, rising to 1,125 metres near the centre, which creates two separate areas of production, one to the north of the range and one to its south. The smaller northern section lies between the Montagne and the Calavon river. This river marks the boundary between Luberon and the stray southern portion of Ventoux (which should arguably also fall under the Luberon umbrella). The more ex-tended southern area of production is between the Montagne and the Durance river, which itself marks the boundary between the Luberon growing region and Coteaux d'Aix-en-Provence further south.

It's a warm and sunny terroir, but not hot, since the rivers act as conduits for cold air from the Alps. The further east you go, the cooler and wetter it gets, and the higher the vine-growing land. There can be 20 days' difference in ripening from the furthest west to furthest east. The central Montagne offers south- and north-facing slopes and plenty of high-altitude sites, with vineyards climbing from 200 to 500 metres. Soils are largely clay limestone, with some deep gravels at the foot of the mountain range, some outcrops of sand and sandstone, and more marl as you travel east.

Vine cultivation goes back to Roman times, but the modern history of Luberon really begins in the 1980s with the establishment of several small domaines, such as Château la Verrerie, joined by a second wave around 2002, and a third around 2014. Cooperatives still dominate the scene however, with around 85 per cent of total production. With global demand for rosé continuing unabated, Luberon has embraced the commercial opportunity, and now makes more rosé than red. Most of it is fashionably pale and inoffensive, but the best can pass for compe-tent examples from Coteaux d'Aix-en-Provence. The red wines tend to be marginally more interesting, ranging from light- to full-bodied, but can lack ripeness, concentration and character. Most are accessible and easy-drinking wines, with the occasional flash of genuine interest. The best are unforced, with a charming aerial, free-spirited demeanour. The white wines, however, are beginning to forge a distinctive character that marks them out from other Rhône whites. They have a zesty brightness that makes them really drinkable aperitif-style wines – not something the Rhône does terribly well as a rule. The key is Vermentino, occasionally still called Rolle locally, which has a distinctly floral, citric, mandarin-like flavour profile when grown here. Philippe Tolleret, the managing director of Marrenon, a union of eight cooperative wineries that produces half of all AOC Luberon, describes the grape as 'the future of Luberon whites' and I can see why.

Luberon still feels a little sleepy compared to its dynamic neighbour Ventoux. It is almost as if the place is simply too beautiful to have to try terribly hard, attracting as it does a never-ending stream of fleeting, moneyed admirers. Though many wines are perfectly adequate and a few are worth seeking out, the style is resolutely conventional, with few names (except perhaps the elusive Guillaume Gros) really trying anything new. Apart from the producers below, you're still more likely to be wowed by the scenery than the wines.

Appellation: AOC Luberon

Birth of the appellation: 1988

Communes: Ansouis, Apt, La Bastide-des-Jourdans, La Bastidonne, Beaumont-de-Pertuis, Bonnieux, Cabrières-d'Aigues, Cadenet, Castellet, Cheval-Blanc, Cucuron, Goult, Grambois, Lacoste, Lauris, Lourmarin, Maubec, Ménerbes, Mérindol, Mirabeau, La Motte-d'Aigues, Oppède, Pertuis, Peypin-d'Aigues, Puget, Puyvert, Robion, Saignon, Saint-Martin-de-Castillon, Saint-Martin-de-la-Brasque, Sannes, Taillades, La Tour-d'Aigues, Vaugines, Villelaure, Vitrolles-en-Lubéron

Total surface area sold under the AOC in 2019: 3,397 hectares

Average yield in 2019: 45 hectolitres per hectare

Colours permitted: red, rosé, white

Production in 2019: 23 per cent red, 61 per cent rosé, 16 per cent white

Grape varieties permitted: Reds must be a blend, and the majority of the blend must come from at least two of the following three varieties: Grenache, Mourvèdre, Syrah. May also contain Bourboulenc, Carignan, Cinsault, Clairette, Grenache Blanc, Marsanne, Marselan, Roussanne, Ugni Blanc, Vermentino and Viognier.

Rosés: same as reds.

Whites must be a blend of at least two varieties; the majority of the blend must contain Bourboulenc, Clairette, Grenache Blanc, Marsanne, Roussanne, Vermentino. May also contain Ugni Blanc and Viognier.

Key producers

Château la Canorgue

Bonnieux

chateaulacanorgue.com

The first thing you notice is the birdsong. 'You hear them all the time,' says Nathalie Margan. 'And insects. But they get eaten by the birds.' Château la Canorgue was the first property in the region to go organic, in 1977, and the local fauna seem very happy here. All being well, they will soon be certified biodynamic. Nathalie is certainly the fifth generation of the family to work here, but that's only as far as written records go. Today they play around with 15 different cuvées, but their Luberon *rouge* Château la Canorgue (a blend of 70 per cent Syrah, 20 per cent Grenache and 10 per cent Carignan, 50 per cent whole bunch) is not to be missed. You can see why the family has stuck around for so long. It's one of the most beautiful estates in the region, near the rickety mountaintop village of Bonnieux. The *bastide* and gardens are so beautiful they supplied the backdrop for the 2006 Ridley Scott film *A Good Year* featuring Russell Crowe and Marion Cotillard. The main challenge they face here is being invaded by fans of the film trying to take selfies.

Domaine de la Citadelle

Ménerbes

www.domaine-citadelle.com

Porn. It's not what it used to be. The *Emmanuelle* series of soft-focus titillation from the 1970s was considered outrageous in its day but would barely get a 15-certificate these days. Anyway, inadvertently the series did wonders for Luberon wines when, in 1990, director Yves Rousset-Rouard subsequently invested in this property near Ménerbes, on the northern slope of the Montagne du Luberon. It was originally just 8 hectares, but now stretches over 50 hectares and is certified organic. The Luberon *rouge* Le Gouveneur is a particularly durable expression of southern Syrah.

Domaine de Fontenille

Lauris

www.domainedefontenille.com

Fontenille is an imposing country house and gardens near Lauris in the southern part of the Luberon. It was built in the late 1500s, and grapes have been grown there for most of its existence. Recently refurbished to include a hotel, spa and restaurant, the estate now has 35 hectares of vines positioned around the house itself and is certified organic. Both whites and reds are measured and harmonious and are clearly the result of a considered hand in both vineyard and cellar. The Vermentino-based whites are particularly good, and to me represent the archetype of contemporary Luberon *blanc*.

Château Val Joanis

Pertuis

www.val-joanis.com

If Château Val Joanis wasn't so famous for its exquisite gardens, it would no doubt still be just as famous, for its beautiful wines. They play to the region's strengths, opting for a brisk, unforced style across all three colours that really captures the floaty, aerial nature that defines Luberon wines.

Château la Verrerie

Puget

www.chateau-la-verrerie.com

One of the first major private domaines in the Luberon, Château la Verrerie was established in 1981 in the west of the region near Puget. It wasn't until 1985 that they built their own winery. It was created by Jean-Louis Descours, and is now owned by his son Christopher Descours, who runs the EPI luxury group. Compared to their neighbours, they make a particularly bold, ripe and concentrated style, and their top cuvées are expensive. The 56 hectares of vineyard is now certified organic and managed by Valentine Tardieu-Vitelli, who says of the estate, 'even in summer there's always a breeze.' A comment which sums up Luberon wines rather nicely.

Other good examples

La Bastide du Claux makes excellent wines, particularly the whites. The elusive ex-sommelier **Guillaume Gros** makes very good reds if you can track them down. The top cuvées of cave cooperative **Marrenon** in both red and white are good options at the more affordable end. The ambitious **La Cavale**, under the guidance of Alain Graillot of Crozes-Hermitage, shows potential.

9

THE VISAN VALRÉAS HILLS

VINSOBRES

The Ventabren massif might be home to the big-name duo of Cairanne and Rasteau, but to the north of the Aigues river is a similar massif that deserves just as much attention. It's built from the same pebbly marl soils as Ventabren and is around four times as large, but this range doesn't have an established name – so let's call it the Visan Valréas massif. Like Ventabren, its viticultural sites are concentrated on its southern face: Visan to the west, Saint-Maurice in the centre and Vinsobres to the east.

When I started working in wine, I'd occasionally ask winemakers what makes the wine from their region special, what marks it out from its neighbours. After a moment's reflection, the answer often went something like this: 'our wine has a lovely freshness and very fine tannins,' followed by a nod and a satisfied smile. The problem is of course that this describes most fine wines from everywhere in the world. I've since learnt that this question is often best directed towards the outsider rather than the native; answering it requires distance, perspective and cold-blooded objectivity. The word that pops up more often than any other in the marketing blurb for Vinsobres is 'freshness'. But it's true; within the Southern Rhône, Vinsobres is eye-wideningly fresh, and there are good reasons for it.

For a start, Vinsobres is the most northerly of all the Southern Rhône *crus*, tucked far into the north-east of the region on the eastern flank of the Visan Valréas hills close to Nyons. The appellation consists of a large south-east-facing slope, the pretty village of Vinsobres itself towards the bottom, near the D94, and the Aigues river that marks its southern boundary. There are four parts to the terroir. Les Collines is the hilly higher-altitude land (300–450 metres, clay, sand) to the north-east of the village. Le Plateau is the flatter higher-altitude land (350–450 metres, red clay, large pebbles) to its north-west. The warmer Coteau section (250–350 metres, clay, sand, pebbles, limestone) runs in a band from east to west below the village. Below that is the thin Première Terrasse (200–250 metres) above the river. Though many good wines are made on Le Coteau, most winemakers covet the vineyards at altitude, where grapes ripen up to 10 days later than those grown at the lowest sites.

Its northerly situation and high-altitude vineyards give this *cru* a long, slow ripening season which helps the grapes retain acidity – tartaric acid additions are relatively rare here. The Syrah in particular gains a florality and spiciness that lies somewhere between Southern Rhône and Northern Rhône in style. Vinsobres feels the effect of the mistral but its proximity to the French Prealps brings other winds into play; the cold pontias comes at night from the east. The resulting diurnal temperature variation is another factor that brings aromatic brightness and clarity. When it comes to the natural freshness of Vinsobres, Cédric Guillaume-Corbin, owner of Domaine la Péquélette, says 'one real bonus is that we are neither north nor south, not totally mountain or totally plain,' and he suggests the proliferation of woodlands interspersed among the vineyards also helps. 'They bring freshness, they transpire. I'm convinced they're important. I'm planting some trees myself.' You'll also find olive trees, lavender and oaks.

For all this talk of freshness, this is still a sunny spot with a very warm climate, growing plentiful Grenache alongside the Syrah. A typical Vinsobres will be dark in colour, with fruit that really attacks your palate. Its structure will be clearly drawn and textural, with taut tannins, piercing acidity and a distinct salinity on the finish. The best wines have an aerial freshness, an aromatic lift, a lightness of touch and drinkability despite their assertive structures. Some, however, mature quicker than you might expect, and if not carefully reined in, their acidity and tannin can run riot, fruit disappearing in their wake. When on song, however, Vinsobres is the Barbaresco of the Rhône.

With such a fresh terroir, you might wonder why they don't produce white wine. When the appellation was promoted from Named Village to *cru* only a handful of estates made any white, and those that did made diverse styles with little common ground – so only reds were permitted. Today, many producers have parcels of white grapes grown within the appellation and the quality can be excellent – check out Domaine Chaume-Arnaud's La Cadène and Domaine Vallot's Le Haut des Côtes *blanc*. Local growers are trying to update the appellation rules but for now they can only be sold under AOC Côtes-du-Rhône – and often represent great value for money.

So why does Vinsobres not share the same visibility and renown as Vacqueyras or Gigondas? For a start, it was only elevated to *cru* level relatively recently. You could also argue its name sounds a little odd. Another reason is that no major négociants bottle and sell one, which can be a huge benefit for appellations trying to establish their regional brand in export markets. The Perrins of Château de Beaucastel, however, have been quick to see its potential and now own 40 hectares of bi-odynamically farmed vineyards in the appellation, making two excellent bottlings. They were followed in 2019 by Louis Barruol of Château de Saint-Cosme in Gigondas, who bought the large Château de Rouanne. Hopefully this will help bring more attention to this northern eyrie.

Appellation: AOC Vinsobres

Birth of the appellation: 2006

Communes: Vinsobres

Total surface area sold under the AOC in 2019: 570 hectares

Average yield in 2019: 33 hectolitres per hectare

Colours permitted: red only

Grape varieties permitted: Grenache must make up the largest part of the blend, and wines must contain Syrah and/or Mourvèdre. May also contain Bourboulenc, Carignan, Cinsault, Clairette, Clairette Rose, Counoise, Grenache Blanc, Grenache Gris, Marsanne, Muscardin, Piquepoul Blanc, Piquepoul Noir, Roussanne, Terret Noir, Ugni Blanc, Vaccarèse and Viognier.

Key producers

Domaine Chaume-Arnaud

Vinsobres

T.: +33 (0) 4 75 27 66 85

Philippe and Valérie Chaume-Arnaud turned their estate organic in 1997, then biodynamic in 2003. It was in response to the increasing temperatures they were witnessing, in an effort to bring balance to their wines. It seems to have worked; both their Vinsobres cuvées are consistently brilliant. Both are fermented and matured in concrete, with no oak ageing. The *cuvée classique* is a bright and zingy red-fruited style thanks in part to containing 20 per cent Cinsault; La Cadène contains more Mourvèdre and is a deeply concentrated and rewarding wine. The estate now covers 35 hectares, almost all of which is in Vinsobres, with some vines as much as 80 years old.

Domaine Jaume

Vinsobres

www.domainepascalrichard-jaume.com

Pascal Jaume claims that it was his grandfather who first planted Syrah in Vinsobres in 1955. His family has been growing vines here since 1905, but only started bottling it themselves in 1960. Pascal joined the family business in 1981, his brother Richard in 1987, and their children represent the fifth generation. The estate extends over 92 hectares. They find managing this size of holding organically too much of a challenge, but they keep chemicals to a minimum. The Vinsobres Altitude 420 is a classic example with plenty of freshness and bite; Référence is more concentrated and spends some time in barriques (one-third new barrels, one-third 1-year-old barrels, one-third 2-year-old barrels, for 12 months) that needs a little time to integrate, but it works well. The new Vinéa Natura is both fleshy and structured and has no added sulphites.

Domaine la Péquélette

Vinsobres

www.lapequelette.fr

La Péquélette means 'the smallest' in Provençale, and for a while at just 6 hectares this estate was the most diminutive in Vinsobres. In size, perhaps, but not in quality. The wines here have a particularly energetic and aerial expression. Owner Cédric Guillaume-Corbin puts it down to the biodynamic viticulture. It was his decision to follow this approach that led him to pull out of the local cave cooperative and follow his own path. 'I don't regret it at all!' he beams, though he admits learning to make and market his wines was a challenge. Increasingly he co-plants so-called 'accessory' varieties such as Carignan, Cinsault and Clairette in with his parcels of Grenache, Syrah and Mourvèdre – he compares his different blocks to classrooms filled with complementary personalities. All new plantings are now in *gobelet,* which he believes gives better quality wines with better balance from longer-living vines. And he's one of the nicest guys you could ever hope to meet.

Domaine Vallot – Le Coriançon
Vinsobres
www.domainevallot.com

If there's one producer that consistently impresses me during blind tastings of Vinsobres, it's Domaine Vallot. The family domaine, established over 100 years ago, is now managed by François Vallot. He is assisted by his daughter Anaïs Vallot, who is also co-president of the Comité des Vignerons de Vinsobres, which benefits hugely from her energy and enthusiasm. The estate is biodynamically farmed and stretches over 30 hectares. The Vinsobres Le Haut des Côtes *rouge* is particularly fine, a perfectly classic example. The Vinsobres L'Exception is concentrated and polished.

Other good examples
Château MontPlaisir and **Domaine Serre Besson** are two new estates already making very good wines, and the first vintage of **Château de Rouanne** under the new ownership of Louis Barruol looks promising. **Domaine l'Ancienne École** and **Domaine Constant-Duquesnoy** are two other reliable names with enviable holdings on the Plateau. **Domaine de Montine** makes a relatively light but highly drinkable Vinsobres, and the Cuvée ++ of **Domaine du Moulin** can be good. **Le Cellier des Dauphins** deserves a mention for its cuvée, widely found in UK supermarkets, that is true to style and good value for money. It sources some wines from local cave cooperative **La Vinsobraise**, a very good cooperative that doesn't shy away from Vinsobres' arcane structure. The unoaked Diamant Noir has good typicity and is very inexpensive (€6.95 direct from the co-op at time of writing). **Domaine Gramenon** La Papesse and Contre Couleur are sometimes granted the appellation, sometimes not, so they are occasionally bottled under AOC Côtes-du-Rhône. Either way, they are thrilling wines.

SAINT-MAURICE

Sandwiched between Vinsobres to its east and Visan to its west is the tiny appellation of Saint-Maurice. It's a diminutive patch of vineyard land with an unremarkable village at its foot, punctured by the D94.

There are only two private domaines to make wine under this appellation. The larger, with 15 hectares, is Domaine la Florane in Visan. The smaller, with 2 hectares, is Domaine Chaume-Arnaud in Vinsobres. It was winemaker Thibaud Chaume's great-grandfather, in fact, who co-founded the cooperative Cave des Coteaux Saint-Maurice, the third and final producer to bottle any Saint-Maurice. One private domaine is situated within the commune boundaries but it dropped out of the appellation altogether in 2013 to produce Vin de France (see Domaine Viret, page 163).

Saint-Maurice is the central south- and south-east-facing section of the Visan Valréas hills. Drive to the top and the land becomes increasingly rumpled and hilly, riven with deep valleys providing multiple different exposures and shadowy corners among the woods. The soils are fairly constant – extremely stony on the surface, with red and brown clays underneath, all on top of deep, pebbly limestone marls. In terms of terroir, 'Saint-Maurice is much closer to Vinsobres than Visan,' says Adrien Fabre of Domain la Florane. He points out that Visan has more clay in the soil, less limestone, and is earlier ripening. Saint-Maurice is a more austere, late-ripening site, which explains why he grows more Syrah here. He likes this terroir as it delivers wines with a naturally low pH. The problem? 'When I serve the wine at tastings, no-one's heard of it,' says Fabre. 'Same here,' agrees Chaume, 'but it brings something to the range, and it is different, it has its own identity.'

Appellation: AOC Côtes-du-Rhône Villages Saint-Maurice
Birth of the appellation: 1967
Communes: Saint-Maurice
Total surface area sold under the AOC in 2019: 159 hectares
Average yield in 2019: 37 hectolitres per hectare
Colours permitted: red, rosé, white
Production in 2019: 87 per cent red, 2 per cent rosé, 11 per cent white
Grape varieties permitted: As per communal Côtes-du-Rhône Villages regulations (see page 54)

The more individual winemakers there are for a defined vineyard area, the more confident you can be when attributing a *goût de terroir*. When there are very few, it's hard to know what originates from the land and what is accentuated (or concealed) by the winemaker. But on tasting the few Saint-Maurice wines that exist, I would say that the style of both red and white wine here is upright and fresh, with a certain straightness, marked tangy acidity and gentle tension – along with slightly dusty, fine-sand tannins in the reds. I've no doubt it's possible to make excellent wine here, in a style close to Vinsobres – and if anything, even more straight and tense. 'I hope that one day it gets recognized for its quality,' says Fabre. With so few producers and lacking any private estates within the commune that bottle wine under the appellation, this will be an uphill struggle. But like so many of the smallest appellations in the Rhône, these are wines with character and interest that could one day beckon others to set up here – particularly if the climate continues to warm.

Key producers

Domaine Viret

Saint-Maurice

www.domaine-viret.com

There is only one private domaine based within the appellation of Côtes-du-Rhône Villages Saint-Maurice, and that's Domaine Viret. As mentioned above, they now bottle their wine under Vin de France rather than the appellation. Despite this, they demand a mention. The question is where to start: the circular planting? The man-made menhirs? The dowsing with rods to locate water and telluric currents? You could write a book on their approach. In fact, that's what Alain Viret, now in his seventies, is currently working on – a treatise on his unique approach to viticulture which he terms Cosmoculture®.

The essentials are as follows: these are natural wines, so they're organically grown, hand-picked, vinified without additions, with very low doses of sulphites and bottled unfined and unfiltered. The approach draws on biodynamics, geobiology, radionics, homeopathy and the use of strategically placed stone menhirs that work as a kind of acupuncture for the earth. It is inspired by ancient civilizations. The gravity-fed cathedral of a winery is built according to local energetic frequencies and the rising and setting of the sun. Vinification with natural yeasts takes place in various vessels, including amphorae (Philippe Viret claims to be the first in France to use them for fermentation in recent times), small porcelain spheres, more conventional wooden barrels of various sizes and stainless-steel tanks.

The domaine now covers 35 hectares in a single block around the winery and farmhouse. The wines are defiantly natural in style and there are 20 different cuvées, running the gamut from 12% abv, gluggable lip-smackers to intense, thickly-textured, velvety reds; fresh white to orange wines. The Virets are constantly experimenting, and a visit to the domaine is dizzying. Alain was born in the farmhouse, but only started domaine-bottling when Philippe finished his oenology studies at Montpellier and made some microvinifications in his garage. The domaine was established in 1999; a tasting of their 1999 Colonnades shows a wine that's still full of life. The occult aspects of their approach won't be to everyone's taste, and neither will the wines, which aren't 'classically Rhône'. It's no surprise that they don't operate within the appellation framework. 'I felt like I couldn't evolve my domaine under these rules,' says Philippe. But these are fascinating wines, made to high standards, and some of the most singular in the Southern Rhône.

Other good examples

Domaine Chaume-Arnaud (see Vinsobres) and **Domaine la Florane** (see Visan) both make excellent red wines that are well worth buying. Chaume-Arnaud's is a little leaner and more aerial, la Florane's is more generous and concentrated, particularly the Guillaume de Rouville cuvée. The Guillaume de Rouville white, a blend of Grenache Blanc, Roussanne, Marsanne and Viognier planted at 400 metres altitude, is if anything even better – a remarkably Burgundian take on white Rhône. Of the bottlings from **Cave des Coteaux Saint-Maurice**, the oaked Grande Réserve is the best.

VISAN

Two Côtes du Rhône Villages sitting side by side in the northern part of the Southern Rhône, both beginning with the letter V, Visan and Valréas, are often mentioned in the same breath, but is this fair? Well, the terroir is largely similar and the wine style is certainly comparable. But, according to at least one winemaker, 'the two villages hate each other.' Just to add some fuel to the fire, I'd say that even though Visan wines have more instances of unbalanced alcohol, overall it's the more consistent appellation of the two.

With 10,000 inhabitants Valréas is more of a town, whereas Visan, 8 kilometres to its south-west, is a picturesque, sleepy village. There are some sandy soils around Visan itself, but there are really two main ter-roirs: the Garrigue and the Coteau. The Garrigue is an old alluvial ter-race, very stony, with sand and some welcome blue marls underneath. The majority of vines are planted here, but the best wines come from the Coteau, which rises to 400 metres. This hillside has a variety of ex-posures, from west to south to east. It's made up essentially of yellow marls and colluvial gravels with 'enormous amounts of clay, right to the top,' according to geologist Georges Truc, which means the vines rarely suffer from hydric stress. He says the terroir is in fact very similar to that of Rasteau and Cairanne – another pair of neighbouring appellations on a different hummock of clay limestone between two rivers.

Appellation: AOC Côtes-du-Rhône Villages Visan

Birth of the appellation: 1966

Communes: Visan

Total surface area sold under the AOC in 2019: 592 hectares

Average yield in 2019: 37 hectolitres per hectare

Colours permitted: red, rosé, white

Production in 2019: 93 per cent red, 3 per cent rosé, 4 per cent white

Grape varieties permitted: As per communal Côtes-du-Rhône Villages regu-lations (see page 54)

Wine production here was, until recently, entirely red and wholly con-trolled by the cooperative winery. Only in the 1980s did private estates start to emerge. Now there are over 30, and most work organically, wheth-er certified or not. They've helped to reveal the remarkable potential of the appellation, encouraged innovation and ushered in white and rosé pro-duction along with the reds. Although examples are relatively few, there are already some excellent non-red wines coming through, and I expect more will follow. As in Valréas and Vinsobres, a combination of northerly location, altitude and north wind brings a natural freshness to the wines. Stylistically neither Visan nor Valréas have the same straightness, tension and inner steel as Vinsobres. Compared to Valréas, Visan is perhaps a little more focused: the same flashlight, but twisted to a tighter beam. Both have a vibrancy and brightness that makes them a source of some beautifully drinkable wines. Adrien Fabre of Domaine la Florane says, 'it's fresher and cooler here than the south – it's the terroir of the future.'

Key producers

Domaine Dieu-le-Fit

La Baume de Transit

www.domainedieulefit.fr

You've heard of biodynamics, but have you heard of geobiology? It's a relatively young field of scientific study that explores the connections between the physical Earth and the biosphere. It's something that Rémi Pouzin has been studying with reference to wine. Originally from Visan, his family has been making wine organically since the 1960s. Though inspired by biodynamics, his wines are no longer certified as such, but he uses no additions in his winemaking except a little sulphite at bottling. He does however use pendulums and dowsing rods to help better understand his parcels. It sounds a little extreme, but Rémi is a down-to-earth character, and his wines are far from bizarre – they capture the freshness and energy of Visan fruit with great precision.

Domaine la Florane

Visan

www.domainelaflorane.com

One of the most exciting domaines of the Visan Valréas hills, Domaine la Florane makes wine in two appellations, Visan and St-Maurice. (Wines from St-Maurice were until recently bottled under the Domaine de l'Echevin label, but they've since been brought under Domaine la Florane.) After a *stage* at Harlan Estate in California, Adrien Fabre returned to work with his father François in 2007. The estate is now biodynamically farmed, and the impressive subterranean gravity-fed winery was finished in 2001. The Visan estate is one large south-facing block of 24 hectares of vines surrounded by woodland, and is one of the two highest domaines in the appellation. Unusually, 25 per cent of their production is white wine and 20 per cent is rosé. 'In the past six or seven years we've really changed our style,' says Adrien, 'less ripe and less extracted to go back and find freshness.' The whole team now is aged under 40, and he says, 'we're just at the beginning.' The energy is palpable and the wines are going from strength to strength.

Vignoble Art Mas

Visan

www.artmas.fr

The south-facing vineyards of old-vine *gobelets* on the Visan Coteau are farmed organically – you couldn't hope for much more really. Xavier Combe's father took the fruit to the local co-op, but when he returned to the domaine in 2009, Xavier started bottling his own. He now farms the vineyards according to biodynamic principles and hand-picks the fruit. He's currently planting more white varieties (he's a big fan of Bourboulenc) and every year he makes a one-off experimental cuvée. A winemaker brimming with ideas and creativity.

Other good examples

The organic **Domaine Coste Chaude** has historically been an outstanding estate and is home to some of the highest terroirs of the appellation. It was bought in 2018 by Vincent Tramier, a solicitor who recently retrained as winemaker – one to keep an eye on. The organic **Au 7ième Clos** make red and white wines with a lifted freshness that really speaks of Visan. Biodynamic **Domaine Roche-Audran** (see Vaison-la-Romaine) is very good, and **Domaine de la Bastide** can also be a source of interesting wine. **Cave les Coteaux** is certainly worth a look, particularly the Visan Rouge Grande Réserve Bio, which is consistently one of the best co-op produced red wines in the Southern Rhône.

VALRÉAS

If you climb to the top of the Visan Valréas hills and look north, you'll see vineyards of Valréas spreading all the way to the foot of the Massif de la Lance mountain range 10 kilometres away. These mountains curve around from north to east, and represent the natural border of the Côtes-du-Rhône. It feels a little greener and less dusty in this far-flung cul-de-sac compared to the Rhône's southern reaches. It may be an hour's drive from Châteauneuf, but don't miss it off the itinerary: the best reds of Valréas offer a compelling combination of vibrancy, drinkability and value for money.

When Valréas was granted its communal appellation in 1967 the growing area covered the entire commune. Studies carried out by the *syndicat* have identified five distinct zones: it's an extensive, complex terroir. The largest section equates to a low alluvial terrace (the Basses

Terrasses) which is accompanied by a smaller, slightly elevated one (the Moyennes Terrasses). Both are flat, pebbly and dry; the lower one is extremely stony, with cement-like compacted layers of rock which stop roots in their tracks. The wines from these terroirs tend to be fruity if sometimes lacking in structure and interest. As you travel south towards the Visan Valréas hills, the land begins to rise, with banks of sand and rolling hummocks of marl, eventually rising to the Massif de la Côte, a higher altitude (250–400 metres) undulating ridge with interspersed vineyards and woods. Soils are mostly stony marls, the terroir here is fresher, with a variety of different exposures, including some north-facing sites. The wines here are more purposeful and attention-grabbing.

Michèle Aubéry-Laurent of Domaine Gramenon praises Valréas' 'strength, energy and incredible acidity'. Grenache as usual leads the way, with a little more Syrah than its southern neighbours, a little less Mourvèdre, and not much Carignan. The white wines are yet to hit their stride, but I have no doubt they eventually will. And although there are many good reds, it feels like Valréas has more to give. As an appellation, it suffers from a lack of visibility and renown. Both large and small producers often find it easier to declassify their wines and sell them as Côtes-du-Rhône. Not many négociants have taken an interest, and it doesn't have the same tourist appeal as the Luberon or the Ardèche. Emmanuel Bouchard of Domaine du Val des Rois says 'we have the potential to be a *cru* in quality, but we need a common will to do it.' In the meantime, it remains an overachieving Named Village.

Appellation: AOC Côtes-du-Rhône Villages Valréas
Birth of the appellation: 1967
Communes: Valréas
Total surface area sold under the AOC in 2019: 557 hectares
Average yield in 2019: 37 hectolitres per hectare
Colours permitted: red, rosé, white
Production in 2019: 98 per cent red, 0 per cent rosé, 2 per cent white
Grape varieties permitted: As per communal Côtes-du-Rhône Villages regulations (see page 54)

Key producers

Clos Bellane

Valréas

www.clos-bellane.com

When Stéphane Vedeau bought the 48-hectare Clos Petite Bellane in 2010, he changed the name to Clos Bellane – 'less is more', he says. The wines were good; now they are outstanding. Les Echallas proves just how successful pure Syrah from this high altitude, northerly spot can be. His Pureté 400 is even better, a soaring expression of unblended Southern Rhône Grenache. Verdeau's négociant arm, La Ferme du Mont, is also worth knowing about – a reliable source of expressive Southern Rhône wines from around the region.

Domaine Gramenon

Montbrizon-sur-Lez

www.domaine-gramenon.fr

Michèle Aubéry-Laurent was a 19-year-old nurse when she married Philippe Laurent. Together they bought a half-ruined house and some ancient Grenache vineyards in Montbrizon-sur-Lez, 5 kilometres north-east of Valréas, in 1978. In 1990, Philippe died. Michèle took over the estate, and continued to make wine to support herself and their three children. One of her sons, Maxime-François, now works alongside her, and he also runs the négociant side of the business, which bears his name. They have always been organic, and converted to biodynamics in 2010. Sometimes Michèle uses a minimal addition of sulphites; sometimes none. She now has 4.5 hectares of Vinsobres, 5 hectares of Valréas, and a further 15 hectares of vineyards, mostly in Côtes-du-Rhône. Hand-harvesting, low yields, natural yeasts and partial destemming are typical for the reds, most of which are fermented in concrete, and matured in concrete or old barrels. Most of her wines are pure Grenache, some parcels of which are over 120 years old. These are intensely concentrated wines of extraordinary energy and impact, wines of incredibe purity, among the most enthralling expressions of Grenache and Syrah in the Southern Rhône.

Domaine Grande Bellane

Valréas

www.grandebellane.com

Next door to Clos Bellane, Domaine Grande Bellane is also worth a stop. It was established in 1919 and Damien Marres' great-grandfather built the tanks, fetching gravel from the edge of the river by horse and cart. Today, the organic estate comprises a 55-hectare block of wines at the summit of the appellation.

Domaine des Grands Devers

Valréas

www.grandsdevers.com

Run by the four Bouchard brothers, Domaine des Grands Devers is situated on the border between Visan and Valréas, and wines are bottled under both appellations. The Valréas is particularly interesting, deliberately made in an old-fashioned way that gives it a very peculiar character. The Grenache is hand-harvested as whole bunches and fermented by semi-carbonic maceration (instead of flushing the tanks with carbon dioxide, it is gradually released by the fermenting berries). The 28 per cent Syrah component is harvested by machine, crushed and destemmed before a traditional fermentation in concrete. The intensely structured wine has complex aromas of elderberry, bay leaf, white pepper and juniper. The texture is similarly detailed: a wine with real interest.

Domaine du Séminaire

Valréas

domaine-du-seminaire.fr

An estate of 40 hectares in one block to the east of Valréas, Domaine du Séminaire was established in 1925 and is now in the hands of the fourth generation of the Pouizin family. The vineyards stretch from 300 to 400 metres altitude and the freshness is evident in the wines. They still use the concrete fermenters built in 1938 for the long, slow vinifications of their reds. Their Valréas cuvées are very good, and their Côtes-du-Rhônes – also from Valréas terroirs – offer unbeatable value for money.

Other good examples

Also situated at altitude, **Domaine du Val des Rois** and **Mas de Sainte Croix** make some fresh and classically-styled Valréas cuvées.

10

MOUNTAIN FRINGES

SAINT-PANTALÉON-LES-VIGNES AND ROUSSET-LES-VIGNES

Of all the ten zones of the Southern Rhône, this is the smallest, and currently the least commercially important. It comprises a few small appellations that skirt along the mountain fringes of the far north and north-east of the Southern Rhône: Saint-Pantaléon-les-Vignes, Rousset-les-Vignes, Nyons and Puyméras. Parts of Grignan-les-Adhémar can be added to this zone too. They share a freshness, lightness and high acidity, along with a relative lack of depth and richness.

As you drive through the low sprawl of the town of Valréas on the way to Saint-Pantaléon-les-Vignes, the Massif de la Lance mountains come into view. That's it; you've reached the edge of the Côtes-du-Rhône growing area. The Montagne de Lance is the highest peak at 1,338 metres, but each one of these triangular peaks has a name: the Oure, the Tison, the Corbieu. They lend a dramatic backdrop to the two furthest north of the Côtes-du-Rhône Named Villages. Both villages are suffixed with 'the vines' as if to say 'don't forget about us' – and with any fewer producers bottling wine under these appellations, they really could drop off the map. Apart from the Cave Saint-Pantaléon-les-Vignes which bottles a little of both appellations, there is currently just one private domaine bottling AOC Côtes-du-Rhône Villages Saint-Pantaléon-les-Vignes (Domaine Gigondan) and two bottling AOC Côtes-du-Rhône Villages Rousset-les-Vignes (Domaine la Bouvade and Domaine la Banate). Both villages are tiny. 'Historically we've always worked together in a lot of ways,' says Philippe Barral, who delivers his grapes to the co-op. 'We each have our own *mairie* but we share a school for example. People often have parcels in both appellations, and both villages were given the appellation on the same day – 18 March 1969.'

The appellations are neighbours and share similar terroir. Both are elevated for the Southern Rhône; the vineyards of Saint-Pantaléon sit at between 300 and 420 metres altitude, whereas Rousset's are a little higher up, between 350 and 450 metres, with the village itself tucked into a niche in the foothills. The mountains have a freshening influence on both. They pick late here, typically 12 days later than at Sainte-Cécile, says Barral, and Bruno Gigondan at Domaine Gigondan picked his 2019 vintage (a very hot year) as late as 19 October.

Most growers concentrate on Grenache and Syrah for reds, with later-ripening varieties like Mourvèdre being relatively rare but increasing in popularity. 'Before, our wines had more marked acidity and we were penalized for it in tastings compared to other appellations,' says Barral. 'But with climate change, we have better balanced wines.' A penetrating natural acidity remains the calling card of both appellations (all producers baulk at the idea of adding tartaric) which helps these wines endure a decade in bottle with ease. Despite this strong natural acidity, whites and rosés are very rare; growers say there is no demand, so there's no immediate benefit in investing in the expensive additional equipment required, such as pneumatic presses.

The main element of terroir that distinguishes the two appellations is their soils. In Saint-Pantaléon-les-Vignes the soils are composed of brown and blue marls with a high proportion of clay and small white pebbles, all on a sandstone bedrock. In Rousset-les-Vignes, the sandstone comes up to the surface where it decomposes into sand, and has far fewer pebbles. This lends the wines of Saint-Pantaléon a richer, rounder mouthfeel, whereas the wines of Rousset tend to be a little finer and paler in colour. Along with Puyméras, the twin appellations of Saint-Pantaléon-les-Vignes and Rousset-les-Vignes represent the mountain tribes of the Southern Côtes-du-Rhône, producing wines with freshness, a natural lightness of expression and bright acidity that was once a weakness in the face of the rich, ripe wines of the *crus* further south. Though they lack the profundity of a good Châteauneuf-du-Pape, these wines do enjoy their own local character – and as the climate heats up, they may have the last laugh.

Saint-Pantaléon-les-Vignes

Appellation: AOC Côtes-du-Rhône Villages Saint-Pantaléon-les-Vignes

Birth of the appellation: 1969

Communes: Saint-Pantaléon-les-Vignes

Total surface area sold under the AOC in 2019: 29 hectares

Average yield in 2019: 40 hectolitres per hectare

Colours permitted: red, rosé, white

Production in 2019: 100 per cent red, 0 per cent rosé, 0 per cent white

Grape varieties permitted: As per communal Côtes-du-Rhône Villages regulations (see page 54)

Rousset-les-Vignes

Appellation: AOC Côtes-du-Rhône Villages Rousset-les-Vignes

Birth of the appellation: 1969

Communes: Rousset-les-Vignes

Total surface area sold under the AOC in 2019: 21 hectares

Average yield in 2019: 39 hectolitres per hectare

Colours permitted: red, rosé, white

Production in 2019: 99 per cent red, 0 per cent rosé, 1 per cent white

Grape varieties permitted: As per communal Côtes-du-Rhône Villages regulations (see page 54)

Key producers

Domaine la Banate

Rousset-les-Vignes

www.labanate.fr

Belgian wine lover Jean T'Kint worked in plastic injection moulding until he could finally afford to fully focus on his true passion. He finally bought a vineyard in 2011, 4 hectares of 60-year-old Grenache and Syrah vines in Rousset-les-Vignes. It's essentially a retirement project, albeit a very active one – and the results are serious. He immediately turned the estate organic, growing grapes 'as organically as possible, with the most respect for nature possible,' he says. He makes no additions during the winemaking process, apart from 30 milligrams per litre of sulphites at bottling. He makes one red wine, harvested by hand, and releases it late (he was selling the 2014 in 2019). It's a detailed, vibrant, upright and highly drinkable wine with the tell-tale piquancy of the appellation, which shows what can be achieved in this corner of the Rhône with love and attention to detail.

Other good examples

The other private domaine in Rousset-les-Vignes is **Domaine la Bouvade**, a 17-hectare estate making several red and white cuvées in the appellation, all displaying characteristic fresh acidity. **Domaine Gigondan** is the only private domaine bottling AOC Saint-Pantaléon-les-Vignes, and theirs is a riper, oakier style. The **Cave Saint-Pantaléon-les-Vignes**, which bottles wines under the **Les Vignerons de Valléon** brand, is small for a cooperative, with just 120 members. It bottles vibrant wines under both appellations, and the quality is impressive.

NYONS

On 15 October 2020, the twenty-second Named Village was inaugurated: Côtes-du-Rhône Villages Nyons. The town of Nyons lies in the far north-east of the Southern Rhône, at the frontier of the Baronnies mountain range. It straddles the river Aigues where it's ejected from the alpine foothills on its way to the Rhône. The growing area skirts around the edge of the Baronnies northwards from Nyons via Venterol until it reaches a border with the growing area of Saint-Pantaléon-les-Vignes; it also follows the Baronnies southwards via Mirabel-aux-Baronnies and Piégon to Puyméras.

This newest appellation in the Rhône has been two decades in the making; local winemakers first applied in 1988. 'The dossier was presented several times,' says president of the appellation Pierre-Michel More, 'but on each occasion, there was a little detail that we needed to work on.' The main sticking point, it seems, was the over-reliance on Grenache, so local vignerons planted more Syrah in response. They also grow some Mourvèdre here, but little else. The appellation is for still, dry, reds only. The soils are clay limestone, with some colluvial limestone pebbles, with hillside vineyards rising to 300 metres altitude. The relatively high diurnal temperature differences here 'bring a freshness to our wines,' says More.

In the past I've enjoyed Côtes-du-Rhône Villages reds from this area, which have often displayed vibrancy and precision, not terribly concentrated, but fuller-bodied than a typical Puyméras. Since the first wines to be labelled Côtes-du-Rhône Villages Nyons will be from the 2020 vintage, released in spring/summer 2021, I can't yet talk about the style of wine from this new appellation with any certainty. I'm told that four cooperatives and a dozen private domaines intend to make wine under the appellation. Nyons has long been associated with other Mediterranean products; it was the first AOC in Europe granted for olives in 1994. Now its wine has a chance to shine too.

Appellation: AOC Côtes-du-Rhône Villages Nyons

Birth of the appellation: 2020

Communes: Mirabel-aux-Baronnies, Nyons, Piégon, Venterol

Total surface area sold under the AOC in 2019: Not yet in production

Average yield in 2019: Not yet in production

Colours permitted: red only

Grape varieties permitted: As per communal Côtes-du-Rhône-Villages regulations (see page 54)

PUYMÉRAS

For a small, sleepy village, the bar on the main road through Puyméras is remarkably busy during the week. The ancient buildings that make up the heart of the village scale a hill and they've been rebuilt on top of each other for centuries. Stroll along the lower alleyways and you can peer through wooden doors that hang open, revealing their foundations inside, like the hollow trunks of old oaks. The inhabited floors at street level are sunny and spotless. It's the kind of place you might imagine yourself retiring to one day.

It's one of five picturesque villages that make up the Puyméras appellation, dotted over a dramatic, contrasting scenery that becomes increasingly mountainous as it stretches towards the Baronnies to the east. The cool air currents that tumble down from the mountains bring a significant chill in the evenings even during summer, and they harvest later than the neighbouring appellations. There is less mistral than average, and more rain. Until fairly recently this was a terroir more suited to vegetable-growing than wine. The appellation is spread out over a series of plateaux at the feet of the Baronnies, between 200 and 400 metres altitude. Soils vary, most are very stony, either *galets roulés* or colluvial limestone pebbles, usually accompanied by red clay and sand. Around Faucon the soils are sandier still.

The Named Village appellation was put in place in 2005, and now there are half a dozen private domaines and two cooperative wineries bottling a Puyméras. Despite the freshness of this mountainous corner of the Rhône, they only applied for an appellation for red wines since there was so little white planted at the time. Perhaps this will change in time, as the whites from this area can be very good. Though Grenache is the principal grape, there is a lot of Syrah planted, in an attempt to darken the colour and bring down overall alcohol levels. The wines are light- to medium-bodied, more often transparent than opaque. Acidulated and raspberry-fruited, their current incarnations are often fresh and lively, but rarely deep, long or resonant. They are best drunk young and fresh, lightly chilled.

Local growers estimate that around 30 per cent of the vineyard area is organic. There are two outstanding natural wine estates near Faucon – Domaine Houillon and La Roche Buissière – and although they don't currently bottle any AOC Puyméras, they're certainly worth knowing about. This land feels like something of a new frontier, and there is undoubtedly potential here, but perhaps there is more work to be done until this is fully realized. It's early days for Puyméras, but in the coming years I suspect it will be the source of some very interesting wines.

Appellation: AOC Côtes-du-Rhône Villages Puyméras
Birth of the appellation: 2005
Communes: Faucon, Mérindol-les-Oliviers, Mollans-sur-Ouvèze, Puyméras, Saint-Romain-en-Viennois
Total surface area sold under the AOC in 2019: 153 hectares
Average yield in 2019: 40 hectolitres per hectare
Colours permitted: red only
Grape varieties permitted: As per communal Côtes-du-Rhône Villages regulations (see page 54)

Key producers

La Roche Buissière

Faucon

www.larochebuissiere.fr

Pierre Joly was one of several local vignerons who decided to start grow-ing organically in the 1980s. 'They thought we were mad!' he says, given the extra work it involves. He now bottles his own wine, and has 17 hec-tares of vines across various AOC Côtes-du-Rhône and Côtes-du-Rhône Villages plots, and was just planting within AOC Puyméras when we spoke in 2019. The reds range from very light Grenaches (Prémices has just a few days of maceration) to more structured Syrahs, not to men-tion an excellent rosé. They use no additions, yeasts or sulphites during vinification, do not fine or filter and sometimes bottle without adding any sulphites at all. The wines are lively, crunchy, drinkable and great value for money.

Domaine Saint-Apollinaire

Puyméras

T.: +33 (0) 4 90 46 41 09

Domaine Saint-Apollinaire lies just outside the village of Puyméras. Remarkably, this 12-hectare estate has been farming organically since 1967. Grapes are hand-harvested and the wines are currently made by Elodie Daumas without using any additives. Her wines – bottled under AOC Côtes-du-Rhône – may not necessarily appear the most 'correct' to some tastes, but I believe they're among the deepest and most char-acterful in the area.

Other good examples

Domaine le Puy de Maupas, **Domaine de Combebelle** and **Domaine Faucon Doré** are good options. Although their offering is mixed, the occasional cuvée from **Cave la Comtadine** can be good, such as their Domaine Jas des Rouves. Natural wine enthusiasts should make a bee-line for the newly established **Domaine Houillon**, near Faucon, bot-tling under Vin de France. The name might be familiar to lovers of Jura wines; Aurélien is the brother of Emmanuel and Adeline Houillon, and all three worked alongside Pierre Overnoy in Arbois. A tasting of their inaugural vintage shows real promise.

GRIGNAN-LES-ADHÉMAR

Appellation: AOC Grignan-les-Adhémar
Birth of the appellation: 1973
Communes: Allan, La Baume-de-Transit, Chamaret, Chantemerle-lès-Grignan, Châteauneuf-du-Rhône, Clansayes, Colonselle, Donzère, La Garde-Adhémar, Les Granges-Gontardes, Grignan, Malataverne, Montségur-sur-Lauzon, Réauville, La Roche-Saint-Secret-Béconne, Roussas, Saint-Paul-Trois-Châteaux, Saint-Restitut, Salles-sous-Bois, Solérieux, Valaurie.
Total surface area sold under the AOC in 2019: 1,318 hectares
Average yield in 2019: 39 hectolitres per hectare
Colours permitted: red, rosé, white
Production in 2019: 75 per cent red, 14 per cent rosé, 11 per cent white
Grape varieties permitted. Reds must contain a majority of Grenache and/or Syrah. May also include Bourboulenc, Carignan, Cinsault, Clairette Blanche, Grenache Blanc, Marsanne, Marselan, Mourvèdre, Roussanne and Viognier. White varieties may contribute up to 10 per cent of the blend.
   Rosés: as for reds, except white varieties may contribute up to 20 per cent of the blend.
   Whites may include the following: Bourboulenc, Clairette Blanche, Grenache Blanc, Marsanne, Roussanne and Viognier. Bourboulenc and/or Clairette Blanche may make up no more than 50 per cent of the blend.

Grignan-les-Adhémar reaches further north than any other Southern Rhône appellation. It is a neck that connects the head of Lyon and the heart of Provence, with vital arteries running through it: the A7 motorway, railways, chains of pylons – the Rhône itself. Landmarks include the Lafarge concrete works and the Tricastin nuclear power plant – this appellation was previously called Coteaux du Tricastin, but it changed its name in 2010 (more on this later). Much of this infrastructure lies close to the Rhône river, which marks the appellation's western boundary. It covers 21 communes, however, so there is plenty more attractive terroir to explore. Away from this industrial corridor, the countryside becomes hilly, then pastoral, more generically Rhône.

This hasn't always been an area known for its viticulture, and it remains far from monocultural; there are more hectares of truffle oak plantations here than vineyards. Henri Bour of Domaine de Grangeneuve says that when his father arrived in 1964 there was only 350 hectares under vine in the region, and none of the local polyculture farmsteads focused entirely on wine. Bour's father, also called Henri, was one of the Pieds-Noirs who returned to France after the Algerian War of Independence (1954–62). Identifying the untapped potential of the terroir, he started ripping out woodland and planting vines, originally to the bemusement of local farmers. By the end of the 1960s, there were six major domaines run by Pieds-Noirs; Domaine de Grangeneuve is the only one that remains in the same family. Today there are eight cave cooperatives and over 30 private domaines.

It's a large terrain and the soils vary. Close to the Rhône you can find sandy clay limestone and *galets roulés*; the northern half is hilly, with more clay limestone, marls and alluvions; further south the soils are dry, gravelly *garrigue*. There is also a small separate island of AOC land tucked away at 350 metres altitude in the Massif de la Lance, to the north of Rousset-les-Vignes, around the village of La Roche-Saint-Secret-Béconne. 'We're equatorial Rhône Valley,' says Vincent Bouyer, winemaker at Château Bizard in the northern part of the appellation. 'Of course the climate is Mediterranean, but we're at the crossroads of continental, alpine and Mediterranean influence.' He points out that the scenery is greener here than further south. Bour says that one of Grignan-les-Adhémar's unique characteristics is the quantity of classically Northern Rhône grapes grown here; Syrah makes up over a third of plantings and Viognier over half. But with Duché d'Uzès following a similar *nordiste* varietal path this is no longer so special. Some growers describe the style here as between Northern and Southern Rhône, but beside a varietal twang, any further Northern Rhône inflection is hard to perceive.

Reds are made mostly from Grenache, Syrah or both – monovarietal wines are permitted here in all colours. There's not much in the way of later ripening varieties such as Mourvèdre and Carignan. Bouyer says that even Grenache wouldn't always reliably ripen here in the past, but today that's no longer an issue. White varieties are planted widely; wines are typically blends of Viognier and Grenache Blanc and range from the early-picked and restrained, to the ripe and exotic, occasionally fermented and matured in oak. But what is the style of Grignan? Not so long ago it was reflective of the landscape – generic Rhône, with an industrial side. It's difficult to describe the attributes of a classic Grignan, if such a thing really exists; as it stands, it's easier to describe what Grignan is not. But quality has been improving of late, corresponding with the appellation's change of name.

It was in 2008 that the local Tricastin nuclear power plant suffered a series of safety incidents. They were minor, but nonetheless the name Tricastin became tainted by association and sales of the local wines were affected. 'It penalized our production, and affected our morale,' says Bour. At that time, he says, the wines were typically very cheap and quality was mediocre. As president of the appellation, he saw an opportunity – not only to change the name, but also to improve quality. Along with the name change, they applied to the INAO to further tighten official quality criteria: producers had to grow at least 30 per cent Syrah amongst red varieties and 30 per cent Viognier amongst whites, maximum yields were reduced and all wines needed to pass an independent tasting assessment. At the time it was hard to find much enthusiasm for the new moniker. Grignan-les-Adhémar was chosen to invoke the ornate town of Grignan and the historic Adhémar family and their links to literature and the nobility. But if you're not familiar with either and don't speak the language it's just an unwieldy gargle of French.

Whatever you think of the name, quality is better than ever and the market bears witness to this: the average price of wine *en vrac* increased substantially between 2008 and 2019. But despite this, identifying a unique *goût de terroir* remains elusive. As it stands, quality viticulture, well-equipped wineries and proficient winemaking is what makes the best wines stand out. This may explain why there have been few new break-out domaines here that have lasted the course. But Tricastin always was – and Grignan-les-Adhémar is – a source of restrained, good value Rhône varieties.

Key producers

Château Bizard

Allan

www.chateaubizard.fr

The handsome Château Bizard has a row of 350-year-old mulberry trees. Their fruit was once used to feed the silkworms farmed here until they were wiped out by a disease that crippled the industry in 1861. The then-owners converted the estate to vineyards in 1862. In 1863 they were hit by phylloxera. Definitely a tough few years. Thankfully, successive owners have persevered, and the estate now makes well-made, polished wines from 20 hectares of vines, a quarter of which are white.

Having worked in Rioja, winemaker Vincent Bouyer has added a few American oak barrels to their stock of French, which bring a subtle but distinctive mark to their wines. Their Grenache-based fortified wine is another point of interest – not to mention their original huge cement tank which has since been converted into a chapel.

Domaine de Grangeneuve

Roussas

domainesbour.com

'Since the start,' says Henri Bour, 'we focused on quality. That is how we survived.' Though he has worked this estate for decades, Bour is not content to rest on his laurels. It is considered by many to be the best estate in Grignan-les-Adhémar, and he has recently invested €1 million in new facilities, and has just achieved HVE certification.[3] The estate has now amassed 82 hectares of vines, including 13 hectares of whites and 15 hectares of organic vineyards. While Bour was president of the appellation, this obsession with quality pulled up standards more widely. The reds here don't reflect his forceful personality – they are gently aromatic, measured in structure and extraction. If there's one wine which most characterizes Grignan-les-Adhémar, it's his 50:50 Grenache–Syrah cuvée La Truffière. His Viognier-based whites proudly and successfully embrace the variety's flamboyant personality.

Domaine de Montine

Grignan

www.domaine-de-montine.com

Have you ever tried to set up a new name for an email or social media account to find it's already been taken? Well the Monteillet family had a similar problem, with Domaine de Monteillet having already been nabbed by the Côte-Rôtie estate owned by Stéphane Montez. So, after pulling out of the local cooperative in 1987, Jean-Luc and Claudy Monteillet named their nascent domaine after a hill nearby that was home to the local water tower. It has since grown to 73 hectares, including a slice of AOC Vinsobres. Mélina Monteillet likes Grignan-les-Adhémar as it gives wines that are 'rich but elegant, and very drinkable.' A style they've embraced at Domaine de Montine.

---

3 'Haute Valeur Environnementale' is a voluntary French environmental certification scheme for farms, based on four criteria: biodiversity, conservation, water management and responsible use of fertilizers.

Domaine du Serre des Vignes
La Roche Saint Secret

serredesvignes.com

Tucked away in the little enclave of La Roche Saint Secret, Domaine du Serre des Vignes is one of the most remote wineries in the Southern Rhône, even further north than Rousset-les-Vignes. The cool microclimate is dominated by the Massif de la Lance mountain range, but vines are grown on slopes with good exposure to the sun. These are wines with balance, freshness and aromatic detail that underline yet again that this far north-eastern corner of the Southern Rhône is increasingly an area to watch. The old-vine cuvée Mas de Merlère offers startling value for money, as does the rosé.

Other good examples
Domaines André Aubert makes elegant, balanced and drinkable expressions in all three colours, and **Domaine Ferrotin** has a particularly characterful, light, low extraction style that's worth seeking out, especially the 100 per cent Grenache Vielles Vignes. Of négociant bottlings, the cuvée made by **Delas** is impressively reliable.

11

MASSIF D'UCHAUX AND SURROUNDING TERRACES

MASSIF D'UCHAUX

Massif d'Uchaux doesn't comfortably fit within any of the ten zones. Geologically and stylistically, it is unique. It really deserves a zone of its own, though it does share some terroir with Rochegude, an appellation that sits on its north-east flank and acts as something of a link between Massif d'Uchaux and the surrounding appellations of Suze-la-Rousse, Sainte-Cécile and beyond.

Of all the massifs that are key to understanding the wines of the Southern Rhône, the Massif d'Uchaux is the largest, but it has the smallest area under vine. The area gained its Named Village appellation in 2005, and covers parts of five communes. It's an island of forest surrounded by rivers: the Rhône to the west, the Lez to the north and the Aigues running around it to the east and south. Aside from Châteauneuf-du-Pape, which lies 18 kilometres due south, it's some of the closest vine-growing area to the Rhône on this side of the river.

At its centre, the appellation lacks landmark villages such as Cairanne and Rasteau on Ventabren, instead the growing area has a chain of small villages stationed around its perimeter, as if to shield the vineyards within. Once you've made your way onto the massif, the mountains that encircle the Southern Rhône and help you navigate are hidden by trees: you're lost. On arriving at Domaine la Cabotte, Eric Plumet greeted me with a cheery, 'you have to be brave to visit Massif d'Uchaux!'

> **Appellation**: AOC Côtes-du-Rhône Villages Massif d'Uchaux
> **Birth of the appellation**: 2005
> **Communes**: Lagarde-Paréol, Mondragon, Piolenc, Sérignan-du-Comtat, Uchaux
> **Total surface area sold under the AOC in 2019**: 212 hectares
> **Average yield in 2019**: 28 hectolitres per hectare
> **Colours permitted**: red only
> **Grape varieties permitted**: As per communal Côtes-du-Rhône Villages regulations (see page 54)

It might lack renown amongst wine lovers, but not for geologists and naturalists. The respected entomologist Jean-Henri Fabre lived in Sérignan-du-Comtat, and it's an area of particular geological interest. Note that the appellation is not simply named Uchaux after the nearby town of the same name, nor is it named after one of the constituent communes, but after the massif itself. Historically villagers have settled on the perimeter rather than the centre of massif since the farmland is more fertile and productive at the edges. The soils on the higher ground (up to 280 metres altitude) at the centre where the vineyards are concentrated today are particularly meagre, a trait that only a vigneron could find arousing. Unlike the surrounding soils that have been brought here by rivers, the vines in Massif d'Uchaux are planted directly into the bedrock. Yields are among the lowest in the Southern Rhône.

Small-scale family winemaking isn't new here, but winemaking estates only sprang up here after the Second World War with the arrival of heavy machinery; it takes more than a horse to break up and work this rocky terrain. These limestone and sandstone soils were laid down in the late Cretaceous Period and often only have a shallow layer of clay overlaid with angular yellowish limestone pebbles the size of your hand. They break when thrown, and glint with quartz within. Winemakers regularly find fossilized ammonites, sponges and coral among the stones. The soils aren't entirely homogeneous. Towards the east, the fragments of limestone get increasingly large, and you can walk across them like stepping-stones in the vineyard; you may also find outcrops of flint. Further south the pebbles become smaller, with red, white and yellow sands becoming more immediately visible, mixed in with clay. Vineyards are typically found on the south-facing slopes of hills, with various oaks and pines elsewhere, along with heather, juniper and rock rose.

The surrounding appellations of Suze-la-Rousse, Saint-Cécile, Rochegude, Plan de Dieu and Grignan-les-Adhémar all feature more recent free-draining alluvial terraces within their boundaries. Massif d'Uchaux does not. One of the benefits of this limestone and sandstone bedrock is that it soaks up water and releases it gradually, so the vines rarely suffer from lack of water. The woodland that covers 70 per cent of the appellation also helps retain a certain humidity. Irrigation is rare. The climate is a little cooler than in lower-lying villages. Plumet says that when he leaves Orange, it's usually a couple of degrees cooler when he arrives at the domaine. The pine trees rarely grow tall before they get blown down by the mistral; their roots can't penetrate deep enough to withstand it.

For such a diverse and savage terroir, it's great to see that more than half of the 16 private estates pursue organic or biodynamic viticulture. Despite some very good whites being grown on the terroir, the appellation only allows red wines, and there's an identifiable style here. Rather than a spoonful of berry coulis or stewed fruit, these are berries plucked from the bush. They don't lack weight or ripeness, but all the same they enjoy a gentle tension, upright and animated. They have a red-fruited perfume, often raspberry or wild strawberry. Rather than the tannic swell of *galets roulés*, the tannins here are finely pixelated.

Vineyards secreted in the woods and no emblematic centre – Massif d'Uchaux isn't as easy to define as, say, Gigondas. And to an American audience, the name may not appear terribly alluring. Plumet admits 'it's not that simple in terms of marketing.' But local winemakers understand its appeal; Louis Barruol cites it as a terroir of interest, and the Charavin family of Domaine des Coteaux des Travers is renovating a dilapidated estate here. It won't be long before the word gets out more widely: Massif d'Uchaux is a unique terroir with thrilling potential.

Key producers
Domaine la Cabotte
Mondragon
www.cabotte.com

A *cabotte* is a small vineyard hut in which Burgundian vignerons store their tools. Gabriel d'Ardhuy, owner of Domaine d'Ardhuy near Ladoix-Serrigny in the Côte de Beaune, often used to take holidays in the Rhône, and had long dreamed of owning vineyards there. When cycling across the Massif d'Uchaux he passed an estate that was for sale and bought it immediately. This was in 1981. He was joined by one of his seven daughters, Marie-Pierre, and together they replanted 20 hectares of vines. In 1986, they were joined by her husband Eric Plumet, and the estate now covers 30 hectares of Massif d'Uchaux and 1 hectare of Châteauneuf-du-Pape, all of which is farmed biodynamically. The two red Massif d'Uchaux cuvées have a natural balance and the freshness you'd expect from this lovely appellation.

Domaine Cros de la Mure

Mondragon

T.: +33 (0) 4 90 30 12 40

The last time I visited Eric Michel it was the day after his sixtieth birthday, and he still works his 28-hectare organic estate almost single-handedly. 'I don't like delegating,' he says, preferring to spend his days tending to his vines personally. He's an affable vigneron, modest and quick to laugh, and plays down his knowledge and achievements. But he's one of the most quietly influential vignerons in the Southern Rhône; even luminaries like Jérôme Bressy cite him as an inspiration.

Michel is based in the northern part of the appellation and has a number of parcels in Massif d'Uchaux, including some of the oldest vines, planted in 1960. His Côtes-du-Rhône *rouge* could be labelled AOC Côtes-du-Rhône Villages Massif d'Uchaux; it's a blend of different parcels, including around 25 per cent Syrah, which naturally gives yields of around 18 hectolitres per hectare. His Massif d'Uchaux is a parcel selection from his oldest vineyard, a blend of 75 per cent Grenache and 25 per cent Mourvèdre. He makes a particularly rich and unctuous dry white wine from Massif d'Uchaux terroir, labelled as Côtes-du-Rhône, which could only be from the Southern Rhône. His wines display the natural acidity and youthful tension that marks out Massif d'Uchaux, and he believes the best terroirs deserve to be elevated to *cru*. Taste his wines and it's hard to disagree. He also owns a small parcel in Gigondas (*lieu-dit* La Fouille et les Florets) and an even smaller one in Châteauneuf-du-Pape (*lieu-dit* Pignan).

He picks late, after the first rains of autumn, in order to wash the grapes and help them relax. Fermentations are very long; reds are vinified, then aged in concrete for 18 months 'to guard the purity of the fruit.' Whites are fermented and aged for 12 months in 450-litre and 600-litre oak barrels, using new oak only if barrels need replacing. 'You need to make a wine like you feel it in the vineyard,' he says, 'it needs to have a soul.' And they do.

Château de Fonsalette

Lagarde-Paréol

chateaurayas.fr

The smallest of the three estates owned by Emmanuel Reynaud of Château Rayas, Château de Fonsalette is 10 hectares of vines tucked away in woodland on the eastern edge of Massif d'Uchaux near Lagarde-Paréol. Naturally there is no sign, but you can see the small château from the road. The soils are ochre-coloured sands littered with small pebbles. Wines are however sold under the regional AOC Côtes-du-Rhône. The wines are vinified at Château Rayas: a red (50 per cent Grenache, 35 per cent Cinsault, 15 per cent Syrah), a white (80 per cent Grenache Blanc, 10 per cent Clairette, 10 per cent Marsanne) and occasionally a pure Syrah. The wines are very much in the Rayas vein, and also enjoy the fresh, upright nature of Massif d'Uchaux terroir. They are particularly fine and can age for ten to twenty years, or more in good vintages.

Le Mas de Casalas

Mondragon

www.lemasdecasalas.com

Jérôme Hue and Isabelle Supparo bought a house in Mondragon in 2004. Jérôme is a PE teacher, but they decided to make some wine with the 3 hectares of vines that came with the property – some planted as far back as 1922. 'Whenever I've been surprised during a tasting, it's been with a natural wine,' he says, so they immediately converted the estate to biodynamics and make wine in the natural spirit, using minimal sulphites, if any, at bottling. The Carignan-heavy Ma Reveuse is particularly animated and fresh with stunningly vibrant aromatics. Wines are bottled as Vin de France.

Other good examples

Vincent Baumet (see Rochegude) makes one of the best wines in the appellation. **Domaine de Dionysos**, **Domaine des Coteaux des Travers** and **Famille de Boel France** all make fine examples of Massif d'Uchaux with a good sense of typicity. **Château Simian** is inconsistent, but when on form the wines are excellent. **Château Saint-Estève d'Uchaux** is one of the first estates to establish itself on this terroir, and makes relatively punchy examples. The Richard family of Château la Nerthe bought the 51-hectare **Domaine de la Renjarde** in 1986 and it is now the source of their very good Les Cassagnes de la Nerthe range.

ROCHEGUDE

Appellation: AOC Côtes-du-Rhône Villages Rochegude
Birth of the appellation: 1967
Communes: Rochegude
Total surface area sold under the AOC in 2019: 154 hectares
Average yield in 2019: 36 hectolitres per hectare
Colours permitted: red, rosé, white

Production in 2019: 97 per cent red, 0 per cent rosé, 3 per cent white
Grape varieties permitted: As per communal Côtes-du-Rhône Villages regulations (see page 54)

Rochegude is the stepping stone that connects the Massif d'Uchaux to the surrounding terraces as it has vineyards spread across both. The village of Rochegude was built around the twelfth century Château de Rochegude, which sits on the north-east-facing slope of the massif. The appellation covers much of the commune of Rochegude that surrounds the village. There's sand and sandstone around the village itself and into the massif, and heavier clay at the foot of the village, but the largest part (around 70 per cent of the surface area) lies on the more recent alluvial *'garrigues'* terraces that it shares with neighbouring appellations Suze-la-Rousse and Sainte-Cécile.

The wines of Rochegude were once enjoyed by the likes of Thomas Jefferson, but today they are less renowned. A drive around the north of the village with local winemaker Vincent Baumet is instructive but sobering. The sandy vineyards are interspersed with woodland – look carefully among the trees and you can still see the drystone walls that would once have divided up parcels of vines. 'Now the trees have taken over,' he says. Closer to the village he points out several sites on sandstone soils that were once covered in vines, but have since been concreted over to build houses. 'There aren't enough vignerons with conviction,' he shrugs, 'they'd prefer to sell their land.' This loss of this terroir is permanent.

It's a shame, as the wines from the sandier soils have a distinct lightness and drinkability; those issuing from the *garrigues* are much more concentrated. Baumet believes having a choice of soil types to work with is a benefit, however, bringing complexity to the finished wines. Only a handful of producers bottle their wines under the appellation today, and although some of the wines are very good, Rochegude feels dormant considering its former prominence. Perhaps one day it will rise again.

Key producers

Vincent Baumet

Rochegude

T.: +33 (0) 6 80 44 04 36

There is no better way to understand Massif d'Uchaux and its surrounding appellations than visiting Vincent Baumet in Rochegude. He works 40 hectares of organic vineyards in and around Massif d'Uchaux, Rochegude and Suze-la-Rousse, previously taking all of the fruit to the Rochegude cooperative, but now bottling half of it himself. An unassuming, salt of the earth vigneron, he pays close attention to the individual needs of each variety on each terroir, favouring old vines, traditional *gobelets* and hand-harvesting, eschewing irrigation and fermenting with natural yeast. The results speak for themselves, with each of his wines expressing their origins with clarity: his Suze-la-Rousse is dense, dark and supple, his Rochegude is gently floral and bright and his Massif d'Uchaux is spicy, tense and thrilling.

Other good examples

Domaine de Roquevignan was purchased in 2015 by Nicolas and Magali Rougeot and is now producing fresh and juicy wines at very reasonable prices. **Domaine du Gourget** and **Château de Lignane**, both organic, are also good options.

SUZE-LA-ROUSSE

Appellation: AOC Côtes-du-Rhône Villages Suze-la-Rousse

Birth of the appellation: 2016

Communes: Bollène, Bouchet, Suze-la-Rousse, Tulette

Total surface area sold under the AOC in 2019: 200 hectares

Average yield in 2019: 36 hectolitres per hectare

Colours permitted: red only

Grape varieties permitted: As per communal Côtes-du-Rhône Villages regulations (see page 54)

The first mention of the village of Suze dates back to 852. The origins of its longer name are not known for certain, but legend has it that one of the original owners of the castle, Marguerite des Baux, was known as 'La Rousse' due to her red hair. The magnificent castle that dominates the village – and it's certainly more castle than château – was originally owned by the Prince of Orange in the twelfth century. In 1426 Marguerite's daughter, Antoinette, married Louis de La Baume. That was the start of the Baume-Suze family, which owned the castle privately until 1958. In 1965 it was bought by the Drôme *département*, which has leased out the top floor to the Université de Vin since 1978.

From the château's ramparts you can see the vineyards stretching out forever, beyond the town and into the distance. Most of it embodies that classic Southern Rhône terroir of ancient alluvial riverbeds – flat, low-lying, stony and well-drained with some red clay underneath, which helps to keep the vines hydrated during the baking summer, all over a bed of deep blue marl. To the north of the village, however, where the terrain becomes increasingly wooded, there are remarkable outcrops of gaudily ochre-coloured sand so coarse and friable that at first I assumed it had been dumped by rogue builders. As you travel west towards Bollène the gravels give way to sandstone and limestone.

Suze-la-Rousse only gained Named Village status in 2016, the same year as neighbouring Sainte-Cécile. Both appellations are solely for red wine, and they share two of their communes, both laying claim to a portion of Tulette and a portion of the commune of Suze-la-Rousse. Some local vignerons are happy to admit they couldn't tell the difference between Sainte-Cécile and Suze-la-Rousse wines in a blind tasting, and I doubt I could either. They both display that Grenache-rich, generous, potent style you'd expect from a classic Côtes-du-Rhône Villages. Perhaps their unique styles will become more apparent over time.

There is a sense of purpose among local growers, aided no doubt by the fact that 'there's been a change in generation, all at the same time,' according to Rafaël Knapp of Domaine la Borie. He only recently bought the domaine after fifteen years as a wine importer in California. Another dynamic new domaine is LePlan-Vermeersch, established by former racing driver Dirk Vermeersch and run by his daughter Ann, producing appropriately full-throttle wines. Though the Suze-la-Rousse style may not have any strong defining features compared to its neighbours, there is some value to be found among the best producers.

Classic stony garrigue terroir of Suze-la-Rousse

Key producers

Domaine des Gravennes

Suze-la-Rousse

www.domainedesgravennes.com

Les Gravennes is a 100-hectare *lieu-dit* to the north of Suze-la-Rousse. Domaine des Gravennes owns 25 hectares of it, along with a further 5 hectares near Bollène. Brothers Luc and Rémi Bayon de Noyer, both in their early 30s, recently took the reins after completing their studies and various *stages* around the world. They represent the fourth generation to be working vines here, but the domaine has only been bottling its own wines since 1996. Now certified organic, they also use some bio-dynamic practices in the vineyards. 'I want to keep it small,' says Luc, '30 hectares is enough. We want to keep the wines good value, and just sell to restaurants, wine shops and export.' The wines have real vivacity and clarity of expressions. And he's right about the value – these wines are a steal.

Other good examples

Domaine du Jas is owned by a different branch of the same family that owns Domaine des Gravennes, and makes reds in a punchier style. At the other end of the spectrum is **Domaine Gabriel Monier**, producing a bright, fine and drinkable style, along with La Petite Verdière, the organic label of **Domaine de la Bastide**. **Domaine la Borie** is currently in a state of flux as its new owners bed in, but early signs suggest this is an estate to follow. **Vincent Baumet** (see Rochegude) makes a very good example.

SAINTE-CÉCILE

Having only secured Named Village status a few years previously, there was still a good sense of energy among the winemakers of Sainte-Cécile when I attended their open day to taste their brand new 2018s. Given that there are only twelve independent wineries in the appellation (and four co-ops), it took quite some determination and teamwork to push it through. Each had played its part, and it felt something like chatting to a band after a successful gig – fittingly, Sainte Cécile is the patron saint of musicians.

The appellation is made up of two separate areas, the larger section to the south of the village, the smaller to its north. The southern part (known locally as the *garrigue*) is a large, flat, alluvial terrace, with brown marl sandwiched between the sandstone beneath and plentiful alluvial pebbles above. The stones get larger and larger as you approach the village. The clay gradually releases any stored water, which is hugely beneficial in this sunny, dry, drought-prone terroir. Thomas Bertrand of Domaine Rouge Bleu says, 'you often see storms passing on the other side of the Aigues that don't touch us, especially in summer.' Drip irrigation is increasingly common here. The northern terrace is more recently deposited, smaller in size, marginally lower in altitude, and has white marl close to the surface instead of brown. The vines in this section don't suffer from water stress, thanks to deep blue marls underneath. Winemakers who own vineyards in both sections tend to blend between the two.

The wines are typically generous and concentrated in style; while the Sainte-Cécile imprint isn't clearly defined, quality is a step up from a typical generic Côtes-du-Rhône. Though some of the wines are prone to overexuberance and unbalanced alcohol, there is a certain natural charm and elegance to them. But as the runaway climate starts to bring into question the viability of the hottest, driest parts of the Côtes-du-Rhône, you can't help but wonder how much longer sites like this will be able to produce balanced wines.

Appellation: AOC Côtes-du-Rhône Villages Sainte-Cécile

Birth of the appellation: 2016

Communes: Sainte-Cécile-les-Vignes, Sérignan-du-Comtat, Suze-la-Rousse, Travaillan, Tulette

Total surface area sold under the AOC in 2019: 339 hectares

Average yield in 2019: 35 hectolitres per hectare

Colours permitted: red only

Grape varieties permitted: As per communal Côtes-du-Rhône Villages regulations (see page 54)

Key producers
Domaine les Grands Bois
Sainte-Cécile

www.grands-bois.com

President of the appellation, Marc Besnardeau, co-owns one of the most successful domaines in Saint-Cécile with his wife Mireille. It was her grandfather who established the estate in 1920. It now stretches over 46 hectares, and has been certified organic since 2011. Alongside three Côtes-du-Rhônes, four Cairannes and a Rasteau, they also make two Sainte-Céciles. Philippine is a blend of Grenache and Syrah and stands out for its juicy delicacy; Gabrielle is the same blend but aged for 9 months in oak. The wines here are prone to tip over into high alcohol, but when balanced can offer vibrancy and impressive concentration.

Other good examples
Domaine Rouge Bleu, **Domaine Moun Pantaï** and **Le Cri de l'Araignée** all follow a low intervention approach, making characterful wines that are well worth trying. **Château de Ruth** and **Domaine Philippe Plantevin** are more traditional. Cave cooperative **Cave Cécilia** makes some impressive Sainte-Cécile cuvées.

PLAN DE DIEU

In the Middle Ages, the Plan de Dieu looked very different from how it looks today. It was once densely forested, with endless green oaks.

These woods were owned by the nuns of the Abbaye de Prébayon near Gigondas, long since destroyed. That's the likely origin of its sanctified name, the 'Plain of God', although others claim that the woods were so infested with bandits that travellers would pray to the Almighty before attempting to cross them.

Appellation: AOC Côtes-du-Rhône Villages Plan de Dieu

Birth of the appellation: 2005

Communes: Camaret sur Aigues, Jonquières, Travaillan, Violès

Total surface area sold under the AOC in 2019: 1,111 hectares

Average yield in 2019: 37 hectolitres per hectare

Colours permitted: red only

Grape varieties permitted: As per communal Côtes-du-Rhône Villages regulations (see page 54)

This was the first Named Village to take its title from a geographic feature rather than a specific commune (such as Sablet or Séguret). It took prolonged lobbying by local winemakers, but the terroir is so homogeneous it's clear where the boundaries lie, spread over the intersection of four different communes. To use the name of one over another would be arbitrary and inaccurate; eventually the authorities agreed. The Plan de Dieu is a triangular plain of deep, free-draining gravels. It's the old river bed of the Aigues and Ouvèze rivers, which today flow along two of its sides. The boundaries of the plain are easy to spot as they stand 5 metres higher than the surrounding brown soils. The triangle's base, 5 kilometres long, stretches along the foot of the Ventabren massif (the appellations of Cairanne and Rasteau have both claimed a small portion of the plain at the foot of their hillside home). The two lengthier sides of the triangle, 12 kilometres long, reach a point just south of Camaret sur Aigues. The terrace is a little higher near Rasteau (120 metres), a little lower near Camaret (80 metres). After the Second World War, it was increasingly planted with vineyards, and now is effectively a monocultural block of trellised vines as far as the eye can see. It's so flat there's an airstrip in the middle.

The middle of the plain is a great way to get your bearings since you can spot half a dozen other appellations, all on higher land around the edges of the plain: Cairanne, Rasteau, Séguret, Sablet, Gigondas and Vacqueyras. Plan de Dieu winemakers love this spot as it's so easy to work. Rain drains away quickly, keeping diseases at bay and vineyards accessible; it's flat and therefore easy to farm mechanically. The appellation is dominated by large estates (some over 100 hectares), which explains why few are organic, even though it would be relatively straightforward here compared to neighbouring appellations. Yields aren't terribly high but the overall output is massive, making more wine than any other Named Village appellation, twice the volume of the second biggest (Côtes-du-Rhône Villages Laudun).

'The only problem we have here is dryness,' says Bernard Latour of Domaine de l'Espigouette. 'But with irrigation it's no longer a problem.' Drip irrigation systems are an increasingly common sight; about half the vineyards here now have them installed and their use is increasingly regular. Some winemakers claim this is an ideal situation – no problems with ripening grapes, and no problems with blockages in maturity thanks to an unbridled supply of water. But as the climate grows ever hotter and more unpredictable, the Plan de Dieu is beginning to look increasingly less like the winemaking paradise some would paint it. There is no shade, no cooling effects of altitude, no east- or north-facing sites to escape from the sweltering summer sun, and soils are so free-draining that young vines have trouble quenching their thirst.

Only red wines are made here, and many are big, boozy brutes, powerful and attention-grabbing but lacking in elegance and subtlety. For now, there are still a handful of wines – often old vines, dry grown – that are bold, elemental expressions of Grenache, scented with *garrigue* herbs.

Key producers

Domaine les Aphillanthes

Travaillan

www.domainelesaphillanthes.fr

Domaine les Aphillanthes was created in 1999 by Daniel and Hélène Boulle. They make a diverse collection of wines across Côtes-du-Rhône, Côtes-du-Rhône Villages, Plan de Dieu, Rasteau, Cairanne and Gigondas. All the wines are worth trying and their Plan de Dieu Vieilles Vignes often leads the pack: deeply vinous and powerful but retaining a sense of finesse and style. This blend of Grenache and Mourvèdre is as good as many Châteauneuf-du-Papes, and it proves just what can be achieved here with old vines, low yields, sensitive viticulture and skilled winemaking.

Plan de Dieu

Domaine de l'Espigouette

Violès

www.espigouette.com

'We go for quality, not quantity,' says Bernard Latour. His vines across his three plots of Plan de Dieu in Camaret sur Aigues and Trevaillon are naturally low yielding as they get older – they have an average age of 45 years, and are unirrigated. His sons Julien and Emilien work with him now, and represent the fourth generation. They also make Côtes-du-Rhône, Vacqueyras, Gigondas and Rasteau, and quality is solid throughout the range.

Domaine la Manarine

Travaillan

T.: +33 (0) 4 90 46 51 19

When Gilles Gasq was young his father bought an estate in Figari, Corsica, intending to make wine, but it was an unrealized dream – the land was too arid to bear fruit. When Gilles established his own estate in 2001 with 4 hectares of Plan de Dieu, he used the same name as his father's estate – La Manarine. Thankfully he's had more success, and has since built a house and winery in Travaillan. Now he has 36 hectares, including 9 hectares of Plan de Dieu which he farms organically. He says the Grenache here has 'plenty of character, with *sucrosité* and no rough edges.' He makes a fresh and savoury Plan de Dieu of notable drinkability.

Other good examples

Domaine Bois de Meges, **Domaine Bois des Dames** and **Domaine de l'Arnesque** all make bright, expressive examples. **Domaine Martin** makes enjoyably powerful, ageworthy bottlings. The organic **Domaine le Renard** is worth trying, as is **Château Malijay**.

The decline of Syrah?

There is a disease peculiar to Syrah currently affecting plants, most notably in France and California. It has been studied since 1999 but there doesn't yet seem to be a universally agreed name – it's usually a combination of 'Syrah/ Shiraz' and 'disease/decline/disorder', depending on the region. Leaves turn red prematurely, and swellings and cracks appear around the graft union, eventually leading to vine death. Some clones appear to be worse affected than others, and there is currently no cure.

The other factor working against Syrah is the changing climate. Along with Muscardin, Syrah is one of the earliest red grapes to ripen in the Rhône, and is looking increasingly ill-adapted to the hottest terroirs of the South. Speaking about the recent history of winemaking in the Southern Rhône, Yves Gras of Domaine Santa Duc points out, 'We replaced Carignan with Syrah from the north as things were getting hotter – it's madness.' Robert Charavin of Domaine des Coteaux des Travers in Rasteau agrees. He stopped planting Syrah 15 years ago due to the warming climate, and now favours the later-ripening Mourvèdre. Laurent Robert of Domaine Combe Julière, also in Rasteau, doesn't grow any Syrah at all now as he finds the alcohol levels too high and the tannins too drying. One grower in Plan de Dieu confided that within 25 years' time, he believed there would be no more Syrah grown in his appellation.

Although hotter terroirs are becoming challenging for Syrah there are still plenty of excellent examples from fresher corners of the Southern Rhône. Here, in no particular order, are ten from around the region that contain at least 75 per cent Syrah.

- Clos Bellane Côtes-du-Rhône Villages Valréas *rouge* Les Echallas
- Domaine la Florane Côtes-du-Rhône Villages Saint-Maurice *rouge* Guillaume de Rouville

- Domaine le Sollier Duché d'Uzès *rouge* Les Linthes
- Domaine du Bramadou Roaix *rouge* Le Montagne de Mars
- Domaine Gramenon Côtes-du-Rhône *rouge* L'Emouvante
- Domaine du Serre des Vignes Grignan-les-Adhémar *rouge* Sarrazine
- Domaine Camp Galhan Duché d'Uzès *rouge* Perassières
- Domaine de Fondrèche Ventoux *rouge* Persia
- Château Pesquié Ventoux *rouge* Artémia

- Saint Jean du Barroux Vin de France *rouge* Entrevon (Vin de France, but from Ventoux terroir)

Above: Vineyards in the north of Châteauneuf-du-Pape, dusk.

Below: Gigondas vineyards high in the Dentelles de Montmirail.

Above: Les Briguières, Sablet, looking towards Gigondas.

Below: Séguret.

Above: Pebbly marls of the Visan hillside.

Below: Limestone and sandstone soils of Massif d'Uchaux.

Above: Limestone *lauzes* soils, Tavel.

Below: Côte-Rôtie.

Above: Pale gneiss surrounded by dark schist in *lieu-dit* La Côte Brune, Côte-Rôtie.

Below: Planting *en échalas* (wooden stakes) in *lieu-dit* La Landonne, Côte-Rôtie.

Above: The vineyards of Château-Grillet.

Below: Ploughs, presses and small stainless steel tanks at Domaine Thierry Allemand.

Above: Cornas *lieu-dit* Chaillot in the foreground, looking south towards Saint-Péray and the ruined Château de Crussol.

Below: Saint-Joseph vineyards in the foreground to the left, with cuttings burning in *lieu-dit* Les Oliviers at the foot of *lieu-dit* Saint-Joseph; the south-facing hill of Hermitage is in the background to the right.

Above: Rebuilding drystone walls in Hermitage.

Below: Hermitage terraces.

12

UPPER WEST BANK

LAUDUN

In 2015, Cairanne was the last Named Village to be elevated to *cru* level. With a critical mass of excellent domaines, stylistic unity and consistently exceptional quality, it was head and shoulders above the other Named Villages. Foolish though it is to make predictions when it comes to French administration, it looks highly likely that the next Named Village to be promoted to *cru* will be Laudun. In 2020, no Named Village stands quite as tall as Cairanne did in 2015. But if more *crus* must be minted, then when it comes to terroir, style and history, Laudun does have a case for upgrading. In the Southern Rhône, the west bank is relatively light in *crus* compared to the east bank, and this part of the Rhône deserves the renewed attention another *cru* would bring. It would effectively make Laudun the capital of the Upper West Bank.

The appellation consists of three communes sitting within an extensive, enclosed valley that runs 12 kilometres west to east, directly to the north of AOC Lirac. The little river Tave dawdles along the valley floor, emptying into the Cèze briefly before the Cèze in turn empties into the Rhône. The growing area was described to me by Luc Pélaquié of Domaine Pélaquié as 'like a skateboard park' – a flat valley floor, sloping up on three sides. The ramps don't rise too high – just 220 metres on the north-facing slope (the commune of Saint-Victor-la-Coste) and 270 metres on the south-facing slope (communes of Tresques and Laudun). Most of the vines are on the flat and the lower parts of the slopes; vineyards are often interspersed with woodland around the villages.

The north-facing Saint-Victor-la-Coste ripens later than the surrounding terroirs – partly due to exposition, partly due to cool air currents from the surrounding hills. Soils are sand over sandstone with significant limestone gravels. On the valley floor (around 100 metres altitude) there are large expanses of *galets roulés* mixed with red clays, particularly towards the east. The village of Laudun has complex soils, a patchwork of *galets roulés*, silty clay, limestone, sandstone and loess. The Tresques terroir is similarly complex but generally sandier.

Roman artefacts have been uncovered in many of the appellations of the Southern Rhône, but Laudun is a detectorist's dream. Amphorae dating back to between 200 and 300 BC have been discovered at Cesar's Camp, the plateau behind Laudun. Château Courac has a room full of relics that have sprouted from its vineyards in recent times, including, somewhat poetically, a Roman coin minted in Sicily – the island where current owner Joséphine Arnaud was born. Laudun continued to be appreciated through the ages, praised by the great author and soil scientist Olivier de Serres (1539–1619) and appreciated by the courts of King Henry IV and King Louis XII. In Jacques Peuchet's *Dictionnaire Universel de la Géographie Commerçante* (1799), he states that white wine from Laudun was shipped from Roquemaure to Bordeaux and Burgundy.

White wine has always been Laudun's speciality. There are four Southern Rhône *crus* that produce white wine (Châteauneuf-du-Pape, Lirac, Vacqueyras and Cairanne) and Laudun comfortably produces more white wine by volume than all except Châteauneuf. In 2019, 21 per cent of Laudun's output was white, more than double the global Rhône Valley average of 10 per cent. Given the naturally elegant style of the west bank (see box below), it's well suited to whites; the main factor here would appear to be the large proportions of sand, which often produces wines that are lighter in body with more finesse. Cool westerly air currents also bring a freshness to the terroir. None of the permitted white grapes are strongly favoured, nor is any particular commune. That said, the Rhône's wine culture is rooted in reds, and white wines in Laudun are still in the minority. The finesse and straightness of style carries over to the reds. Laudun *rouge* has a slimmer, neater, more tailored frame than the more generous east bank reds, and in my experience even straighter than Lirac. Those grown on sand tend towards paler colours, with lighter structures and less capacity to age.

Looking back once more to Cairanne, the last village to be promoted, its situation was very different: over 40 private domaines, several of which were the most exciting in the Rhône, and a waning co-op (since revived). Laudun is the opposite: it has fewer than 20 private domaines, few of whom are household names, but it has been thrust forward by two overachieving caves cooperatives. Les Vignerons des 4 Chemins was instrumental in the region in the 1960s, particularly in improving the quality of white wines, and its output remains good to this day. Maison Sinnae (formerly Laudun Chusclan Vignerons) has recently been even more dynamic. Under president Philippe Pellaton (who since 2020 has also been president of professional association Inter Rhône) it has continued to grow and build on its position as one of the most dependable co-ops in the Southern Rhône.

According to Luc Pélquié, *cru* status for Laudun would be 'an engine that will push people forward'. It does indeed feel that there is more track ahead of Laudun for it to move even further forward in terms of quality. Organic viticulture is still relatively rare; rows of irrigation hoses are common. *Cru* status would surely attract more talent to this oasis of vines on the west bank of the Rhône: let's hope that the inevitable rise in land prices doesn't discourage young vignerons and talented outsiders from building on what has been centuries, if not millennia, in the making.

Appellation: AOC Côtes-du-Rhône Villages Laudun
Birth of the appellation: 1967
Communes: Laudun, Saint-Victor-la-Coste, Tresques
Total surface area sold under the AOC in 2019: 579 hectares
Average yield in 2019: 37 hectolitres per hectare
Colours permitted: red, rosé, white
Production in 2019: 79 per cent red, 0 per cent rosé, 21 per cent white
Grape varieties permitted: As per communal Côtes-du-Rhône Villages regulations (see page 54)

Key producers
Château Courac
Tresques
T.: +33 (0) 4 66 82 90 51

On deciding to sell Château Courac, the previous owners wanted most of all to keep it in local hands. Fredéric Arnaud's family has a long history of winemaking in Treques, and when he and his Italian wife

Joséphine went to visit in 1994, she says 'it was love at first sight.' It's an ornate, charismatic property, and since taking it on in 1995 they've gradually built the vineyard up to 100 hectares, largely grown on sand with a little clay. They make 150,000 bottles of red Laudun, 30,000 of white Laudun, and both are highly typical and ageworthy examples of the appellation. Prices are however very keen: if you're building a cellar on a budget, some magnums of their red Laudun would be a shrewd addition.

Domaine Pélaquié

Saint-Victor-la-Coste
www.domaine-pelaquie.com

Domaine Pélaquié is something of a west bank specialist, owning 100 hectares from Tavel, via Lirac, up to Laudun and beyond. The family has been cultivating vineyards in Saint-Victor-la-Coste since the sixteenth century. They sold wine in barrel until they first bottled wine in 1924 – very early for the region. Luc Pélaquié was a doctor when he and his brother took on the estate from his grandfather in 1976. It was in a dilapidated state, so they set to work improving it. 'I didn't want to give it to my children in the same state that I found it,' he says 'and quality is the only way to move forward.' His brother died shortly after, but Luc soldiered on and has been instrumental in the evolution of Laudun. Only the best 70 per cent of their Laudun wines take the appellation, the rest he declassifies. Not a great fan of Syrah, Luc believes 'Mourvèdre has a more interesting personality.' His 100 per cent Mourvèdre Luc Pélaquié, grown locally but bottled under AOC Côtes-du-Rhône, settles the argument.

Other good examples

Caves cooperatives **Les Vignerons des 4 Chemins** and **Maison Sinnae** (see Chusclan) both make a range of Lauduns, some of which are very good. The excellent **Rocca Maura** makes one red Laudun Les Barryes, which is a particularly fine and aerial example. Other good white cuvées are made by **Domaine des Maravilhas**, **Domaine d'Antonin** and **Brotte**. Good red cuvées are made by **Domaine de Rabusas**, and the Laudun made by **Domaine Duseigneur** of Châteauneuf-du-Pape is unquestionably among the best. **Frédéric Agneray** makes delicious natural wines not far from Tresques, from vineyards in Margelet and, closer to Chusclan, Sabran.

West bank finesse

The differences between the various Rhône *crus* are frequently discussed, but what is less commonly acknowledged is the difference in style between the wines of the west bank (which is mostly in the Gard) and those of the east bank (principally the Vaucluse). While the wines of the east bank often display the classic richness and generosity of Côtes-du-Rhône wines, those of the west bank tend to be straighter and leaner in profile; a little stricter, not quite so rosy-cheeked. There are a number of possible reasons for this: soil types, vineyard exposure, humidity and the effect of Rhône tributaries.

The most important factor is likely to be soil. There are plentiful deposits of sand close to the Rhône on the west bank in Laudun, Lirac and Tavel, and this tends to produce whites with an elegant profile and reds with fine tannins. As you travel further north from Saint-Gervais towards the Ardèche plateau there is an increasing amount of limestone, which gives a sensation of freshness and tension in reds and whites alike. There are more *galets roulés*, old alluvial terraces and clay on the east bank, all of which deliver wines with greater concentration, richness, and more rounded textures. True, there are large banks of *galets roulés* and pebbles from Signargues down to Costières de Nîmes on the west bank, but the characteristic west bank finesse is less marked south of Tavel.

Another source of this natural elegance could be exposure; generally speaking, there are more east-facing vineyards on the west bank and more west-facing vineyards on the opposite bank. East-facing vineyards take in the gentler morning sun and shield the grapes from the heat of the afternoon, helping to temper alcohols and preserve acidity.

Robert W. Mayberry in his book *Wines of the Rhône Valley* also notes the 'somewhat more elegant' style of the wines of the west bank, and suggests that the tributaries of the Rhône on each bank play an important role. He points out that the main tributaries of the east bank originate in the Alps, the same as the Rhône itself, so when the Rhône is low, these tributaries are almost dry, resulting in a drier overall climate. The west bank tributaries of the Rhône, the Ardèche, Cèze and Tave, originate elsewhere (the Cèze from the Cevennes, the Ardèche from the Massif Central), resulting in a more regulated ambient humidity on this side. He adds to this the importance of the orientation of these tributaries. On the east bank, they run broadly north-east to south-west, acting as channels for the drying mistral. The tributaries on the west bank tend to run west to east, perpendicular to the north wind, and thus not channelling it through the growing area.

> Rather than one single factor, it's likely to be a combination of these different aspects of terroir that results in the phenomenon of west bank finesse. Whatever the cause, you can taste it in the wines.

CHUSCLAN

The Named Village appellations of Laudun and Chusclan have a lot in common. Both are wide, flat valleys that follow small tributaries of the Rhône. Laudun surrounds the Tave that meanders west to east. Chusclan, immediately to the north of Laudun, follows the larger Cèze, which flows north-west to south-east. The two appellations are separated by a high, wooded plateau, on top of which is the Roman oppidum known as Cesar's Camp. At the northern limit of Chusclan is another range of hills, topped by the ruined Château de Gicon. Looking south from the ruins, you survey a carpet of vines flowing from Bagnols-sur-Cèze in the west, past the villages of Chusclan and Orsan, to Codolet, next to the Rhône. Look north for the vineyards of Saint-Étienne-des-Sorts. The vines scale the slopes a little higher than in Laudun, and the terroir is perhaps marginally warmer.

There are some similarities in soils between Laudun and Chusclan, but if anything, Chusclan is sandier – in some places shallow and rich in quartz over sandstone and limestone; in other places, metres deep. But it's not just sand; there are deposits of layered limestone to the north and west near Bagnols-sur-Cèze, a massive hill of galets known as Monticaut to the south-east, and down on the plain plentiful alluvions, pebbles and clay.

Gilles Chinieu of Domaine la Romance explains that in the 1960s and 1970s Chusclan was famed for its rosé, which made up around 60 per cent of production, but gradually red wine has taken the upper hand. For now, 'the ultimate aim is to become a *cru*,' he says, but it looks like a distant prospect compared to Laudun. Having a strong, quality-focused local co-op means it's less likely that local growers will drop out and set up their own domaines. So it is in Chusclan – apart from Château Signac, there are no long-established private domaines, and few recent ones – just six in total. With so few private domaines, building Chusclan's reputation is slow-going. Most Chusclan is sold by cooperatives, and there can be a certain consumer and journalistic bias against such structures, which doesn't help in building the appellation's image. The commercial reach and expertise of négociants can be instrumental in building a regional brand, but so far only one has shown an interest here. Another problem is rivalry; producers in Orsan, for example, may not want to sell their wine under the name of the neighbouring village of Chusclan. Lastly, the major town within the appellation, Bagnols-sur-Cèze, is hardly the most picturesque.

Nevertheless there is a certain Chusclan style. The wines are similar to Laudun, but tend to be a little riper, juicier, fruitier. This roundness can lead to an overly fruity and potent character from time to time, but others can be every bit as good as those from their better-known neighbour.

Appellation: AOC Côtes-du-Rhône Villages Chusclan

Birth of the appellation: 1967 (rosé); 1971 (red)

Communes: Bagnols-sur-Cèze, Chusclan, Codolet, Orsan, Saint-Etienne-des-Sorts

Total surface area sold under the AOC in 2019: 291 hectares

Average yield in 2019: 35 hectolitres per hectare

Colours permitted: red and rosé only

Production in 2019: 98 per cent red, 2 per cent rosé

Grape varieties permitted: As per communal Côtes-du-Rhône Villages regulations (see page 54)

Key producers

Domaine la Romance
Bagnols-sur-Cèze
www.domainelaromance.com

Gilles Chinieu has something of the science teacher about him. The fifth generation of his family to grow vines, he started converting his vineyards to organics in 2009 and began bottling a proportion of his crop himself. His vineyards are built on layers of limestone, along with some silt and sand. 'In the Gard we're less well-known than in the Vaucluse,' he says, 'but we also have quality terroirs.' Leading the push for promotion to *cru* status, he describes it as 'a great collective project' for the community which will help Chusclan be recognized for quality wines – 'that's what motivates me,' he says. His reds have a dab of ripe sweetness at their core and can lack consistency from vintage to vintage but when they're good, they're very good.

Château Signac

Bagnols-sur-Cèze

chateausignac.com

Situated on the border between Bagnols-sur-Cèze and Orsan and built on an old Roman site, Château Signac is an old fortified farm that was inhabited by Benedictine monks until the French Revolution. The property has changed hands many times, and is now managed by Burgundian négociant Maison Chanzy, which has installed Benjamin Boyer to farm the 33 hectares of north- and east-facing vines and make the wines. The rosé Cuvée d'Or is full but finessed, the reds enjoyably chunky – Chusclan Cuvée Combe d'Enfer is particularly worth trying.

Other good examples

The Chusclan of **Domaine Clavel** is authentic and complex, offering incredible value for money – it is worth seeking out (see Saint-Gervais). The Chusclan of **Domaine de Rabusas** is less oaky than their Laudun and just as good. Dependable caves cooperatives include **Maison Sinnae** and **Les Vignerons des 4 Chemins**.

SAINT-GERVAIS

If you follow the Cèze river north-west upstream from Chusclan, a few kilometres past Bagnols-sur-Cèze you'll reach Saint-Gervais. A small, low-rise village built mostly from white stone, it is slightly grubby and essentially featureless but pleasant. One of the smallest Named Villages, it has just three producers at the time of writing. The whole commune of Saint-Gervais can use the appellation but the terroir is far from homogeneous. There are vineyards on the pebbly marl and loess surrounding the village itself, but as you ascend the winding paths that snake north and north-east from the village, after a few kilometres the best sites reveal themselves. There are two clay limestone plateaux surrounded by dense woodland: the Soleillan to the north of the village, and the larger Cellettes to the north-east. Both are late ripening sites, the Soleillan sitting at 150 metres altitude, the Cellettes at up to 200 metres. Soils are similar – clay with significant patches of angular limestone scree. The sunsets are spectacular here – if marred slightly by the chain of domineering pylons barging their way through the vines.

The local cave cooperative was swallowed up by Les Celliers des Chartreux in 2015, and in doing so they've become the largest producer of AOC Saint-Gervais. Director of production Frédéric Sablayrolles says that the wines of neighbouring Chusclan are 'much more rich, powerful and concentrated,' while those of Saint-Gervais are more 'fine and elegant'. This is a fresh terroir; he's never needed to acidify them. 'It has fantastic potential,' he says, but with so few producers and no consumer reputation 'it's going to be a long process to lift it up.'

Tasting the wines of the two private domaines, Domaine Sainte-Anne and Domaine Clavel, their bright freshness and elegance in both colours is notable even by west bank standards. Jean Steinmaier of Domaine Sainte-Anne puts this down to three factors: the soil, the altitude and the diurnal temperature differences. Claire Clavel of Domaine Clavel adds the west bank situation and its proximity to the Cevennes. This aromatic spark and electric acidity give the wines refreshment when young, and enough charge to last for years in bottle.

Most Named Villages have a *syndicat* of local winemakers, but Clavel has never known the appellation to have one. She's trying to set one up herself. 'I want to defend the appellation,' she says. 'It's a real terroir, with real quality behind it that I believe in.' And so she should.

Appellation: AOC Côtes-du-Rhône Villages Saint-Gervais

Birth of the appellation: 1974

Communes: Saint-Gervais

Total surface area sold under the AOC in 2019: 68 hectares

Average yield in 2019: 34 hectolitres per hectare

Colours permitted: red, rosé, white

Production in 2019: 91 per cent red, 0 per cent rosé, 9 per cent white

Grape varieties permitted: As per communal Côtes-du-Rhône Villages regulations (see page 54)

Key producers

Domaine Clavel

Saint-Gervais

www.domaineclavel.com

At 75 hectares, Domaine Clavel is more than twice the size of Domaine Sainte-Anne. It doesn't share the same (slightly faded) picturesque allure, nor the same noble backstory, but the wines are every bit as good. 'The challenge for me,' says Claire Clavel, 'is to sell it all in bottle.' And she's nearly achieved it. Claire is the fourth generation to make wine here; it was her father Denis who pulled out of the local co-op to go it alone in 1991. 'He was passionate,' says Claire, 'and he wanted to see what his grapes could do.' Today they make Vin de Pays d'Oc, Côtes-du-Rhône and Côtes-du-Rhône Villages Chusclan and Saint-Gervais. Their estate isn't organic, but it's Terra Vitis[4] certified and 20 per cent of their production is white. She has two ranges within Saint-Gervais, with a red and a white in both: Syrius, and the more expensive Claire de Lune, which sees more oak. Arguably the latter are the better wines, but for a clear image of what Saint-Gervais is all about without any make-up, try the former.

Domaine Sainte-Anne

Saint-Gervais

T.: +33 (0) 4 66 82 77 41

'For a long time, it was just the cave co-op and us,' says Jean Steinmaier. 'And they didn't make much Saint-Gervais.' Originally from Burgundy, his parents Guy and Anne Steinmaier bought the dilapidated property in the little hamlet of Les Cellettes in 1965 as a holiday home. It came with 12 hectares of vineyards, which needed replanting. It didn't take them long to realize the potential here. Domaine Sainte-Anne quickly gained a reputation for quality, and along with the cave cooperative, it was the Steinmaier family that pushed for a Named Village appellation, granted in 1974. Jean studied winemaking in Beaune, before joining them in 1977. Today the 35 hectares of vineyard are all harvested by hand in small cases. Farming is *raisonée* but not organic, in case he needs to treat certain diseases such as black rot, which they saw in 2015. There is a range of Côtes-du-Rhônes, Côtes-du-Rhône Villages and Côtes-du-Rhône Villages Saint-Gervais – their Mourvèdre-based Les Rouvières is particularly expressive, and their pure Viognier, bottled as Vin de France, is another highlight.

Other good examples

Les Celliers des Chartreux makes a good red and an even better white Saint-Gervais, which at €7.70 each direct from their boutique offer great value for money.

---

4 An independent French organisation that promotes environmentally and socially responsible practices among wine producers.

SAINT-ANDÉOL

Appellation: AOC Côtes-du-Rhône Villages Saint-Andéol
Birth of the appellation: 2017
Communes: Bourg-Saint-Andéol, Saint-Just-d'Ardèche, Saint-Marcel-d'Ardèche, Saint-Martin-d'Ardèche
Total surface area sold under the AOC in 2019: 43 hectares
Average yield in 2019: 38 hectolitres per hectare
Colours permitted: red only
Grape varieties permitted: As per communal Côtes-du-Rhône Villages regulations (see page 54)

Travel north from Saint-Gervais and eventually you reach the Ardèche river; cross to the other side and you're no longer in the Gard, but the Ardèche *département*. This triangular nook of land between the Ardèche and Rhône rivers has always felt like an insider secret. It has long been home to a number of overperforming estates making wines with real local interest and colour (often at very low prices). It was only promoted to a Named Village in 2017, but if I were to choose a candidate to be promoted to *cru*, on the quality and consistency of the wines being made here, Saint-Andéol would be among the runners.

The appellation is a group of four communes, all of which have a saint in their name: Bourg-Saint-Andéol, Saint-Just-d'Ardèche, Saint-Marcel-d'Ardèche and Saint-Martin-d'Ardèche. After phylloxera, many vignerons in this part of France replanted with disease-resistant hybrid vines, which often produced inferior wines. President of the appellation, Philippe Faure, explains that even in the 1970s and 1980s much of the output here was Vin de Table, and only in the late 1980s was part of the area classified as Côtes-du-Rhône Villages, as the classic Rhône *Vitis vinifera* varieties took over.

In the 1990s, Jean-Luc Dorthe of Domaine de Couron led a *syndicat* of growers towards further recognition, putting a dossier together to lobby the INAO, which they delivered in 1999. It took 19 years for it to be accepted. The name was a sticking point; local vignerons thought 'Bourg-Saint-Andéol' was too ungainly, but the powers that be refused to shorten it. During a visit to the area, local vignerons took the officials from the appellation authorities to places of interest within the proposed growing area, including the church that houses the remains of the martyr Saint-Andéol. When they walked in, a beam of light shone through the windows and lit up the tomb – and it seemed to sway the visiting representative: 'We didn't do it on purpose!' says Faure.

There are two main types of terroir. The prevailing kind is *galets roulés*, making up 80–90 per cent of the surface area, the same Villafranchian deposits found in Châteauneuf-du-Pape and further south. What's unusual here is that they cover steep hillsides rising to 150 metres altitude known locally as *moures*, creating valleys and amphitheatres that give a variety of different exposures to the vines. This terroir is concentrated around Saint-Marcel. The other, less prevalent, type of soil is clay limestone, most of which is found further north in Bourg-Saint-Andéol. As you climb the gentle slopes towards the limestone plateau of the Côtes du Vivarais the sharp white stones become like rubble in the vineyards.

Frédéric Dorthe of Domaine du Chapitre explains that they enjoy cool nights here thanks to the proximity to the high plateau which is 'good for conserving colour and concentration of aromas,' he says. He also claims the 'more vertical' style of the wines here comes from elevated levels of acidity in the underlying soils compared to the more central Southern Rhône vineyards, as evidenced by the number of chestnut trees here. Olive trees, by contrast, become increasingly rare in this latitude, as do other emblematic Mediterranean plants. 'We're really at the limit for Mourvèdre here,' says Dorthe, with Grenache and Syrah (along with a little Carignan) being much more common. The red wines still display the characteristic generosity of Grenache but they stand upright, in contrast to some of the laid-back styles from more southerly east bank appellations. White wines were omitted from the appellation when it was first established but plantings are on the increase, and growers are hoping to amend the rules in due course. There's no doubt they deserve to be included – Domaine Saladin's white cuvée Per El is as *rhodanien* a white as you could hope to find in the Southern Rhône.

This is a Rhône terroir, but it is distinctively Ardèche. There is a northern sobriety to the people and their wines, and the landscape has a different accent. Its recent strides up the appellation ladder give the impression of a new area, but that is only partly true; some of the winemaking families here are hundreds of years old. What it does demonstrate, however, is the dynamism and optimism among local vignerons, and a decision to make their voice heard more widely. It's a voice worth listening to.

Key producers

Domaine du Chapitre

St-Marcel-d'Ardèche

www.domaine-chapitre-ardeche.com

Frédéric Dorthe has a more Burgundian air than some of his Provençal neighbours. He studied in Beaune in fact, and in 2000 returned to the family domaine in Saint-Marcel. His family has close links to the Saladins, and originally grew fennel along with grapes, until his father concentrated increasingly on vineyards in the 1960s and 1970s. 'My father sold it all *en vrac* to Guigal,' he says, but when Frédéric joined the domaine they started bottling themselves. He also planted white varieties and started replanting using massal selection. The estate isn't organic, but has HVE certification. He makes a fairly wide range, including some IGP which he crops at 40–50 hectolitres per hectare, and some Côtes-du-Rhône and Côtes-du-Rhône Villages Saint-Andéol with yields of 25–30 hectolitres per hectare. His Grenache vines, the oldest of which are 50 years old, are grown on galets; his best Syrah is grown on calcareous soils. His wines have a Burgundian lilt; his reds are lean and piquant, whereas his whites are more well-fed. These are quietly serious, unshowy wines in keeping with the local terroir.

Mas de Libian

St-Marcel-d'Ardèche

www.masdelibian.com

Another ancient property in St-Marcel-d'Ardèche, Mas de Libian has been in the Thibot family since 1670. It was originally a hunting lodge and manor house, but over the years the estate became focused on grapes. The first cellar was built in 1970, and the vines have always been grown organically. They were certified biodynamic in 2015. They now have 33 hectares of mixed agriculture, including vegetables, beehives, olive trees and cereals. Twenty-five hectares are dedicated to vineyards, the soils for which comprise *galets roulés* and clay. They don't currently bottle any of their wines under AOC Saint-Andéol, but some of their wines are nonetheless born of this terroir, and display a lush and succulent style that is texturally rich and full of warmth.

Domaine Saladin

St-Marcel-d'Ardèche

www.domaine-saladin.com

When Henri Saladin failed to come home at the end of the First World War, his family assumed he was dead. Two years later, he reappeared. He'd been convalescing in hospital in northern France after being gassed during fighting. When his family saw what had happened to him, they swore never to touch the chemical farming products that were beginning to arrive on the market. So they claim they have always been organic – since 1422. Sisters Marie-Laurence and Elisabeth Saladin now run the estate, representing the twenty-first generation. They own 17 hectares of vineyards, some co-planted, some in blocks, and make wines across three colours. They like to use some white grapes in the red ferments, and use semi-carbonic maceration for their Grenache. 'A hundred years ago it was traditional,' says Marie-Laurence. 'There were no destemming machines back then,' she points out. The resulting wines are pale in colour, with an easy, refreshing drinkability and great sense of purity and peace.

Other good examples

There's a solid level of quality in this appellation. Sound, balanced wines with good typicity can be found at **Domaine Coulange**, **Domaine la Pierre-Laine**, **Domaine de Couron**, **Domaine Delorme** and **Domaine de Notre Dame de Cousignac** (see Côtes du Vivarais). **Château Rochecolombe** also makes good wines, with some cuvées in a more oaked style.

CÔTES DU VIVARAIS

The Ardèche *département* follows the west bank of the Rhône from Pont-Saint-Esprit all the way up to Condrieu. The Côtes du Vivarais is at its southernmost limit, and the growing area even straddles the Ardèche river, placing a foot in the Gard. The area corresponds to an undulating limestone plateau that's been weathered to create countless caves and gorgeous gorges. The Côtes du Vivarais is hilly and densely wooded, some trees cling on to raw limestone with the barest covering of topsoil. Vineyards surround a series of villages; some industrial, and others, like Saint-Montan, achingly pretty. Most are at high altitude, such as Saint-Remèze, which sits at 360 metres. Many of the better vineyards are on south-facing slopes, where they catch the sun but take shelter from the mistral. Altitude, latitude and forest all combine to give a feeling of freshness.

Its recent history is one of cooperative wineries, twelve of which have conglomerated to create Vignerons Ardéchois, which makes some respectable inexpensive cuvées. The appellation also sees bottlings from fifteen independent domaines. During the mid-nineteenth century the region was known for growing hybrids, but most of these have been ripped out and replaced with Syrah and Grenache.

Appellation: AOC Côtes du Vivarais

Birth of the appellation: 1999

Total surface area sold under the AOC in 2019: 232 hectares

Average yield in 2019: 38 hectolitres per hectare

Communes: Barjac, Bidon, Champclos, Gras, Issirac, Labastide-de-Virac, Lagorce, Larnas, Le Garn, Montclus, Orgnac-l'Aven, Saint-Montan, Saint-Privas-de-Champclos, Saint-Remèze, Vinezac

Colours permitted: red, rosé, white

Production in 2019: 53 per cent red, 40 per cent rosé, 7 per cent white

Grape varieties permitted: For reds Syrah must make up at least 40 per cent of the blend and Grenache at least 30 per cent. Reds may also contain Cinsault and/or Marselan.

For rosés Grenache must make up 60–80 per cent of the blend. Rosés may also contain Syrah, Cinsault and/or Marselan.

Whites must contain at least 50 per cent Grenache Blanc; Clairette and/or Marsanne must make up at least 30 per cent; Viognier and Roussanne must be no more than 20 per cent.

Quality here is highly variable; the best are captivating, but some are curiously old-school and others rather lacking. With such diversity it's not easy to discern a unifying style, but the best reds show dark fruits – blackberry, blackcurrant – with a proud, edgy tannic structure and an inner tension. They are savoury, and tend towards Northern Rhône sobriety rather than Southern generosity. Whites lean towards the floral and apple-flavoured, but are stylistically diffuse; rosés are pale and largely commercial.

Some producers, such as Vignerons Ardéchois and Notre Dame de Cousignac, are experimenting with maturing wines in barrel or bottle in some of the local caves. It's too early to say whether the darkness, silence and high humidity make a noticeable difference to the finished wines but it's encouraging to see producers trying something new. Hopefully this spirit of innovation and exploration will help the local growers to unlock the potential and reveal the true character of what could be an exceptional terroir.

Key producers

Domaine Gallety
Saint-Montan
gallety.fr

One domaine stands head and shoulders above all others in Côtes du Vivarais and that is Domaine Gallety. This organic, family-owned estate lies on the edge of the appellation, barely a kilometre from the Rhône, a 15-hectare south-facing slope that surrounds the house and winery. Altitude and limestone may be what define Côtes du Vivarais, but this has little of either. The vineyard stretches between 72 and 125 metres altitude and although the Grenache is planted on clay limestone, the Syrah is planted on very deep pure clay.

Work in the vineyard and winery is fairly classic for a quality-minded Rhône estate: hand harvesting, fruit sorted multiple times, stems removed if green, indigenous yeasts, varieties fermented separately, fermentation in epoxy-lined concrete, weekly pumping over and punching down, juice and wine moved by gravity and top cuvées aged in large used barrels. Their untitled Domaine Gallety is a 50:50 blend of Syrah and Grenache and has a measured drinkability and northern sensibility that exemplifies this part of the Rhône. Their highly concentrated, captivating 100 per cent Syrah cuvée Syrare, from 40-year-old vines, starts reaching its peak after 10 years or so, taking on extraordinary truffle and pot-pourri complexity – as if bolstered by a little Cornas. Their 100 per cent Grenache cuvée La Ligure, from 85-year-old vines, may not be as consistent as their Syrare but has a polished elegance and northern freshness in good vintages.

Domaine de Notre Dame de Cousignac
Bourg-Saint-Andéol
www.domainedecousignac.fr

'We're certified organic,' says Rafaël Pommier, seventh-generation winemaker. 'This place is fifteen centuries old, so we want to maintain it.' The beautiful domaine is steeped in history and well worth a visit – they have a bed and breakfast and are soon to open an organic restaurant. The estate is now owned by large négociant Ogier but the family is still very much involved. They farm 60 hectares across IGP Ardèche, Côtes-du-Rhône and Côtes du Vivarais. Rafaël would describe the style of Côtes du Vivarais as 'juicy, refreshing, not heavy,' and this is also a fair description of the estate's range. Quality is consistently high, including the clean, fresh and expressive no-added-sulphite cuvées. His Vinolithic cuvée is barrel matured in limestone caves.

Other good examples

Domaine Vigier produces well-made wines with a good sense of typicity at very affordable prices. **Clos de l'Abbé Dubois** is a long-established domaine making wines that are proudly characterful even if they can stray into esoteric rusticity on occasion. Newcomer **Domaine les Terriers** shows promising polish and concentration in its first two vintages.

Plant de Brunel

The village of Saint-Remèze is home to just one domaine, Clos de l'Abbé Dubois. It is also where winemaker and nurseryman René Brunel was based before he retired. In 1982 he noticed a vine growing out of some marc on the ground near his cellar. He decided to cultivate it, and eventually planted an experimental block. Happy with the results, he sought to get it recognized by the INRA. It transpired it was a spontaneous natural crossing of Grenache and Jurançon Noir. This highly fertile variety, with small clusters and a very short stalk, is very resistant to downy mildew, powdery mildew and grey rot. It's also resistant to drought. Brunel's grandson Sébastien Etienne says that it's similar to Grenache but more deeply coloured and more tannic. It has since been accepted as a permitted grape variety for IGP Ardèche. Not many places make a pure version, but Clos de l'Abbé Dubois makes a 100 per cent Plant de Brunel cuvée called L'Originel.

DUCHÉ D'UZÈS

The newly-created Other Rhône Valley appellation of Duché d'Uzès picks up at the western limit of the generic AOC Côtes-du-Rhône growing area, continuing westwards until it hits the Cevennes, gathering up a vast tract of vineyard land and countless villages and towns across 77 communes.

Appellation: AOC Duché d'Uzès

Birth of the appellation: 2013

Total surface area sold under the AOC in 2019: 322 hectares

Average yield in 2019: 33 hectolitres per hectare

Communes: Aigaliers, Aigremont, Arpaillargues-et-Aureillac, Aubussargues, Bagard, Baron, Belvézet, Blauzac, Bourdic, Bragassargues, Brignon, Canaules-et-Argentières, Cardet, Cassagnoles, Castelnau-Valence, Collorgues, Cruviers-Lascours, Dions, Durfortet-Saint-Martin-de-Sossenac, Flaux, Foissac, Fons, Fontarèches, Fressac, Gajan, Garrigues-Sainte-Eulalie, Goudargues, La Bastide-d'Engras, La Bruguière, La Calmette, La Capelle-et-Masmolène, La Rouvière, Lédignan, Lézan, Logrian-Florian, Martignargues, Maruéjols-lès-Gardon, Massanes, Massillargues-Attuech, Monoblet, Montaren-et-Saint-Médiers, Moussac, Ners, Puechredon, Ribaute-les-Tavernes, Saint-André-de-Roquepertuis, Saint-Bauzély, Saint-Bénézet, Saint-Césaire-de-Gauzignan, Saint-Chaptes, Saint-Christol-lès-Alès, Saint-Dézéry, Sainte-Anastasie, Saint-Félix-de-Pallières, Saint-Hippolyte-de-Montaigu, Saint-Jean-de-Ceyrargues, Saint-Jean-de-Crieulon, Saint-Jean-de-Serres, Saint-Jean-du-Pin, Saint-Laurent-la-Vernède, Saint-Maurice-de-Cazevieille, Saint-Maximin, Saint-Nazaire-des-Gardies, Saint-Quentin-la-Poterie, Saint-Siffret, Saint-Théodorit, Saint-Victor-des-Oules, Sanilhac-Sagriès, Sauve, Savignargues, Serviers-et-Labaume, Seynes, Tornac, Uzès, Vallabrix, Verfeuil, Vézénobres.

Colours permitted: red, rosé, white

Production in 2019: 55 per cent red, 20 per cent rosé, 25 per cent white

Grape varieties permitted: Reds must contain at least 40 per cent Syrah and at least 20 per cent Grenache; may also contain Mourvèdre, Carignan and/or Cinsault.

Rosés must contain at least 50 per cent Grenache and at least 20 per cent Syrah; may also contain Mourvèdre, Carignan and/or Cinsault.

Whites must contain at least 40 per cent Viognier and at least 30 per cent Grenache Blanc, along with at least 20 per cent Marsanne, Roussanne and/or Vermentino. Clairette and Ugni Blanc are also permitted.

The town of Uzès is particularly worth a detour if you're exploring the region. It was originally a Roman settlement, and has enjoyed a rich and eventful history. Today it has something of a Bobo vibe and is popular with tourists for its ornate architecture and its good shopping and eating. The Duke of Uzès is historically the most important peerage in France, and it was the owner of this title who would proclaim 'The King is dead, long live the King!' at royal funerals. Uzès is the family seat, currently occupied by Jacques de Crussol d'Uzès, the seventeenth duke.

The growing area of Duché d'Uzès is currently covered by five different Vin de Pays, including Vin de Pays des Cevennes and Vin de Pays d'Oc. In 1989, local producers came together to put forward a request for the best terroirs to be considered for AOC status. On the back of exhaustive soil studies, this was eventually granted in 2013 for the higher, best-exposed vineyards, most of which are composed of clay limestone.

The appellation has a whopping footprint, stretching 50 kilometres west to east, and 20 kilometres north to south. The area is pinched in the middle to form a western and an eastern lobe. There are no official names for these two lobes, but the western side is often referred to as the 'Cevennes part' and the eastern side is often called the 'Uzès part'. Considering its humongous size, very little wine is yet bottled under this appellation: just 10,642 hectolitres in 2019 (for comparison, AOC Ventoux bottled 252,240 hectolitres).

The Uzès part is larger, and has some outcrops of sandier soils closest to the Rhône. The overall terrain is fairly level with a gently pastoral feel to it: muddy fields studded with small villages that vary from the adorably pretty to the grey and functional. The similarly rural Cevennes part is never steeply sloping but neither is it totally flat. It is visibly encircled by higher land that marks the appellation's boundaries: the Lussan hills to the north, the Cevennes to the west and raised limestone bluffs that separate it from Nîmes to the south. Both the western and eastern sides have plenty of *garrigue* terroir, particularly the Cevennes part, a jumble of truffle oaks, olive trees and herbs. It's a little wetter towards the Cevennes; there's more mistral towards the Rhône. Differences are however mild, both in the countryside, and in the wines.

It's rare for an appellation to be granted for red, white and rosé, but Duché d'Uzès is one of them. Permitted varieties and proportions in the blend are quite specific and fairly unusual for the Southern Rhône: majority Syrah with Grenache for reds; majority Grenache with Syrah for rosés; majority Viognier with Grenache Blanc for whites (to this will soon be added an obligatory dollop of Marsanne, Roussanne and/or Vermentino). Over half of the 35 private domaines are now organic or in organic conversion. Patrick Chabrier of Domaine Chabrier says these Northern Rhône varieties began to be widely planted in the 1990s, and they suit the terroir thanks to the freshening mountain influence. Nicolas Souchon of Mas de Volques says, 'the freshness of the nights is very clear, and it can get very cold in winter.' He says this helps to retain aromatic freshness and acidity in the wines. 'The closer to the mountains, the fresher it gets,' he says, partly due to the tramontane wind that flows in from the west. Though some claim this is felt by the whole appellation, it's a stretch to imagine a strong mountain influence reaches as far as Uzès, let alone beyond.

It's true however that the style of wine is fairly homogeneous across the appellation. Reds have that slimmed-down west bank finesse; discrete and drinkable, they often feature blackberry and liquorice with a slightly charred quality to the aromas. Some can feel pallid, sober or a little hollow, but there are some very good, distinctive wines here that have detailed aromatics, lightness of touch and a fine-boned but tensile tannic frame. It's not unusual to find reduction in some of the wines, but this should be easy to remedy. The blend of Viognier and Grenache Blanc is often a successful one in this terroir. The perfumed side of Viognier is rarely overtly heady except when overoaked, and the Grenache Blanc brings a grounding influence. The best wines have an easy-going and amenable style, with good precision if rarely great complexity. Rosés shoot for the centre in terms of colour and style: neither pale nor dark, pleasantly drinkable and authentically Rhône.

Gaining the appellation has proved to be a real boost for local growers. They can charge higher prices for their wines as a result, which should lead to a virtuous circle of further investment and improving quality. The homogeneity of style is no doubt due at least in part to the strict appellation rules: Duché d'Uzès is one of the few Rhône appellations to have an official panel tasting every wine before it's granted the AOC. Whether such strict regulations are wholly beneficial for an appellation still finding its feet is up for debate. But the ingredients for success are here: a sense of dynamism and purpose among producers, widespread commitment to responsible viticulture and some stand-out domaines. No doubt some smaller distinct terroirs will rise to prominence within the larger appellation in years to come – it will be fascinating to watch their progress.

Key producers

Domaine Camp Galhan

Ribaute-les-Tavernes

campgalhan.com

The commune of Ribaute-les-Tavernes in the Cevennes part of Duché d'Uzès is one of the very few to feature any *galets roulés* in the appellation (the other is Saint-Chaptes). This is what makes the wines of Camp Galhan so distinctive – they are one of the rare estates to produce AOC Duché d'Uzès cuvées issuing from this type of soil. Not organic, but working in *agriculture raisonnée*, Alain and Lionel Pourquier harvest the crop by hand for their top cuvées and process their grapes in a custom-built gravity-fed winery. The result is wines that are measured, pure and focused.

Domaine Chabrier

Bourdic

chabrier.fr

Of the 130 hectares grown by Christophe and Patrick Chabrier around Bourdic in the Uzès part of the appellation, 30 hectares are in AOC Duché d'Uzès, the rest are in IGPs Cévennes and Coteaux du Pont du Gard. Patrick says that this was historically very much a terroir for red wines, but whites are now on the up. Their top cuvée La Garrigue d'Aureillac displays their potential – tasted in 2019, their 2012 was mature but still fresh, with a citrus tang. The vineyards were bought by their grandfather in 1925, and they've been bottling their own wine since 1998. Theirs is an approachable, undemonstrative style that makes for enjoyably drinkable wines.

Mas des Volques

Aigremont

T.: +33 (0) 6 87 28 98 95

Working as a cellarmaster at Domaine des Escaravailles in Rasteau and Clos Saint Jean in Châteauneuf-du-Pape was good training for Nicolas Souchon of Mas des Volques. (It also put him in touch with consultant Philippe Cambie, who continues to work with him here.) His great-grandfather bought the original vines in 1930, and Nicolas gradually expanded the holdings until he was ready to start bottling in 2010. The estate now covers 12.5 hectares, which is farmed without herbicides, and produces 30,000 bottles of wines a year. He believes in the AOC: 'The appellation is the recognition of what we can do, it's the identity of the place, the expression of everything you see all around you,' he says. The freshening mountain influence 'is like the effect of altitude in the wines,' he explains, despite the vineyards lying at 130 metres above sea level. He makes assertive wines in a fairly lavish style.

Domaine le Sollier
Monoblet
www.domainelesollier.fr

Domaine le Sollier is the most westerly domaine in Duché d'Uzès, up in the foothills of the Cevennes. Getting out of the car, our ankles are nipped by a furious Jack Russell, a master truffle hunter as it turns out. They bottle some wines under AOC Duché d'Uzès, 'but geologically we're closer to the Languedoc in terms of soil,' says Nicolas Olivier. The 12.5-hectare estate, worked organically by Nicolas and his brothers, sits on a geographical fault that makes for a patchwork of different soils. Sandstone and marl can be found, but most of their vineyards are planted on dolomite terroir, very well draining sandy limestone soils that produce a captivating style of Syrah. Nicolas says he aims to make wine 'with the least intervention possible,' but they usually add a low dose of sulphites. Though the vineyards have been in the family for generations, they bottled their first estate wine in 2006. It's a unique site with few immediate neighbours, so Nicolas says, 'we can create our own identity, a bit like Mas de Daumas Gassac or Granges de Pères.' Wishful thinking? Not at all. Their wines have a clarity, sense of detail, and beguiling otherness that draws you in.

Other good examples
Domaine Reynaud, **Domaine de l'Orviel** and **Domaine de l'Aqueduc** are also strong contenders, while **Les Vignes de l'Arque**, **Domaine Natura** and **Domaine St Firmin** are also worth checking out. In terms of local cooperatives, some good value wines can be sourced from **La Cave Durfort** and **Les Collines du Bourdic**.

13

LOWER WEST BANK

LIRAC

Lirac is one of the oldest *crus* in the Rhône Valley. It's had over 70 years to refine and define itself, to prove itself. Yet what Lirac represents remains a little hazy. As an appellation, it lacks self-confidence. There are reasons for this: its history is chequered, the terrain is heterogeneous and piecemeal, and wine production has not always focused on optimizing quality. It's an appellation of long-unrequited potential. But choose carefully and Lirac can be the source of affordable wines of real finesse in all three colours.

If you look to the other side of the Rhône from the riverside village of Roquemaure, one of the four communes that make up the appellation of Lirac, you can spy Châteauneuf-du-Pape. It's a reminder of better times and changing fortunes – the wines of the west bank were once more highly prized than those of the east. In the fourteenth century Roquemaure was a major port. By the sixteenth century, Lirac wines were held in great esteem and served in royal courts both in France and abroad. Like so often in France, it was phylloxera that rammed Lirac off the highway and into the dust. It was the first appellation to be infected, in fact – Lirac is phylloxera's ground zero. It was here that vines sent from America were planted by Monsieur Borty in his garden in 1862 (see page 17). Aphids housed in the vines went on to destroy over a million hectares of French vineyards. It wasn't until 1925 that the appellation rebuilt itself in earnest, thanks in part to the hard work of Comte Henri de Régis de Gatimel of Château de Ségriès, an important estate to this day.

Appellation: AOC Lirac

Birth of the appellation: 1947

Communes: Lirac, Roquemaure, Saint-Geniès-de-Comolas, Saint-Laurent-des-Arbres

Total surface area sold under the AOC in 2019: 857 hectares

Average yield in 2019: 25 hectolitres per hectare

Colours permitted: red, rosé, white

Production in 2019: 87 per cent red, 3 per cent rosé, 10 per cent white

Grape varieties permitted: For reds the majority of the blend must be composed of Grenache, Syrah, Mourvèdre and Cinsault. The following accessory varieties may be used, but can't make up more than 10 per cent of the finished blend: Carignan, Clairette Rose, Counoise, Grenache Gris, Marsanne, Piquepoul Blanc, Piquepoul Noir, Roussanne, Ugni Blanc and Viognier.

Regulations for rosés are the same as for reds, but the accessory varieties above can contribute up to 20 per cent of the finished blend.

For whites the majority of the blend must comprise Bourboulenc, Clairette, Grenache Blanc and Roussanne. Marsanne, Piquepoul Blanc, Ugni Blanc and Viognier may also be used.

More recent history isn't all glowing either. The early 1960s saw an influx of Pieds-Noirs from Algeria. These dynamic agricultural pioneers weren't afraid of getting their hands dirty, but they planted without a nuanced understanding of the terroir. Since then, a lot of vineyard land has been purchased by large estates from neighbouring appellations attracted by inexpensive land with great possibility. Some vineyards have been bought by Tavel estates, looking to add red and white wines to their range as dark rosé has become increasingly difficult to sell. Still more vineyards have been bought by wealthy Châteauneuf-du-Pape producers who can see an opportunity to diversify their offering with more affordable wines. You could argue that their modern facilities and commercial networks can only be good for Lirac's global reputation. But very good though these wines often are, Châteauneuf producers are less likely to be invested in the appellation than Lirac-based estates that only make Lirac wines, and to consolidate and move forward, this is what Lirac needs.

You can understand the interest from Châteauneuf producers. Much of the terroir is like that of Châteauneuf, and it costs one tenth of the price. There are beds of *galets roulés* over clay in and around the villages of Saint-Laurent-des-Arbres and Lirac, particularly on the plateau of Vallongue. There's more sand and clay around Saint-Geniès-de-Comolas and Roquemaure. There are also some jagged outcrops of limestone colluvial deposits. Generally speaking, the soils are a patchwork. It feels more hilly and rolling than Châteauneuf, more closed in, and there are some deep wooded valleys that tunnel into the mountains to the west.

Lirac is the only Rhône *cru*, except for Vacqueyras, to make all three colours, and although reds make up the clear majority of the volume, the whites are just as convincing. Bernard Duseigneur of Domaine Duseigneur in Châteauneuf also owns land in Lirac. 'People are still looking for their identity,' he says, 'they were previously trying to make a mini Châteauneuf-du-Pape, but the race for power is long gone now.' Though you can still find uncomfortable expressions of full-throttle Lirac, there is a move towards a more transparent, elegant style that feels like a more genuine expression. What characterizes Lirac for me is a slimmed-down finesse compared to Châteauneuf, less rich in body and less generous than much of the east bank, with a particularly fine tannic expression and front-loaded acidity. If Châteauneuf is powerful, Lirac is svelte. It is feline.

The white wines are in a similar style – finer and more tense than the other *cru* whites of Châteauneuf-du-Pape, Vacqueyras and Cairanne. That said, there are essentially two styles of white Lirac: a concentrated, palate-coating, sometimes oak-influenced style that can err towards the tropical (such as the Château Saint-Roch Confidentielle and Domaine Pelaquié's Luc Pélaquié), and a finer, more floral style that seems more identifiably Lirac. There are excellent examples of both styles Lirac produces the most drinkable white wines of the Southern Rhône.

Lirac's rosés are also among the best in the Rhône Valley, and vary from the very pale to a medium depth of hue, but rarely as deep as Tavel. Unlike Tavel, there's no mandatory intensity of colour for Lirac rosés. Unsurprisingly, therefore, most are fashionably pale, though sometimes at the expense of character and flavour. Although some estates make excellent examples, such as Château de Montfaucon, Castel Oualou, Château le Devoy Martine and Château Boucarut, some even better rosés can be found next door in Tavel.

Duseigneur confirms that Lirac prices *en vrac* are still close to those of generic Côtes-du-Rhône, and around a third of the wine that could be sold under AOC Lirac is sold under other appellations such as Côtes-du-Rhône – you couldn't imagine that happening in Châteauneuf. Rodolphe des Pins of Château de Montfaucon is also the president of AOC Lirac, so it's no surprise to hear him state, 'I think Lirac has enormous potential.' Tasting his wines, however, you see that it really does. However, for the foreseeable future, Lirac remains more a story of specific terroirs and individual producers rather than that of a unified style.

Key producers

Domaine des Carabiniers

Roquemaure

www.biodynamicwine.bio

I've rarely encountered a domaine so enthusiastic about and wedded to biodynamics as Domaine des Carabiniers – their web address bears witness to that. The family domaine dates back to the 1930s. In the 1980s and 1990s fourth generation Christian Leperchois greatly expanded the estate to its current 50 hectares and converted it to organic viticulture. His son, current winemaker Fabien, joined in 2006 and converted it to biodynamics. He attributes the fact that the estate escaped the coulure of 2017 and the downy mildew of 2018 to this approach. Fabien makes no additions to his wines, except for minimal sulphites with certain cuvées when necessary. He puts the widespread acidification of wines in the Rhône down to a desire to please American critics who favour powerful, tannic wines. 'My goal is to harvest the grapes with correct acidity, correct alcohol and good fruit,' he says. There is some IGP Pays d'Oc and AOC Côtes-du-Rhône, but they also make red and white Lirac, Tavel and a red Châteauneuf-du-Pape. Output can be inconsistent, but when at their best the vibrant Liracs and Tavel are among the best in the appellation.

Domaine Coudoulis

Saint-Laurent-des-Arbres

T.: +33 (0) 4 66 50 02 59

Currently in conversion to organic viticulture, Domaine Coudoulis has quietly been going from strength to strength since being bought by Bernard Callet in 1996. It's a single 28-hectare block of vines in Saint-Laurent-des-Arbres, mostly old-vine Grenache grown in *gobelets* among *galets roulés*, along with some Syrah, Carignan and Cinsault. They now make five Lirac cuvées. Dedicace is a fine and measured style, made

LOWER WEST BANK 225

of Grenache, Syrah and Cinsault; Evidence a little more concentrated, using Mourvèdre instead of Cinsault. Hommage is a parcel selection of the best fruit of the domaine. Cuvées S (pure Syrah) and G (pure Grenache) are only made in exceptional years. The new cellar, built in 2012, has given the estate a further leg up. The style is elegant, tailored, and very true to type.

Domaine Maby

Tavel

www.domainemaby.fr

The Maby family has been growing vines in neighbouring Tavel since the beginning of the nineteenth century, but it was really in the 1950s and 1960s that the estate grew significantly, eventually covering 120 hectares across Lirac and Tavel. The estate split in 1996, and today Richard Maby owns 60 hectares, including his Côtes-du-Rhône and IGP land in nearby Pujaut. Today he makes a red IGP, a red Côtes-du-Rhône, three Tavel cuvées, and six Liracs. His top-of-the-range Tavel and white Lirac are distinctly oak-influenced, but the entry-level Fermade trio of Liracs and two less expensive Tavels are delightfully drinkable and offer remarkable value for money.

Château de Montfaucon

Montfaucon

www.chateaumontfaucon.com

Montfaucon is the area nearest to the river to the north of Roquemaure. The château towers above it and is visible for miles – it's an imposing edifice, the first tower of which was built in the eleventh century. It was enlarged in the Middle Ages then again in 1880, and the winery at the foot of the château was used from the sixteenth century until 1936, when the owners began selling their grapes to the local cooperative. In 1995, on inheriting the estate, Rodolphe des Pins rebuilt the winery and started bottling again. He is a rare mix of the visionary and the personable which is exactly what is needed in his position as president of AOC Lirac.

They now own 60 hectares of vineyards and amongst other appellations make two red Liracs, two white Liracs and one rosé Lirac. All are consistently excellent wines, arguably the best in the appellation, made in a straight and savoury style that's designed to age – and they age very well indeed. Their top white cuvée Vin de Madame la Comtesse is particularly intriguing. It's a field blend from a terraced vineyard of sand, clay and pebbles planted in 1870 but almost entirely Clairette and Clairette Rose. Fermented in used barriques, it's aromatically discreet, with pear, aniseed and citrus pith, but on the palate it's electric. A deeply intellectual and consistent cuvée that is emerging to be one of the most distinctive white wines of the Southern Rhône.

Other good examples

Domaine de la Mordorée, **Château d'Aqueria** and particularly **Domaine l'Anglore** (see Tavel, below, for full profiles) are also among the best producers of Lirac, as is **Château de Ségriès**. Other strong local producers to consider are **Château le Devoy Martine**, **Château de Manissy**, **Domaine du Joncier**, **Domaine Lafond Roc-Epine**, **Château Saint-Roch**, **Mas Isabelle**, **Château de Bouchassy**, **Vignobles Assemat** and **Domaine la Lôyane**. Newcomers **Clos des Serènes** and **Domaine Jocelyn Raoux** show promise. Very good Liracs are made by the following producers based in Châteauneuf-du-Pape: **Domaine de Marcoux**, **Domaine Roger Sabon**, **Château Mont-Redon**, **Domaine Duseigneur**, **Domaine Pierre Usseglio** and **Domaine Grand Veneur**. **Famille Brechet** of **Domaine des Bosquets** in Gigondas makes a Lirac cuvée called Le Plateau des Chênes which is a good, affordable option. Local cave cooperative **Rocca Maura** is a source of some very good, occasionally really excellent, Lirac cuvées. Négociants **Ogier** and **Chapoutier** are also good sources.

TAVEL

There's no argument over which appellation is the most famous in the Southern Rhône. For decades, this has deservedly been Châteauneuf-du-Pape, and there's no sign of that changing. The prize for the most unusual appellation, however, would surely go to Tavel – the only one to make exclusively rosé wines. And not just any rosé: a particularly dark, deeply coloured one. By their nature, fashions change, so by the time this book is published perhaps dark rosé will be the Next Big Thing. But the trend for pale rosé that has dominated the first two decades of the twenty-first century shows no sign of slowing down. Tavel has not benefited from the rosé boom. If anything, sales have dipped.

Châteauneuf may be more famous now, but that wasn't always the case. If anything, it would appear that Tavel's history is equally, if not more, illustrious. The popes who established Châteauneuf's reputation only arrived in the fourteenth century. Though the first text mentioning the vines of Tavel dates back to 897, earthenware vases decorated with grapes have been found nearby that date back to the first century AD. Vines were so important to Tavel during the nineteenth century that, following the phylloxera crisis, the population of the village dropped by 75 per cent. It didn't take long to bounce back, however, and in 1936 – along with Arbois, Monbazillac, Cassis and Châteauneuf-du-Pape – Tavel was one of the first French wine regions to be awarded *appellation d'origine contrôlée* status. At the time, Tavel was known for the quality of its light red wines, but it was awarded the appellation for rosé wines only; Châteauneuf-du-Pape got whites and reds. At the time, being anointed one of the first AOCs in France was a boost. But being precluded from making red wines from this beautiful terroir was the price it had to pay.

Tavel sits directly to the south of AOC Lirac. Like most of the major west bank appellations, the original growing area follows a small tributary of the Rhône, the Malaven in this case, that flows in from the west. There are three main subzones, each home to a different type of soil. The most striking of these is the *lauses*, angular, white limestone scree that is poor and infertile. This litters the floor of an extended oval bowl to the west of the village that is created by a range of low hills surrounding it, known as the Combe de Malaven. The Malaven river trickles across this valley floor. Jean-Claude Viaud owns vineyards across different terroirs and explains that the *lauses* reflect the sun away (rather than storing the heat like *galets roulés*) meaning it ripens later than other terroirs and the wines, he says, are more mineral. The second soil type is *galets roulés*, a large bed of which is found to the north-east of the village on the plateau of Vallongue. This is a relatively new terroir that was only cleared and established with the arrival of heavy machinery in the 1960s. The galets are accompanied with fine gravels and clay, and give particularly full-bodied, powerful wines. Administratively speaking, Vallongue is bisected east to west in the middle: the southerly half of the plateau is AOC Tavel; the northern half is AOC Lirac. There's nothing to the naked eye which suggests the southern half is any different from the northern half. Appellation boundaries feel distinctly arbitrary sometimes. The third main soil type is sand, found mostly to the east of the village, where many of the more historic estates are situated. It's easy to cultivate, and produces wines of finesse. Another terroir allied to this is the *terres blanches*, but there is some disagreement between winemakers as to whether this constitutes a distinct fourth terroir. It's a deep, fine, friable soil made of up clay, silt and a high proportion of colluvial limestone.

The wines are grown from the typical smorgasbord of Rhône varieties, centred around Grenache, but 18 per cent of the growing area is made up of Cinsault, a greater percentage of the vineyard area than any other appellation. It grows twice as much as Châteauneuf, despite being a third of its size. This thin-skinned variety could account for why Tavel was historically famous for light-coloured reds. Once picked, grapes are cold macerated for between 12 and 48 hours before being pressed, then the press and free run juices are fermented at low temperature, typically around 14–18°C. The wines are sometimes clarified by 'flotation' (sparging with nitrogen to make suspended matter rise to the top, with the wine then racked off from below), malolactic is usually blocked to retain acidity and wines are usually filtered. Tavel has become quite a technical style of wine.

That Tavel is a dark rosé is stipulated in its *cahier des charges* – a spectrometer is used to measure colour density, and if the wine is too light or too dark, it's rejected. The winemakers of Tavel may have missed out on the global craze for pale rosé, but even if they could change the tint of their wine, many producers would proudly refuse. 'I don't want to surf a trend,' says Dominique Le Dantec of Domaine Amido. 'Trends pass. Tavel remains.' You could argue that the appellation laws are doing precisely what they are meant to do: defending a traditional style of wine. But some winemakers are beginning to question whether this truly is a terroir exclusively for rosés (see box, page 230). Tavel wines aren't just deep in colour, they are also peerlessly deep in flavour. They have all the generosity and roundness of neighbouring reds and a certain edge that brings drinkability. The best have genuine complexity and remarkable longevity – they can easily last 10 years in good vintages, losing a little brightness of colour and taking on slightly maderized notes of caramel, honey and tobacco. They are highly versatile with food, particularly lightly spiced dishes. Less successful bottles can be heavy, however, overly full in body, with unbalanced alcohol and confected flavours ('Haribo' as one producer accurately pointed out).

The appellation has seen many highs and lows over its remarkable history. The current situation isn't easy. This once-great terroir currently sells over half its wines in supermarkets at low prices. 'It's a difficult market,' says Luc Pélaquié, with admirable understatement. Some producers such as Domaine Lafond Roc-Epine and Domaine Maby have experimented with oak barrels, but results haven't been overwhelmingly positive. Raphaël de Bez of Château d'Aqueria says 'there was a very difficult time, 2005 to 2010, when *rosé de Provence* really exploded in France, but quite a few [consumers] are questioning that now. I think it will change. It's a fashion thing … I'm confident in the future.'

Appellation: AOC Tavel
Birth of the appellation: 1936
Communes: Roquemaure, Tavel
Total surface area sold under the AOC in 2019: 898 hectares
Average yield in 2019: 33 hectolitres per hectare
Colours permitted: rosé only
Grape varieties permitted: Wines must be a blend, and must include Grenache. Other principal varieties are Bourboulenc, Cinsault, Clairette, Clairette Rose, Grenache Blanc, Grenache Gris, Mourvèdre, Piquepoul Blanc, Piquepoul Gris, Piquepoul Noir and Syrah. Minor permitted varieties are Calitor, Carignan, Carignan Blanc.

Key producers

Domaine l'Anglore

Tavel

T.: +33 (0) 4 66 33 08 46

Who are the greatest winemakers in the Southern Rhône? Perhaps it's a matter of opinion, but I'd be surprised if Eric Pfifferling wasn't in the Top 10. He originally took his grapes to the local cave cooperative but increasingly he found he couldn't drink the resulting wines, describing them as 'very chemical, very technological – they gave me a kind of indigestion.' He pulled out in 2002 and struck out on his own after travelling around France, spending time with natural wine luminaries such as Thierry Puzelat, Jean Foillard and Pierre Overnoy. He now just makes the best wines possible, usually by carbonic maceration, from his 20 hectares of vineyard spread across Tavel, Lirac, Côtes-du-Rhône and IGP Gard. If this means blending across Lirac and Tavel, or making red wines from Tavel terroir, so be it, even if it means bottling them as Vin de France. He usually, but not always, uses minimal amounts of sulphites. Get hold of his wines if you can. They are among the most exciting in the Rhône.

Tavel – a terroir for reds?

Some local winemakers argue that the tradition for Tavel is rosé wine so Tavel should stick to rosé, even if the market is tough. But how far back should we look when talking about tradition? In his book *Tavel: The people and the wines*, Rolf Bischel quotes Monique Fraissinet of Domaine Fraissinet, who says: 'Tavel is not a *rosé de saignée*, it is a wine somewhere between rosé and red, but since there is no name for this, it is called a rosé. Tavel was always deep in colour. I have a document from Tavel's first winemaking *syndicat* that states: "Tavel is not a rosé, it is a gold-tinted ruby wine."' The entry for Tavel in the 1933 edition of the *Larousse Encyclopaedia* agrees: 'Red wine, harvested from around Tavel (Gard). It's a pale wine, but light and pleasant and lasts well.'

So if Tavel was historically a red wine (albeit a pale one), why was it described as a rosé in the original *cahier des charges*? In all likelihood it was to distinguish it from the powerful, dark reds of Châteauneuf-du-Pape over the river – after all, these two were part of the original group of five *appellations d'origine contrôlées* of 1936. That this legislation was championed by Baron Le Roy of Châteauneuf-du-Pape is an interesting detail – no doubt he was keen to avoid any competition between the two.

Rosé wine at the time was a broader church than it is today, running from dark Bordeaux Clairet and Tavel to the pale rosés of Provence. Our idea of what a rosé wine is today is closer to a white, and as Tavel rosé has attempted to stay commercially relevant, its stretch towards a paler style, within the limits of appellation rules, has pushed it even further from its pale red roots.

To walk around the appellation there's nothing that outwardly suggests that this terroir should be one solely for rosé wine. That the Vallongue plateau is sliced in half, with rosé being made in the Tavel half, and reds being made in the Lirac half, underlines this impression. Some producers, such as Domaine l'Anglore and Domaine Moulin la Viguerie, are already making Tavels as dark as many Ploussards from the Jura, Mencias from Bierzo and Pinot Noirs from Burgundy – with excellent results.

That Tavel produces some of the most characterful rosés in France is beyond doubt; the wines are complex, mineral and long-lived. But as the wine has evolved, becoming ever more technical in its production, is it genuinely a wine of terroir, or one that has simply forged a strong style? I'm sure that Domaine de la Romanée Conti could make a complex, mineral and long-lived rosé from La Romanée Conti. But would it be better than their pale red?

Château d'Aqueria

Tavel

www.aqueria.com

The story of d'Aqueria begins when Louis Joseph d'Aqueria bought a plot of land in Tavel, called Puy Sablonneux, from the monks of the Abbey of Villeneuve-Les-Avignon. His son Robert built a home that was then transformed in the eighteenth century into the impressive country house that still stands today. It's had many owners over the centuries, but is currently owned by the Olivier family, who bought it in 1919. It is now run by the third generation, brothers Vincent and Bruno Le Bez. There are 70 hectares in a single plot around the château, spread across Lirac, Tavel and Côtes-du-Rhône. They are strong in both *crus*, but 80 per cent of their output is Tavel (just one cuvée), a blend of Grenache, Grenache Blanc, Clairette, Cinsault, Mourvèdre, Syrah, Bourboulenc and Piquepoul Blanc. They opt for a short maceration time (18–24 hours), producing a particularly fine, straight style that ages remarkably well. Despite the size of production (around 250,000 bottles) quality is consistently excellent.

Domaine Lafond Roc-Epine

Tavel

www.domaine-lafond.com

Pascal Lafond has recently been joined by his two sons to help farm this 80-hectare organic domaine, which is often the source of excellent value Lirac and Tavel. Around half of the holding is in Tavel, mostly on *lauses* and *galets roulés*. The L'Esprit de Roc-Epine is partly aged in new oak (a third of the blend for a month).

Domaine de la Mordorée

Tavel

www.domaine-mordoree.com

Perhaps better known for its powerfully ripe Châteauneuf-du-Pape, year after year Domaine de la Mordorée also makes some of the best wines in Tavel. The estate was established in 1986 by Francis Delorme and his son Christophe. Following Christophe's early death at the age of 52, the 50-hectare estate is now managed by his wife Madeleine and their daughter Ambre. They make two cuvées. La Dame Rousse is taken from a variety of Tavel terroirs. La Reine des Bois is the top cuvée and comes from a 3-hectare plot of 40-year-old vines on the Vallongue plateau, which is cold macerated for 48 hours. It represents a big step up in quality, bold and complex, and is arguably the greatest 'traditional' Tavel.

Domaine Moulin la Viguerie

Tavel

T.: +33 (0) 6 83 51 40 54

Gaël Petit's family has been at the heart of the Tavel appellation for centuries, and he himself was president of the Tavel appellation for 5 years, until 2018. A deep thinker, he owns one of the largest libraries of wine books I've seen in the Rhône. Like Eric Pfifferling, he believes at some point Tavel 'forgot how to make wine,' relying increasingly on mechanization and technological methods that wouldn't have been available for much of Tavel's existence. He is starting to experiment with darker rosés and the results are spectacular.

Other good examples

The following all make reliable, classic styles of Tavel. In a lighter, crisper style are **Prieuré de Montézargues**, **Roudil Jouffret**, **Domaine la Rocalière** and **Domaine Pélaquié** (see Laudun). Reliable, classic examples can be found at **Château de Trinquevedel** and **Domaine Amido**. Dark, fuller wines are more common at **Château de Manissy** and **Château de Ségriès** (see Lirac). The biodynamic **Domaine des Carabiniers** (see Lirac) is a particularly good exponent. **Balazu des Vaussières** make extraordinary, highly idiosyncratic and sometimes brilliant natural wines; their white and red Vin de France cuvées are declassified Lirac and the rosé Vin de France is declassified Tavel.

SIGNARGUES

You won't find a village called Signargues on the map. Like Massif d'Uchaux and Plan de Dieu – two other Named Villages created in 2005 – its name refers to a feature of the local landscape. Outcrops of pebbly soils are what all the Lower West Bank appellations have in common, and the plateau of Signargues is a particularly large bank of *galets roulés*, the same Villafranchian deposits that are found in Châteauneuf-du-Pape and Gadagne. It's a sizeable appellation, and along with Gadagne is one of the furthest south of all the Named Villages. The growing area lies just across the Rhône from Avignon as the river redirects southwest. It's the gateway to Costières de Nîmes, and the Mediterranean beyond. This flat plateau sits at 150 metres above sea level and wanders across four communes. Within are two valleys, effectively creating three raised terraces; in the dips the vineyards are classified as AOC Côtes-du-Rhône or Vin de France. Otherwise, it's a strikingly uniform pebbly landscape, criss-crossed by pylons. The galets here can reach a depth of 1.5 metres before you hit the clay beneath. President of the local *syndicat* Francis Fabre says that any differences apparent in the wine are more likely derived from vignerons' choices than fluctuations in the terroir.

The hot and sunny climate is 'the most Mediterranean possible,' according to Jean-Marie Granier of Les Vignerons d'Estézargues. It is particularly pummelled by the mistral; if you're planning on bringing your caravan here for a holiday, choose your plot carefully as the wind has been known to blow them over. Syrah is no fan of strong winds either, but one third of plantings are made up of this variety (Grenache makes up half, the rest is Mourvèdre, Cinsault and a little Carignan). Fabre explains that much of the Syrah was planted in the 1960s and 1970s, when only certain varieties were permitted by the INAO. Carignan wasn't allowed, and most growers weren't familiar with Mourvèdre, so Syrah proliferated.

Some wines can have a charismatic swagger, but I remain unconvinced that growing abundant Syrah on this hot bank of stones is the obvious choice. Wines can often feel uncomfortable: high in alcohol, overripe, like drinking fists. There are glimmers of elegance, however, particularly from Domaine des Romarins, and certain cuvées from Les Vignerons d'Estézargues are muscular and sinewy but not overbearing. It's home to some very competent and passionate vignerons which is good news for the future, but for now at least many of the wines could be described as 'work in progress'.

Appellation: AOC Côtes-du-Rhône Villages Signargues
Birth of the appellation: 2005
Communes: Domazen, Estézargues, Rochefort de Gard, Saze
Total surface area sold under the AOC in 2019: 445 hectares
Average yield in 2019: 35 hectolitres per hectare
Colours permitted: red only
Grape varieties permitted: As per communal Côtes-du-Rhône Villages regulations (see page 54)

Key producers

Domaine des Romarins

Domazan

domainedesromarins.wordpress.com

As well as being president of the appellation, Francis Fabre owns Domaine des Romarins, where he works with his two sons. The vineyards have been in the family for generations, with some vines over 50 years old. The first estate-bottled wine came in 1980. Unusually for Signargues, most of the grapes are hand-harvested. The wines have a distinct drinkability and finesse.

Les Vignerons d'Estézargues

Estézargues

T.: +33 (0) 4 66 57 03 64

Natural wine and cooperative wineries are two worlds that rarely meet, but Les Vignerons d'Estézargues is rather special. Set up in 1965, it's a society of 12 winemaking families making around three million bottles a year. Although most of the wine is blended into large volume cuvées across all the different properties, member domaines also make a wine under their own name using their own fruit. Wines are 'as natural as possible,' according to Jean-Marie Granier: 80 per cent is organic and some wines are bottled unfiltered, while others only use minimal sulphite additions at bottling, if at all. These days, it's rarely a cooperative that makes the best wine in any given appellation, but Les Vignerons d'Estézargues makes some of the freshest, most characterful and exciting wines of Signargues.

Other good examples

Domaine de la Rouette, **Domaine des Andrines** and **Domaine de la Charité** are three other names to look out for in Signargues.

COSTIÈRES DE NÎMES AND CLAIRETTE DE BELLEGARDE

Sometimes Rhône appellations have natural borders: soil types, rivers, woods, mountains. More often they share borders with neighbouring appellations, and there can be stylistic blurring at the edges. And just as appellations can blur and blend, so can entire wine regions. Costières de Nîmes, neatly described by wine writer Andrew Jefford as 'the *cru* wine of the Camargue', is the most south-westerly appellation in the Rhône Valley, stretching down to the Mediterranean and abutting onto the neighbouring wine region of the Languedoc. Its furthest vineyards from Avignon certainly feel very different from the Rhône heartland; you pass white horses grazing on pasture and blue-green cacti standing tall. Under its former name of Costières du Gard it fell under the Languedoc-Roussillon family of vineyards; since changing its name in 1989, it sits under the Rhône umbrella. It may have a feel all of its own, but a look at the soils beneath your feet demonstrates clearly that the terroir here is undeniably more Rhône than Languedoc.

The soils here are composed of the same *galets roulés – terraces Villafranchiennes* laid down in the Quaternary Period – made famous by Châteauneuf-du-Pape, and also commonly found in Lirac, Signargues and Gadagne. The deposits here are larger still, with thousands of hectares of rounded red, brown and ochre stones over water-retaining clay. It's a massive appellation, covering over 4,000 hectares, a quarter of which is either organically or biodynamically farmed.

The appellation covers 24 communes, which follow the bank of stones that sits just south of Nîmes and runs north-east to south-west. It can be broadly split into two halves, a northern part and a southern part. Though all the galets originate from the Alps, they were deposited by different rivers: the northern part by the Rhône, the southern section by the Durance. The northern section is largely flat, sitting at around 60 metres above sea level. There's a small limestone outcrop as well as *galets roulés*, with some loess covering patches of the galets. Some of these stones are huge: Cyril Marès of Mas Carlot says he once found one weighing 78 kilograms. The dominant wind here is the mistral. The southern section gently slopes down to sea level, with a mix of different sizes of pebble, some very small. It's also swept by the mistral, but the dominant wind here in summer is the dewy marin. During the afternoons, hot air rises as the sun hits the pebbles, sucking in cooler sea air as a result. Fanny Molinié-Boyer of Château Beaubois says that although her domaine near Saint-Gilles is marginally further south than Nîmes, it is regularly 3–4°C cooler during the summer as a result of this effect. She explains that there are more white varieties planted in the southern part of the appellation as a result, and the reds here display 'elegance, finesse and fruit' compared to the northern part, whose reds exhibit more 'concentration, power and spiciness'.

Costières de Nîmes

Appellation: AOC Costières de Nîmes
Birth of the appellation: 1986
Communes: Aubord, Beaucaire, Beauvoisin, Bellegarde, Bernis, Bezouce, Bouillargues, Le Cailar, Caissargues, Garons, Générac, Jonquières-Saint-Vincent, Lédenon, Manduel, Meynes, Milhaud, Nîmes, Redessan, Rodilhan, Saint-Gilles, Sernhac, Uchaud, Vauvert, Vestric-et-Candiac.
Total surface area sold under the AOC in 2019: 3,680 hectares
Average yield in 2019: 48 hectolitres per hectare
Colours permitted: red, rosé, white
Production in 2019: 50 per cent red, 43 per cent rosé, 7 per cent white
Grape varieties permitted: Reds must be a blend of at least two varieties, and must include at least one of the following principal varieties: Grenache, Mourvèdre and Syrah (principal grape varieties must make up at least 50 per cent of the blend). Accessory varieties include Carignan, Cinsault and Marselan. No more than 10 per cent Marselan allowed.

Rosés: as for reds.

Whites must be a blend of at least two varieties, and must include at least one of the following principal varieties: Grenache Blanc, Marsanne and Roussanne (principal grape varieties must make up at least 60 per cent of the blend). Accessory varieties include Bourboulenc, Clairette, Macabeu, Vermentino and Viognier. No more than 20 per cent Viognier allowed.

In 2012 the local winegrowers' *syndicat* began steps to make these two distinct zones more official, and by 2021, hopes president Bruno Manzone, they will be able to use more specific geographical terminology on labels to specify the wines' origins. The northern part will be known as 'Costières de Nîmes Saint-Roman' and the smaller southern part 'Costières de Nîmes Franquevaux' (the names refer to nearby abbeys). Both sub-appellations will necessitate more stringent production criteria, and are likely to include only red and white wines, not rosés.

This may be Rhône terroir, but Grenache here plays second fiddle to Syrah. When most of the Carignan was pulled up, the relatively fresh climate here was seen as more preferable for this *nordiste* variety. The results have an unmistakable Rhône fullness, but are rarely as concentrated, powerful or extracted as those from more central Rhône vineyards; they are more Victoria plum than damson in flavour, often with *garrigue* herbs and sage. Use of stems is rare, and although some oak-aged cuvées are made to last, most reds are for early drinking. The rosés here can be impressive. For such an extensive appellation, it's not surprising that there's a large amount of very pale, commercial, forgettable pink, but it is possible to find some delicious wines that combine fresh, precise fruit flavour without excess body or gloop. The potential for rosé here is every bit as good as, if not better than, rosés from more illustrious Southern *crus* – and without the price tags. Whites too are strong, and the best of them can go head-to-head with most other Southern Rhône appellations. If Luberon whites can be identified by a vibrant freshness and expressiveness of aroma, and Ventoux whites are marked by an inner steel, then Costières de Nîmes whites are notable for their pillowy softness. They tend to be low in acidity, but compensate with a tense quality and a positive bitter twang. Flavours vary from floral to pithy citrus, and frequently almond. Much of this is thanks to the quality of the local Clairette (see Clairette de Bellegarde), and although this has long been planted here with Grenache Blanc and Roussanne, newcomers Vermentino and Viognier are gaining ground.

This is a large appellation, and the more local growers can be supported in expressing the detail of their terroirs the better; the new geographic designations are a step in the right direction. As one of the eight Other Rhône Valley appellations, it may theoretically sit at the bottom of the appellation pyramid, and if you buy at random, you're more likely to get misses than hits, but there is an energy and enthusiasm here that is heartening and bodes well for the future.

Most appellations have their own section in this book, but the section on Clairette de Bellegarde surely belongs within the section on Costières de Nîmes – just as the appellation sits within the terroir of Costières. Bellegarde is one of the communes included in the Costières de Nîmes appellation, near its heart. To the eye there is nothing to distinguish it from its near neighbours; its 15 hectares of *galets roulés* soils are the same, the land fairly flat, the climate no different. However, producers in this one commune can choose to produce wine under a different appellation, if that wine is a 100 per cent Clairette.

Church records in Nîmes dating back to 1774 mention the importance of Bellegarde in Clairette production, and other local papers dating back to the start of the nineteenth century state that in the Gard *département*, Clairette typically sold for twice as much as other wines. Bruno Manzone of Domaine Manzone says that during this time it was used for communion wine. The oldest parcels here date back to 1929, and the appellation was awarded as early as 1949, but being such a tiny appellation it has never gained a popular following. In 2019 there were just five bottlers: Mas Carlot, Domaine Mazone, Clos des Boutes, Terre des Chardrons and the co-op Vignerons Créateurs, almost all of whom work organically. It remains no more expensive than Costières de Nîmes *blanc*. For a unique and special wine, this is great news for consumers, if not producers.

The wines must be dry, still and made only from Clairette Blanche, not Clairette Rose. Mas Carlot is the master; owner Cyril Marès describes Clairette as 'a blank page, it expresses terroir, and the winemaker's choices.' Some opt for lees stirring, some ferment or age in oak, others don't. It's not strongly aromatic; it has a soft, gentle fragrance that turns around honeysuckle, the peels and piths of citrus fruits, liquorice, honey and almond. It's petal soft and gently oily on your palate with a mineral seam that brings balance and drinkability. Acidity is low; malolactic fermentation is often blocked. A 2010 tasted in 2019 was as fresh and bright as a buttercup. The best can age twice as long as this, picking up hazelnut and petrol notes along the way. It is the quintessential expression of Clairette – the most emblematic white grape of the Southern Rhône.

Clairette de Bellegarde

Appellation: AOC Clairette de Bellegarde
Birth of the appellation: 1949
Communes: Bellegarde
Total surface area sold under the AOC in 2019: 7 hectares
Average yield in 2019: 36 hectolitres per hectare
Colours permitted: white only
Grape varieties permitted: Must be 100 per cent Clairette Blanche

---

Key producers

Château Beaubois

Franquevaux

chateau-beaubois.com

Overlooking the Scamandre *étang* (coastal pond), Château Beaubois sits at just 10 metres above sea level. Fanny Molinié-Boyer and her brother

François work their 55 hectares organically, achieving biodynamic certification in 2019, just in time for the estate's 100-year anniversary in 2020. 'We work on purity,' says Fanny, who pays close attention to picking dates, and uses hands-off winemaking, gentle extraction and larger barrels to achieve it. Around 20 per cent of their output is white. They make ripe, rounded wines in all colours, and are particularly worth visiting if you're looking for good rosé.

Domaine Michel Gassier and Château des Nages

Caissargues

www.domainegassier.com

A winemaker who has done more than his fair share to raise the profile of Costières de Nîmes, Michel Gassier makes wines under two different estates in the appellation. Château des Nages is the family domaine, in which he represents the fourth generation, and recently he has also established a separate domaine under his own name, Domaine Michel Gassier. Both are farmed organically. He has a particularly sensitive touch both in the vineyard and the winery, and makes authentic, balanced wines that deliver real satisfaction. Unusually, he makes a sparkling wine, and it's one of the best in the Southern Rhône.

Mas Carlot and Mas des Bressades

www.mascarlot.com

www.masdesbressades.com

These two estates owned and run by Cyril Marès are just a stone's throw from each other, but are situated in two different communes. Mas des Bressades (45 hectares) is in Manduel and Mas Carlot (65 hectares) in Bellegarde. Cyril is the seventh generation of winemaker in his family; his ancestor Henri Marès (1820–1901) discovered that powdery mildew could be successfully treated with sulphur. Cyril, who took over in 1996 after winemaking *stages* in California and Chile, makes the wines from both estates in the same way. Each estate expresses itself slightly differently, however; the wines of Mas Carlot are fresh and bright, those of Mas des Bressades deep and concentrated. They have been certified organic since the 2020 vintage. Both estates make a range of Costières de Nîmes, and Mas Carlot also produces a particularly fine and ageworthy Clairette de Bellegarde.

Château de Montfrin

Meynes

www.chateaudemontfrin.com

This imposing château, with extensive surrounding vineyards and olive groves, is currently owned by actor and film producer Jean-René de Fleurieu. The estate produces nine organic wines across Vin de France, IGP, Côtes-du-Rhône, Côtes-du-Rhône Villages and Costières de Nîmes. The wines, like their labels and cuvée names, are original and highly individual.

Château Mourgues du Grès

Beaucaire

www.mourguesdugres.com

François Collard's father was something of a pioneer in Costières de Nîmes. He bought an old agricultural estate, owned by the local Ursuline nuns since the sixteenth century, with the intention of focusing on arboriculture (*Mourgues* is an old Provençale term for nuns, *grès* for *galets roulés*). But he also planted vines, and they flourished. He was one of the first in the region to plant Syrah. François joined the property in 1990, and they bottled their first wine in 1994. He and his wife Anne now farm 65 hectares organically, only adding sulphites at bottling, and they are moving towards biodynamics. They make 11 different cuvées to mirror the subtle gradations of their terroir, aiming to make tense, mineral, elegant and aromatic wines – and doing so with great success. Their Capitelles bottlings are among the most stylish in the appellation.

Other good examples

Château l'Ermitage, **Château de Campuget**, **Domaine du Vistre**, **Château d'Or et de Gueules**, **Domaine de Boissière**, **Domaine Renouard**, **Château Font Barrièle**, **Mas du Notaire**, **Château Vessière**, **Clos des Centenaires** and **Château Guiot** are worth exploring in Costières de Nîmes. **Domaine Mazone** and **Terre des Chardrons** are additionally notable for the quality of their Clairette de Bellegarde.

14

THE DIOIS

If the wines of the Rhône Valley can be divided into the Northern Rhône and the Southern Rhône, then where should we place the wines of the Diois? The valley of the Drôme lies north of Montélimar, which is generally considered to be the frontier between North and South, but the majority of plantings are of Southern Rhône varieties: Muscat à Petits Grains and Clairette, mostly for sparkling wine. Cut off from the rest of the Rhône growing area, this is very much a region apart.

Getting there is easy enough. If you're leaving the Southern Rhône by car, you're likely to travel north along the A7 motorway. Halfway between Montélimar and Valence you can come off at the D104, which follows the river Drôme east up the Drôme valley towards the Alps. Within a few minutes you're treated to a breathtaking view of the hill of Brézème on the opposite bank. Drive for a further 20 minutes and the hills begin to rise and fold. Pass the town of Crest and you're in the vineyards of the Diois, which continue for 30 kilometres as the crow flies. As you step out of the car, the grassy air feels a little more scintillating than when you got in. There are fields of lavender – but olive trees are rare.

Just like the Tave, the Ouvèze and the Aigues further south, the Drôme is a tributary of the Rhône. The terrain here, however, is very different compared to these other waterways: the Drôme valley is tight, it cuts deep, with hills and mountains rising high around it. Half of the land is covered in forest. There are around 1,700 hectares of vines, planted on both sides of the river, so roughly the same surface area as Crozes-Hermitage. But this is no monocultural sea of vines; the parcels are small, concealed and dispersed, surrounded by fruit and nut trees, vegetables, hay and livestock. The average vineyard holding of a private domaine here is just 6 hectares. Even the villages are small; the biggest is Die with just 4,500 inhabitants. This is a peaceful, rural setting hemmed in by mountains; the Vercors to the north, the Baronnies to the south, the Ecrins to the east. It feels very different to the rest of the Rhône Valley vineyards. Wink Lorch features the Diois in detail in her book *Wines of the French Alps,* and says that the region 'is nothing like the Rhône Valley; it lies on the Alpine foothills.'

Administratively speaking, however, the four appellations of the Diois are now considered part of the Other Rhône Valley appellations. The growing area is the same for all of them (31 communes), except for Chatillon-en-Diois, which can be made in just 12 of these 31, in the fresher, higher eastern half of the growing area. Here are the appellations in a nutshell.

Clairette de Die

Méthode ancestrale: a sweet sparkling white wine made mostly or entirely from Muscat à Petit Grains Blancs. It's a sweet and frothy, naturally low-alcohol, highly aromatic wine, typically featuring floral (jasmine, rose) scents along with fresh fruit (lychee, green apple).

Méthode brut: a dry sparkling white wine made from 100 per cent Clairette. Only 5 per cent of Clairette de Die is made this way, and it rarely has the same freshness or purity of expression as the *méthode ancestrale*.

Crémant de Die

A traditional method sparkling white wine made mostly from Clairette. This is always dry (though sometimes only just), and typically displays pear and apple aromas, sometimes gently floral, rarely marked by much toastiness or lees character.

Coteaux de Die

A dry still white wine made from 100 per cent Clairette. Very little is made. It's a full-bodied, low acid white, the only one from the region that bears any resemblance to a Southern Rhône white, and can certainly rival Clairettes from further south.

Châtillon-en-Diois

Dry still wines in three colours. Whites are either Chardonnay, Aligoté or both. Wines are typically light and precise, often straightforward, and closer in style to Jura than Mâcon. The Chardonnays are occasionally oaked, and are more accessible than the Aligotés, which are particularly mineral, sometimes austerely so.

Red and rosés are mostly Gamay, with optional Pinot Noir, Syrah or both. The reds range from the light, fruity and simple to fairly concentrated, medium-bodied, deeply coloured and fruity wines similar to a *cru* Beaujolais. I'm yet to encounter a rosé.

Let's face it: it's a confusing range of wines that would benefit from clearer nomenclature. Clairette de Die Méthode Brut is gradually being phased out in fact, but while there is still an established market for it, it's difficult to finish it off. In the 1950s there were talks about changing the name from Clairette de Die to Muscat de Die, which again would be helpful for consumers, but the motion failed to pass.

At around 95 per cent of production, AOC Clairette de Die is by far the most important of the four appellations. It's a wine with a long and well-documented history: Pliny the Elder praises a sweet and a sparkling wine made by the Voconces (the local gallic tribe at the time) in his *Natural History* written in the first century AD. The first written mention of Clairette (spelt *clerete*) in the region was in 1748, in a letter written by a notary from Châtillon-en-Diois. The wine became so popular that before phylloxera struck there were 6,000 hectares of vines here. It was devastated like everywhere else in the Rhône, but quickly bounced back, and was one of the first wines to be given an appellation, in 1942. By the 1960s there were around 300 hectares under vine, but with the advent of temperature control, this expanded by the 1980s to around 1,000 hectares. Today there are around 1,600 hectares planted.

It's similar in style to Moscato d'Asti, but made in a different way. After pressing, the must is settled, filtered, and chilled to between 0 and 10°C. Legend has it this once took place in large jars in cold mountain streams, but now methods are more prosaic. Natural yeasts are used for a very long, slow fermentation taking between one and two months. One reason for using the local yeast population is that it has become highly adapted to low temperature fermentation; producers claim that fermentation with these yeasts can even take place below zero degrees centigrade. Part-fermented juice (at around 4 to 5% abv) is then bottled, and the alcoholic fermentation continues at low temperature (around 12°C) to around 8% abv, and the carbon dioxide produced dissolves into the wine, creating the effervescence. There's a minimum time on lees of four months. Fermentation stops when the pressure becomes too high for the yeasts to function. The wines don't go through malolactic. To remove the lees, the bottles aren't usually disgorged by freezing the necks, instead they are emptied into tanks, the wine is filtered again, the bottles are washed to remove any residual yeasts and the wine is rebottled.

A bottle of AOC Clairette de Die Méthode Ancestrale must have at least 35 grams per litre of residual sugar, but 50–55 grams per litre is more typical; there is no maximum limit. No sugar is added during the process. By contrast, Clairette de Die Méthode Brut and Crémant de Die are both dry, with a maximum of 15 grams per litre residual sugar.

The *méthode ancestrale* is a highly technical process requiring considerable financial investment in powerful refrigeration equipment with concentrated glycol. For this reason much of the production is still made by the large cooperative Jaillance, which makes around 80 per cent of all Clairette de Die. It's a unique style of wine, characterized more by the strongly aromatic grape used and the particular vinification process than terroir. This is something of a shame, as there is clearly some very good vine-growing land in the Diois. The vineyards aren't on the valley floor, but on higher banks, often gently sloping, up to 700 metres altitude. There are three principal types of soil: yellow or black marls, colluvial limestone scree and alluvial terraces. The limestone soils give fine, energetic wines, the marls slightly rounder ones – the black marls are less delicate. The grapes from alluvial soils, with more rounded stones, all go into blends, so it's hard to know for certain what particular characteristics they offer.

The Diois is cooler (particularly at night) and wetter than much of the Southern Rhône, with around 800 millimetres of rain a year. Another difference is that the valley is shielded from the mistral. 'The [Massif du] Vercors makes the microclimate here,' according to Franck Monge of Domaine Monge Granon. 'It acts as a barrier to the north wind.' Over a quarter of vineyards are farmed organically. As the climate becomes warmer, planting of red varieties is increasing, but 'for now it's still marginal,' says Fabien Lombard of Domaine Peylong, 'the DNA of the Diois is still sparkling.' He has recently planted Grenache and Mourvèdre; he is using them for IGP rosé while the vines are young, but is looking forward to seeing if they could make red wines as the vines age.

It's hard to predict what the future will look like for this region. It's intimately tied to Clairette de Die, which is both a blessing and a curse: there is an existing market for the wines, but one that's in steady decline due to the growth of rivals such as Prosecco that employ cheaper methods. Clairette de Die has been with us for 2,000 years – it's not going to die out any time soon – but, rather like Tavel, it has become a highly technical, commercial product largely sold at low prices in super-markets, with a small number of committed producers making really delightful examples. But as long as it doesn't really reflect terroir, the interest for the committed wine lover is limited. This isn't the case for the fresh, weightless still wines of the Diois, however, which have a style all of their own. Lombard predicts that over time the production of still wines will increase, and sweet wines will decrease. I suspect he's right.

Clairette de Die

Appellation: AOC Clairette de Die

Birth of the appellation: 1942

Communes: Aix-en-Diois, Aouste-sur-Sye, Aubenasson, Aurel, Barsac, Barnave, Beaufort-sur-Gervanne, Châtillon-en-Diois, Die, Espenel, Laval-d'Aix, Luc-en-Diois, Menglon, Mirabel-et-Blacons, Molière-Glandaz, Montclar-sur-Gervanne, Montlaur-en-Diois, Montmaur-en-Diois, Piegros-la-Clastre, Ponet-et-Saint-Auban, Pontaix, Poyols, Recoubeau-Jansac, Saillans, Saint-Benoît-en-Diois, Sainte-Croix, Saint-Roman, Saint-Sauveur-en-Diois, Suze, Vercheny, Véronne

Total surface area sold under the AOC in 2019: 1,638 hectares

Average yield in 2019: 53 hectolitres per hectare

Colours permitted: sparkling white only

Grape varieties permitted: Must contain at least 75 per cent Muscat à Petits Grains Blancs; can also contain Clairette, Clairette Rose and Muscat à Petits Grains Rouges.

Crémant de Die

Appellation: AOC Crémant de Die

Birth of the appellation: 1993

Communes: as for Clairette de Die

Total surface area sold under the AOC in 2019: 20 hectares

Average yield in 2019: 53 hectolitres per hectare

Colours permitted: sparkling white only

Grape varieties permitted: Principal grape is Clairette; may also contain Aligoté, and no more than 10 per cent Muscat à Petits Grains Blancs. Mutation to Clairette Rose or Muscat à Petits Grains Rouges is tolerated within individual parcels to a maximum of 10 per cent

Coteaux de Die

Appellation: AOC Coteaux de Die

Birth of the appellation: 1993

Communes: as for Clairette de Die

Total surface area sold under the AOC in 2019: 1.5 hectares

Average yield in 2019: 40 hectolitres per hectare

Colours permitted: still white only

Grape varieties permitted: Only Clairette Blanche is permitted, but mutation to Clairette Rose is tolerated within individual parcels to a maximum of 10 per cent

Châtillon-en-Diois

Appellation: AOC Châtillon-en-Diois

Birth of the appellation: 1975

Communes: Aix-en-Diois, Barnave, Châtillon-en-Diois, Laval-d'Aix, Luc-en-Diois, Menglon, Molières-Glandaz, Montlaur-en-Diois, Montmaur-en-Diois, Poyols, Recoubeau-Jansac, Saint-Roman

Total surface area sold under the AOC in 2019: 43 hectares

Average yield in 2019: 44 hectolitres per hectare

Colours permitted: still red, still rosé, still white

Production in 2019: 31 per cent red, 15 per cent rosé, 54 per cent white

Grape varieties permitted: Reds and rosés must contain at least 60 per cent Gamay, may also contain Syrah and/or Pinot Noir, and can only be grown in the communes of Châtillon-en-Diois and Menglon.

For whites Chardonnay and Aligoté, as a blend or a single variety, are permitted.

Key producers

Domaine Achard-Vincent

Sainte-Croix

www.domaine-achard-vincent.com

When they describe themselves as 'organic pioneers' they're not exaggerating: Achard-Vincent has been organic since 1968. Now in the hands of the sixth generation, the 11-hectare estate has been converted to biodynamics, and has been certified since 2005. Perhaps this is the secret behind the great freshness and purity of expression in the wines, all of which are sparkling: six Clairettes and two Crémants. The Crémant de Die P'tit Jules is even more extraordinary for being made with no added sulphites. A highly recommended source of Diois sparkling.

Cave Monge Granon

Vercheny

www.clairette-mongegranon.com

Since the Monge and Granon winemaking families joined forces in 1985, Cave Monge Granon has been one of the biggest estates in the Diois, with 39 hectares of vineyards. In 2006, they established Verdie, a négociant arm, taking their annual production to 600,000 bottles. They might be big, but their wines are among the best in the Diois. They also take their environmental responsibilities seriously, and make some organic and biodynamic cuvées. Their pure Muscat Clairette de Die Très' Or has great purity and freshness, their Crémant de Die is elegant and floral, and wines in the Châtillon-de-Diois range are also very fine, particularly their austerely alpine Aligoté Bio and their single-vineyard Chardonnay Clos de Beylière.

Domaine Peylong

Suze

www.peylong.com

Suze is a small village in the valley of the Gervanne, a tributary of the Drôme in the eastern part of the Diois. This is where you'll find Domaine Peylong, a small, open-minded organic estate owned by Christelle and Fabien Lombard, who represent the sixth generation. Fabien is also co-president of the local *syndicat*. They grow a dozen different varieties of Burgundian and Rhône grapes and even some Cabernet Sauvignon, which flow into seven different IGP and AOC wines across three colours, still and sparkling, dry and sweet. They are one of the few producers of Coteaux de Die, and their barrel-aged cuvée Oublié from a parcel of 45-year-old Clairette demonstrates the potential of still, dry Clairette in the Diois. I hope it will encourage others to move in the same direction.

Cave Poulet & Fils

Vercheny

www.poulet-et-fils.com

Based in the viticulturally important village of Vercheny, this is a modern, fairly large estate that produces a consistently high-quality range of Diois wines, across Crémant de Die, Clairette de Die and

Châtillon-en-Diois. Emmanuel Poulet, the fourth generation, took over in 2004, and by 2012 had achieved HVE certification. He has also developed the export side of the business, now selling wines in 15 countries. His Châtillon-en-Diois *rouge*, from a south-facing slope at 550 metres altitude, is a particularly concentrated and deep example. He'd plant more if he could find more vineyards, but the growing area is minuscule. Label design is generally atrocious in this part of the world, but Poulet's are much better packaged than most.

Other good examples

Jean-Claude Raspail et Fils makes particularly fine Crémant de Die, the Cuvée Flavien being one of the most richly flavoured and characterful of all. **Domaine de Maupas** is the address to visit to experience varied expressions of Châtillon-en-Diois. **Jaillance** makes an extensive range of wines, mostly sparkling. Some cuvées are very good, particularly the Crémant de Die Grande Cuvée Icône and the Clairette de Die bottlings Tradition Bio and Icône Cuvée Blanche. **Cave Carod** (now owned by French wine behemoth Les Grands Chais de France) presents something of a mixed bag but the pure Muscat Clairette de Die Jasmée is light, fine and fresh. **Domaine Lattard** is based just outside of the Diois growing area in Autichamp, a few kilometres south-west of Crest, and the crisp, clean natural wines are worth discovering if you're in the area.

PART 3
THE NORTHERN RHÔNE

15

AROUND AMPUIS

CÔTE-RÔTIE

Even to walk these vineyards is tiring; the smashed panes of schist slip and slide beneath your shoes. To spend day after day here in the beating sun, clearing woodland, building walls and tending vines is hard to imagine. If these craggy folds didn't produce a unique wine, there's no way people would still be farming here. But they do, and have done for over two thousand years. When you look upon these irregular, rickety terraces, you can't help but ask questions: who started this extraordinary endeavour, when and why?

The Northern Rhône inhabits the narrow eastern edge of the raised shelf of igneous and metamorphic rock known as the Massif Central. At its foot runs the Rhône, north to south. There are vineyards on the other side of the river, and even these consist in part of granite hewn off by the river. For many, granite is almost synonymous with the Northern Rhône, but it's not the only rock here. At its southern pole there's limestone, and at the north, at Côte-Rôtie, schist and gneiss. The village of Ampuis is at the centre of the appellation, on the flat land close to the river. When the sun isn't shining it can feel a little dour; a village in need of a haircut and a new pair of shoes. It's the slopes beyond the houses that catch your eye, rising up abruptly from 180 metres to 325 metres altitude. It might not sound much, but the effect is dramatic.

From the heart of Ampuis, the schist runs north and the gneiss goes south. There is some granite here too, at the southern tip of the appellation at the border with Condrieu. Naturally, the real situation is more irregular and detailed; sometimes you see gneiss and schist in the same vineyard, there are thin bands of sparkling white flint, and even banks of small *galets roulés* at the far north of the appellation. The river flows mostly north to south in the Northern Rhône, but between Vienne (just north of Ampuis on the other side of the river) and Condrieu, the river briefly flows north-east to south-west. A series of streams and rivers that tumble down from the plateau above have sliced into the edge of the rock as they snake their course to the Rhône, creating these corrugated, jagged vineyards. Most vineyards face east, south-east and south, but such is their chaotic state some even face south-west and west. These valleys are severe and difficult to cross – often you have to return to the village before taking alternative hairpins back up.

No doubt this terroir caught the eye of Roman winemakers on their journey up the river by boat. Wines were certainly produced here in Roman times, being mentioned by Pliny the Elder, amongst others. There are theories that viticulture may have been started here significantly earlier in fact, around 600 BC by Phocaean Greeks coming up-river from their settlement in Marseille. The wines from around Vienne at the time were known as *picatum*, meaning flavoured with pitch or resin – whether this came naturally or was an added flavouring remains unclear. Due to the punitive taxes on wine shipped via Burgundy, the wines only became better known throughout France from the seventeenth century, once the Loire was opened up as a shipping route (it runs closer to Ampuis than you might imagine, just 43 kilometres away at its closest point). Their early renown was cut short by phylloxera, which arrived around 1880, and by 1893 the vineyards were totally destroyed, with just a few solitary vines remaining according to contemporary reports. The vineyards were slowly rebuilt, but two successive world wars claimed the lives of many local vignerons. In 1949, Côte-Rôtie was fetching around 1 franc per litre and by 1973 there were just 72 hectares in production. Only the most dedicated stuck to the slopes, ignoring more comfortable, better paid jobs in the nearby factories of Vienne and Lyon. As recently as the 1960s, estates bottling large parts of their production were rare. It was only in the late 1970s and 1980s that the wider world began to take notice. Since then, plantings have increased rapidly.

It's often the coolest sites that can still successfully ripen a given grape variety that create its most compelling expression. On the fringes you see the subtle gradations of non-fruit aromas which define a grape variety. So it is with Syrah in Côte-Rôtie. It translates as 'roasted slope', and it's true that the south-facing slopes don't want for ripeness, but this is the most northerly appellation in the Rhône. Compared to Châteauneuf-du-Pape – or even Hermitage – the climate here is far from roasting. The result is a wine with multiple aromatic registers. There are floral notes, particularly violet. Herbs are common, especially juniper, thyme, rosemary and bay leaf, not to mention black olives. Smoky aromas sometimes curl from the glass, smoked meats like duck or bacon, wood smoke, tobacco. There is fruit of course, but it sometimes appears almost as an afterthought – raspberry, redcurrant, blackberry. White, black and pink peppercorns sometimes make an enlivening appearance, but as the climate gets warmer, they're not as common as they once were (see box on rotundone, page 30). It's a wine that is rarely heavy or solid and at its best is haunting, transparent, elegant and tender.

Some of this perfume is thanks to Viognier – up to 20 per cent is allowed in the blend. This is a well-known feature of Côte-Rôtie, but it's worth mentioning that other Northern Rhône appellations can use a proportion of white grapes too: Saint-Joseph can contain up to 10 per cent of Marsanne and/or Roussanne in their reds, and Hermitage up to 15 per cent (but this is much rarer compared to Côte-Rôtie). Another source of this particular fragrance is down to using old local iterations of Syrah such as Serine (see page 256). The historical basis for using Viognier in Côte-Rôtie is uncertain. It's been suggested that Condrieu and Côte-Rôtie both used to make red and white wines, but when appellation rules were drawn up in the 1930s, Condrieu was given white wine production and Côte-Rôtie red. Given the similarity of these terroirs, this is entirely believable. In fact, I've seen labels for white Côte-Rôtie (and even sparkling red Côte-Rôtie!) dating back to 1900. After these two appellations were established, presumably there were a lot of white plants remaining in the vineyards of Côte-Rôtie, hence the 20 per cent rule.

Appellation: AOC Côte-Rôtie

Birth of the appellation: 1940

Communes: Ampuis, Saint-Cyr-sur-le-Rhône, Tupin-et-Semons

Total surface area sold under the AOC in 2019: 323 hectares

Average yield in 2019: 38 hectolitres per hectare

Colours permitted: red only

Grape varieties permitted: Wines must be made of Syrah, with up to 20 per cent Viognier allowed in the blend.

René Rostaing of Domaine Rostaing describes the 20 per cent rule as a 'tolerance' rather than a feature, and only his Côte Blonde contains any Viognier. He says it can be overly prominent in a wine and can 'denature' a Côte-Rôtie, making it flabby. It's rare to find any winemakers using the full tolerance, however – more than 10 per cent is rare, and even at this level it can feel destabilizing. According to the *cahier des charges*, any Viognier must be co-planted in the vineyard, and must be co-fermented. A problem with this is that Viognier ripens before Syrah. One option is to undertake a first pass through the vineyard to hand-pick the white bunches then store them at low temperature before co-fermentation – but this is labour-intensive and expensive. Viognier is much more commonly found in the southern vineyards of Côte-Rôtie, and is rare at its most northerly point.

The appellation is split into 73 *lieux-dits* across three communes. The original decree included just two: Ampuis and Tupin-et-Semons. The more northerly commune of Saint-Cyr-sur-le-Rhône was added in 1966. The two best-known *lieux-dits* are neighbouring sites Côte Blonde and Côte Brune. Occasionally, you might hear the whole of the southern part of Côte-Rôtie described as 'the Côte Blonde', and the northern half 'the Côte Brune'. This is unhelpful to outsiders trying to understand the appellation, but it is understandable: the soils south of Côte Blonde are paler, consisting largely of pale-yellow gneiss; the soils north of Côte Brune are a dark, brown-green schist.

It is the difference in soils of these two hallowed *lieux-dits* that gave rise to the somewhat hackneyed local legend about the two daughters. It goes something like this: once upon a time, a local nobleman called Maugiron lived in the Château d'Ampuis. He owned some of the best vineyards in Côte-Rôtie and gave half of them to each of his two daughters; the blonde daughter was given the Côte Blonde and the brunette was given the Côte Brune. The blonde daughter was very beautiful in youth (like the wines of *lieu-dit* Côte Blonde, which are highly perfumed and approachable young), whereas the brunette had hidden depths and took time to get to know (like the wines of *lieu-dit* Côte Brune, which are less perfumed and more structured). I'm inclined to agree with Jean-Paul Jamet of Domaine Jamet when he says, 'you need to forget this legend; it's for tourists.' To look at the soils in more detail, the paler soils are mostly made up of gneiss mixed with calcareous loess soils from the plateau. These give very perfumed, open and floral wines that are elegant and silky. The darker soils are from weathered micaschists, easily breakable and crumbly, with thin bands of clay within. They also have plentiful iron oxide, visible as crimson staining on the rock. The wines from these soils are darker and more intense, with weightier tannins, appearing more robust in youth but tending to age well. Those grown on granite tend towards a lighter style, but with a distinct saline freshness.

Due to the steepness of the slopes the soils need to be kept in place by drystone walls, here called *cheys*. The terraces that these walls create are known as *chaillés*. They collapse like drunken soldiers when it rains. 'You've never finished repairing the walls,' says Jean-Paul Jamet. 'You could spend your whole life doing it.' Though some vines are trained on wires on the flatter parts at the foot of the slopes and on the plateaux, the Syrah bush vines are traditionally trained on pairs of wooden stakes called *échalas*. It makes for a unique landscape. The scenery is further embellished with an ever-increasing number of billboards popping up among the vines. Since the end of the 1800s, certain producers have painted the larger walls in their vineyards with the names of their domaines and most prestigious cuvées, an early form of advertising to passing train passengers. There are now at least 20, of different shapes and sizes, some professionally painted on walls, others crudely daubed on planks. It doesn't exactly add to the natural beauty of the place. There is legislation being drawn up to prevent any more.

Vineyards on steep slopes and narrow terraces are expensive to work – everything must be done by hand. In common with other Rhône estates, growers in Côte-Rôtie are turning towards organic viticulture, but while pesticides and some fungicides are relatively easy to forgo, finding a way to keep the weeds under control without recourse to herbicides is proving difficult. It can't be done mechanically in the more challenging vineyards, and finding the staff to do it by hand isn't easy – not to mention the significant added expense. Some producers such as Domaine Clusel-Roch, Domaine Georges Vernay and Domaine Pierre-Jean Villa are managing to work without herbicides, but compared to Hermitage and Cornas, progress in Côte-Rôtie is slow. Villa's domaine covers 17 hectares and he started going organic in 2011; by 2021 he should be certified. 'It's a question of investment,' he says, and taking it slowly rather than trying to convert all at the same time. Instead of spraying or ploughing he's been experimenting with using cover crops that don't compete for water around the base of vines, using local plants like mouse-ear hawkweed and sedum. Early experiments are encouraging.

Regarding organics, Christine Vernay of Domaine Georges Vernay says 'Yes it's difficult. But it's possible. And terroir speaks more clearly when you take care of it.'

The traditional method of vinification in Côte-Rôtie was to use whole bunches – sometimes crushed, sometimes not – fermenting in large open-top wooden containers with punching down followed by submerging the cap under the surface of the juice. Wines would then be matured in old barrels, either 225-litre barriques, 600-litre demi-muids or larger foudres of various sizes. The 1980s and 1990s saw numerous new approaches. There was an influx of stainless-steel fermenters, the destemmer was introduced, and producers began using new oak barrels. This 'modern' style no doubt improved many of the more rustic wines at the time, and produced a more polished style of wine that was favoured by the some of the powerful critics of the day. The Côte-Rôties of Guigal – mostly destemmed and matured in 100 per cent new oak barriques – quickly garnered high praise and high prices. Other producers adopted similar approaches, but not always with the same expertise. Overoaking in Côte-Rôtie became widespread, and remains a problem to this day, rubbing out the subtler details of terroir and adding drying, pinched tannins to the wines. The trend now is swinging back towards larger oak barrels, particularly demi-muids, and using a smaller proportion of new oak. Use of whole bunches is also increasing, which, when used sensitively, can add freshness, texture and aromatic interest. Mastering the use of stems will be increasingly important in creating balanced wines as the climate gets hotter.

Côte-Rôtie is a dynamic and exciting appellation, particularly in relation to Hermitage, which is considerably more static. There have been extensive new plantings over the past few decades, and there is still space to plant – both within the appellation, and on some exceptional land on the slopes which happens to be classified as AOC Côtes-du-Rhône. Côte-Rôtie can be expensive, and often overpriced. But find an excellent up-and-coming producer and, unlike regions such as Burgundy, there are spellbinding wines to be found without breaking the bank.

The changing climate is a challenge for the whole of the Rhône Valley, but Côte-Rôtie still appears relatively well placed: a northerly location, a variety of expositions, positive trends in both viticulture and vinification, talented young winemakers and a naturally exceptional terroir. There is still space for Côte-Rôtie to grow and improve: a mouth-watering prospect.

Côte-Rotie échalas

Key producers

Domaine Barge

Ampuis

www.domainebarge.com

A long-established, pioneering estate in Côte-Rôtie, Domaine Barge has been making wine for over 100 years, and was bottling Côte-Rôtie as early as 1929. It is one of the few producers to have a presence on the main street in Ampuis (it's worth calling ahead if you're planning a visit) and the estate is managed today by Julien Barge, who took over from his father Gilles in 2019. He immediately put a stop to all herbicides, effectively turning the estate organic, but is not yet looking for certification. The approach here has always been sensitive, and is increasingly so – rather than looking to expand the 8-hectare estate, if anything the opposite is true. The result is a joyfully vivid and satisfyingly textural range of Côte-Rôties, fermented with stems and bottled unfined and unfiltered. As Julien takes over fully from Gilles, it will be interesting to see how this estate develops.

Domaine P&C Bonnefond

Ampuis

www.domaine-pcbonnefond.fr

Brothers Patrick and Christophe took over the 2.5-hectare family domaine in 1990. The first of the family's vineyards were bought by their great-grandfather, but before they arrived the harvest was sold to négoci-ants. They now have 10 hectares of vineyards, making for a dependable range of wines: 7.5 hectares are in Côte-Rôtie, 1 hectare is in Condrieu and 1.5 hectares are IGP Syrah and Viognier. Their Côte-Rôties have reached a satisfying balance between modern and traditional in style, offering firm but not heavy wines, fine but not overly polished, all with a good sense of finesse and local typicity. All are 100 per cent Syrah, all destemmed, with élevage of 18–20 months in 400-litre barrels. They use 10 per cent new oak for the blended Colline de Couzou and 30 per cent for the single-vineyard cuvées Côte Rozier and Les Rochains. The single-vineyard wines are considerably more intense than the blend, Les Rochains being the more assertive and grippy of the two. Their Condrieu Côte Chatillon is good; succulent and plump, towards the oakier end of the scale.

Domaine Clusel-Roch

Ampuis

www.domaine-clusel-roch.fr

This estate – pronounced *rock* not *rosh* – has farmed vines organically since the end of the 1990s. Attention to detail and quality here is impres-sive – they've been producing their own massal selections from old-vine Serine since 1990. There are three Côte-Rôties. Les Schistes was originally called Classique and is blended from *lieux-dits* La Viallière, Champon and Le Plomb; La Viallière and Les Grandes Places are both single-vineyard wines. All are partially destemmed, fermented with natural yeasts and spend two years in barriques, 15 per cent new oak for the blend, 25 per cent new oak for the *sélections parcellaires*. The style is fairly soft and juicy, with a relatively open-knit feel to the structure. Both single-vineyard wines are elegant, with the old-vines of Les Grandes Places giving a par-ticularly concentrated and complex wine that takes longer to reach its peak. There is also a juicy and affordable range of more straightforward wines from AOC Coteaux Lyonnais to the north of Côte-Rôtie, planted with Gamay and Chardonnay. Their Côte-Rôties aren't the most consist-ent, but when they're good, they're excellent.

Domaine B&D Duclaux

Tupin-et-Semons

www.coterotie-duclaux.com

Brothers Benjamin and David run this estate, which was purchased by their great-grandfather Frédéric Caillet in 1928. It has remained curiously under the radar, perhaps because their holdings are in Tupin-et-Semons, but they show just how good this gneiss terroir can be. The style is strict and savoury and the wines are remarkably structured and ageworthy for this part of the appellation. The two original cuvées – the blended La Germine and single-vineyard Maison Rouge – have long been reliable options, both using around 20 per cent stems, with 20 and 40 per cent new oak respectively. They have recently been joined by two further cuvées. La Chana is a straightforward young-vine cuvée without any great mystery. Les Prunelles (first vintage 2018) sits at the top of their range; a selection of their best parcels from *lieu-dit* Coteaux de Tupin, it is vinified with a higher proportion of stems, around 80 per cent. Another recent addition to the range is their Condrieu, made from young vines in a fresh and precise style that's best drunk young.

Domaine Yves Gangloff

Condrieu

T.: +33 (0) 4 74 59 57 04

Yves Gangloff's brother Pierre was a painter living in the Château d'Ampuis when Yves came to visit him in 1978. Yves wasn't intending to stay for long, but he fell in love. So he stayed in Ampuis, got a job with Delas as a vineyard worker, and eventually got married. The price of land was rather different in the 1980s: he bought his first parcel, 0.8 hectares of Côte-Rôtie, for 85,000 francs in 1983 (approximately €8,000). It would cost him €1m today. He now has 3.3 hectares in Côte-Rôtie, 2.5 hectares in Condrieu and 2.5 hectares in Saint-Joseph near Serrières, making both red and white. He makes three Côte-Rôties, which have short macerations and brief élevage in barriques, with around 15 per cent new oak. He uses a proportion of stems, less for the Serine Noire, even though it comes from older vines. Softly spoken, but with the looks and charisma of an ageing rock star, Yves has always had a sensitive and traditional approach in the vineyards, and makes ethereal, tender wines of extraordinary finesse. His brother still paints; his work adorns Yves' labels.

Domaine Xavier Gérard

Condrieu

T.: +33 (0) 4 26 05 38 70

The last time I visited Xavier he had recently moved into his new gravity-fed cellar in Condrieu and was preparing to receive some visitors

– the whole Lyon rugby team – for an impromptu tasting and barbecue. Clearly the word is starting to get out – Xavier is one of the most exciting new talents in the Northern Rhône. Well I say new; he took over from his father François in 2013 after a stint at Boekenhoutskloof in Franschhoek, South Africa. François' first vintage of Côte-Rôtie was 1980, and he first bought land in Condrieu in 1984.

Gangly, scruffy and full of enthusiasm, Xavier now farms 8 hectares, and is aiming for 12 hectares in total. He wants to keep the business on a small scale so he can continue to work the vineyards and cellar himself. His blended Côte-Rôtie (*lieux-dits* Le Mollard, La Landonne, La Viallière and La Brosse) and his single-vineyard La Landonne – a plot that normally delivers a particularly rugged Côte-Rôtie – have a lightness of touch and impeccable balance. His Condrieus are equally good: they don't shy away from Condrieu's natural richness, but they find an uncommon drinkability and clarity of expression. Even his Saint-Joseph from *lieu-dit* Le Blanchard in Chavanay has a Burgundian elegance. His wines are currently at the cheaper end of what is available in these appellations. They won't be for long.

E. Guigal

Ampuis

www.guigal.com

No producer has played a greater role in the modern history of Côte-Rôtie than négociant house E. Guigal. Based in the heart of Ampuis, it was established in 1946 by Etienne Guigal, but when he was struck temporarily blind in 1961, his son Marcel took over management of the business. Unusually for such a large company, the family is still directly involved in making the wine – Marcel's son Philippe is the chief winemaker. Today the figures speak volumes: they make 8.5 million bottles of wine a year, employ 68 full-time members of staff and own 152 hectares of vineyards, a whopping 40 hectares of which are in Côte-Rôtie. Their success has enabled them to buy other properties, such as nearby négociant house Vidal-Fleury, and Domaine de Bonserine. In 2017 Domaine de Nalys in Châteauneuf-du-Pape was acquired and renamed Château de Nalys; and in 2020 Domaine les Clefs d'Or was added, giving the company a robust presence in the Southern Rhône. They have even bought local landmark the Château d'Ampuis.

Despite making such a huge range of wines, the best known are the three single-vineyard Côte-Rôties – La Mouline, La Turque and La

Landonne – collectively known as the La-Las. La Turque is from the middle section of *lieu-dit* Côte-Brune, while La Mouline is from the heart of *lieu-dit* Côte-Blonde. The parcel of *lieu-dit* La Landonne was planted in 1975 to celebrate the birth of Philippe. La Mouline (89 per cent Syrah) and La Turque (93 per cent Syrah) are usually destemmed, whereas La Landonne (100 per cent Syrah) is made with whole bunches. One thing that makes Guigal's La-Las wines unique is their élevage: 42 months in new oak barriques. In fact, since 2003, an in-house cooper has been employed to keep on top of barrel requirements.

The wines quickly gained very high scores from Robert Parker in his heyday, along with other contemporary critics. Prices rose dramatically, and these are now some of the most expensive wines in the Rhône. Other local growers started to pursue a Guigal-style élevage in the hope of a slice of the action, and this winemaking approach has persisted in the appellation. This long élevage has become part of the Guigal signature style, not just with the Côte-Rôties, but also with other wines in the range, such as the top Saint-Josephs. It certainly imbues the Côte-Rôties with great longevity.

Although the Côte-Rôties tend to hog the limelight, the humble Côtes-du-Rhônes deserve a mention too. Guigal makes 4–4.5 million bottles a year across all three colours – a titanic amount – but for a generic Côtes-du-Rhône the standard is consistently impressive. This company has retained notable quality and consistency throughout its range, despite its vast scale.

Domaine Jamet

Ampuis

www.cote-rotie-jamet.com

There is no obvious single factor that makes Domaine Jamet the greatest estate in Côte-Rôtie. Somehow Jean-Paul Jamet captures the essence of each parcel, managing to remove himself from the finished product, producing beautiful wines that display their terroir in the most pure and vivid way possible. It's a combination of a number of elements: exceptional plots, a traditional way of working, a certain single-mindedness and, quite simply, a natural flair for his work.

The key of course is owning mature vines across some of the best vineyards in Côte-Rôtie, including Fongeant, Côte Blonde, Landonne, Côte Rozier, Le Plomb and Chavaroche. Almost all are entirely Syrah planted on schist, mostly in the commune of Ampuis. While the trend over the past few decades has been to produce a range of single-vineyard wines, the emphasis here remains on blending the 25 parcels from 17 *lieux-dits* to produce one principal domaine Côte-Rôtie. It's true they make a single-vineyard Côte-Brune – consistently among the very finest, most breathtaking wines of the Rhône – but since the start this has been bottled separately. This was the first vineyard that Jean-Paul's father Joseph Jamet started out with in 1950. Jean-Paul started at the domaine in 1976, and worked with his brother Jean-Luc to expand their holdings until they went their separate ways, Jean-Luc establishing a separate domaine under his own name in 2013.

In 2008 another Côte-Rôtie, called Fructas Voluptas, was added to the range. Partly made from bought grapes, this is the only red wine that is destemmed, and is designed to be more approachable than the others. Using stems is an important part of the philosophy here, as is minimizing the use of new oak – two factors that serve to display the wine's origins with clarity. Their Condrieu Vernillon was first produced in 2015 – the year Jean-Paul's eldest son Loïc started working at the estate. A blend of *lieux-dits* Vernon and Côte Chatillon, it is currently the only Condrieu to be matured entirely in amphorae, and the results are already highly impressive. Their Côtes-du-Rhônes, two red cuvées and a white, are from beautiful parcels bordering Côte-Rôtie and represent great value picks.

The case for *premiers crus* and *grands crus* in the Rhône

As the legend of the Seigneur de Maugiron demonstrates, there is already tacit agreement among growers about some of the best *lieux-dits* in Côte-Rôtie. Would it make sense to draw up something more detailed and concrete, a list of *premier* and *grand cru* sites akin to the system in Burgundy? After all, there are significant differences in style – and some quite marked differences in quality – between the 73 *lieux-dits*.

The *cru* system of Burgundy, though not infallible, helps wine lovers explore and familiarize themselves with the endless subtleties of the region. As it stands, there is little for Rhône lovers to hold on to but the crude and confusing distinction between the *blonde* soils of the South and the *brune* soils of the North. 'It's been discussed in Côte-Rôtie a lot,' says Christine Vernay. 'It's more pertinent for Côte-Rôtie than for Condrieu or Saint-Joseph, where a selection has already been made by limiting the highest vineyards to 300 metres – that hasn't been done in Côte-Rôtie. In Côte-Rôtie you have the plateau and the hillside. So you could imagine that the hillside would be *cru* vineyards, the plateau wouldn't be.'

Almost all winemakers would agree on the quality of *lieux-dits* Côte Blonde, Côte Brune and La Landonne. And we would no doubt find broad agreement on *lieux-dits* La Viallière, Les Grandes Places, Lancement, Côte Rozier and probably Chavaroche. After that, what about *lieux-dits* Maison Rouge and Coteaux de Tupin in Tupin-et-Semons? Le Mollard and Fongeant – *premiers crus*? Well, *parts* of Fongeant, and therein lies the problem. Some *lieux-dits* are large, covering different expositions and soil types – and a *grand cru* surely implies consistency of quality and style. Fongeant contains both schist, which gives 'all the elegance of Syrah,' according to Jean-Paul Jamet, and loess, which is 'much less elegant, but more structured.' Jamet also underlines the importance of altitude when it comes to quality, and some *lieux-dits* stretch nearly the height of the slope.

Single-vineyard wines might have become popular over the past few decades, but the tradition here, as in Hermitage, is to blend. When Pierre-Jean Villa bought a parcel of vines dating back to 1934, he intended to make a special cuvée. 'But by itself, it didn't work,' he shrugs. 'Commercially I could have charged more,' he says, 'but I preferred it in the blend.' Jean-Paul Jamet points out that even the most famous *lieux-dits* aren't exceptional every year – sometimes even La Landonne is just too intense and tannic to show well by itself.

Another issue is the question of who should draw up the classification. A newly classified *grand cru* vineyard would explode in value, so producers would no doubt want as much of their own vineyards to be included, worthy or not. And if not producers, who else is qualified to do such a job? 'You'd start a war!' warns René Rostaing. Jean Gonon in southern Saint-Joseph remembers the reclassification of his appellation: 'we laugh now but there were death threats.' Better to keep the peace.

Domaine Jasmin

Ampuis

T.: +33 (0) 4 74 56 16 04

Amiably brusque and without airs and graces, Robert Jasmin sees himself as the custodian of his terroir and bottles the results without fanfare. He's the fourth generation to be working these blonde soils, and has a traditional approach to production, though his grapes are destemmed. Until 2014 he only made one, unnamed, Côte-Rôtie. In

2015 he introduced a new cuvée, Oléa, and has since christened his *cuvée classique* La Giroflarie. The new wine is a selection of the best barrels, typically containing more from *lieu-dit* Le Mollard, and sees a more intensive élevage, resulting in an oakier style. For such a well-built specimen, La Giroflarie remains a notably fine and elegant wine.

Domaine Levet

Ampuis

www.coterotielevet.fr

If there's anything that sums up the faded, unembellished ambience of Ampuis, it's Domaine Levet's storefront on the main road. Levet is to Côte-Rôtie as Clape is to Cornas: tannic, savoury wines, traditional almost to a fault, and even the most approachable wine takes years to come around. Agnès Levet describes them as 'traditional, typical, *vins de garde.*' Softly-spoken Agnès is the fourth generation to guide the estate established by Christophe Chambeyron in 1929, back when the slopes were worked with oxen. She has just 4.5 hectares of vines, all planted with massal selection Serine with an average age of 45 years. The parcels are in the Ampuis *lieux-dits* of La Landonne, Côte Brune, Côte Blonde, Le Mollard, Lancement, Chavaroche, Leyat, Baleyat, Le Truchet and Fongeant. Agnès doesn't use insecticide, and works in *agriculture raisonnée* – she can't find the workers to weed the slopes by hand. She makes three Côte-Rôties, some destemmed, others not, depending on the parcel, with three-week macerations with a submerged cap. Élevage is in demi-muid with 20 per cent new oak. Améthyste is a blend of different parcels, Maestria is a blend of *lieux-dits* La Landonne and Côte Blonde, and La Péroline is 100 per cent whole-bunch *lieu-dit* Chavaroche designed for long ageing. Not all of the estate looks to the past: she made her first Condrieu in 2019.

Domaine de Monteillet

Chavanay

www.montez.fr

It's hard to know where to shine the spotlight when it comes to Domaine de Monteillet's range of wines. Stéphane Montez is based in Chavanay, and his Saint-Josephs are among the finest – but his Côte-Rôties are so good they demand to be mentioned alongside the other masters of the appellation. However, you can also say the same about his incredible Condrieus. Ninth-generation winemaker Stéphane Montez is something of a magician – and one of the most talented Rhône wine-makers of his generation. His family has lived on the same property, making wine (amongst other things), since 1741. Bottling began more recently, as did the rapid acquisition of vineyards, of which Stéphane now has 35 hectares. His first Côte-Rôtie vineyard, bought in 1997, was a parcel of *lieu-dit* Les Grandes Places planted in 1951. He now has several dotted around the slopes.

His reds are in a contemporary style – the wines are precise, aromatic and textural with a distinct freshness and drinkability. He typically destems around 70 per cent of the crop in a ripe vintage, and opts for a long, cold maceration, followed by warm fermentation with natural yeasts, and then a long, gentle extraction of around 5 weeks (submerged cap with no punching down, just pumping over). He favours demi-muids over barriques for élevage and ages without racking on the fine lees, which he calls the 'the umbilical cord of the wine.' His whites successfully combine richness with tension. Stéphane is still young and has boundless energy – this is an estate to watch.

Domaine Stéphane Ogier

Ampuis

www.stephaneogier.fr

In the recent history of Côte-Rôtie, the rapid rise of Domaine Stéphane Ogier is particularly noticeable. His extra-terrestrial new winery installation in Ampuis is rivalled only by Domaine de Monteillet's *cigare volant* up on the plateau. The name of the estate until recently included the name of his father Michel, whose first vintage was in 1983 (before this the family sold grapes to négociants for generations). Stéphane, who was six years old in 1983, was inspired by his father's work. He studied winemaking in Burgundy and returned to the estate in 1997, when there were still frequent opportunities to buy land. He now owns parcels across the length of the appellation and beyond. Many of these are bottled separately under the name of each *lieu-dit* (except La Belle Hélène from Côte-Rozier, named after his mother). His winemaking recipe for each is subtly different in order to most accurately display the character of each.

He also makes some exceptional IGP Syrah and Viognier called La Rosine, a very good Saint-Joseph, one of the most convincing Seyssuels and some of the greatest Condrieu. It would appear there's nothing this good-looking young guy can't do. The style here straddles modern and traditional; it is a ripe and polished style, but fresh, detailed and compelling – these are vivid expressions, writ large. As he ventures into the Southern Rhône to make a négociant Côtes-du-Rhône, it'll be interesting to see what he does next.

Serine

Syrah has gone by many names in the Rhône over the centuries. Pierre Charnay in his *Vignobles et Vins des Côtes du Rhône* lists Sirrah, Sirac, Serine, Marsanne Noire, Entournerein, Plant de Biaume and Lasira. Serine, or Petite Serine, is also used to refer to an ancient pre-clonal variety of Syrah found in and around Côte-Rôtie.

Recommended clones of grape varieties were introduced in the 1960s by government agencies looking to improve vineyard health and quality. What was considered desirable in a clone then – high yields and high alcohol, for example – does not always chime with what vignerons are looking for today. Some producers have therefore used massal selection to propagate pre-clonal old vine material such as Serine. Agnès Levet in Côte-Rôtie says that all of her 4.5 hectares of vines are planted with massal selections of Serine (or Petite Serine as she calls it). She says that the bunches are longer, with olive-shaped berries, and it is less productive than normal Syrah, especially when young. Its attraction is its flavour; 'it's a bit spicier,' she says, 'and more mineral.'

The belief in Serine is centred around Côte-Rôtie, rather than vineyards further south. 'We never say Serine here,' says Jean Gonon, who lives in Mauves, at the southern end of Saint-Joseph, 'and we don't really believe in it.' He does however confirm that there are various sub-types of Syrah, some that grow more upright, some outwards, some with smooth leaves, some with rougher ones. Pierre-Jean Villa lives in Chavanay, at the northern end of Saint-Joseph, and he's not entirely sure whether Serine is better than Syrah. 'I've got both,' he says, 'it's a selection of Syrah. The bunches aren't exactly the same, but qualitatively I can't say it's better. My 1930s to 1950s vines are my best Syrah vines, that I know.' There is still some disagreement about whether there is even such a thing as Serine. 'Myth or reality?' Villa ponders. 'I'm not sure.'

Domaine Rostaing

Ampuis

www.domainerostaing.com

René Rostaing stepped back from the family domaine he created after the 2014 vintage. Smiling and effervescent, he resembles a priest when speaking about wine, relaying his sermon with unfailing lucidity. His son Pierre, more laidback but no less meticulous, has been in charge since 2015. The story begins a little further back, with René's grandfather-in-law, Jean Dervieux. When Jean retired, he shared his Côte-Rôtie holdings between his two children: Albert and Yvonne. Mayor of Ampuis and president of the Côte-Rôtie growers' *syndicat* after the Second World War, Albert Dervieux-Thaize was René's father-in-law. René describes him as 'the most important pioneer' of the appellation, and the first local of this era to focus his activities solely on growing vines. 'He was very kind, very open,' says René, 'always listening and ready to help.' Albert Dervieux-Thaize made powerful wines that were considered among the best in this northernmost point of the Northern Rhône. When he passed away, the vineyards were bequeathed to René. Albert's sister Yvonne married Marius Gentaz, and in doing so established Domaine Gentaz-Dervieux. Marius was 'very discrete, very meticulous, very strict,' says René, who praises the immaculate state of his vineyards. If you can find a bottle of his wine for sale today, it will cost over £1,000. These parcels were also handed down to René, and thus the original estate of Jean Dervieux was reunited. This is how Domaine Rostaing came to possess coveted old-vine parcels of some of the finest *lieux-dits* in Côte-Rôtie.

All the wines are fermented in stainless steel with natural yeasts. Neither René's forebears nor René himself have sought to use new oak barrels to age the wines. René believes that 'it hides typicity and terroir,' and the estate still only uses older barrels where possible (228-litre and 600-litre) for between 18 and 24 months. He also uses as many stems as possible in the wines as they give the wine a 'vertebral column'. Ampodium is a blend of 25 parcels over fifteen *lieux-dits*. It's almost pure Syrah, except for a few Viognier vines. Their single-vineyard wines are where the real fireworks are found, however. Every year they make an aromatically compelling Côte Blonde and muscular La Landonne. In the best years they bottle a towering Côte Brune. From time to time, they also produce an exquisite La Viallère. When on form, these wines are unforgettable.

Maison Stéphan

Tupin-et-Semons

maison-stephan.fr

Though there are a handful of producers in Côte-Rôtie who work organically, there are very few who identify as producers of natural wine.

In 1994, with 2 hectares of wines, Jean-Michel Stéphan started creating natural wines. He now makes a range of Côte-Rôties, some from vines planted as far back as 1896. Most of his holdings are in Tupin-et-Semons, and he works with both Serine and Syrah, with some cuvées including 20 per cent Viognier. It would appear that this is the only estate in Côte-Rôtie that vinifies grapes using carbonic maceration. Given the sparkling aromatics and depth of textural relief, it's surprising that more haven't followed his lead – these can be some unforgettably delicious wines of great transparency that reflect their terroir beautifully. But not always – I have encountered some deviant bottles from time to time. When Jean-Michel's son Romain joined the business in 2017, the estate changed its name from Domaine JM Stéphan to Maison Stéphan. They are now working biodynamically.

Domaine Pierre-Jean Villa

Chavanay

www.pierre-jean-villa.fr

Pierre-Jean Villa was born in Chavanay but trained and worked in Burgundy – which gives you an idea of the style you might expect from his Syrahs. He was enticed back to the Rhône to help set up négociant Les Vins de Vienne, but in 2007 he bought a hectare of Saint-Joseph for himself, and has since amassed 17 hectares, including land in Condrieu, Côte-Rôtie, Seyssuel and Crozes-Hermitage. By 2021 he is due to be certified organic across the whole estate. Biodynamics is next. 'I'm most passionate about the viticulture side,' he says, and he's not kidding – he's a mine of information that would keep any vine-growing geek entranced for hours. We covered pruning: he's recently started working with François Dal of Sancerre and changed his whole approach to *taille Poussard*, with a resulting 30 per cent drop in vine mortality. We talked about climate change: he suggests 'before changing varieties, we should think about rootstocks,' and is experimenting with several new ones. We discussed ploughing, new cover crops, clones and more. He may be busy but he manages to keep on top of current thinking. The result is a very likeable range of wines, all expressive of their individual site. It's very much a contemporary style, medium-bodied and very fine, with great freshness and purity. Burgundian in more ways than one.

Other good examples
There are many other exceptional producers of Côte-Rôtie. The whole-bunch style of **Domaine Benetière** and **Domaine Champet** would also deserve an entry to themselves, even if the wines are hard to find. **Domaine Bernard Burgaud** can also be fantastic, in a destemmed style. **Domaine Billon** makes punchy Côte-Rôties, and you can find lots to enjoy at **Domaine Lionel Faury**, **Domaine Chambeyron**, **Domaine de Rosiers**, **Domaine François et Fils**, **Domaine François Merlin** and **Domaine Pierre Gaillard**. The slender Côte-Rôties of **Domaine Georges Vernay** combine delicacy and longevity. Up-and-coming producers include **Domaine Benoît Roseau**, **Domaine Martin Clerc**, **Vignobles Verzier**, **Vignobles Chirat** and new estate **Domaine Bott**. No négociant is more strongly associated with Côte-Rôtie than Guigal, but there are others making good – sometimes excellent – examples. **Tardieu-Laurent** in particular makes a thrilling Côte-Rôtie. **Saint-Cosme** also makes a very good wine. Two other cuvées worth trying are **Delas** La Landonne and **Les Vins de Vienne** Les Grandes Places. **Chapoutier's** range of Côte-Rôties is very good, but its real strength is Hermitage.

SEYSSUEL

Appellation: Seyssuel does not (yet) have its own appellation; wines are bottled under IGP Collines Rhodaniennes
Communes: Seyssuel, Chasse-sur-Rhône, Vienne
Colours permitted: red and white
Production in 2019: approximately 80 per cent red, 20 per cent white
Grape varieties used: Reds are typically made with 100 per cent Syrah, whites with 100 per cent Viognier

Just as some domaines, négociants and cooperatives eventually become extinct, so it can be with entire appellations. It nearly happened to Condrieu. If it wasn't for the belief and commitment of Georges Vernay, the last few hectares might have been abandoned, and swiftly reclaimed by encroaching woods. If that had happened, there would of course be no section on Condrieu in this book; I wonder which other once-great wines of the Rhône, names long since forgotten, are missing their entry. Thirty years ago this book would have had no section on Seyssuel; until the late 1990s, this once-great terroir was lying dormant, asleep under the oaks and oblivious grazing livestock. But, thanks to the work of another individual, Pierre Gaillard, it has been brought back to life. 'If we hadn't set out like we did,' he says, 'the terroir would have stayed like it was.'

The Rhône river flows broadly north to south, but as it exits Lyon, it zigzags. From Givors to Vienne, it zigs north-west to south-east. From Vienne to Ampuis, it zags south-west. Both of these stretches create favourable growing conditions, with southern slopes that catch the sun. But until recently, only the lower stretch, known as Côte-Rôtie, has been producing wine. The upper stretch is Seyssuel, which, officially speaking, is simply a section of IGP Collines Rhodaniennes. Famous once, it was abandoned for a hundred years – until Gaillard started to do some research.

Gaillard has his roots in a village near Chasse-sur-Rhône, one of the three communes that make up the proto-appellation of Seyssuel. The locals were proud of their wine, but he remembered as a boy hearing them say that the wines of Seyssuel were once considered even better. On reading the work of French agronomist Olivier de Serres (1539–1619) he learned that de Serres compared these ancient vineyards favourably to Côte-Rôtie. He discussed replanting this land with friends François Villard and Yves Cuilleron. 'It was just curiosity to start with,' says Gaillard, 'throwing ourselves into the archives.' Pierre-Jean Villa, who also owns some land here, says that documents in the Seyssuel *mairie* showed there were once 140 hectares of vines in the area, the main source of revenue for the village, but they simply weren't replanted after phylloxera.

In 1996, Gaillard, Villard and Cuilleron bought some south-facing land from a local sheep farmer and each planted a hectare of Syrah. 'We had interesting wines practically from the first vinification,' says Gaillard. Louis Chèze was quick to follow, as was Stéphane Ogier, and there are now over a dozen Côte-Rôtie estates in on the act, with plantings stretching across three communes, from Chasse-sur-Rhône in the north, via Seyssuel, to Vienne, with some vineyards within the city limits. Both Syrah and Viognier are now planted, with similar training methods to Côte-Rôtie – usually cordon de Royat on the flatter land, *gobelet* on the slopes.

These are some of the most northerly red wine vineyards in the Rhône, but the microclimate here is peculiarly warm. Some of the flora, such as the holm oak and the *gagée des rochers*, are more commonly found in the Southern Rhône. The land here is less intensively planted than Côte-Rôtie, and it feels a little more open and pastoral. Though largely south-facing, this stretch of the river acts as a wind-tunnel, which dries the soils and concentrates the berries. Villa points out however that the vines never suffer from hydric stress, perhaps due to the large bank of clay that sits behind the stony schistous slopes. Gaillard adds that these schists also contain thin layers of clay, which also helps fight drought.

Despite this being a fairly hot terroir, the reds are less full than a typical Côte-Rôtie. Gaillard notes aromas of 'ripe raspberry, crushed raspberry' in the wines; I also often find a whiff of exotic spices. The whites, too, tend to be less broad and opulent than Condrieu, a little straighter in style and not so proudly aromatic. The red wines of Seyssuel are often silky, elegant and pure, with great transparency and I've been impressed by the quality of many recent examples. Stylistically they are closer to Côte-Rôtie than anything else, but for now the best Saint-Josephs are still more compelling. I haven't yet been moved by a Seyssuel in the same way as a great Côte-Rôtie, nor have I experienced the same levels of complexity or intensity.

It's important to bear in mind however that it's still early days: the vines are young. And there are additional valleys and slopes here that haven't yet been planted, which could equal or surpass the current sites. This isn't likely to happen any time soon, however. Thanks to the unusual microclimate and flora here, environmental groups have pushed for a temporary moratorium on planting more vineyards. It will at least give local winemakers time to concentrate on lobbying for this terroir to be granted its own appellation. How long this will take, nobody knows; it might have to pass through the whole appellation hierarchy, or it might be promoted more directly. What is certain is that this sleeping beauty deserves to be the ninth *cru* of the Northern Rhône.

Key producers
Les Vins de Vienne
Chavanay

www.vinsdevienne.com

When Pierre Gaillard, Yves Cuilleron and François Villard all planted vines in Seyssuel in 1996, they clubbed together to build a cellar and buy equipment on this side of the Rhône. They also set up a négociant business, Les Vins de Vienne. They now own 12 hectares in Seyssuel and produce three wines from this terroir: Sotanum (first vintage 1998), a straight and direct style of Syrah with 70 per cent whole bunch; Taburnum (2000), a neat and distinctly saline Viognier; and Heluicum (2004), a lighter Syrah with a shorter élevage. The first two are excellent wines by any standards, the third also shows good finesse.

Seyssuel is now just a small part of the company's output. Today they produce 600,000 bottles a year under 43 labels, half of which are from northern *crus*; the rest is made up of AOC Côtes-du-Rhône and southern *crus*. The three owners still work on the blending, and the main winemaker is Pascal Lombard. As with any négociant, not every cuvée is a winner, but the standard here is impressive, with some very good wines, especially in their Lieux-Dits range.

Other good examples

All three partners in Les Vins de Vienne also produce a red Seyssuel from their personal domaines. **Domaine Pierre Gaillard** Asiaticus is a dense style that underlines the innate spiciness of the terroir, **François Villard** Seul en Scene is brooding and textural, and **Cave Yves Cuilleron** Ripa Sinistra is a more polished and powerful expression. **Domaine Billon** is heavily invested and makes an assertive style called La Batie. **Domaine Pierre-Jean Villa** L'Esprit d'Antan is a particularly pure and suave example, and **Domaine Stéphane Ogier** L'Ame Soeur is also very good, expressive and perfumed. In white, **Les Vignobles de Seyssuel** Sixtus is slim, fine and clear-cut.

CONDRIEU

The rehabilitation of Viognier was one of the most striking wine success stories of the late twentieth century. In 1965 there were only 8 hectares remaining, all in its original heartland of Condrieu. Fifty-five years later there are over 1,000 hectares planted throughout the Rhône, with total global plantings topping 16,000 hectares by 2016. But in the words of Rémi Niero, 'there aren't many terroirs on earth where you can make a good Viognier.' It can certainly make an enjoyably exuberant wine outside of the Northern Rhône, but I'm yet to find an example that comes close to the best wines of Condrieu. Here, the wines find the necessary salinity, tension and freshness to balance the natural aromatic opulence of the grape, and in doing so it can – on occasion – produce some of the finest white wines in the world.

Appellation: AOC Condrieu
Birth of the appellation: 1940
Communes: Chavanay, Condrieu, Limony, Malleval, Saint-Michel-sur-Rhône, Saint-Pierre de Boeuf, Vérin
Total surface area sold under the AOC in 2019: 203 hectares
Average yield in 2019: 37 hectolitres per hectare
Colours permitted: white only
Grape varieties permitted: Wines must be 100 per cent Viognier

The northern tip of Condrieu is essentially a continuation of the granite slopes of Côte-Rôtie – once you pass the little river Bassenon, you're in Condrieu country, swapping red wines for white. The boundary is somewhat arbitrary of course, but that's the nature of appellations. To the naked eye the vineyards are very similar – a series of rumpled slopes lined with irregular drystone walls, all shaped by a series of streams that flow down from the plateau above. In fact, the name Condrieu comes from *coin de rieux* ('corner of streams'), as there are three small rivers that run through the village.

These largely south-, south-east and east-facing slopes follow the river as it flows south past the village of Condrieu, through the communes of Vérin and Saint-Michel-sur-Rhône. These are the three original communes of AOC Condrieu, minted in 1940. In 1967, the appellation was extended further south to include a succession of remote islands of terroir dotted along the communes of Chavanay, Malleval, Saint-Pierre-de-Boeuf and Limony. In 1986, there was a further revision, to remove all vineyards over 300 metres in altitude from the appellation, just to include the best exposed slopes. Now the appellation runs through three different *départements* (Rhône, Loire and Ardèche) and is made up of 88 *lieux-dits*. From north to south, the vineyards of Condrieu stretch across 14 kilometres. It's climatically similar to Côte-Rôtie, with cold winters, and summers whose warmth is accentuated by the sloping vineyards and captured by the dark granitic soils. There are several different types of granite in Condrieu, and they each give slightly different expressions. The central part of the original 1940 appellation (and the separate appellation of Château-Grillet, embedded within Condrieu) is grown on granite containing a dark mica called biotite. At either end, there are small outcrops of granite that contain a light mica called muscovite, and to the north near Côte-Rôtie there is a large south-west-facing slope comprising dark migmatite, a composite rock made up of both metamorphic rock and igneous granite.

Of the additional vineyard land added in 1967, the largest part is in the commune of Chavanay. There are two hefty slopes: one made of muscovite granite, the other, dark migmatite. One peculiarity here is that some of the AOC Condrieu land is shared with AOC Saint-Joseph – you can make either, depending on which *cahier des charges* rulebook you follow. Travelling further south, the demarcated Condrieu vineyards get smaller, more morcellated and more geologically diverse. Malleval's thirteen small *lieux-dits* contain biotite granite, dark migmatite, pale leucocratic migmatite and gneiss. Saint-Pierre-de-Boeuf's two tiny *lieux-dits* are both dark migmatite and the vineyards of Limony are as diverse as Malleval's. There are also a few small patches of loess. Of the two main types of soil, biotite granite seems to give a slightly straighter expression with a saltier edge to the wines. Wines from migmatite are often more ample in texture; Xavier Gérard says he frequently finds pear flavours from wines grown on migmatite. Some excellent wines are made in every commune, but the best come from the original heart of the appellation, particularly from the *lieux-dits* Vernon and Chéry, and from Château-Grillet.

Winemaking has been practised here since the Romans inhabited the area, and just to look at these sites you can see their outstanding viticultural potential. So why did plantings drop down to such a small area in the mid-1900s? It's the same story as Côte-Rôtie, albeit more severe: the region was hit by phylloxera, then two world wars, and in the aftermath wine production concentrated on quantity and ease of production – so the slope was overlooked in favour of the flat. Young people found easier jobs in nearby factories. But a handful of growers kept the faith. One man in particular deserves our thanks: Georges Vernay. He took on his father's vineyard on the Coteau de Vernon in 1953, when production had dwindled and hillside vineyards were in disrepair. While others abandoned the slopes, he believed; he cleared another hectare of woodland, built stone walls and planted more vines. A well-built, charismatic man, he went on to lead the growers' *syndicat* for 30 years, convincing the next generation that Condrieu was worth fighting for. Initially, progress was slow: in 1971 there were 12 hectares, by 1986 this had increased to 20 hectares and in 1990 the figure reached a healthy 40 hectares. Today there are 227 hectares.

Though not all of the slopes of Condrieu are quite as crumpled as those of Côte-Rôtie, growing Viognier is in some ways even more difficult than growing Syrah (see page 40). It has difficulty withstanding strong winds, it's early ripening so prone to spring frost, it suffers from coulure, and it drops acidity and gains sugar rapidly at the end of the growing season. Picking early isn't an option. Christine Vernay explains that if you pick early, you emphasize the varietal character of the grape rather than the terroir, but equally 'there's a moment when it tips over … there's a frontier that you can't cross, because then you lose a lot, you're in over-maturity, another universe, one where it loses its salinity.' Pierre-Jean Villa agrees that the date of picking is crucial: 'it's not yesterday, it's not tomorrow – it's today.'

Once the grapes are picked and pressed, there are plenty of options open to the winemaker. To begin with, there's the proportion of suspended solids (*bourbe*) after settling in the juice – the question of whether to work with totally clear juice or not. Winemakers can then ferment in stainless steel (relatively unusual, e.g. Domaine Rostaing) or in oak barrels (Domaine Georges Vernay uses a variety of different sizes) or a combination of both (e.g. Domaine Niero). Sizes of vessel vary considerably, and the option to ferment in new oak barrels can have a strong effect on the final wine. The current trend is towards larger barrels, lighter toast, and less new oak – Lionel Faury made all of these changes when he took over from his father in 2006. He also introduced a number of acacia barrels, which he believes contribute freshness and vivacity. Condrieu does take well to new oak, with some cuvées, such as Guigal's La Doriane being fermented and then matured in 100 per cent new barriques.

Yeasts can be indigenous or selected, and some producers such as Delas for their Condrieu Clos Boucher use both, but in different barrels. Lees stirring is common, but is less fashionable than it once was. It has multiple benefits: it protects the wine from oxidation, it can reduce unpleasant reductive aromas, it keeps fermentation moving, and it can reduce the impact of new oak on the wine. The downside is that it can add weight and fat to an already fairly corpulent style of wine. Xavier Gérard says that the fruity side of Viognier comes from both the skins and the lees, so he doesn't stir. 'I've never had a Viognier that needs *more* fruitiness,' he says.

Whether to allow or restrict malolactic fermentation is another choice. Neither Domaine Rostaing La Bonnette nor Ferraton Les Mandouls are put through malo, largely to help retain acidity and freshness. It's much more common to let malo take its course, however; Pierre-Jean Villa says it helps the wine to age and François Villard says it accentuates minerality, which, in any case, he says is 'the greatest freshness you can get in a wine'. Élevage typically lasts from 6 to 12 months. The vast majority today is fermented to dryness, though 3 or 4 grams per litre residual sugar isn't that unusual. It wasn't always this way: in the middle of the nineteenth century Condrieu was sweet. Some producers still produce a small amount of sweet Condrieu, typically made with clean grapes and leaving around 60–80 grams per litre residual sugar. It can be delightful. Though today sweet Condrieu is usually made with clean grapes, this hasn't always been the way with dry wines. In the 1990s, François Villard often included a proportion of botrytized grapes when vintages allowed and found it had a positive impact on the wines. Sadly, it's no longer an option as the grapes take on sugar faster than they used to due to the warming climate, so he can't wait for the necessary autumnal conditions for botrytis to take hold. Chaptalization was once common in Condrieu; now it's no longer required.

The question of whether Condrieu improves with age is one that comes up regularly. To answer this question, I would say that it is not the grape variety that predicates the longevity of a wine but the terroir. So while it's true to say that Viognier isn't a variety that tends to age well, it's also true that Condrieu is a wine that can age brilliantly. 'We're convinced Condrieu can age,' says Rémi Niero, and I've tasted enough old wines to share his conviction. That said, most standard cuvées are best enjoyed within the first few years of vintage, in their vibrancy and pure fruitiness. Though straightforward cuvées often show well for longer than you might expect, they don't necessarily improve. Wines from the very best sites, however, can develop great depth and complexity at around 15–20 years of age, taking on notes of grilled nuts, gingerbread and petrol but losing nothing of their glistening mineral freshness.

Sixty years ago, only a handful of Condrieu wines were being bottled. Now there are nearly 100 private domaines producing at least one cuvée, not to mention a proliferation of négociant bottlings. Though it has a strong character, quality is mixed, and it is still easy enough to find overly fat, gloopy wines that lack freshness and tension, particularly in hot vintages. But as the years go by, I'm finding more and more impressive wines to choose from. The current global taste for white wines tends toward delicate, fine, high-acid styles. Condrieu isn't fashionable, nor will its voluptuous charms ever be to everyone's taste. But it is undeniably one of the most striking, unmistakable terroir wines on the planet, and it can be one of the most luxurious, mesmerizing wines imaginable.

Key producers

Cave Yves Cuilleron

Chavanay

www.cuilleron.com

Reaching its one-hundredth birthday in 2020, this estate was established by Yves' grandfather Claude Cuilleron in 1920. Considering he took over just 3.5 hectares of vineyards in 1987, Yves has achieved a staggering amount. He now produces around 40 different cuvées, amounting to 430,000 bottles a year, from 75 hectares of Northern Rhône vineyards, from Saint-Péray to Seyssuel. In 1996, he also set up négociant house Les Vins de Vienne with Pierre Gaillard and François Villard. He is probably best known, however, for his Condrieu, of which he makes five dry and one sweet.

Given the extent of his vineyard holdings some herbicides are used, but no insecticide, and all treatments are minimized where possible. Replanting is carried out using massal selection and only indigenous yeasts are used for fermentation. Winemaking is kept as simple as possible, without enzymes or adjustments; reds are partly destemmed and bottled unfiltered. His wines have strong personalities, and can make quite an impact – the occasional cuvée can feel overly polished and oaky, but others can be bold and brilliant. In 2015 he restructured the range, and renamed many of the top cuvées to reflect their *lieux-dits*; thus his Condrieu Vertige became Condrieu Vernon, etc. His newest project is to work with ancient local varieties such as Persan and Durif, the results of which are just coming to fruition.

Domaine Rémi Niero

Condrieu

www.vins-niero.com

This is one of those rare Rhône estates that makes more white wine than red. It was established in 1985, when Rémi's father Robert acquired some vineyards from Robert's father-in-law, the esteemed Jean Pinchon. Rémi, who could quite easily have been a model such are his good looks, took over in 2004 and has since doubled the holdings to 8 hectares, half of which is in Condrieu. These enviable parcels are in some exceptional *lieux-dits* which he is gradually converting to organic.

With parcels in *lieux-dits* La Viallière and Coteaux de Bassenon, the Côte-Rôties here are good, in a destemmed, polished style (with plentiful, sometimes excessive, new oak at the top of the range). But the range of Condrieu is the real strength – also fairly modern in style but with a detail and terroir expression to match their flamboyance. Opening the range is his reliable Condrieu Les Ravines, a blend of five terroirs in the commune of Condrieu. Héritage is a barrel selection, typically expansive and intense but retaining good balance. Chéry is a single-vineyard wine from 30-year-old vines on *lieu-dit* Coteau de Chéry, a wine that captures the tension and drive of the site. Coeur de Roncharde was first made in the 2018 vintage, a single-vineyard wine from 75-year-old vines on *lieu-dit* La Roncharde at the north of the appellation. It's the most delicate and perfumed of the range, a wine with great purity and elegance that shows the huge potential of this terroir.

Domaine André Perret

Chavanay

www.andreperret.com

The wines of André Perret aren't as storied as those of Domaine Georges Vernay. André is a quiet, unassuming man and his estate doesn't share such a remarkable back story, but for me this is the other great producer of Condrieu, albeit in a very different style. When he took over from his father in 1982, the estate was mostly fruit trees, which André gradually converted to vineyards. He now has 13 hectares of vineyards in total, and although he isn't certified organic he uses no systemic products on his vines. His Condrieus aren't as broad-framed as many, in fact they're surprisingly petite, almost cherubic. He makes three: his unnamed classic cuvée and Clos Chanson from Chavanay are gentle, pure expressions of Condrieu, but his single-vineyard Chéry from the *lieu-dit* Coteau de Chéry is consistently one of the most beautiful, pitch-perfect wines of the appellation. His red Saint-Josephs are perfumed, structural wines that can be a little skinny in cooler vintages, fresh and precise in warm ones.

Domaine Georges Vernay

Condrieu

domaine-christine-vernay.fr

As mentioned above, without Domaine Georges Vernay, there might not be a chapter on Condrieu at all. Georges' father François Vernay planted his vines on the Coteau de Vernon, and Georges took over in

1953. The estate is now run by Georges' daughter Christine Vernay and her husband Paul Amsellem, who both joined the estate in 1996. They will soon be accompanied by their daughter Emma, who is finishing her training. The estate is now one of the few in Condrieu to be certified organic, and Christine, who makes the wine, is now moving towards biodynamics. They make three Condrieus. Les Terrasses de l'Empire is a blend of many small parcels in a dry but approachable style that's best enjoyed young. Les Chaillées d'Enfer is a blend of two 50-year-old south-facing parcels on biotite granite in a more imposing, assertive wine that ages well. Finally, the Coteau de Vernon, a single-vineyard wine from a favourable part of the best *lieu-dit* in Condrieu, gives a driving, intense, savoury and complex expression and is often described as the greatest wine of the appellation.

Though they are best known for their Condrieu, the red wines shouldn't be overlooked. Christine makes Côte-Rôtie, Saint-Joseph *rouge* and IGP Collines Rhodaniennes *rouge*, all in a fine, cool and collected style. Her Côte-Rôtie Maison Rouge from the *lieu-dit* of the same name is particularly elegant, subtle but self-assured, and ages well despite its diminutive frame.

François Villard

Saint-Michel-sur-Rhône

www.domainevillard.com

François Villard grew up near Chavanay, his parents were farmers. In typically teenage fashion, he decided to go his own way and become a chef instead, a path he followed between 1979 and 1989. Thankfully, by his own admission, he wasn't the most gifted cook, and instead became interested in wine, buying books, tasting wine and walking the local vineyards. By 23, 'I had to work in wine,' he says, 'it had become an obsession.' He bought his first Condrieu parcel in 1988. Land wasn't expensive at the time, so he invested in more parcels including some Saint-Joseph and Côte-Rôtie. By 2000, he had 9.5 hectares. In 2002, he set up a négociant business which enabled him to expand his business. By 2007, he had acquired 27 hectares, and today he owns 40. Including bought-in grapes, he now bottles the equivalent of 75 hectares a year – so the same amount as Yves Cuilleron, with whom he owns Les Vins de Vienne along with Pierre Gaillard.

Unlike his two partners in this separate enterprise, his range is relatively tight, but it stretches from Saint-Péray to Seyssuel. Even more so than Cuilleron, his strength lies in Condrieu, of which he makes four. Les Terraces du Palat was originally from two parcels in Chavanay, but now includes *lieux-dits* Riollement and Tinal, 80 per cent vinified in barriques, of which 20 per cent are new, giving a fruity and approachable, but not simple, style of Condrieu. Le Grand Vallon is from *lieu-dit* Le Grand Val in Saint-Pierre-de-Boeuf, an east-facing slope which helps retain acidity. It sees 35 per cent new oak, and produces to a more perfumed, structured style. Deponcins comes from *lieux-dits* La Roullière and Poncin in Saint-Michel-sur-Rhône, granitic sands rich in clay, which contributes to a more concentrated, saline style, also seeing 35 per cent new oak. These three wines vie to be his best each year, but the final wine in the range is particularly impressive. Villa Pontiana, first produced in 2009, is a selection of the best, most mineral barrels of Le Grand Vallon and Deponcins, making for a powerful, sapid expression that is only produced in the best vintages.

Villard is now converting the estate to organic viticulture; 2019 was the first year without using herbicides. Another project is to plant vines in La-Côte-Sainte-Anne, 40 kilometres to the east of Chavanay, which once had vineyards before phylloxera. Considering Villard's success in Seyssuel, it should be a project worth watching.

Other good examples

Other particularly fine and balanced examples that are often the equal of those featured above can be found from **Domaine Jamet, Domaine Xavier Gérard, Domaine Lionel Faury, Domaine Stéphane Ogier, Domaine de Monteillet, Domaine Pierre-Jean Villa** and **Domaine Yves Gangloff** (all featured in more detail in the section on Côte-Rôtie, except Domaine Faury which appears in the Saint-Joseph section). The following producers can also be a good source, and most are towards the cheaper end of the spectrum: **Cave Christophe Blanc, Domaine Benoît Roseau, Domaine du Chêne, Domaine Aurélien Chatagnier, Domaine Rostaing, Domaine B&D Duclaux, Domaine de Bonserine, Domaine Barge, Domaine Pierre Gaillard, Tardieu-Laurent, M. Chapoutier** and **E. Guigal**'s classic label Condrieu. If you're looking for a richer expression, try **Domaine Chambeyron, Domaine Mouton, Domaine Christophe Pichon, Delas Frères** and **E. Guigal** La Doriane.

CHÂTEAU-GRILLET

AOC Château-Grillet stands out as distinctive in the Rhône, an appellation with one estate – or is it an estate with its own appellation? Monopoles like this are scarce, but not unique. For a single producer to own an entire *lieu-dit* is unusual, but to own all the terrain of an entire appellation is even rarer. This occurs most commonly in Burgundy; Domaine Lamarche 'La Grande Rue', for example, and Domaine du Comte Liger-Belair 'La Romanée' are both *grand cru* monopoles. What's rarer still is for the name of the estate to reflect the name of the appellation they control, such as Domaine de la Romanée-Conti 'La Romanée-Conti' and Clos de Tart 'Clos de Tart' in Burgundy. In the Rhône, there is Château-Grillet – the name of the producer, the appellation, and the *grand vin* all rolled into one.

Its history is intimately entwined with that of Condrieu, the larger appellation that surrounds this tiny 3.5-hectare estate. Château records date the property back to the reign of Louis XIII (1610–43) and in 1787, it was sufficiently well-known to attract a visit by US President Thomas Jefferson. An inventory dating back to 1814 from the Château de Malmaison (the residence of Empress Joséphine de Beauharnais, first wife of Napoléon I) counts 296 bottles of 'Château Grillé'. It was presented to King George IV of England in 1829. From 1827 to 2011 it was owned by the Neyret-Gachet family, until it was sold to François Pinault, and is now part of his Artémis Domaines portfolio under the management of Frédéric Engerer (which also includes, as it happens, Clos de Tart).

The estate itself straddles the border between two communes, Vérin and Saint-Michel-sur-Rhône, and Château-Grillet shares the same grape variety and soils as the Condrieu vineyards that surround it: Viognier grown on biotite granite, with plenty of mica and quartz under a sandy topsoil. The vineyards inhabit a south-facing nook, a vertiginously steep, tight amphitheatre all held up by 104 drystone walls that start at 150 metres altitude and climb to 250 metres. This formation creates a particularly warm microclimate, sheltered from the north wind, and this is the main factor that distinguishes the appellation from Condrieu. When I visited in the month of March it was filled with wheeling, screeching swallows.

The château building itself is something of a hodgepodge; some parts date back as far as 1760, other additions in brick are clearly more recent. It's more functional than fairy tale, in keeping with its Northern Rhône setting. The vines, ranging in age from 30 to 45 years, are all planted on *échalas*. Standing there in the sun, with vineyards rising up on all sides, there is no doubt as to the quality of this terroir.

So how, exactly, is Château-Grillet different to Condrieu? Their *cahiers des charges* are broadly similar, but there are some differences. Generally speaking, Château-Grillet's rules of production are slightly more restrictive: vines must be planted on *échalas*; at 37 hectolitres per hectare maximum yields are slightly lower; minimum planting density is higher; wines have a longer stipulated élevage before release. Another important difference is that Château-Grillet has to be dry. And, distinctively, it must be sold in fluted Alsace-style bottles. What marks out a Château-Grillet from a typical Condrieu in the glass is a searing tension and salinity, they certainly have less of the rich abundance of aroma you would expect from, for example, the Côte Chatillon. It's more about tension and energy than aroma, though there's plenty of perfume to enjoy as well. It's similar to Domaine Georges Vernay's Coteau de Vernon in this respect, and it's undoubtedly this tension and minerality that helps sustain the wine as it ages – a decade or two is not unusual.

But in the past, it wasn't a wine's production method and style alone that determined whether it was granted its own appellation. In the 1930s, appellation laws were different. If you had a property designated a château (a building with at least two turrets) and your vineyards in one block around the property, you could apply for your own appellation. The owners at the time were wealthy Lyonnais, not local *paysans*, so perhaps they were more aware of these administrative quirks – either way, they were successful in their application. Going on style alone, Château-Grillet deserves its own appellation no more than *lieu-dit* Reynard in Cornas. You could argue they both do. There is no definitive answer. But even if you were inclined to argue that Château-Grillet should be subsumed into the rest of the Condrieu appellation, one thing is clear – this particular site is exceptional.

In his book *The Wines of the Rhône*, published in 1992, John Livingstone-Learmonth observes that 'it's expensive (a case of the 1988 in Britain was on regular sale at around £440, or over US$70 a bottle, with the bottles containing 70, not 75 centilitres) and it's not worth the money.' Today in London, a single 75 centilitre bottle of the 2017 costs £414. As Artémis Domaines no doubt recognized on purchasing this property, a monopole attracts a premium. Whether it's worth it or not is down to the palate, or perhaps the pocket, of the beholder.

Appellation: AOC Château-Grillet
Birth of the appellation: 1936
Communes: Saint-Michel-sur-Rhône, Vérin
Total surface area sold under the AOC in 2019: 3 hectares
Average yield in 2019: 18 hectolitres per hectare
Colours permitted: white only
Grape varieties permitted: Wines must be 100 per cent Viognier

Producer

Château-Grillet

Verin

chateau-grillet.com

Jaeok Cramette, a winemaker of South Korean descent, is the technical director and looks after both vineyard and cellar. She told me that one of the first things the new owners did in 2011 was to stop using herbicides. Working the soils cut many superficial roots, 'a sacrifice', she says, which led to a temporary drop in yields for the 2013 vintage, down to 11 hectolitres per hectare from a typical 19. They also adapted the style of pruning, at great expense. Certified organic since 2016, the estate now practises biodynamic viticulture. The new owners inherited a dated cellar, which was fully replaced with small presses and diminutive stainless steel thermoregulated tanks. Different parcels are vinified separately according to soil type, vine age and picking date. Indigenous yeasts are preferred, and temperatures kept to around 18°C, finishing with selected yeast if required. The wine is then transferred into 228-litre and 300-litre lightly-toasted barrels; a new one is bought every year, with others between 2 and 5 years old. The wine goes through malolactic, and barrels are stirred around once a week. Wines are fined if necessary, and are put through a light filtration. Sulphite additions are kept to a minimum.

Since changing hands the domaine has seen the addition of two new wines. A second wine, declassified to Côtes-du-Rhône, was named Pontcin in 2011 and 2012, but this cuvée name has since been dropped. It consists mostly of young vines but made in the same way as the *grand vin*, albeit with a shorter élevage of 13 months instead of 18. It is more varietal in character than the Château-Grillet but shares a fresh salinity, and is best drunk young. The new owners also bought a few rows of vines at the very top of the Château-Grillet amphitheatre (in AOC Condrieu). This 0.25-hectare plot is in the *lieu-dit* of La Carthery, from which the wine takes its name. Its first vintage was 2017, and to date it has not been commercially released or shown to journalists.

The *grand vin* itself has been variable in quality during its long history. The last decades of the twentieth century were up and down: mostly down. 'Sometimes it was great because the terroir is magical,' says Cramette, 'but sometimes less so.' Since rehabilitating the vineyards and cellar she says, 'you can taste the difference now, it's an enormous qualitative change resulting in much more regular quality.' A tasting of recent vintages does suggest that the estate has turned a corner.

16

AROUND TAIN-L'HERMITAGE

SAINT-JOSEPH

'You can talk about Hermitage for hours; it has its place in history, it's easily defined. It's impossible to talk about Saint-Joseph as an appellation. It's very spread-out from north to south … No-one can say what Saint-Joseph is,' says Jean-Louis Chave. This is an inconvenient truth for those trying to write about Saint-Joseph. It is an appellation with no centre: there is no village called Saint-Joseph. Its growing areas have little in the way of collective history. It is easier to define Saint-Joseph by what it is not, rather than what it is.

Before we try to understand it, let's consider the whole of the Northern Rhône for a moment. It is not one homogeneous place but rather a region with two very different poles. At the northern limit are Côte-Rôtie, Condrieu and Château-Grillet; the remaining appellations cluster to the southern end, close to Hermitage. Before wine grapes became the prevailing crop, farmers around Ampuis grew a lot of vegetables; around Tain l'Hermitage, fruit trees were more common. Even the local people have subtly different dispositions: those in Ampuis are more guarded to begin with; around Tain they're quicker to smile. Saint-Joseph is a 50-kilometre-long shoelace of an appellation that dangles down the west bank of the Rhône river, connecting these two ends. There is a week's difference in the date of harvest between the two poles and the styles of wines are very different. Buy a Saint-Joseph and it could come from the northern pole, the southern pole – or somewhere in between.

The best way to appreciate this appellation is to drive up the D86 from Guilherand-Granges near Saint-Péray to Chavanay. It directs you through most of the 26 communes included in the appellation via a succession of villages, the impressive slopes looming into view one after another. As in Côte-Rôtie and Condrieu, this eastern edge of the Massif Central has been scored by streams and rivers that follow its fault lines, producing a succession of steep south- and south-east-facing granite outcrops, now lined with rickety terraces. Even from a distance it is clear that there are some exceptional terroirs along the way.

In a sense Saint-Joseph is the heart and soul of the Northern Rhône, a succession of abrupt slopes, perhaps too small to be appellations in their own right, that have been swept together under an umbrella appellation. In a blind tasting, the wines of Cornas, Hermitage and Côte-Rôtie make themselves known by their distinct and assertive characters; the Saint-Josephs are likely to be those left behind. That's not to say they are weak in comparison; they can still be beautiful expressions of the Northern Rhône. Jean-Louis Chave goes on to say that Saint-Joseph is 'an idea of a wine, Syrah on granite,' and that is essentially what these wines share. It is also what distinguishes them from the Crozes-Hermitage in our imaginary blind tasting; the lean, upright tension derived from granite soils is comparatively rare in Crozes-Hermitage, where most of the vines are grown on old alluvial terraces, giving a rounder, fruitier expression.

Most of the soils of Saint-Joseph are granitic, but they are not all the same type of granite. At the northern tip, around Chavanay, there is a lot of muscovite granite and migmatite, and also plenty of gneiss along much of the more northerly half of the appellation, and near Tournon. There are regular small patches of loess dotted along the whole stretch, and some small calcareous outcrops, particularly in the far south; Domaine Courbis' best Saint-Joseph *blanc* is named 'Les Royes' after its Châteaubourg *lieu-dit*, a steep limestone amphitheatre. The soil around Tournon and Mauves consists of particularly coarse-grained, heavily de-composed granite. There are also some flat alluvial terraces within the appellation, and more recent alluvions, mostly at the southern end, that tend to give more basic wines.

The appellation was originally granted in 1956 for the southern end, a growing area that covered just six communes: Glun, Mauves, Tournon, Lemps, Saint-Jean-de-Muzols and Vion. The quality of the wines coming from this area has been known for centuries. In the Middle Ages the wine from here was known as the 'Vin de Mauves', and some 'Vin de

Tournon' was supplied to King François I (1494–1547). Victor Hugo even mentions 'Vin de Mauves' in *Les Misérables*, published in 1862. The name Saint-Joseph comes from one of its finest *lieux-dits*, just to the north of Mauves: a beautiful cone-shaped hill with expositions curving round from south-west to east. Jean Gonon recounts a story in which local vignerons had a meeting with Baron Le Roy to give a name to the appellation when it was first established. He suggested Vin de Tournon, but the then-president of the appellation, a Monsieur Sauzon, explained that this wouldn't be fair to the other nearby villages making wine, and started to list his parcels: 'Saint-Joseph …' Baron Le Roy didn't wait to hear the others, he jumped on Saint-Joseph and wrote it down.

There are other *lieux-dits* especially around Mauves, Tournon and Saint-Jean-de-Muzols which are gaining a name for themselves among Rhône lovers, albeit it in a more embryonic way than the respected names of Côte-Rôtie or Hermitage. 'There are some quarters that have more history, where you can make more interesting wines,' says Jean-Louis Chave. 'The idea of a *cru* system in Saint-Joseph is a logical one. Every time you have perpendicular valleys to the Rhône river – Les Chalaix, Les Oliviers, La Dardouille, *lieu-dit* Saint-Joseph, Sainte-Épine and Bachasson. Those are the historic *crus* of the region, all these slopes between Mauves, Lemps and Saint-Jean-de-Muzols.' To this list, some would add the *lieux-dits* Le Paradis, Le Clos and the Vignes de l'Hospice. Logical or not, Chave recognizes the practical impossibility now of creating any kind of official *cru* system, and Jean Gonon agrees.

The other 20 communes now included in the appellation were added in 1969. Most of these lie to the north of the original six, and it's arguable that this should have been a new, distinct appellation instead of an extension to Saint-Joseph. But it's too late to change that now. As in Condrieu, it was only in the 1980s that many of the best slopes were rehabilitated. At this time, farming apricots still rivalled winemaking when it came to making a living, and Gonon reminds us that 'wine has only been a big thing here since the 2000s.' Saint-Joseph still doesn't have the same cachet as Hermitage, Cornas or Côte-Rôtie. Despite the work in the best sites being just as laborious and time consuming, prices are lower, so investment is slower.

In terms of quality, however, the best Saint-Josephs of Chavanay, such as Domaine de Monteillet Cuvée du Papy, Domaine Lionel Faury La Gloriette and Domaine Xavier Gérard Le Blanchard can outperform the Côte-Rôties of inferior addresses, while still displaying a similarly *nordiste* expression of Syrah – fine, spicy, red-fruited. The same is true of the best Saint-Josephs of the southern end – there are some exceptional wines, such as Domaine Gonon and Domaine J.L. Chave Clos Florentin, which have their own unique Saint-Joseph character that's analogous to neither Cornas nor Hermitage. Nor is there much to gain from comparing these Saint-Josephs to those further north; in the south they are typically bolder and more extracted, with a denser tannic mass and darker aromatic profiles.

The vast size – or more specifically, length – of the appellation, and the inescapable fact that it includes some terroir of inferior quality, means that the words 'AOC Saint-Joseph' will never guarantee quality or style. But if you know what you're looking for, it can be a source of some excellent, highly characterful, remarkably good value wines.

Appellation: AOC Saint-Joseph

Birth of the appellation: 1956

Communes: Andance, Ardoix, Arras-sur-Rhône, Champagne, Charnas, Châteaubourg, Chavanay, Félines, Glun, Guilherand-Granges, Lemps, Limony, Malleval, Mauves, Ozon, Peyraud, Saint-Désirat, Saint-Etienne-de-Valoux, Saint-Jean-de-Muzols, Saint-Pierre-de-Boeuf, Sarras, Sécheras, Serrières, Talencieux, Tournon-sur-Rhône, Vion

Total surface area sold under the AOC in 2019: 1,348 hectares

Average yield in 2019: 37 hectolitres per hectare

Colours permitted: red and white

Production in 2019: 86 per cent red, 14 per cent white

Grape varieties permitted: Reds must be made of Syrah, with up to 10 per cent Marsanne and/or Roussanne allowed in the blend.

　　Whites must be made of Marsanne, Roussanne or a blend of the two.

Key producers

Cave Julien Cécillon

Saint-Jean-du-Muzols

www.juliencecillon.com

Julien Cécillon is one of those people who everyone seems to like – no-one has a bad word to say about him. A bit like his wines. He set up the estate in 2011 with his American wife Nancy Kerschen. Wine, however, is in his blood – his uncle is the renowned Jean-Louis Grippat. His first wines in 2012 were small volumes of Saint-Joseph, and he has now installed himself in Saint-Jean-du-Muzols. His Saint-Joseph *rouge*, Babylone, is from 35-year-old Syrah and his *blanc* Victoria from 45-year-old Marsanne, both planted on granite. His two old-vine Crozes-Hermitage *rouges* are also granite-born, as is his Cornas Saint-Pierre. Only his Saint-Péray Gemini differs, a Marsanne–Roussanne blend grown on clay limestone. The whole range is impressive, depicting each terroir with clarity, and displaying a deft winemaking hand that's been well-honed making wine around the world. An estate to watch.

Domaine Coursodon

Mauves

www.domaine-coursodon.com

Another Mauves mainstay (along with Chave, Gonon, Gripa, Marsanne, etc.) is Jérôme Coursodon, fifth generation at this historically important Saint-Joseph domaine. They only make Saint-Joseph, and have 16 hectares of exceptional hillside parcels around Mauves. The style here is bold, ripe and sometimes quite glossy, particularly at the top of the range – reds are destemmed and the cuvée Sensonne is matured in 100 per cent new oak barriques. Whites are just as good, again in a concentrated style. Silice is 100 per cent Marsanne, fermented in stainless steel with blocked malolactic. The decidedly richer Le Paradis Saint-Pierre is from *lieu-dit* Le Paradis, 95 per cent Marsanne, 5 per cent Roussanne, malolactic completed, fermented and matured in 50 per cent new oak barriques.

Domaine Guy Farge

Saint-Jean-de-Muzols

www.vigneron-guy-farge-rhone.com

Tucked away in Saint-Jean-de-Muzols, this domaine has been going from strength to strength in recent years. Thomas Farge took over from his father in 2018 and is doing great things. At 22 hectares it's a fairly large private estate for the Northern Rhône, including terroirs in Saint-Péray, Cornas, Saint-Joseph and Condrieu, not to mention some IGP land. The house style here is one of gentle extraction, producing wines of transparency and finesse across the range. The Saint-Joseph *rouge* cuvées are made with whole bunches and natural yeasts, and matured in old demi-muids. Passion des Terraces, made from vines over 100 years old, grown on steep granite terraces, is consistently one of the best in the appellation. The new single-vineyard Cornas bottling Reynard, first vintage 2016, has also got off to a strong start.

Domaine Lionel Faury

Chavanay

www.domaine-faury.fr

Lionel Faury makes such uniformly excellent wines across his holdings in Saint-Joseph, Condrieu and Côte-Rôtie, that it was not immediately obvious in which chapter his estate should feature. But seeing as he lives in Chavanay, and his Saint-Joseph La Gloriette is so exceptional, I choose to place him here. La Gloriette is a blend of three vineyards planted in the 1950s, some of the most northerly in the appellation, a wine of great freshness and finesse that is so texturally deep it's like bathing in a forest. His Côte-Rôties are arguably better wines however, particularly his Emporium from *lieu-dit* Fourvier. His Condrieus are rich but not heavy, and La Berne, from massal selections supplied by Georges Vernay in the 1960s planted in a south-facing amphitheatre, has great concentration and length that marks it out as one of the best from Chavanay. When Lionel took over from his father in 2006 aged just 23, he immediately increased the usage of whole bunches for his reds, reduced the amount of new oak and stopped stirring the lees of his Condrieus. The result is a range of traditional, slightly old-school wines that are still somewhat under the radar, offering excellent value for money and immensely enjoyable drinking.

La Ferme des Sept Lunes

Bogy

T.: +33 (0) 4 75 34 86 37

Another natural wine estate that's the source of some thrilling and peculiar expressions of Saint-Joseph, La Ferme des Sept Lunes is based in the village of Bogy up on the Ardèche plateau, between Saint-Désirat and Serrières. It's been in Jean Delobre's family since the 1930s, but the vineyard has been farmed biodynamically since 1997 and since 2005 Jean has been working almost entirely without added sulphites. As a result, he finds his wines more generous and more complex, with longer lasting flavours. Sometimes an oxidative element can come into play, but he believes as long as it isn't too marked that can bring complexity. Don't expect a 'classic' Saint-Joseph from this address – the wines can be surprising, even challenging. For those with an open mind, they are well worth trying.

Domaine Pierre Gaillard

Malleval

www.domainespierregaillard.com

Along with Yves Cuilleron and François Villard, Pierre Gaillard is the third of the three dynamic, modernizing musketeers based around Ampuis who have had such success from the late 1980s to the present day. Gaillard is a particularly imposing figure, more economical with his words than the others, but happy to share his knowledge and no-nonsense opinions. After studying winemaking in Beaune, Gaillard made his first purchase in 1981 with the Clos de Cuminaille vineyard in Malleval. Since then, he's bought vineyards throughout the Northern Rhône, Banyuls and Faugères. He now owns 77 hectares in total, and I have great admiration for how he manages to keep tabs on such a vast and varied estate. The standard is high across the whole range of Northern Rhône appellations, and the approach remains fairly 'modern', that is to say reds are all destemmed and use of new oak is fairly intensive – up to 100 per cent new oak barriques for his Côte-Rôtie Rose Pourpre from *lieu-dit* Côte-Rozier, but the wine handles it well. The Saint-Joseph *rouge* Clos de Cuminaille, an east-facing slope in Chavanay whose Syrah sees 40 per cent new oak for 18 months, is a highlight of the range, as is the fine, perfumed, elegant Condrieu L'Octroi. What he will be remembered for no doubt is the key part he has played in the renaissance of Seyssuel.

Domaine Gonon

Mauves

T.: +33 (0) 4 75 08 45 27

Whenever I visit brothers Pierre and Jean Gonon, they always have company – other winemakers, restaurateurs from Lyon, friends and family, all eating, drinking, talking. Over the past 20 years, the estate has gained quite an international following, and is now recognized as the leading estate in Saint-Joseph. And they still don't have a website.

Their father, also called Pierre, was among the first to bottle in Saint-Joseph, in 1964. The brothers didn't train formally, but learned from him, and took over the estate in the late 1980s. It now amounts to 10.5 hectares, with vineyards in Mauves, Tournon and Saint-Jean-de-Muzols, and is worked organically. The Saint-Jean-de-Muzols vineyards were originally owned by revered local winemaker Raymond Trollat, and the brothers occasionally make a separate Vieilles Vignes cuvée with these vines, planted by Trollat's grandfather in 1920. The body of the production is their largely destemmed Saint-Joseph *rouge*, a deliciously deep, sprawling, textural style that ages well. Les Oliviers is their Saint-Joseph *blanc*, a blend of 80 per cent Marsanne and 20 per cent Roussanne that comes from the Mauves *lieu-dit* of the same name that has long been known for the quality of its whites; it's unabashedly Rhône in its natural opulence, finding energy despite its low acidity. They also make an appealing IGP Ardèche Syrah Les Iles Feray, and, surprisingly, a Vin de France Chasselas.

Catherine & Pascal Jamet

Arras

www.catherineetpascaljametvignerons.com

The wiry and energetic Pascal Jamet (no relation to the estates in Côte-Rôtic) is an expert in ampelography, and spent 10 years at a vine nursery before establishing his own vineyards. He started out in 1994, and met Catherine in 1996. They have now planted 4 hectares of Saint-Joseph on the gneiss slopes of Arras, not to mention a further hectare in Saint-Péray and 3 hectares of IGP Collines Rhodaniennes. They have a hands-off approach in the cellar, preferring to create balance in the vineyards, with some parcels cultivated organically. Pascal's previous work has informed his viticulture; he works with unusual varieties for the region such as Merlot, Cabernet and Dureza, and imported training techniques. The wines are expressive and authentic, with satisfying textural character.

Domaine Monier-Perréol

Saint-Désirat

T.: +33 (0) 4 75 34 20 64

Philippe Perréol's vineyards are mostly on loess and limestone. Jean-Pierre Monier's are on granite. They originally both took their grapes to the cooperative Cave Saint-Désirat, but now have their own estates, and sometimes bottle their wines under Domaine Monier or Domaine Perréol. But since they work with the same biodynamic philosophy, and have complementary terroirs, they sometimes blend their wines and bottle under Domaine Monier-Perréol. What great friends they must be. Between them they have 12 hectares, and make a range of red and white Saint-Josephs and some IGP Collines Rhodaniennes. For their Saint-Josephs, they have destemmed until recently, and now are beginning to experiment with 50 per cent whole bunch. They use larger

400-litre and 500-litre old barrels for the classic Saint-Josephs, and a small percentage of new oak for the single-vineyard wines. The Châtelet is a perfect illustration of a classic Saint-Joseph that isn't trying too hard, and is all the more charming for it. Whichever of the three domaine names you have on the bottle, you're in for a treat.

Domaine Romaneaux-Destezet

Arlebosc

romaneaux.destezet.free.fr

The river Doux empties into the Rhône at St-Jean-de-Muzols. If you follow it back up to the Ardèche plateau for 12 kilometres, eventually you reach the village of Arlebosc, where you might find, if you're lucky, the elusive Hervé Souhaut. He established his estate here in 1993, and the wines quickly gained a following, particularly on the natural wine scene. He works his land organically, avoids any additives and uses very low doses of sulphites. The only wine to bear the name of the estate is his white wine, a blend of Viognier and Roussanne, the rest bear his name instead. He makes a Syrah and a juicy old-vine Gamay, La Souteronne, but his Saint-Joseph *rouge*, Sainte-Epine, from 100-year-old vines with no destemming and bottled unfiltered, is a particularly captivating and fascinating expression of this extraordinary *lieu-dit*.

Domaine Benoît Roseau

Pélussin

www.closdupigeonnier.fr

When I first visited Benoît Roseau in the village of Pélussin, 4 kilometres west of Chavanay, he was mending his van in the cellar he built with his own hands. He is the first of his family to make wine, but even as a young boy he always envisaged himself running a domaine. He planted his first vines in the grounds of his parents' house in the village, and has since managed to weave together an estate of 4 hectares, including 1.38 hectares of red and white Saint-Joseph in Serrières, 24 ares (0.24 hectares) in *lieu-dit* Coteaux de Tupin in Côte-Rôtie and 20 ares in *lieu-dit* Le Riollement in Condrieu. He also buys some grapes and wine in Cornas and Saint-Péray. He works 70 per cent of his own vineyards organically, and won't be totally content until they are all converted. Benoît makes fine, measured wines with great clarity and sense of place. He has achieved a great deal since he struck out in 2010; this is a domaine to watch.

Other good examples

Because of the disparate, slightly tenuous nature of the appellation, choosing the best producers of Saint-Joseph isn't as straightforward as choosing the best of Cornas or Côte-Rôtie. Many of the best wines are made by estates that also own more prestigious vineyards, and so are better known for other, more expensive or higher-reaching cuvées. And there are a lot of producers to choose from. I've split the selection into northern Saint-Joseph and southern Saint-Joseph (for those producers with more centrally-located vineyards I've taken a stylistic, rather than strictly geographic, view).

Northern Saint-Joseph

The very best Saint-Josephs from the more northerly reaches of the appellation are from **Domaine Yves Gangloff**, **Domaine de Monteillet** and **Domaine Xavier Gérard**. There are plenty of other exceptional Saint-Josephs to be found here from **Domaine du Chêne, Domaine Georges Vernay, Domaine André Perret, Domaine Aurélien Chatagnier, Domaine Christophe Pichon, Domaine Vallet, Domaine Stéphane Ogier, Domaine des Amphores** and **Domaine Pierre-Jean Villa**.

Southern Saint-Joseph

From the southern part of the appellation, wonderful wines can be found at **Domaine Laurent Habrard, Domaine Bernard Gripa, Dard & Ribo, Domaine Alain Voge, Domaine Jolivet, Domaine Vincent Paris, Domaine Rouchier** and **Domaine Marsanne**. Other excellent examples can be found at **Domaine du Tunnel, La Vigne des Pères, Domaine Gérard Courbis, Domaine du Coulet, Domaine Jean-François Jacouton, Domaine Aléofane, Domaine des Pierres Sèches, Domaine des Miquettes** and **Domaine Courbis**.

Négociant bottlings

Négociant bottlings are a mixed bag; I often find more generic wines to be disappointing, but some top négociant bottlings are among the best wines in the appellation. **Chapoutier** Saint-Joseph Les Granits, in both white and red, are phenomenal wines; the Les Granillites white and red are also reliably good, and the Alléno et Chapoutier range is also worth trying. **Ferraton** makes a good range of Saint-Josephs, including some interesting single-vineyard wines. The Saint-Joseph *rouge* Paradis and Saint-Joseph *blanc* Les Oliviers are particularly noteworthy.

Guigal Saint-Joseph Lieu-dit in white and red are both very good, with plentiful spicy oak. **Delas Frères** Saint-Joseph *rouge* Sainte-Epine is very good in a rich, bold and spicy style. **Alain Jaume's** Saint-Joseph *rouge* La Butte d'Or can be impressive. The cooperative **Cave de Tain** Saint-Joseph *rouge* Esprit de Granit can also be excellent.

Past masters[5]

Who are the greatest French painters of the nineteenth century? There are so many to choose from: Paul Cézanne, Edouard Manet, Henri de Toulouse-Lautrec, the list goes on. What about the greatest French winemakers of the nineteenth century? Or indeed any century before that? A great artist's creations live on eternally, but a great winemaker's only a hundred years at best. That their work has a finite lifespan doesn't necessarily lessen their achievements, but once we can no longer taste and discuss a vigneron's wines, our collective memory of them begins to fade.

If an estate takes a family name, like Domaine Clape in Cornas, it can serve as a memorial to those who have passed – the revered Auguste died in 2018 – as much as a reference to the current generations – Pierre and Olivier who still work the vines today. Some surnames are so entrenched in a village that even when a great estate runs its course, these names spring up once again. The great Robert Michel of Cornas may be long retired, but Johann Michel represents a new generation of Michels making great wines in the village. Another Cornas veteran is Noël Verset, whose estate was sold off when he died. Today you can buy the wines of Alain Verset, a tiny estate that produces lovely, classical wines; but Alain is Noël's nephew, not his successor, and the wines don't come from the same vineyards.

Since he has no successor, and his domaine is unlikely to be sold as it stands, the name of Michel Juge will no longer be so visible. His 1991 Cornas Cuvée Spéciale made an indelible impression on me in 2010; though he has passed on, he and his wines will live on in the memory of wine lovers far and wide. Two of the greatest names in Côte-Rôtie have also been extinguished for now – Marius Gentaz of Domaine Gentaz-Dervieux, and Albert Dervieux-Thaize of Domaine Dervieux-Thaize. Both of their estates were built on vineyards handed down from Jean Dervieux, and then eventually put back together again by René Rostaing, under his name, not theirs (see entry on Domaine Rostaing).

5 For detailed information on all of these and other past masters, I can recommend *The Wines of the Rhône* by John Livingstone-Learmonth.

In Saint-Joseph, there are two winemakers who made great strides in their time but are now retired without direct successors – Raymond Trollat and Jean-Louis Grippat. Grippat sold his vineyards to Guigal in 2001, and Trollat sold vineyards to Domaine Gonon in stages, from 1988 to 2006. 'In 1988 these were old vines on the slopes,' says Jean Gonon, 'nobody wanted them.' The Domaine Gonon Saint-Joseph Vieilles Vignes that is made from time to time is from vines planted by Trollat's grandfather in 1920, and it serves, says Gonon, 'to keep a trace of him.'

Old bottles from all of these past masters do surface from time to time, but with each bottle drunk they become more rare – and expensive. Some, such as those by Gentaz-Dervieux, now cost thousands of pounds a bottle. I'd love to devote more space to all of them here, but it seems perverse when these are wines that few of us are ever likely to encounter. However, these are names that deserve to live on among wine lovers, and are men to whom we owe so much.

CORNAS

Red wines, pure Syrah, all from one commune. Surely of all the appellations of the Northern Rhône, Cornas is the easiest to grasp. And at just over 150 hectares under vine, along with Hermitage, it's also one of the smallest. Walk from one end of the village to the other and you can take in most of the best vineyards, an east-facing slope that serves as a breathtaking backdrop to the rows of plain houses. If you're not a wine lover, there's little else to tempt you here.

Was it winemaking that attracted the Romans to Cornas? Though they settled here, there is no concrete evidence of viticulture from that period, but it's immediately obvious that this is excellent terroir. The first written reference to wine in Cornas dates back to 1000: a gift of a vine to a member of the Abbey of Saint-Chaffre du Monastier. Due to the high taxes imposed on wines travelling north, it wasn't until the eighteenth century that Cornas gained a foothold on Paris wine lists. Like the other west bank appellations of the Northern Rhône, the slopes were largely abandoned after suffering phylloxera and the shocks of two world wars. After the Second World War there was plenty of work in nearby Valence that offered more money for less sweat. Thankfully some committed vignerons stayed on, and bit-by-bit, Cornas hauled itself back onto its feet. It wasn't until the 1950s that winemakers began bottling wine in Cornas, and it was common for winemakers with small holdings to have other jobs to support them. That said, there are no large domaines in Cornas. Most of the vineyards are simply too labour intensive to work at scale, and only Domaine du Coulet has much more than 10 hectares of Cornas.

Cornas hasn't always had the same consistency or modern standards as its more prestigious neighbours. Less than twenty years ago, Cornas still had a reputation for displaying a particularly rustic, gamey side. It has been described as the *gout de terroir* in the past, but it was more likely down to poor cellar hygiene and brett. One man who brought a modernizing thrust to Cornas was Jean-Luc Colombo. Originally from Marseille, he set up as a winemaker and winemaking consultant in the late 1980s. On his advice, many local winemakers experimented with alternative approaches to vinification and viticulture, particularly destemming and the use of new oak barrels. Today the pendulum is swinging back towards more traditional methods, with most of the new generation of winemakers moving towards more neutral containers and the use of whole bunches. The past twenty years have seen the installation of a new generation of winemakers, and a number of exciting new domaines. Cornas is one of the most dynamic and collegiate appellations in the Northern Rhône in this regard. Cornas terroir will always deliver wines with muscle and grit, but the movement is towards a fresher and more elegant expression. There is still plenty of land left to plant, so the story isn't finished yet.

The appellation can be crudely split into two sections: the slope and the plateau. The slope is what you can see from the village. Though it's broadly east-facing it's particularly rumpled, as if pulverized from above. It consists of a succession of contorted hillside nooks and crannies, with vineyards facing in all directions. 'That's what expresses Cornas,' says Olivier Clape of Domaine Clape, 'all the valleys and changes in direction, it's not like Hermitage,' which has a more regular face to the sun. There are some more uniform slopes, such as *lieu-dit* La Côte. But even these are quite abrupt; the village of Cornas sits at around 120 metres above sea level, and the slopes rapidly rise to 400 metres. The steepness of the slope is just one of the factors that creates a particularly hot microclimate here. South-facing slopes such as top *lieux-dits* Reynards and part of La Geynale bask in the sun, and most of the slope is protected from the north wind.

The soils are made up of heavily decomposed granite that easily breaks between your fingers. It creates a sandy topsoil, but there's little humus. It's not the most inviting terrain, but it can be penetrated by vine roots once the plants get established. It's also very free draining. Though granite dominates the appellation, there are significant limestone deposits at the northern limit along *lieux-dits* Pied la Vigne and Le Coulet, and also some silt and clay along the foot of the slope, which usually give less powerful wines.

It would be easy to assume that Cornas was just the slope until you drive up into the plateau above. It's hilly, high in altitude and more exposed to the wind than the slope, which makes for a cooler terroir. The wines from these sites tend to be less tannic and concentrated, ready to drink sooner. Although the slope is fully planted, vineyards on the plateau are interspersed with woodland and grazing land, with plenty of potential still to plant. I'm yet to hear any local winemakers argue the case that this land is the equal of the slope, but as the climate warms and the vines here age, perhaps this will change.

Lieu-dit *Reynards*

Cornas has always been known for the thunderous power of its wines. Even with a light touch in the cellar, these are invariably concentrated, dense wines, very different from the feathery finesse of Côte-Rôtie. They are closer in spirit to the very best southern Saint-Josephs, but mightier, and make themselves known by their texture and volume. They are not necessarily more tannic than those of Hermitage, but whereas the tannins of Hermitage are typically very fine and integrated into the wine, in Cornas they are very much a standout feature; the wine is built around a deeply textural, sometimes grainy or sinewy tannic heft. There is a wild, untameable aspect to the wines of Cornas, it's a wine that cannot easily be contained or shaped. That's not to say they can't be elegant, fine wines – they can. But on their own terms.

With all this natural concentration and tannin, you might expect these wines to have great longevity. They can be long lived, but are less predictable than Saint-Joseph and Hermitage in this respect. A wine you'd expect to stride on for years can come to an abrupt end, while relatively simple bottlings sometimes retain their youth and vigour for longer than you might imagine. They are also less constant and steady in their development. There is no doubt that Cornas can – on occasion – produce wines equal to the best of Hermitage and Côte-Rôtie. They are assertive and spirited wines that sometimes seem to have their own agenda. Not all the wines will be elegant, but at least Cornas should never be boring. It's an appellation that has greatly evolved over the past twenty years, and shows no signs of slowing down.

Appellation: AOC Cornas

Birth of the appellation: 1938

Communes: Cornas

Total surface area sold under the AOC in 2019: 156 hectares

Average yield in 2019: 33 hectolitres per hectare

Colours permitted: red only

Grape varieties permitted: Wines must be 100 per cent Syrah

Key producers

Domaine Thierry Allemand

Cornas

T.: +33 (0) 4 75 81 06 50

When Thierry Allemand finished his studies, he got a job as an electrician but – fortunately for us – he didn't enjoy it. So instead he took a job as an assistant to Joseph Michel, father of Robert Michel (see box, page 295), in Cornas. Thierry wasn't from a winemaking family, but, seeing his potential, Joseph convinced Thierry's father to buy him some vines.

This was in 1982. Thierry didn't take a day's holiday in 12 years, re-investing all his earnings into buying new parcels. When I visited him in 2020, Thierry, who is still full of energy, was sporting a white, whiskery moustache. He now works with his son Theo, who has just completed some *stages* with Domaines Durand, Clape and J.L. Chave. They now have 5 hectares in Cornas, mostly *lieux-dits* Pigeonnier, Tézier, Chaillots and Reynards. 'We're already overcome with work from 5 hectares,' says Theo, 'we'd prefer just to do the work as it should be done rather than buy more vineyards.'

They make two main Cornas cuvées, both named after *lieux-dits*, but they are not single-vineyard wines. Chaillots is made with younger vines from the estate (around 40 years old on average). Reynard is the old-vine cuvée: their oldest parcel, originally owned by Noël Verset, was planted in 1908. They work organically, and consider the phases of the moon when making decisions. The wines are not destemmed and are punched down by foot twice a week, then aged for 2 years on the lees without racking, avoiding new oak barrels. Addition of sulphites is reduced as much as possible. In a few vintages a *sans souffre* Cornas cuvée has been made, but due to speculation on the secondary market, the 2014 is likely to be the last. Since 2015, however, in the best years they have been quietly making a Spéciale Cuvée instead. To date it hasn't been released commercially, but a tasting of the 2015 in 2020 revealed one of the most beautiful Cornas wines I've ever tasted. 'We can bring elegance without losing the traditional ways,' says Thierry. And he's right.

Domaine Franck Balthazar

Cornas

+33 (0) 6 20 05 41 79

The Balthazar name is another with deep roots in the village. The do-maine was established in 1931 by Casimir Balthazar, taken over by his son René, and has been in the hands of his grandson Franck since 2002. The estate was 2 hectares when Franck took it on, and he has bought new parcels making it up to 3.5 hectares. His approach is quietly tra-ditional, and he also makes a *sans souffre* cuvée from his young vines, which can be juicily compelling. The jewel of the estate however is his centenarian parcel of vines from *lieu-dit* Chaillot, bottled under the name of the *lieu-dit*. He added a négociant side to the business in 2015, so now makes a range of wines from bought grapes from other Rhône appellations, north and south.

Domaine Clape

Cornas

T.: +33 (0) 4 75 40 33 64

There is no sign on the building – not even a buzzer. The dingy cellar, hidden under a row of anonymous houses and accessed by a cramped lift, contains rows of ancient black oval foudres and concrete bins of old bottles almost entirely swallowed up by tufts of black mould. It's a remarkably low-key set-up for one of the Rhône's most emblematic estates.

Bottles in the cellar at Domaine Clape

Since Auguste Clape's death in 2018, the estate has been in the hands of his son Pierre and grandson Olivier, both unfailingly cheerful and welcoming. The approach here is determinedly traditional: whole bunches are vinified in unlined concrete tanks, then aged for two years in small foudres before bottling. They don't try to tame or soften the elemental force of Cornas with racking or new oak, preferring to leave that to time. The *grand vin* is best left for a decade before opening, when it emerges like a grizzly bear from hibernation. It's a dark, ferric, tempestuous wine of great complexity and textural depth.

The Cornas is a blend of parcels from the slope including Sabarotte, Patou, Tézier, Mazards, La Côte and old-vine Reynards. They have never made single-vineyard bottlings, nor do they intend to. In 1997, they started making a second wine called Renaissance, a barrel selection that tends to come from younger Cornas vines. The inaugural year was ruined by a faulty batch of corks – so the first vintage is really 1998. They produce two other Syrahs, a Côtes-du-Rhône, and a Vin de France called Vin des Amis; they're from vineyards near to Cornas, and share some of the savage nature of their big brothers. They also make an excellent Saint-Péray.

Domaine du Coulet

Cornas

domaineducoulet.com

Bearded, brash and constantly cracking jokes, Matthieu Barret cuts a very particular figure in the Cornas landscape. Domaine du Coulet is a relatively large estate for Cornas, with much of the land being spread over steep terraces to the far north of the appellation in *lieu-dit* Le Coulet, which features some limestone outcrops among the granite. He has 11 hectares of Cornas and 7 hectares of Côtes-du-Rhône, along with a growing négociant business, Matthieu Barret Sélections, offering wines from all over the Rhône Valley.

His vineyards are farmed biodynamically, and his Cornas wines are highly distinctive. They often have the aromatic and textural profile of natural wines, with a potent herbal, resinous dimension that gives an impression of whole-bunch fermentation, even though the bunches are destemmed. Sometimes they are less concentrated and less tannic than you might expect from a typical Cornas, and they have a remarkably drinkable side, coupled with an intriguing complexity. No doubt this is in part due to their élevage in large cement eggs. Brise Cailloux is the most voluminous cuvée, a selection of both old and young vines from around the domaine. Billes Noires is more intense and structured, from a parcel of old vines (over 50 years old) from the extreme north of the appellation at *lieu-dit* Les Arlettes. Gore (sometimes spelt 'Ogre' depending on the year) is his top cuvée from north- and east-facing slopes of *lieu-dit* Les Arlettes, which is similarly intense but even more piercingly energetic. An estate with plenty of personality.

Domaine Guillaume Gilles

Cornas

T.: +33 (0) 4 75 55 38 26

'I've been in the vines since I was very young,' says Guillaume Gilles, and you can tell; he's young and spritely with piercing brown eyes, but built like a rugby prop. Twenty years of working these hillsides by hand will do that. His path to owning his own domaine has been gradual. He worked with Robert Michel, and when Michel retired, he sold Gilles 2.5 hectares of his old-vine *lieu-dit* Chaillot. More recently he has added a hectare of *lieu-dit* Les Rieux, a high-altitude parcel of young vines that go into his new cuvée Nouvelle R, first vintage 2015. The estate has been worked organically since 2009, and is in the process of being certified. Guillaume works traditionally, and says, 'The principle is to have the best possible grapes. Then in the cellar – nothing.' He doesn't destem, avoids winemaking additions such as yeast or tartaric acid, and vinifies in concrete with no temperature control. He avoids new oak as much as possible, and uses 400-litre barrels and demi-muids to mature the wines, 18 months for his classic Cornas, 12 months for Nouvelle R. He also produces some Côtes-du-Rhône and Vin de France.

Domaine Johann Michel

Cornas

domainejohannmichel.monsite-orange.fr

The Michel name is well-established in Cornas. Johann's great-grandfather helped to set up the appellation in 1938, but his is a different branch of the family to the celebrated winemaker Robert Michel. So it was far from obvious that Johann should embark upon a career as vigneron. But he bought half a hectare of Cornas in 1997, set up a domaine, and has never looked back. He now has 3 hectares over four *lieux-dits*: Les Saveaux, Patou, Les Côtes and Chaillot, and describes his approach as *agriculture raisonnée*. Considering that his vines are only up to 20 years old, results so far have been remarkable. His classic Cornas cuvée is destemmed, but Jana (*lieu-dit* Chaillots, used demi-muids) and 'Mère Michel' (*lieu-dit* Les Côtes, new demi-muids) are not. The style is vibrant, concentrated, lush and powerful.

Domaine Vincent Paris

Cornas

www.vin-paris.fr

Lieu-dit La Geynale, next to Reynards at the heart of the appellation, creates some of the most thunderous Syrahs in the world. In person, Vincent Paris is slight of frame and quietly modest, but his single-vineyard bottling from 100-year-old vines is a roaring black hole of a wine that all Rhône-lovers should experience if they can. He has 6 hectares in total in Cornas and makes two other bottlings, Granit 30 (destemmed young vine cuvée from 30° slopes, early drinking) and Granit 60 (old vines grown on 60° degree slopes, mostly destemmed, drink young or up to 15 years old). Chemicals are kept to a minimum here, with only some herbicide used on the steepest parcels. No new oak is used, and wines are unfiltered. They have the natural power of the appellation, but with finesse. His Saint-Joseph *rouge* can be overlooked, but this would be a mistake; from high-altitude vines in Ardoix, it's a fine-boned, precise expression that offers great value for money.

Tardieu-Laurent

Lourmarin

tardieu-laurent.fr

Though based in the breathtakingly beautiful village of Lourmarin in the Luberon, the négociant Tardieu-Laurent is probably best known for its Cornas, and is one of the few négociants to make a cuvée that can rival the best estates. Michel Tardieu was a civil servant, but decided to follow his passion and set up the business in 1996. He has since been joined by his son Bastien. Compared to the ocean liners Chapoutier and Guigal, Tardieu-Laurent is more of a yacht – a haute couture négoci-ant, if you will. They make wines in all the possible appellations of the Northern Rhône, and most Southern *crus* too, often across multiple cuvées. Their size allows a certain attention to detail – working with reliable growers with old vines in the best *lieux-dits* has led to good results. The wines are polished, elegant, and some cuvées can be oaky. They have begun to move away from such obvious élevage in recent years, and have started using whole-bunch fermentation to good ef-fect. Their Cornas Vieilles Vignes and Côte-Rôtie Vieilles Vignes are top picks from the range, and their Côtes-du-Rhônes often taste rather more expensive than they actually are.

Domaine du Tunnel

Cornas

www.domaine-du-tunnel.fr

Though he started out making wine as early as the mid-1990s, Stéphane Robert's wines soon came to represent a refreshing new era for Cornas. They seemed to take the best of the appellation's 'modern' phase – clean wines, with polished, concentrated fruit – but quickly stepped away from an over-reliance on new oak. Perhaps this was taken on board during his time with Jean-Louis Grippat. He has since developed the estate to 11 hectares, mostly in Cornas and Saint-Péray. There was a time when his top of the range bottlings could verge on the exaggerated, but his style is gradually moving in a more measured direction. His Saint-Joseph *rouge*, from vineyards in Mauves, Glun and Tournon, is also highly recommended, and he has even added some Condrieu to his expanding domaine. Though not organic, the domaine has been HVE certified since 2018.

Domaine Alain Voge

Cornas

www.alain-voge.com

Alain Voge, who sadly died in 2020, joined the family farm on his return from Algeria in 1961. He didn't have long to learn the ropes, as his father Louis died in 1965. After falling out with the négociant who bought their crop of grapes, it wasn't long before he started bottling himself. By 1980, he had given up his sidelines, as fruit grower, nurseryman and distiller, to concentrate solely on making wine. He started converting the domaine to organics in the 2000s, and achieved organic and biodynamic certification in 2016.

Today the estate sits somewhere between traditional and modern. More straightforward Cornas cuvée Les Chailles is destemmed, but Vieilles Vignes and single-vineyard Les Vieilles Fontaines see a small proportion of whole bunch. Élevage is in 228-litre barriques, with no new oak for Les Chailles, then a little as the range progresses. Vines are cultivated *en gobelet* and fermented using natural yeasts, using minimal sulphite additions. He has several parcels on the slopes (and the plateau at *lieu-dit* Saint-Pierre), but his 80-year-old vines at *lieu-dit* La Fontaine are some of the most enviable in all of Cornas.

Just as his Cornas wines are among the best of the appellation, so are his Saint-Pérays. Though once excessively oaky, they are now brighter and more drinkable than in the 2010s, particularly the old-vine 100 per cent Marsanne Fleur de Crussol. His traditional method Les Bulles d'Alain is also a particularly enjoyable example of the style. And don't miss his Saint-Joseph *rouge* Les Côtes. Alain leaves a great Northern Rhône estate at the top of its game.

Other good examples

Two excellent producers in a traditional style are **Domaine Alain Verset** (tenacious, energetic) and **Domaine Dumien-Serrette** (fine, precise). Enjoyable expressions of a more 'modern', ripe and often oaky style can be found at **Domaine Durand** and **Domaine Courbis**. The wines of **Domaine Lionnet** and **Domaine Guy Farge** are highly recommended, both making wines that sit somewhere between these two styles. Don't miss **Domaine Mikael Bourg**, a very good source of Cornas and Saint-Péray in a more contemporary, fresh and open style. The paucity of good négociant and cooperative bottlings is perhaps another reason why Cornas has taken longer to establish itself than Côte-Rôtie and Hermitage. Two stand out alongside **Tardieu-Laurent: Ferraton** is particularly adept at expressing the essence of Cornas, and **Delas** Chante Perdrix is a polished and bold Cornas cuvée that ages well.

SAINT-PÉRAY

Appellation: AOC Saint-Péray

Birth of the appellation: 1936

Communes: Saint-Péray, Toulaud

Total surface area sold under the AOC in 2019: 92 hectares

Average yield in 2019: 39 hectolitres per hectare

Colours permitted: white only

Grape varieties permitted: Wines can be made from Marsanne, Roussanne or both.

The story of Northern Rhône viticulture is based on granite, but the history of little Saint-Péray, its southernmost appellation, includes another type of rock: a huge hill of limestone known as the Montagne de Crussol that rises up near the river. At nearly 400 metres altitude, it has long served as a valuable vantage point, looking both upstream and down, and across the river to Valence. It has been occupied since Roman times, and the ruined Château de Crussol on top dates back to the twelfth century. It's also home to the Château de Beauregard, built in 1652, which spent much of its life as a prison, later becoming a gigantic cellar.

Robert Bailly mentions that in the early part of the sixteenth century this calcareous corner of the Northern Rhône was recognized for its pale reds, and especially for its whites, but today the appellation only allows for whites. The appellation covers more than just limestone soils, with granite also playing a major part, particularly on the other side of the valley from Crussol, with vineyards stretching north all the way to the communal border with Cornas, where plantings suddenly switch from white to red. On the valley floor there's also plentiful stony alluvial deposits and clay. The slopes here are more gentle than much of Saint-Joseph, and so are the wines.

Winemakers can choose between Marsanne or Roussanne, or can blend the two, but they perform differently on different soils. Laure Colombo, daughter of winemaker Jean-Luc, has established her own independent estate in Saint-Péray, Domaine de Lorient. 'Roussanne on granite gives more aromatic wines, with a noble bitterness which brings a lot of freshness,' she says. 'Marsanne on richer soil brings more opulent wines but also with pleasant freshness in hot vintages.' The best wines however tend to major on Marsanne.

Sharing the same grapes, climate, and sometimes soils as a southern Saint-Joseph *blanc*, Saint-Péray inevitably shares many gustatory similarities. What marks out a classic Saint-Péray however is a certain puppyish softness to the wine, if anything it's gentler and more generous in body on the mid-palate. It has a sunnier disposition and is less severe than a typical Saint-Joseph. It also has a freshness and drinkability that makes it more appealing to drink without food. In the late 1990s and 2000s there was a trend towards a more pumped-up Saint-Péray, more concentrated, riper, oaky. Some are still made this way, but this can end up smothering the aromatic and textural details that make Saint-Péray unique. In the 1997 edition of *Wines of the Rhône Valley*, Robert Parker summarizes the wines of Saint-Péray as follows: 'Dull, somewhat odd, uninteresting wines that are heavy and diffuse.' The worst wines of Saint-Péray still are, but a lot must have changed since then.

Though increasingly hard to find, the other form of Saint-Péray that we mustn't forget is sparkling. At the start of the twentieth century, around 90 per cent of Saint-Péray was made this way, but today the clear majority is made without bubbles. The first successful attempts at making Saint-Péray Mousseux were by Maison Faure in 1829, in an experiment in the Château de Beauregard with the help of a winemaker from Champagne. The wine quickly took off, and prices soon rivalled those of its northerly competitor. Today it is still made using the Champagne method, with a second fermentation in bottle and disgorgement, which, depending on the dosage, usually results in a dry sparkling wine. Saint-Péray and Champagne share some limestone soils, but this is where any similarity ends. Marsanne and Roussanne aren't obvious choices for sparkling wine production – they tend to make rich, fairly full-bodied wines with moderate acidity. Picking early and blocking malo can help, but sparkling Saint-Péray never has the freshness, clarity and detail of the best Champagnes. That's not to say they're entirely without merit; good sparkling Saint-Péray typically has a fairly full-bodied feel on the palate, with stone-fruit aroma, and a fine if not always terribly elegant mousse. When placed among other sparkling wines from around the world at the same price level, however, it's easy to see why it's now the still wines of the region that are in the ascendant.

Fabrice Gripa of Domaine Bernard Gripa describes Saint-Péray as a 'sleeping beauty'. Plantings are on the rise, but perhaps what the appellation lacks is a leading domaine that devotes itself to white wines – so often an estate's Saint-Péray plays second fiddle to a Cornas or a Saint-Joseph *rouge*. Until then, this tiny appellation will likely remain something of an insider secret.

Key producers

Domaine Bernard Gripa

Mauves

+33 (0) 4 75 08 14 96

The Gripa family, of Spanish and Italian descent, arrived in the area 400 years ago. Fabrice Gripa took over the estate from his father Bernard in 1997. They have long made wines in Saint-Péray, and in more recent times added some top red and white Saint-Joseph from *lieu-dit* Saint-Joseph, taking the estate to 17 hectares. Despite the impressive quality of the Saint-Joseph wines, for me they remain the reference in Saint-Péray.

Fabrice makes two still Saint-Péray cuvées. Les Pins is 70 per cent Marsanne, 30 per cent Roussanne whereas Les Figuiers is 60 per cent Roussanne, 40 per cent Marsanne, from a very old plot of vines on a low-lying gentle slope. They are fermented in demi-muids and 12-hectolitre foudres, with very little, if any, new oak, then matured for 10 months. They are stirred occasionally and always go through malo – there is very little malic acid to convert, and Fabrice says it brings complexity. He compares white wine making to making *pâtisserie*. A pragmatic, down-to-earth winemaker, Fabrice says 'there are no miracles' when it comes to making quality wine – just good terroir, paying close attention in the vineyard and taking care to avoid any oxidation in the winery. For a wine style that's typically drunk shortly after bottling, his wines age remarkably well. He suggests drinking them within 5 or 6 years, as at around 8 years they can enter an oxidative stage, that can last between 3 and 5 years, before entering a new phase. A 1997 I tasted with him in 2020 still had plenty of interest.

Other good examples

Domaine Clape is best known for Cornas, but its Saint-Péray is consistently one of the best in the appellation. The same can be said for **Domaine Alain Voge**, which makes a range of different styles. For those who prefer a richer expression, **Domaine du Tunnel, Jacques Lemenicier, Jean-Luc Colombo** Le Belle de Mai and **Chapoutier** Lieu-dit Hongrie are all worth exploring. Those who prefer to accentuate freshness and tension include **Domaine de Lorient, Domaine Mikael Bourg, Domaine Guy Farge, Domaine Fayolle Fils et Fille, François Villard, Chapoutier** Pic et Chapoutier and **Cave de Tain** Fleur de Roc. **Domaine de la Sarbèche** and **Domaine Benoît Roseau** both produce a successful natural wine take on Saint-Péray. The most successful sparkling examples are made by **Domaine Rémy Nodin, Domaine du Biguet, Domaine Alain Voge** and **Chapoutier**.

HERMITAGE

The hill of Hermitage exists thanks to a lucky kink in the river Rhône. During its long history, instead of skirting around a fringe section of west-bank granite, the river gradually sliced through it, leaving a granitic island on the east bank, onto which other types of rock have fused and bonded during successive geological ages. Though broadly running north to south, the river suddenly turns at the foot of this outcrop, running past its south-facing slope. Most of the favourable sites of the Northern Rhône lie on the west bank of the river, but Hermitage, sitting proud on the east bank, is arguably the greatest site of all.

It's hard to imagine a more perfect terroir. You don't need to be an expert to recognize it; the majestic hill rises up behind the town of Tain l'Hermitage, steep but not precipitous, face to the sun, protected from the wind. Despite the occasional crevice, it's not contorted like

Côte-Rôtie; it has a more uniform surface, totally covered in vines. You couldn't design or perhaps even imagine a better place to grow grapes; it's almost enough to make you believe in Bacchus. Some earlier inhabitants did. Thanks to the remains of a temple to Hercules not far from Tain, we know there were Roman settlements here. In Roman times, Tain went by the name of Tegna, and according to John Livingstone-Learmonth it was acknowledged as being a wine-producing community, mentioned in both Pliny's *Natural History* and Martial's *Epigrams*.

Town records at Tain l'Hermitage note the presence of several hermits living on the hill from 1598, giving the place its current name (back then it was known as Saint Christopher's Hill), which can be spelt either Hermitage or Ermitage on wine labels, both are permitted. The most famous hermit features in a local legend that dates back to 1224, when an injured knight by the name of Henri Gaspard de Stérimberg came across the hill on his return from the Albigensian Crusade (1209–1229) against the Cathars in the Languedoc. He made a request to the Queen of France, Blanche de Castille, to build himself a shelter, which she granted, and he remained there until his death. It's said he tended vines around the little chapel of Saint-Christophe which still sits (since rebuilt) at the top of the hill today. If you visit Tain, take a walk to the chapel. It's easy to access from the *place du Taurobole*, taking little over 40 minutes, and the trek will make you appreciate the work that goes into cultivating this hillside.

The wine's reputation strengthened over successive centuries of famous admirers. When Louis XIII visited in 1642, he was given the local wine and subsequently served it at the royal court. It was also served at the court of Tsar Nicholas in Russia. American President Thomas Jefferson visited Tain during his time as ambassador to France in 1787, and was so taken with it he bought 550 bottles. Price lists from négociant Nacker & Fils from 1835 show that white and red (and especially sweet) Hermitage were easily the most expensive wines from the Rhône Valley at that time, though not as expensive as top Bordeaux. A price list from French wine merchant Nicolas dating from 1828 however (reproduced in Robert Parker's *Wines of the Rhône Valley*) shows Hermitage was offered at the same price as top Burgundy *grands crus* such as Le Chambertin and La Romanée, and Bordeaux *premiers crus* Château Lafitte (sic) and Haut Brion.

During the late eighteenth century and for most of the nineteenth century, the best wines of Bordeaux were often blended with Hermitage to add structure and power, producing a 'Bordeaux hermitagé'. This wasn't a covert practice, it was stated on the labels, and could sell for higher prices than standard Bordeaux. The practice may have been beneficial for Bordeaux, but was less so for Hermitage. Jean-Louis Grippat points out that 'they only bought the good years. In the bad years they didn't buy. So only the lesser wines stayed here; all the best wines left for Bordeaux.'

According to Jean-Louis Chave, the first traces of phylloxera appeared in 1865 in the *lieu-dit* Les Rocoules. Up to this point, Hermitage was owned exclusively by the church and wealthy bourgeois families, but the combination of phylloxera and the allure of new industries created by the Industrial Revolution opened Hermitage up to new ownership. 'So these grand families lost their vines to phylloxera,' says Chave, 'and they reinvested their money in nascent new industries, textiles, silk, paper, leather. They left Hermitage, and that was how my family were able to buy land there.' It was Chave's grandfather who worked the vineyards in the post-war period of the 1950s and 1960s, a difficult era which saw less interest in the wines of Hermitage, and prices dropped. There were even some ugly flats built on vineyard land at the foot of the hill. Interest only began to build again in the late 1970s and the 1980s.

Hermitage might have a towering reputation, but it's worth remembering that the appellation only amounts to 140 hectares – not much bigger than a large Bordeaux estate. Today the land is concentrated in the hands of just a few major players; négociants Chapoutier and Jaboulet, and cooperative Cave de Tain have the largest holdings. The private domaine with the largest holding is Domaine J.L. Chave, and a further 16 private domaines make wine here, though the volumes of some of their cuvées are minuscule.

The hill itself is divided into 20 *lieux-dits*. The western flank closest to the river is the highest at around 320 metres altitude. This is the granite section, covered with decomposed granitic sands; major *lieux-dits* are Les Bessards, L'Ermite and Les Grandes Vignes. These give a powerful, athletic, straight, saline style of Hermitage, and are mostly planted with Syrah. Many of the best red Hermitage wines are based around Les Bessards. Bernard Faurie says it's Les Bessards that give his wines their 'skeleton'. The next section, immediately to the east of this granitic zone on the other side of a ravine, contains the other key *lieu-dit* – Le Méal. This large mid-slope vineyard has very different soils, with limestone, flint and patches of large, rounded pebbles. The style is richer, fuller and darker than that of Les Bessards, and complements it well in a blend. Again, it's mostly red, but there are significant plantings of white varieties too. Above it lies the sandier loess section of L'Hermite, and towards the bottom of the hill beneath Le Méal is *lieu-dit* Les Greffieux, a site with heavier clay and alluvial soils that can be very good if rarely as interesting as Le Méal or Les Bessards.

Further to the east comes the third section, after another, smaller incision into the hillside. It shares a similar geological pattern to the second section. The highest *lieux-dits* at around 190 metres (Maison Blanche, La Pierrelle and L'Homme) are usually planted with white varieties. *Lieux-dits* Les Beaumes and Péléat both contain some compacted alluvials known as *poudingue* among the clay limestone and are important vineyards for Domaine J.L. Chave. *Lieux-dits* Les Rocoules and Les Murets are much larger in area and are preferred for white wines, giving a generous, opulent but upright style. *Lieu-dit* Les Dionnières (sometimes spelt Les Diognières), sitting at the bottom of the slope, is planted with both red and white varieties and tends to give a less dense or ageworthy, though enjoyably precise, style of wine.

The traditional approach was to blend across the different *lieux-dits* and soil types of Hermitage. In the early 1990s, a new, single-vineyard approach was spearheaded by Michel Chapoutier. It has to some degree been followed by other producers such as Ferraton and Delas. Others, such as Jean-Louis Chave, usually keep to a single blended cuvée for each colour. (Many smaller producers only own vineyards in a single *lieu-dit*, so produce a single-vineyard wine by default.)

Commercially speaking, producing a range of single-vineyard wines instead of one blended wine is a shrewd move. It isolates exceptional parcels, leading to critical praise and high scores for certain wines in the range, providing a halo effect. It encourages collectors to buy multiple Hermitage wines instead of just one. It also creates rare cuvées, which helps to drive up prices. From a wine lover's point of view, it's certainly fascinating to see the character of the different vineyards, and note how they remain true to type year after year. But there is also satisfaction and enjoyment to be had from tasting a wine that's blended to represent the whole of this magnificent place, balancing, say, the mineral drive of Les Bessards, the rich fleshiness of Le Méal and the fruity approachability and elegance of Les Greffieux.

One curious aspect of the red wines is that they were traditionally destemmed by hand as far back as the 1800s. 'That was the finesse, the delicacy, the elegance of Hermitage,' says Jean-Louis Chave. Though up to 15 per cent Marsanne or Roussanne are permitted in the case of field blends, I'm yet to come across a red Hermitage that is anything other than pure Syrah. While remarkably dense and clenched when young, some more approachable bottlings such as Delas Domaine des Tourettes and Chapoutier Monier de la Sizeranne can be enjoyed on release, though even these benefit from long ageing. The best wines routinely need 20 years before opening. To broach them sooner is tempting, but you're only robbing yourself of the untold complexity these wines take on when mature. They typically start with black olive and berry fruits, with oregano, bay leaf and occasionally, but rarely, black pepper. With age they add hung game, forest floor, noble woods and the unmistakable whiff of woodsmoke and fireworks. Mature Hermitage exhales the breath of Smaug.

Both Marsanne and Roussanne are allowed for white wines, either varietal or blended, allowing for more stylistic variation. Michel Chapoutier only grows Marsanne on the hill, and a traditional blend contains around 80 per cent Marsanne. Pure Roussanne Hermitage *blancs* do exist, but they are rare, and tend to lack structure and cut. Young white Hermitage is irrepressibly delicious, all apricot and peach flesh, honeysuckle, mango, sometimes rhubarb, often with a subtle bitter twang bringing structure to what is always a low acid wine, and a generously flowing one at that. Nonetheless the whites last as long as, if not longer than, the reds, so try to age some if you can. They take on barley sugar, heather honey, box tree, hazelnut and eventually dried flowers and dried mushroom as they mature. Condrieu is famous for its richness and oiliness, but white Hermitage is an even bigger, fuller wine, its fat not quite so rendered.

Sweet white Hermitage Vin de Paille is rare now, but still produced by Domaine J.L. Chave and Cave de Tain. Like the dry wines, it can be made from Marsanne, Roussanne or both, but bunches must be dried for at least 45 days and reach a minimum of 350 grams per litre residual sugar before pressing. The resulting yields are far smaller than for dry wines, so the prices are correspondingly higher – no wonder it's a style that's disappearing. Let's hope it doesn't vanish completely, as the results can be kaleidoscopically complex, with an imperial wealth of texture. Dry white Hermitage ages for decades; Hermitage Vin de Paille, longer still.

Needless to say, not all of the wines produced here are of the same quality. But there is a certain consistency compared to Côte-Rôtie and Cornas, which fluctuate much more. After all, it is a smaller, more consistent terroir, with an older stock of vines. No matter the colour, what marks out the better wines of Hermitage is the kind of inscrutable regal character that you would expect from a *grand cru* site. Hermitage is not the most dynamic appellation. If we were keen to find fault, we could glibly accuse it of a lack of innovation. A more valid complaint would be the ongoing tediously gratuitous use of small oak barrels. Hermitage is a powerful, tannic beast, but new oak can still mask or smudge the finer details of terroir even in wine such as this. Over the past couple of decades prices have been rising steadily, but at the time of writing it's still possible to find good mature examples for £60–70 a bottle. In a global fine wine context, I believe this offers compelling value for money. It may sound high to some, but for dedicated wine lovers, perhaps not. Hermitage is, after all, the very apogee of one of the greatest grape varieties of all.

Appellation: AOC Hermitage

Birth of the appellation: 1937

Communes: Crozes-Hermitage, Larnage, Tain l'Hermitage

Total surface area sold under the AOC in 2019: 140 hectares

Average yield in 2019: 35 hectolitres per hectare

Colours permitted: red and white

Production in 2019: 68 per cent red, 32 per cent white

Grape varieties permitted: Reds are typically made from 100 per cent Syrah, but up to 15 per cent Roussanne and/or Marsanne is permitted.
Whites are made from Marsanne, Roussanne or both.

Key producers

M. Chapoutier

Tain l'Hermitage

www.chapoutier.com

The first Chapoutier to work in the family business was Marius, in 1897, but by the time the irrepressible Michel Chapoutier took over the business in 1990, it was in the doldrums. He didn't hesitate to transform the company, and it's now one of the biggest operations in the Rhône. He is best known for his Sélections Parcellaires (single-vineyard wines), seven of which are from Hermitage. They are consistently among the best in the appellation. He owns a whopping 34 hectares of Hermitage in fact, more than anyone else, and at his négociant business it's hard to think of many Rhône Valley appellations that aren't produced. Top picks from the range include Ermitage *blanc* De l'Orée, Ermitage *rouge* L'Ermite, Saint-Joseph *rouge* Les Granits and at the more affordable end, Crozes-Hermitage *rouge* Les Meysonniers.

Shortly after joining the company, Michel converted his vineyards to biodynamics, which continues to be a focus today, including the vineyards he has bought in Australia, Portugal, Roussillon, Alsace and Spain. Often brash and controversial, Michel is a dynamo; he never sits still or stops talking, and always has a new project to trumpet. He was named President of the AOC Côtes-du-Rhône and Vallée du Rhône in 2014, and has recently been joined by his daughter Mathilde and son Maxime.

Domaine J.L. Chave
Mauves
www.domainejlchave.fr

'The local nobleman made a gift of the property – a vineyard and a farm – to the family, for services rendered. We don't know what for. That's the origin of viticulture in our family,' recounts Jean-Louis Chave. This was in 1481, and the Chave family have been making wine ever since. The original farm was Bachesson, in the commune of Lemps, in what today is the appellation of Saint-Joseph. By the 1800s they were prosperous, with nearly 80 barrels of wine in their cellar – a huge amount at the time. Then phylloxera arrived. 'In 15 years, they lost it all. It was a brutal change … but it opened the door to Hermitage.' As Hermitage vineyards were sold off in the wake of phylloxera, local farming families finally had the opportunity to buy land. Little by little, the family bought parcels across different *lieux-dits*. A major purchase was made by Jean-Louis' father Gérard in 1982, when he bought Domaine de l'Hermite from a wealthy Irish aristocrat and Egyptologist named Terrence Gray, a 4-hectare estate spread across some of the finest *lieux-dits* in Hermitage. 'It was an enormous turning point for the domaine,' says Jean-Louis. Today it is the largest private domaine in Hermitage, with 15 hectares. Jean-Louis Chave joined his father Gérard in 1992 and now runs the estate with his Californian wife Erin.

Their principal *lieux-dits* for red wines are Péléat, Les Beaumes, Les Bessards, L'Hermite and Le Méal. Each parcel is fermented separately using natural yeasts, then aged for 18 months, with around 20 per cent new oak, before blending and bottling. The wines express the natural power and weight of the site, but are never forced or exaggerated. Since 1990, in exceptional years they make another red Hermitage, Cuvée Cathelin. *Lieux-dits* vary, but it tends to be from Les Bessards and Le Méal, and is a particularly refined and elegant style, even by their standards. Key parcels for the white Hermitage are L'Hermite, Les Rocoules and Péléat. Each parcel is fermented separately then matured in barrel, around 30 per cent new oak, before blending. Compared to many Hermitage whites, the style is straighter, less opulent, and certainly less oaky. It's a generous but not corpulent style with the freshness and precision required to stay the course. Tiny quantities of Vin de Paille are also made.

They also make an exceptional domaine Saint-Joseph *rouge*. Saint-Joseph has been a strong focus for Jean-Louis since his arrival at the domaine. 'My generation was never able to buy on Hermitage like that,' he says, referring to the purchase of Domaine de l'Hermite. 'And we'll never be able to again. It's for that reason my generation is going back to Saint-Joseph.' His first single-vineyard Saint-Joseph was in 2015 with the first vintage of his Clos Florentin, from a beautiful site in Mauves. More are planned.

A quality-focused négociant arm, Domaine J.L. Chave Sélections, makes red and white wine in Crozes-Hermitage, Saint-Joseph and Hermitage, and a red Côtes-du-Rhône called Mon Coeur, a 60 per cent Syrah blend sourced from Vinsobres, Cairanne and Visan.

Domaine Yann Chave

Mercurol

www.yannchave.com

Bernard Chave established the family domaine in 1979 after pulling out of the local cave cooperative. Yann joined in 1996, and in 2007 gained organic certification. Aside from running the 20-hectare estate, he is president of Crozes-Hermitage appellation. He also coaches youth rugby teams – he used to play a lot himself. Most of his holdings are in Crozes; he makes a red and a white cuvée, and a powerful, ageworthy red cuvée called Le Rouvre. He also has 1 hectare of 40-year-old Syrah high up in *lieux-dits* Les Beaumes and Péléat. This is another case of the wine reflecting the man: his Hermitage embraces the density and thunder that this site is capable of, and needs time to come round; his

2010 was far from ready in 2020. It's one of the most solid Hermitage cuvées outside of the more established names, and remains one of the best value in the appellation.

Delas Frères

Tain l'Hermitage

www.delas.com

The roots of Delas go back to 1835, nearly as far as Paul Jaboulet Aîné, and it too has been recently purchased by an outside entity – in 1993 it was acquired by the Champagne Louis Roederer group. In 1997, Jacques Grange joined as technical director, and in 2010 Claire Darnaud joined the winemaking team. In 2015, they bought the old family home of the Jaboulet family in the centre of Tain, building a state-of-the-art winery which is surely the most modern and architecturally ambitious for its size in the Rhône. Today they own 20 hectares in Crozes-Hermitage and 10 hectares in Hermitage, all of which have been farmed organically (without certification) since 2017.

At the top of the range is Hermitage *rouge* Les Bessards, but a new single-vineyard Hermitage *rouge* Ligne de Crête may even eclipse it in time. It comes from a 2.6-hectare block, the highest site on the hill and a Delas monopole; the first vintage was 2015. Also worth noting is the consistent quality of the entry-level wines, including a Ventoux and the Côtes-du-Rhône Saint-Esprit. Since the purchase by Roederer the improvements in quality have been impressive to witness, and today it is arguably the most improved and dynamic négociant house in the Rhône.

Domaine Bernard Faurie

Tournon-sur-Rhône

T.: +33 (0) 4 75 08 55 09

Bernard Faurie lives in a townhouse on the outskirts of Tournon. His immaculate small cellar lies underneath. There is no sign, no buzzer. The grand domaine buildings were sold off by a previous generation – Bernard represents the fourth. When I last saw him in 2020, he had just returned from a skiing trip and had recently turned 71. 'Hermitage is a magical place. When I go there to work, I get back less tired than when I arrived!' he says. His hair is white now, but he's still slim and sprightly, well-groomed and ageing handsomely. He speaks quickly and quietly, occasionally chuckling to himself.

He has less than 2 hectares of organically-grown Syrah in Hermitage across three *lieux-dits*, most of which was planted in 1914: Les Bessards, Le Méal and Les Greffieux. He blends Les Bessards and Le Méal (gold capsule) and Les Greffieux and Les Bessards (white capsule). For some markets he blends all three, and from 2015 he has bottled some pure, late-harvest Les Bessards. In the past he has made some pure Le Méal. All are whole-bunch fermented. He also makes a pure, precise, crystalline white Hermitage from Les Bessards. Though he has now passed on most of his Saint-Joseph vineyards to his son-in-law Emmanuel Darnaud, he has kept a little for his Vin de France Cuvée du Papi. The wines reflect the wine-maker and these are the most gentle, elegant expressions of Hermitage. Every time I visit, he is threatening to retire. But he can't bring himself to give up his vines, especially his beloved Le Méal: 'my elixir!'

Ferraton Père et Fils

Tain l'Hermitage

www.ferraton.fr

The Ferraton domaine was established in the heart of Tain in 1946 by Jean Oréns Ferraton, and it quickly came to be a highly respected pro-ducer. When his son Michel took over, with the aid of his friend Michel Chapoutier, he converted the estate to biodynamics and Ferraton also started a négociant business on the side. Michel Ferraton's son Samuel joined the business, but was badly injured in a motorbike accident. In 2007, they sold the business in its entirety to Chapoutier. The business (far smaller than Chapoutier) is run separately however, and the wines are different in style. Winemaker Damien Brisset joined the company from Bordeaux in 2005, and oversaw the new cellar installation in 2013. For their Northern Rhône bottlings, he only uses indigenous yeasts and uses no additional winemaking products (except sulphur dioxide). The wines are typically made in a fairly bold style. The company owns 18 hectares today, including 3 hectares in Hermitage (*lieux-dits* Les Dionnières, Le Méal and Les Beaumes). The focus today, however, is on Saint-Joseph, where Ferraton is making some eye-catching wines. Cornas is another area of strength, but the jewel in the crown is the Hermitage *rouge* Le Méal.

Paul Jaboulet Aîné

La Roche de Glun

www.jaboulet.com

One of the oldest négociant houses in the Northern Rhône, Paul

Jaboulet Aîné was established in 1834 by Antoine Jaboulet; Paul was the older of his twin boys. After the unexpected death of Gérard Jaboulet at the age of 55 in 1997, the firm struggled. In 2005, they sold the business to the Frey family, owners of Château la Lagune in Bordeaux, and Caroline Frey installed herself as winemaker in 2006. One of her first actions was to start working the soils of the estate-owned vineyards instead of using herbicides. They received organic certification in 2016, and have been working biodynamically (uncertified) since 2018. Today the house makes around 200,000 bottles from the domaine vineyards, and around 1 million bottles from the négociant business (just under half of which is the Côtes-du-Rhône Parallèle 45 range).

The company is best known for the Hermitage *rouge* La Chapelle, a blend of *lieux-dits* Le Méal, Le Bessards, Les Greffieux, Les Rocoules and Les Murets (though some vines were pulled out from Le Méal and Les Murets when the Freys arrived), with an average vine age of 80 years. Quality was always inconsistent, but the 1961, 1978 and 1990 vintages are often hailed as some of the finest wines ever made in the Rhône Valley. The 1978 and 1990 are certainly among the most impressive Hermitage wines I've ever tasted (I'm yet to taste the 1961), and the 1991 is also incredible. Today the wine is destemmed and sees around 15 per cent new oak. Quality has remained inconsistent with the new owners, but the 2016 is extremely fine. Second wine La Petite Chapelle changed its name to Maison Bleue from the 2015 vintage. The two Hermitage *blanc* cuvées can be very good indeed, especially the 2010 La Chapelle *blanc*.

Domaine Marc Sorrel

Tain l'Hermitage

T.: +33 (0) 4 75 07 10 07

Marc Sorrel's workshop cellar is on the main street that runs through Tain. It looks a little dilapidated from the outside, but inside is neat and functional. The domaine was established in 1928, and Marc retired in 2019, handing over to his son Guillaume Sorrel (one of the three founders of Maison Les Alexandrins). Marc, still spry, remains on hand to show his wines, however. The domaine makes two red Hermitage cuvées and two whites. The top red, Le Gréal, is a blend of *lieux-dits* Le Méal (85 per cent) and Les Greffieux (15 per cent), old vines aged around 60 years, fermented with the stems. The single-vineyard Les Rocoules is the top white, vines again 60 years old, that makes for a particularly rich, ripe and opulent style. There is also a superb red Crozes-Hermitage. Quality here can be exceptional, but is not the most consistent; these are old-fashioned wines, authentic and genuine if not always perfectly measured and balanced. But the wines always have something to say. It will be interesting to see the direction of the estate now Guillaume is in the driving seat.

Cave de Tain

Tain l'Hermitage

www.cavedetain.com

Cooperative cellars are far less common in the Northern Rhône than in the South; producers typically have much smaller surfaces to farm, and the gaggle of négociants based here has long offered growers a market for their grapes. There are a handful however, the most notable of which is the Cave de Tain, established in 1933 by Louis Gambert de Loche. The co-op owns 27 hectares of vineyards, including 22 hectares on Hermitage, making it the second biggest land owner. Almost all of this is farmed organically, the rest sustainably. Daniel Brissot is *chef de culture*, having started working at the Cave in 1980. Xavier Frouin is head winemaker. Together they lead a committed band of 263 growers, farming 1,055 hectares in total and producing 5 million bottles of wine a year. The results can be excellent; this is one of the most impressive cooperative cellars in France.

Like all co-ops, some cuvées are stronger than others. Consistently good however is the Saint-Joseph *rouge* Esprit de Granit and Saint-Péray Fleur de Roc. In Hermitage, the white Au Coeur des Siècles is often up there with the best names in the appellation, and the Hermitage *rouge* Classique is a smart buy in good years. The Hermitage *rouge* Gambert de Loche can impress, but the Epsilon can sometimes feel overworked. With a cellar investment to the tune of €11 million in 2014 and an ongoing taste for innovation, it's an enterprise that goes from strength to strength.

Other good examples

Domaine du Colombier makes very good, representative Hermitages in both colours, as does **Domaine Belle**, albeit in a richer style. **Dard & Ribo** makes beautifully expressive red and white Hermitage cuvées, with less extraction but more drinkability than most. **Domaine JC & N Fayolle** makes a curious, stemmy, old-school expression from *lieu-dit*

Les Dionnières that is stylistically atypical but nonetheless interesting. Small-scale white bottlings are made by **Domaine Laurent Habrard**, which focuses on freshness, and **Domaine Betton**, which embraces opulence. **Tardieu-Laurent** and **J.L. Chave Sélections** can also be very good. **Guigal's** white and red Ex-Voto bottlings have many fans, but others find it hard to get past the oak.

CROZES-HERMITAGE

Of the eight *crus* of the Northern Rhône, six are on the west bank, and it's essentially a tale of granite. On the east bank, even Hermitage has granite at its heart. But Crozes-Hermitage, the massive 2,000-hectare appellation that surrounds Hermitage, is on the whole a very different terroir. It wasn't always this way; the appellation has expanded enormously over the years, itself from a granite core. When it was established in 1937, the appellation of Crozes-Hermitage was just for the wines of one village, that of Crozes, just to the north of Hermitage. In the same way that the village of Gevrey-Chambertin in Burgundy appended the name of its most famous nearby vineyard, so did Crozes, in the hope of a little radiated glory. Much of the vineyard here is granitic, but the microclimate is different; it doesn't share the same south-facing aspect or the height of its imperial neighbour.

Crozes was certainly known for the quality of its wines in the nineteenth century, as were neighbouring villages Gervans and Mercurol – back then, wines were labelled according to their respective villages, and considered minor *crus* in themselves. In 1952 these three were grouped together, along with a further eight communes, into the larger conglomerate AOC Crozes-Hermitage. The reasons for this were largely economic, an agenda pushed by local négociants. From a terroir point of view, it was nonsensical, as the appellation can be divided into at least two distinct parts: the small-scale granitic part to the north of Hermitage and the alluvial terraces to its south and south-east known as the Châssis. They produce two divergent styles of wine.

Like Crozes, the village of Gervans is situated to the north of Hermitage, and sits on the same jagged granite outcrop, here covered with loess. The vineyards mirror those across the river in Saint-Joseph, sloping, often steeply, with drystone wall terraces. The vineyards face a different direction, but otherwise the spirit is the same. The vineyards here are defenceless against the cold north wind, and you feel it in both the reds and the whites, which are slender, with a strict correctness, and the salinity and tension derived from granite vineyards. The communes of Erôme and Serves-sur-Rhône have an even smaller area under vine but share a similar, albeit tighter, terroir as they briefly follow the river northwards.

To the south and south-east of Hermitage it's a very different story. These extensive, largely flat, alluvial terraces were until recently covered with apricot trees, but as wine grapes have become a more profitable crop, there are few trees remaining in this monocultural landscape. These are much younger soils, terraces laid down by successive ice ages, consisting of medium-sized *galets roulés* and red clay over a deep gravel base. A major benefit to growers is that this area can be farmed mechanically, unlike the surrounding granite slopes. Land holdings here are relatively high; domaines of 20–25 hectares are not uncommon, and some even have twice that. But the soils here are free draining and prone to drought, creating blockages in maturity, which can result in wines that lack balance and finesse. Compared to the northern part, the wines from this sector are full-bodied, generous, fruity and warmer.

Laurent Habrard is a particularly bright and gifted winemaker located in Gervans who owns land in both parts of the appellation. He says neither terroir is necessarily better than the other, and there is no difference in terms of viticulture or vinification. Stylistically, however, he says they are 'completely different'. The wines from the Châssis are 'coloured, ample, concentrated, and expressive when young.' From the north, they are 'a bit more closed, less coloured, elegant, refined, with complexity and structure.'

Though there are two main areas within the appellation, there are a few smaller micro-terroirs that deserve highlighting. The first is around the village of Mercurol to the east of Tain – low hills of particularly ancient *galets roulés* mixed with silt and white clay. It was historically famed for its white wines, particularly on the Coteau des Pends; Domaine des Entrefaux is one domaine that keeps the tradition alive. Another area known for its whites is Larnage. An area of very fine white clay, known as kaolin, around the ruined Château de Larnage creates wines of remarkable finesse. Mark Romak of Domaine Melody describes it as 'the link between the north and the south' of Crozes-Hermitage. Other good examples are made by Domaine Rousset, Domaine Belle and Dard & Ribo. One area of growing interest used to be considered the least remarkable. Beaumont-Monteux is in the far south-east near the snaking Isère river that acts as the appellation's southern and eastern boundary, with the Rhône its frontier to the west. David Reynaud played a central role in demonstrating just how good the wines from this corner could be, and he has since been joined by other talents such as Gaylord Machon. Machon says the wines from this terroir have a distinctive peppery, bloody note.

That the land in Crozes-Hermitage has – until recently – been available and relatively affordable, so it has been attractive to those from outside the region looking to establish themselves. It's also long been home to members of the Cave de Tain, who are gradually dropping out to create their own private domaines. These factors give the appellation a dynamism and vibrancy that is rare for this part of the Rhône. Growers are willing to experiment – David Reynaud and Dard & Ribo have both attracted well-deserved attention for original, characterful and hugely enjoyable wines from these terroirs. Until recently, Crozes-Hermitage was considered the place to go to get an inexpensive taste of the North. And it's still possible to find examples from producers such as Cave de Tain in supermarkets in the UK for around £10 – which, in good vintages, can be a real bargain. But it's getting increasingly unusual to find Crozes from good private estates for less than £18 a bottle. Increasingly, IGP Collines Rhodaniennes is doing the job Crozes used to do in this regard.

Is it fair that Crozes should fetch lower prices than other Northern Rhône appellations? Probably; though capable of huge aromatic impact and complexity, the Syrahs from Crozes-Hermitage, particularly from the southern part, rarely have the same depth, salinity and tension as those from the west bank. Nor do they age as long; generally speaking, these are wines to enjoy young. But there are always exceptions: Paul Jaboulet Aîné's Domaine de Thalabert 1991, for example, still had ten years ahead of it when tasted in 2011. Domaine Alain Graillot's Crozes-Hermitage La Guiraude is another example that can age brilliantly. Generalizations about large appellations, whether Crozes-Hermitage, Ventoux or Châteauneuf-du-Pape, have limited value; this is one weakness of a classification system that allows such large and diverse places to go under a single signature. Some villages (and specific *lieux-dits* within those villages such as *lieu-dit* Les Piccaudières in Gervans) will inevitably be better than others. Sometimes it pays to look back to the era before the AOC system was implemented in search of clues. For the savvy buyer, it means there are bargains to be found.

Appellation: AOC Crozes-Hermitage
Birth of the appellation: 1937
Communes: Beaumont-Monteux, Chanos-Curson, Crozes-Hermitage, Erôme, Gervans, Larnage, Mercurol, Pont-de-l'Isère, La Roche-de-Glun, Serves-sur-Rhône, Tain-l'Hermitage
Total surface area sold under the AOC in 2019: 1,778 hectares
Average yield in 2019: 33 hectolitres per hectare
Colours permitted: red and white
Production in 2019: 87 per cent red, 13 per cent white
Grape varieties permitted: Reds are typically made from 100 per cent Syrah, but up to 15 per cent Roussanne and/or Marsanne is permitted.
Whites are made from Marsanne, Roussanne or both.

Key producers
Domaine les 4 Vents
Mercurol
T.: +33 (0) 4 75 06 39 15

Formerly Domaine de Lucie, this domaine changed its name when Lucie Fourel was joined by her sister Nancy Cellier. They now farm 10 hectares of vines organically, picking by hand and producing a series of different cuvées all with low doses of sulphites. Their single-vineyard wines are of particular interest. Crozes-Hermitage *blanc* La Rage is opulent expression from old-vine Marsanne from the sandy *lieu-dit* La Rage in La Roche-de-Glun. Their top red vineyards are even better. Les 4 Vents is a blend of two parcels in La Roche-de-Glun, the stony soils of *lieu-dit* Les Savieux and the sandy soils of La Rage, only half destemmed, producing an aromatic firework display. Saint-Jaimes is from a parcel of 50-year-old vines planted by their grandfather in Mercurol. There is no destemming, leading to a structured but not overly extracted style that is fast becoming one of the most interesting wines in the appellation.

Domaine Aléofane
Mercurol
T.: +33 (0) 4 75 07 00 82

Natacha Chave is the sister of Yann Chave, but instead of following the family domaine, she decided to forge her own path. To begin with, she considered vineyards as far away as the Southern Rhône and even Bandol, but 'I couldn't stand being separated from Northern Rhône Syrah,' she says. Thank goodness for that: she makes some of the most refined and elegant wines in the region. Her first vintage was in 2004, and she started buying mature vineyards in Beaumont-Monteux in 2007. She now makes white and red Crozes-Hermitage, red Saint-Joseph, and her first Cornas (first vintage 2020), the planting of which takes her to 8 hectares (she intends to stop at 10 hectares). Experimenting with selections of Serine in her vineyards has brought further interest and complexity to her wines. She works organically, using natural yeasts and a minimum of sulphur dioxide to create authentic wines of place with detail and clarity.

Domaine Combier

Pont-de-l'Isère

www.domaine-combier.com

Established in 1936 by Camille Laurent, the domaine today is led by Laurent Combier, and has grown to 25 hectares. The body of plantings are on Le Châssis, including the Clos des Grives, a 9-hectare plot planted in 1952, which is used for the top red and white cuvées of the same name. Vineyards are also located in Gervans and Serves-sur-Rhône for the Crozes-Hermitage Cap Nord. Even the entry-level young-vine Crozes cuvée Laurent Combier is high quality, and represents great value. There are also Syrah vineyards in Saint-Joseph: Saint-Jean-de-Muzols for Saint-Joseph Domaine Combier and Tournon for Saint-Joseph Cap Nord. The style here is silky, gentle, not overly extracted, and oak (except for the Clos des Grives *rouge*) is kept in the background. This pioneer of organic viticulture in the Rhône has been working this way since 1970. With Laurent's sons David and Julien now working alongside him, this is one of the most dependable estates in Crozes-Hermitage.

Dard & Ribo

Mercurol

Private domaines built on family bonds are common in the Rhône; those built on a friendship, however, are rare. René-Jean Dard's father had 2 hectares of vines. He died when René-Jean was 15 years old, so at a young age he had to take on the vines and press on. He became friends with fellow local François Ribo a little later. Discovering they shared a similar worldview, they began buying parcels and making wine together in 1983. They worked by horse instead of using herbicides and quickly gave up all chemical products. It wasn't easy to start with. 'We had long hair, we lived differently. It was hard to be accepted here,' says Dard. Over the years, their wines have been ignored, misunderstood and even scorned by closed-minded critics and drinkers. But today they are increasingly receiving the recognition they deserve. They are known as natural wine pioneers with no-added-sulphite wines, but that wasn't the aim. 'The goal was always just to make the best wine possible,' says Dard, and at the time it was normal not to add sulphites to red wines, 'so I already had a taste for wines without sulphur.' They quickly found a market in the natural wine bars that were beginning to pop up in Paris where they sold 90 per cent of their volume in the late 1980s.

They now have 8.5 hectares of parcels scattered around Crozes-Hermitage, Saint-Joseph and Hermitage and make a red and white *cuvée classique* from each; in fact, about one-third of their production is white. They are constantly experimenting, making up to 20 different cuvées a year, but some of the larger volume special cuvées are as follows. Crozes-Hermitage *rouge* C'est le Printemps is a kind of *nouveau* style Syrah mostly from Le Châssis, fresh and aromatic, designed for drinking young. Larnage is an important terroir for them: Crozes-Hermitage *blanc* Pé de Loup is 100 per cent Roussanne, and *rouge* Pé de Loup is from the same kaolin soils; Les Karrières and K are 100 per cent Marsanne, again from Larnage kaolin. Saint-Joseph single-vineyard sites make both reds and whites (mostly Roussanne), including Les Opateyres (Tournon, alluvial soils), Pitrou (Saint-Jean-de-Muzols, granite soil) and Les Champs (Tournon, hard granite soils). The Hermitage *rouge* comes from *lieux-dits* Varogne and Les Dionnières, the Hermitage *blanc* from L'Homme.

'We have no recipe for making wine,' says Dard, but reds use stems where possible, and are neither fined nor filtered, and extraction is light. Whites are sometimes fined, but not filtered. As with many natural wines, careful shipping and storage is crucial, and they are not as cookie-cutter consistent as more conventional wines. When on form, they are among the most thrilling, energetic and characterful wines of the Rhône.

Domaine Fayolle Fils & Fille

Gervans

www.fayolle-filsetfille.fr

Laurent Fayolle farms 11 hectares in the northern part of Crozes-Hermitage. A recent cellar upgrade has led to further improvement in what was already an impressive range, elevating the domaine to the premier league of Crozes producers. There are three stages to the range, and all are made in both red and white. Entry level is Sens, Le Pontaix is from 40-year-old vines and aged in demi-muid and Clos les Cornirets is particularly fine and intense, from 60-year-old vines and aged in barriques. Laurent also makes a little red and white Hermitage from *lieu-dit* Les Dionnières, in a particularly elegant style. His Saint-Péray Montis is from bought grapes, but also bears the refined house style.

Domaine Alain Graillot

Pont de l'Isère

T.: +33 (0) 4 75 84 67 52

Though a well-established name among Rhône lovers, Alain Graillot only arrived in the region from Paris in 1985. His unmarked domaine lies at the heart of Le Châssis, and is a reliable source of savoury and complete Crozes-Hermitage in both colours (his white is 80 per cent Marsanne, 20 per cent Roussanne). What has long characterized the house style is the use of whole-bunch fermentation, contributing complexity, freshness and longevity to the wines. In the best vintages he produces a special cuvée La Guiraude, and other wines in the range include small volumes of Saint-Joseph *rouge* and a few hundred bottles of Hermitage *rouge* from *lieu-dit* Les Greffieux.

Alain's son Maxime Graillot now runs the estate along with his own labels Equis and Domaine des Lises, representing a different take on Crozes-Hermitage from mostly destemmed fruit, in a vibrantly aromatic, fresh, early-drinking style. Maxime believes that Crozes-Hermitage is 'one of the most dynamic appellations in the Northern Rhône, and probably even in France,' thanks to the large areas owned by estates, providing scope for experimental cuvées, and a flat terroir which makes it relatively easy to trial new methods in the vineyard. Winemaking talent also helps of course, and there's no lack of that at this address.

Domaine Laurent Habrard

Gervans

laurenthabrard.com

Laurent Habrard might not be as well known as some of the other names on this list, but he's among the most interesting winemakers of his generation. Based in the granitic nook of Gervans, he's the fifth generation to work the estate. Although sprightly and energetic, he's older than he might appear, having taken over the estate in 1998. It's certified organic and HVE, and Laurent has been experimenting with biodynamics since 2017, which he describes as 'another world'.

Of his 15 hectares of vines, 10.5 hectares are Crozes-Hermitage Syrah; 3 hectares are in the southern part, the rest from the north. He destems the grapes and doesn't add sulphites until bottling. It makes for a satisfying, well-balanced and complex style. He occasionally makes a special cuvée featuring the name of his colleagues, usually a barrel selection that undergoes a longer élevage, but not in new oak. These are worth seeking out. His 2.5 hectares of Marsanne and Roussanne for his white Crozes are all planted on loess in Gervans, which makes for a crisp, precise style. Other cuvées are his Saint-Joseph *rouge* from *lieu dit* Sainte-Epine, which is true to the house style, and a Hermitage *blanc* Les Rocoules from a parcel of 100-year-old Marsanne bought from the son-in-law of President de Gaulle in the 1970s. It's a soft, naked style of Hermitage *blanc* with a mineral spine. Are you handy with a paintbrush? If so, enter the yearly competition to illustrate the label, for which the prize is 2 per cent of the production.

Domaine Gaylord Machon

Beaumont-Monteux

T.: +33 (0) 4 75 85 78 91

When I met with Machon in 2020, he was recovering after having taken a mechanical plough to the head. He was doing his best to laugh it off – thankfully it didn't dent his infectious sense of humour. (In case you're wondering – and I bet you were – his older sister suggested to his parents he should be named Gaylord after a character in her favourite television show.) The vines have been in the family since at least the 1950s, probably much longer. Gaylord started at the family farm in 2002, and the first vintage bottled here was in 2011. He works alone, with all of his 8 hectares of Syrah and 0.5 hectares of white varieties (mostly Roussanne) around Beaumont-Monteux. Now HVE certified, he is in his second year of organic conversion.

His hard work and winemaking talent are starting to pay off. In 2015 he was able to invest in a small, modern cellar, and the wines are improving with each vintage. In Crozes-Hermitage he makes two reds and a white. Ghany is made from 10- to 30-year-old Syrah and aged in older demi-muids; Lhony is made from 30- to 40-year-old Syrah and matured in new and recent demi-muids. All reds are destemmed and fermented in concrete, usually with natural yeasts. La Fille Dont J'ai Rêvé, his white, vinified and matured in concrete eggs, is also very good, ripe but not fat. A rising star of the appellation.

David Reynaud

Beaumont-Monteux

www.domainelesbruyeres.fr

There have been vines in David Reynaud's family since the eighteenth century, the fruit of which had been delivered to the Cave de Tain until fairly recently. Upon his return to the estate in 2000, following military service, David and his mother Marceline converted the estate to organic (then biodynamic) viticulture and starting bottling their own wines. The official name of the estate is Domaine les Bruyères, but the name on the label is David's. He's built like an oak, but has a gentle and friendly disposition. His wines are highly individual. They magnify the herbs, spices and flowers that Crozes fruit exudes, and on the palate are fibrous and textural, providing plenty to get your teeth into. This is no doubt attained in part through very low (sometimes no) sulphite additions. The downside to this is the occasional faulty bottle. The majority of the estate is Syrah from around Beaumont-Monteux, and David also produces two very fine Crozes-Hermitage *blancs*: Aux Bêtises is 80 per cent Marsanne and Lou is 100 per cent Roussanne. Rebelle is his Cornas from 50-year-old vines, a vibrantly fruity, relatively unstructured style.

Other good examples

Had they not been featured in full elsewhere, **Domaine Yann Chave**, **Cave Julien Cécillon** and **Domaine Marc Sorrel** would certainly be featured above. Full-bodied styles can be found at **Domaine Melody**, **Emmanuel Darnaud**, **Domaine du Colombier** and **Domaine Michelas St Jemms**. At the other end of the spectrum, we have **Cave Olivier Dumaine**, **Domaine des Martinelles**, **Domaine Pierre-Jean Villa** and **Domaine Rousset**. Just as good, in their own respective styles, are **Domaine Betton**, **Domaine des Hauts Châssis**, **Domaine des Entrefaux** (including their **Champ Morel** label), **Domaine Gilles Robin**, **Domaine Belle** and **Domaine P&V Jaboulet**. Best négociant bottlings included **Delas** Le Clos and Domaine des Grands Chemins and **Chapoutier** Les Meysonniers and Les Varonniers; a very good more affordable example is **Ferraton** La Matinière. **Cave de Tain**, responsible for nearly half of the production of the appellation, is currently working on single-village Crozes-Hermitage expressions that should shine a spotlight on these different terroirs.

BRÉZÈME AND SAINT-JULIEN-EN-SAINT-ALBAN

We may have covered all eight *crus* of the Northern Rhône, but we're not finished yet, not quite. Two terroirs deserving of your attention have been recently rediscovered to the south of Valence. Like many of the best terroirs of Saint-Joseph, both have been created by perpendicular tributaries to the Rhône. They lie at roughly the same latitude as one another but Saint-Julien-en-Saint-Alban sits on the west bank, just north of the river Ouvèze (a different Ouvèze to the one in the Southern Rhône), and Brézème is found on the east bank, on a south-facing slope to the north of the river Drôme. Though geographically close, these terroirs and their wines are otherwise quite distinct.

From the dishevelled town of Saint-Julien-en-Saint-Alban you can't see any vineyards. To access them you need to climb the low hills to the north. It's not a visually arresting site; there are currently around 60 hectares of vineyards spread over these low, gently sloping hills. It's the junction between Massif Central granite and Ardèche limestone; over these different bedrocks are compacted grey marls. Grape varieties are mixed: Grenache, Cinsault and particularly Syrah dominate the reds, Roussanne, Marsanne, Clairette and Viognier the whites. It's still early days; only five private domaines operate here and bottling only began in earnest 10 years ago. Before that, the wines were sold *en vrac* to négociants. Winemakers here are still feeling out what works, but early signs are promising. Charles Helfenbein suspects it is more of a terroir for Syrah; time will tell.

After crossing the Rhône in search of Brézème, you follow the blue-green snow melt river of the Drôme back through the *département* that takes its name towards the town of Livron-sur-Drôme. Nobody needs point it out; the magnificent hill of Brézème quickly springs into view, facing due south with the river at its feet. Like a miniature Hermitage, it's slightly taller to the west (256 metres), its crest gently rippling down to the east. Unlike Hermitage, there is no granite; it's a large limestone and marl bluff that was laid down during the Cretaceous Period. You can still find the fossils of sea shells and ammonites among the sandy loam, clay limestone and angular limestone pebbles that cover it. Many of the steeper parts of this hot, sheltered microclimate are now skirted with drystone wall terraces, and there's a squat stone tower, La Tour du Diable, poking out of the western flank like a ship's funnel. Why is it called Brézème? 'Everyone has their own story,' says Charles Helfenbein. Does it mean 'hot earth' in an old dialect? Does it come from the word *braises* meaning 'embers', referring to the hot microclimate? Or is the hill named after the large house called Brézème at the foot of the slope?

Though this hill represents the most important site, two other *lieux-dits* are currently included under the Brézème growing area. One is La Rolière, an area of deep, silty clay and *galets roulés* a kilometre to the north of the hill of Brézème. The other is Les Davids, a similar terroir further north, close to Domaine Lombard. I'm yet to taste anything from either of these terroirs that can hold a candle to those from the mighty hill itself. It's hard to believe that such an obviously prime site has lain abandoned for so long. Yves Mengin thought the same thing when he clapped eyes on it in 1984. Retiring to Livron-sur-Drôme after working as an accountant, he could see its potential. 'I saw the abandoned hill,' he says, 'and I thought – why not me?' His estate, Domaine des Quatre Cerises, now farms 2 hectares of the roughly 33 hectares planted on the hill.

Brézème's history is more remarkable than most. The first written records date back to 1422, and further documents dating to the early nineteenth century praise both red and white wines, and note their potential longevity. At this time their prices rivalled those of Hermitage. The series of blows that led to its neglect are shared by other local vineyards: phylloxera, mildew, the financial and societal shocks of two world wars and industrialization. But while others were rebuilt, Brézème was neglected. Finally, its renaissance is gathering momentum. Viticulture never totally died out on the hill: the Pouchoulin family have been grape growers on the hill for generations, and have had their own tiny plot since 1940. But it is newcomers such as Jean-Marie Lombard (previous owner of Domaine Lombard) and Yves Mengin who fanned this last remaining cinder so that we can taste these wines again.

The terroir is classified as AOC Côtes-du-Rhône, but the authorities appear to tolerate Brézème being appended to the name. As such, there is no *cahier des charges* specific to Brézème. Nonetheless, growers stick to Syrah for reds and Marsanne, Roussanne, Viognier and a little Clairette for whites. They hope in time to be promoted to *cru* level, and I see no reason why this should not happen. With a small number of producers covering a range of different winemaking approaches, defining Brézème's style is not easy. But whether made in a full-throated, powerful style or a more measured, transparent one, both the red and the white wines take real bite and tension from the alkaline soils and have a marked energy and freshness. Their relatively high acidities give them longevity, and they build complexity as they age. A 1995 Domaine Lombard Brézème *rouge* tasted in 2020 from magnum still had great spice, freshness and length. The mature white wines I've been lucky enough to taste from here are equally thrilling, built around citrus, lychee, violets and lavender. Helfenbein believes this is more a terroir for white wines than for reds, in fact.

It's strange to think of so many vintages ticking by over the years, so many wines unmade and undrunk as the terroir has lain dormant. Along with Saint-Julien-en-Saint-Alban and Seyssuel further north, how many other unique terroirs are there, just waiting to be discovered, or rediscovered? This is what makes the Rhône such an exciting region. It's one of the greatest, most ancient winemaking regions on the planet. But the story isn't over yet.

Brézème

Appellation: AOC Côtes-du-Rhône (Brézème does not currently have its own appellation)

Communes: Livron-sur-Drôme

Colours produced: red and white (rosé permitted but less common)

Typical grape varieties used: Syrah for reds; Marsanne, Roussanne, Viognier and Clairette for whites (though producers can plant according to generic AOC Côtes-du-Rhône *cahier des charges*).

Saint-Julian-en-Saint-Alban

Appellation: AOC Côtes-du-Rhône (Saint-Julian-en-Saint-Alban does not currently have its own appellation)

Communes: Saint-Julian-en-Saint-Alban

Colours produced: red and white (rosé permitted but less common)

Typical grape varieties used: Syrah for reds; Marsanne, Roussanne, Viognier and Clairette for whites (though producers can plant according to generic AOC Côtes-du-Rhône *cahier des charges*).

Key producers

Domaine Helfenbein

Allex

www.terroirsetvins.com

Young, friendly and unshaven, Charles Helfenbein gives the impression of someone who really puts his all into his work. His name derives from his ancient Swiss-German heritage, but he was brought up in the region, having studied locally and worked in the vines for Jean-Luc Colombo. He bought 4 hectares of Brézème in 2008 and rents 5 hectares in Saint-Julien. His Brézème *rouge* is especially worthy of note; destemmed, fermented with indigenous yeasts, then aged for 12 months in old demi-muids, it has the freshness of the terroir and ages remarkably well. An estate to keep an eye on.

Domaine Lombard

Livron-sur-Drôme

www.domaine-lombard.com

In 1981, with just 1 hectare of land, Jean-Marie and Sylvette Lombard created Domaine Lombard. They were one of the first families to put in motion the renaissance of Brézème. When Jean-Marie retired in 2012, the estate was purchased by a group of individuals including Julien Montagnon, an energetic young Roussillon winemaker who was born in Livron. He returned to his home town to take over the winemaking at the domaine, and converted the vineyards to biodynamics. The estate owns 25 hectares, 12 hectares of which are in production on the hill of Brézème and Les Davids.

Whites are opulent, and can be very rich indeed, and the reds are also in an amplified style that doesn't lack impact. Their basic Brézème *rouge* and Eugène de Monticault don't always have the necessary backbone to bring balance, but their young-vine Brézème *rouge* Raspans and particularly La Tour du Diable, from Syrah planted in 2002 (old for Brézème), show what is possible from this terroir – power, elegance, freshness and balance. Maison Lombard denotes their négociant range.

Domaine des Quatre Cerises

Loriol

T.: +33 (0) 4 75 85 60 01

The contribution that Yves Mengin has made to the renaissance of

Brézème has been noted above, but the tenacity required hasn't been touched upon. The 2 hectares he currently farms once belonged to Baron Blanchard (1774–1853), a general under Napoléon I. He had to track down ten different current ancestors in order to buy the land, taking him four years. It took him another four years to clear the land, rebuild the walls and plant the vineyard. His first vintage was in 1998, taking the name Quatre Cerises (four cherries) in memory of the cherry trees he had to pull out to plant his vines, and as a dedication to his four children. He makes 4,000 bottles a year. His red comes from a plot near the Tour du Diable, and has an upright nature and joyful elegance, reminiscent of a good Saint-Joseph. His white is authentically Rhône, with a floral flourish and mineral edging.

Eric Texier

Charnay

www.eric-texier.com

It's hard to think of a more creative or experimental vigneron than former nuclear engineer Eric Texier. Following a *stage* at Domaine Verget in the Mâconnais, he installed himself in Brézème in 1988 after reading about its illustrious past in books dating back to 1880. He now owns 7.5 hectares in Saint-Julien and 4.5 hectares in Brézème, bottling under the name Domaine de Pergaud. His Syrah is marked as Serine on the label, and his Roussanne takes the old local synonym Roussette. He has a minimal intervention, low-added-sulphite approach and farms his vines organically. He always has plenty of other projects on the go, including white and red Châteauneuf-du-Pape and orange wines from Marsanne. The last time I spoke to him he was moving into pear-based ferments. The Rhône could do with more iconoclasts such as him.

APPENDIX I: AGEING WINES

SOUTHERN RHÔNE

Compared to the Northern Rhône, discussing the ageability of Southern Rhône wines is less straightforward. The terroir is more varied, and a greater number of grape varieties are in play. But generally speaking, Grenache-based reds can be drunk on release. Exceptions include those from the most austere terroirs such as parts of Châteauneuf-du-Pape and Beaumes de Venise; particularly concentrated cuvées made with long ageing in mind; and concentrated blends with large proportions of Syrah and/or Mourvèdre. All of these would benefit from a few years of bottle age to soften.

Because Grenache is so approachable when young, many of the best wines of the Southern Rhone are drunk far too young. This is a shame, as the best of Châteauneuf-du-Pape and Gigondas in particular really need to reach maturity before they reveal their full potential. Ageability isn't just a question of grape however; wines from great terroirs tend to age well and develop with interest in bottle no matter what varieties they're made from.

Vintage also plays an important role. It gives a clue as to how long a wine will age, and it bestows a certain character on the wines made that year. The guides by appellation and vintage below refer to red wines only unless otherwise stated. White wines in the Southern Rhône are best drunk within three years of vintage, and only a very small proportion benefit from ageing. Whites from Lirac and Ventoux can stay the course a little longer than average, up to six years or so. Top Clairettes, such as those from Gigondas and Bellegarde, can endure for 10, even 20 years, despite their low acidity. White Châteauneuf-du-Pape is the exception, the very best can age for two or three decades. Rosés from the Southern Rhône should be drunk as young as possible. Those from good sites in Lirac and Gigondas, however, can easily last for four years, and top Tavels can last for over a decade in good vintages.

The golden rule is this: if in doubt, drink it young. Naturally, any capability for a wine to develop and improve in bottle depends on its being stored in good conditions: dark, still and cool.

Southern Rhône by appellation
The following advice reflects the typical wines that are being made in these appellations at the time of writing.

Around Avignon
Châteauneuf-du-Pape – highly variable: up to 8 years as a rule, but the best reds can last for 40 years or more.

Gadagne – up to 10 years.

The Ventabren massif
Rasteau and Cairanne – up to 8 years as a rule, but the best can last twice this long.

Rasteau Vin Doux Naturel – usually best drunk young, but the best can last for 20 years or more.

Roaix and Vaison-la-Romaine – drink within 4 years of vintage.

Dentelles terroir
Gigondas – should drink well up to 8 years from vintage, but the best can stretch to 20 years or more.

Vacqueyras – typically up to 6 years, but the best can stretch to 15 years or more.

Beaumes de Venise – typically up to 6 years, but the best can stretch to 12 years or more.

Muscat de Beaumes de Venise – most, especially the more modern versions, are best drunk as young as possible. The best traditional styles can last 20 years or more.

Séguret and Sablet – up to 6 years.

Ventoux and Luberon

Ventoux – best drunk young, but the most ambitious can last 15 years.

Luberon – best drunk young, except a handful of top cuvées which last for up to 10 years.

The Visan Valréas hills

Vinsobres – most are best drunk within 5 years, but a small proportion age up to 12 years.

Saint-Maurice, Visan and Valréas – generally speaking drink young, but the best will last up to 8 years.

Mountain fringes

Rousset-les-Vignes and Saint-Pantaléon-les-Vignes – drink young, but can last up to 8 years.

Puyméras – drink young, up to 4 years.

Grignan-les-Adhémar – variable, but most are best drunk young, though some can last up to 6 years or more.

Massif d'Uchaux and surrounding terraces

Massif d'Uchaux – up to 8 years.

Rochegude – drink young, up to 4 years from vintage.

Suze-la-Rousse – up to 5 years.

Sainte-Cécile – up to 5 years.

Plan de Dieu – up to 8 years.

Upper West Bank

Laudun and Chusclan – drink young, up to 6 years.

Saint-Gervais and Saint-Andéol – up to 8 years.

Côtes du Vivarais – drink young, within 4 years.

Duché d'Uzès – generally drink young, but the best can last up to 8 years.

Lower West Bank

Lirac – most reds approachable from vintage, top cuvées last up to 10 or even 15 years.

Tavel – best drunk within the first few years of harvest, but last up to 10 years or more.

Signargues – up to 6 years.

Costières de Nîmes – most are best drunk young, but the most ambitious last 8 years.

The Diois

Clairette de Die and Crémant de Die – drink young, don't keep.

Coteaux de Die and Châtillon-en-Diois – drink within 4 years of vintage.

Vintage guide for the Southern Rhône

2019 ★★★★☆

A year that broke temperature records in France, the exceptionally hot, very dry 2019 vintage was more successful than expected, especially in Châteauneuf-du-Pape. Gigondas also fared well, as did other fresh terroirs. Many reds are overripe, with unbalanced alcohol, but the best are remarkably well balanced, concentrated and intense. Whites were also fresher and more concentrated than the growing season might suggest, but are best drunk young.

2018 ★★☆

A wet spring with no mistral led to a severe attack of downy mildew across the Southern Rhône, hitting organic vineyards the hardest. Old vines were also badly affected. Wines often lack depth and sense of place and display murky aromas. The more fortunate estates in conventional viticulture made juicy, fruity reds for early drinking after a hot, dry summer. Best in Gigondas.

2017 ★★★★☆

A hot, dry year that produced powerful, concentrated wines. Some suffered from leathery tannins and jammy fruit, but those who retained freshness and juiciness made excellent wines. Reds can feel quite four-square.

2016 ★★★★★

One of the truly great vintages in the Southern Rhône, excellent across the board. Charismatic wines with a natural sense of balance, despite some high alcohols. Should be very long lived.

2015 ★★★★☆

Very sunny vintage, producing very flattering red-fruited wines. Often high in alcohol, but still quite lovely.

2014 ★★★

An early spring was followed by a cool, wet July, with more rain in September while many were harvesting. A lean, lighter year. East bank wines much better than west bank; very good vintage in Ventoux. Excellent vintage for whites.

2013 ★★★⯪

A wet spring led to serious coulure with Grenache, making for a small harvest. Very late harvest, producing some quite hard, fairly high acid wines.

2012 ★★★★⯪

Juicy and fresh vintage, full of fruit and generally well balanced, even if acidities were occasionally on the low side. Lovely Châteauneuf vintage.

2011 ★★⯪

A hot spring, followed by a cool, wet July and August yielded some decent, correct wines, but some are mushy, lacking structure and harmony.

2010 ★★★★★

An exceptional vintage producing a crop of powerful, tannic wines, the best of which will take many years to come round – but it will be worth the wait.

2009 ★★★★

A very warm and sunny style, some wines towards the jammy, some deliciously lavish. Won't be as long-lasting as the 2010s.

2008 ★★

A cool and very wet vintage which largely produced scrawny wines lacking fruit and joy. The best retained a sense of freshness and have a certain ascetic attraction, but drink, rather than keep.

2007 ★★★★⯪

A divisive vintage, producing extremely concentrated, dark, powerful, sometimes quite sweet wines. Some are spectacular, others are jammy and baked. The best are extremely good. Arguably better in cooler, fresher sites than hot ones.

2006 ★★★★⯪

A fresh, balanced, easygoing vintage; generally well-balanced, highly drinkable wines. Not for long ageing, but drink now and enjoy.

2005 ★★★★⯪

A season that took its time to get going, then ramped up into a hot, dry summer, producing dark, structured, stylish wines with the depth to repay long ageing.

2004 ★★★

A classic, if minor year compared to many during this era. Some wines lacked full ripeness. Time to drink up.

2003 ★★⯪

Extremely hot vintage. Some wines very hot and jammy; others with green tannins when the vines shut down and stopped ripening, or when growers picked too early. Some successful cuvées, but they didn't last long in bottle. Wines often lack typicity. Safer to drink rather than keep.

2002 ★

Rainfall amounting to 680 millimetres in some places produced flash floods just before harvest, leading to untold damage and multiple casualties. Whites picked before the floods are good.

2001 ★★★★⯪

A very good year that has resulted in impressively long-lived wines, even from relatively unheralded appellations. A hot, dry growing season with a rampant mistral in September produced very concentrated reds.

2000 ★★★★

A classic vintage, and an abundant crop. Good wines, but more for mid-term rather than long ageing. Time to drink.

1999 ★★★★⯪

This was a slightly overlooked vintage, coming after the extraordinary 1998, but it was also very good, albeit in a very different style. It was dry again, but less hot than 1998, leading to wines that were sleek, straight, fresh and often more drinkable than the previous year.

1998 ★★★★★

On a par with 2016, 2010, 1990 or 1978? Not quite, but not far off. Very ripe, punchy wines; some with low acidity and high alcohol, but always dramatic. They haven't all aged as well as some predicted, but the best 1998s are still going strong.

1997 ★★★

Light, easygoing fairly soft wines, not for long ageing. Largely past their best now.

1996 ★★★★

Cooler vintage, leading to a crop of quite austere wines; some surprisingly good, however, and long-lived. Others with enduringly tough tannins.

1995 ★★★★½

A hot summer, but heavy rains in September; those who held their nerve enjoyed warm, dry conditions leading to a crop of richly delicious wines. Some still good today.

1994 ★★★½

A very hot and dry summer that looked like it was going to be an exceptional year until the vintage was spoiled by an extremely wet September and October. Wines lack structure.

1993 ★★

Another very wet September. Austere wines without much fruit.

1992 ★½

Very wet vintage, particularly around Gigondas, leading to a light vintage without great longevity.

1991 ★

A very wet vintage in the Southern Rhône that made for thin wines. Much better in the Northern Rhône.

1990 ★★★★★

Very little coulure, a hot and dry summer and an early harvest produced a crop of powerful, concentrated, opulent wines. High yields, but nonetheless exceptional quality, many of which are still going strong today.

Alcohol levels were high for the period, which has helped them to age. Best wines still going strong.

1989 ★★★★★

An exceptionally dry year, but arguably the equal of 1990, especially in Châteauneuf. Very early harvest. Wines of exceptional balance and great longevity.

1988 ★★★★☆

A very good, if extremely tannic, vintage in the Southern Rhône. It doesn't have the same renown today as the two that followed, and can represent a smart buy.

1987 ★★

A damp summer and a wet harvest. Dilution and rot resulted in a crop of light wines.

1986 ★★★

A large crop, very mixed in quality, with some harshly tannic wines. Those who waited for the autumn rains to pass and picked late, however, made excellent wines. Time to drink up though.

1985 ★★★★

Very good across the Southern Rhône, and a particularly good vintage for Gigondas. A wet spring was followed by a beautifully warm and sunny growing season. Fairly soft, approachable wines, but very complete and well balanced. Though an excellent vintage, acidity was fairly low, and the wines haven't lasted as well as expected. Some wines are still showing well today, but most need drinking up now.

1984 ★★☆

A cool summer and a wet September led to highly structured wines that often lacked ripeness.

1983 ★★★★☆

A tricky vintage in the Southern Rhône. Severe coulure on the Grenache thinned the crop early. A very hot July followed, then rain in August and mid-September. Some very good to excellent wines, however, though few will still be drinking well today.

1982 ★★★

A very hot summer, followed by sweltering conditions at harvest and a huge crop. Sweetly ripe, opulent, high-alcohol wines. They aged rapidly.

1981 ★★★★

Rain throughout the summer, followed by downpours throughout September, producing a fairly large crop of intensely structured wines, brusquely tannic with high acidity. They took a long time to come round, but have proved to be excellent and very long-lived.

1980 ★★★⯪

A huge crop offering a well-balanced, robustly structured vintage at the time, but now unlikely to offer much interest.

1979 ★★★★

A somewhat forgotten vintage, in the shadow of the great 1978. But a very good one, concentrated, darkly coloured, slow to evolve, but with very good longevity.

1978 ★★★★★

A great vintage, both in quality and quantity. A steady, warm growing season leading to a late vintage.

Previous exceptional vintages: 1970, 1967, 1964, 1961, 1959, 1954, 1953, 1949, 1947, 1945, 1937, 1929.

NORTHERN RHÔNE

Longevity and ageability of wine are more pertinent issues in the Northern Rhône. Syrah is a variety high in polyphenols, so tends to benefit more from ageing than Grenache. Some wines such as Hermitage really demand long ageing in order to soften their tannins to an acceptable degree before the wine feels ready to drink. In general, it's the red wines from the southern pole of the Northern Rhône that call for the longest ageing; they tend to be fuller-bodied and more muscular. That said, certain Côte-Rôties, particularly pure Syrahs grown on schist, have a hard, angular tannic profile that also benefits from long ageing. Northern Rhône whites also age well, better than those from the Southern Rhône. The dreaded 'hole' in maturity – the mute phase typically between four and eight years after vintage – is particularly prevalent in Northern Rhône reds. It's a phenomenon that seems to be accentuated when using whole bunches, but it's felt less acutely in warm, sunny vintages.

Northern Rhône by appellation

Côte-Rôtie – can usually be drunk on release, then up to 4 years from vintage. After this they are best left alone until 8 years from vintage. They typically last for 12 years but the best can last for several decades.

Seyssuel – whites are best drunk young, reds up to 8 years.

Condrieu – generally speaking, drink young, though the very best terroirs age for 20 years or more.

Château-Grillet – wines can be drunk on release; Grand Vin can age for 20 years or more.

Saint-Joseph – whites can be drunk on release, and as a rule drink young, but can last up to 8 years or more. Reds can be drunk on release and typically age up to 8 years or so, the very best twice that.

Cornas – up to 4 years from vintage, then leave until 8 years from vintage. They typically last for 12 years; the best can last for 30 years or more.

Saint-Péray – best drunk young, within 4 years of vintage, though the very best can age for 10 years or more.

Hermitage – whites can be drunk young, but are better at around 8 years, then develop to 20 years, sometimes much longer. Reds can usually be drunk up to 4 years from vintage, then are best left until 10 years from vintage (and are better with age). They typically show their best at around 20 years; the best can last for many decades.

Crozes-Hermitage – whites are best drunk young; reds too, but the best last 12 years or more.

Brézème and Saint-Julien-en-Saint-Alban – whites can be drunk on release but the best age for 20 years. Most reds are fine to drink young, but the best age for 20 years or more.

Vintage guide for the Northern Rhône

2019 ★★★★

An exceptionally hot vintage but not quite as dry as the Southern Rhône, producing rich, opulent wines that were particularly good around Côte-Rôtie. Hermitage also performed well, but Cornas suffered from the heat, as did white wines (except for white Hermitage). Crozes-Hermitage suffered from hail.

2018 ★★★☆

Only a little mildew compared to the Southern Rhône, so a much better vintage here. Nonetheless it was a very hot, dry year which resulted in an opulent vintage, very ripe, and often with high alcohol – particularly in Crozes-Hermitage.

2017 ★★★★

A hot, dry vintage that led to some chunky, muscular wines. Those who avoided overextraction and retained a sense of freshness made very good wines.

2016 ★★★★☆

A cool, wet start compared to the Southern Rhône, so the wines here don't have the same sense of richness. A classically-styled year in the Northern Rhône, less showy than the 2015s but very well balanced. Better in Hermitage than Côte-Rôtie, where some wines lack concentration.

2015 ★★★★★

An exceptional vintage. Very rich, very ripe but without the tendency towards jamminess sometimes found in the Southern Rhône – a fresher vintage in the North. Occasionally a little overripe in the more southerly appellations, but very special in Côte-Rôtie.

2014 ★★★

A very wet summer produced some slightly drab wines though the best are lean and athletic. Fruit flies (*Drosophila suzukii*) caused widespread damage and rot, especially in Crozes-Hermitage. An exceptional year however for many white wines.

2013 ★★★☆

A gradual start to the season, very long and slow, resulting in a very late harvest. Not all the wines are fully ripe, but the best show real typicity. Good white wines.

2012 ★★★★

A very consistent year, good quality across the board from north to south. For mid-term rather than long ageing.

2011 ★★★⯪

Better in the North than the South, but a season hampered by rains, leading to some dilution in the wines. Consider drinking up soon.

2010 ★★★★★

A spectacular vintage. A cool, wet spring led to very low yields, producing concentrated tannic wines that are taking an age to come round. Not as good in Cornas as Côte-Rôtie, where the wines are approaching readiness now. The monolithic Hermitage wines need much longer ageing – hands off until 2030.

2009 ★★★★⯪

A hot, sunny, dry vintage resulting in a rich, generous style of wine, and very consistent throughout the region. Not as structured as the 2010s, ready sooner, and won't last quite as long.

2008 ★★⯪

Lean, mean and often green vintage in the Northern Rhône. Wet, cool conditions made for wines that lacked concentration and ripeness. Drink up soon. Whites better than reds.

2007 ★★★⯪

Decent vintage producing classically styled, fresh wines that are better drunk sooner rather than later. Much better in the Southern Rhône.

2006 ★★★★

Not hugely structured, but approachable and well-balanced wines. Not a vintage for long ageing, but a consistent, dependable one.

2005 ★★★★⯪

A hot, dry year that made for intense, concentrated and structured wines that require long ageing.

2004 ★★★

Fresh, crisp and crunchy reds that can lack depth – drink soon. Excellent vintage for whites.

2003 ★★★⯪

Extreme heatwave, giving very mixed results. Most are jammy, with high alcohol, and are better avoided. Some excellent wines, however, in a highly opulent, exotic style. Hermitage performed relatively well.

2002 ★⯪

The torrential rains weren't as bad in the Northern Rhône, but it was still a very wet season, leading to dilute wines that lack full ripeness. Whites were better than reds.

2001 ★★★★

A very good, classically-styled vintage. Tannic to start with, the wines have taken time to come round, but are excellent throughout the Northern Rhône. A good time to drink.

2000 ★★★⯪

Large crop. Some slightly dilute wines that lack depth, others neat and well balanced. Not one for long ageing, so consider drinking soon.

1999 ★★★★★

A very good vintage in Hermitage and exceptional in Côte-Rôtie. Ripe wines, with clarity, freshness and definition.

1998 ★★★★

Very structured wines that have rewarded long ageing. Very good in the Northern Rhône, but generally speaking a better vintage in the Southern Rhône.

1997 ★★★⯪

Soft, fresh, approachable wines, not for long ageing, so drink up if you have any.

1996 ★★★

Wines with high acidity and robust tannic structures, not the most friendly. Time to drink up.

1995 ★★★★☆

A small crop that enjoyed a hot, dry season leading to an early harvest. Full, rich, complete wines.

1994 ★★★☆

A very hot vintage, marred by rains in mid-September. Most wines will be past their peak now.

1993 ★☆

Light, soft wines, the result of torrential rains in mid-September.

1992 ★★

Another year of rain during harvest, producing easy-drinking wines that didn't age well.

1991 ★★★★☆

Was there ever a vintage with such a great contrast in quality between the Northern and the Southern Rhône? They didn't suffer such heavy rain here, and the result was a very classically-styled vintage, slim and straight, well balanced, and remarkably long-lived. Particularly excellent in Côte-Rôtie, but don't underestimate the Hermitage – Jaboulet's La Chapelle *rouge* and Domaine J.L. Chave's Hermitage *rouge* are both stunning.

1990 ★★★★★

One of the greatest modern vintages. A hot, dry year that made for concentrated, rich, majestic wines that aged superbly. Better in Hermitage than Côte-Rôtie, where the wines aren't quite so consistent. The best are still going strong, no hurry.

1989 ★★★★★

Hot and extremely dry conditions led to a very early harvest. Perhaps marginally below the quality of the slightly more opulent and long-lived 1990s, but still an exceptional vintage. Consider drinking soon.

1988 ★★★★☆

Another excellent vintage in the Northern Rhône, more structured than the two that followed, sometimes displaying slightly more fibrous tannins. Particularly good in Côte-Rôtie. Only the best are still on good form, consider drinking up soon.

1987 ★★★

Inconsistent, fairly lightweight vintage in the Northern Rhône, September rains spoiling any chance of greatness. Drink up.

1986 ★★⯪

A large crop of medium-bodied wines, prone to astringent tannins. Not a vintage for long ageing. Drink up.

1985 ★★★★

Round, generous, sometimes soft wines, but they've aged better than some predicted. A highly consistent vintage, but it's time to drink now.

1984 ★★

Lean, light, acidic reds from a cool, dull growing season; white wines generally better this year.

1983 ★★★★⯪

A hot, dry season producing some extremely structured wines, particularly tannic and long-lived in Hermitage. Not the most consistent, but the best wines, such as Domaine J.L. Chave's Hermitage *rouge*, are still phenomenal.

1982 ★★★★

Better in the Northern Rhône than in the Southern Rhône, but still a very hot, dry vintage that was picked under sweltering conditions, leading to occasional problems with the vinifications. Rich and velvety wines, particularly good in Hermitage, but not one for long ageing. Drink up.

1981 ★★⯪

Largely lean, light reds in the Northern Rhône; much better in the Southern Rhône.

1980 ★★★

A large crop, yielding gentle, medium-bodied wines that were best drunk young.

1979 ★★★★

Fine, elegant, balanced wines, particularly in Côte-Rôtie, but they haven't aged as well as the 1978s. Drink up.

1978 ★★★★★

A sensational vintage throughout the Northern Rhône, producing concentration and powerful but balanced wines that have proven to be extraordinarily long-lived and show no sign of falling apart any time soon.

Previous exceptional vintages: 1970, 1969, 1966, 1964, 1961, 1959, 1955, 1949, 1947, 1934, 1929.

APPENDIX II: THE MYSTERIES OF RAYAS BY SIMON LOFTUS[6]

One of the things that fascinated me as a wine merchant was discovering how often the most strikingly wonderful wines reflected the character of their makers. But some winemakers proved so elusive, so wilfully determined to avoid all contact with pestering customers and journalists, that their reputation became a matter of myth, hiding any sense of true identity. The only clues were in the character of their wines. In no case was this more intriguing than with the legends surrounding Louis Reynaud and his son Jacques, successive owners of Château Rayas, the greatest estate of Châteauneuf-du-Pape. I was determined to meet them.

I tried to telephone (number unobtainable) and wrote to request a visit – no reply. So I took a chance and announced my intended arrival at 3 p.m. on a certain date in May, 1979. Despite losing my way and stopping several times to ask directions, I made it on time. The modest, ramshackle building was firmly shuttered and there was no sign of life, except the rasping of cicadas. I waited a while, without much hope, then turned the car to leave. As I did so, a very old man rose from a ditch beside the dusty track. The day was hot, but he was dressed in crumpled elegance – grey flannel trousers, old-fashioned striped shirt with collar and tie, linen jacket and a venerable Panama hat. He had the dignified but slightly bemused air of a time traveller from another age, an elderly lepidopterist who had mislaid his butterfly net.

6 © Simon Loftus, 2019

'Monsieur Reynaud?', I hesitated. 'Oui, monsieur.' I asked if it was possible to visit the chais and taste his wine. 'Non.' Without explanation but with great courtesy of manner he refused. I drove slowly down the lane and stopped at the corner to turn and wave. He had disappeared.

I treasure that memory because Louis Reynaud was one of the great traditionalists of Châteauneuf-du-Pape, and by far the most elusive. The fact that he had been there at the appointed time, waiting to refuse me entry, was a very rare honour, from a man notorious for shunning visitors.

He was equally averse to the authorities who laid down rules for wine production. His white wines included Chardonnay (not one of the thirteen permitted grape varieties of Châteauneuf-du-Pape) and the labels of Château Rayas proclaimed, quite illegally, that it was a 'Premier Grand Cru'. The magic words 'appellation contrôlée' were missing. To which Reynaud's response was uncompromising – 'Appellation contrôlée! C'est la garantie de la médiocrité!' But his wines were superb.

Louis Reynaud died soon after that brief encounter, and the estate was taken over by his son Jacques. I managed to obtain an occasional, modest allocation of some fabulous vintages, stretching back to 1957, but it took fifteen years before I was able to arrange a visit.

I arrived full of hope, in September 1994, thinking that I might finally be able to unravel the mysteries of Rayas. Almost immediately I realised that I was doomed to disappointment.

Jacques Reynaud was an enigma. Looking like a tramp but with the shy, confiding smile of a child, he made some of the most extraordinary wines of Châteauneuf apparently by chance, in ill-kempt cellars piled with rubbish. My tasting with him was a bizarrely random experience, with some wines superb, others out of condition. He poured a glass of Pignan, the second wine of Rayas, and I asked the vintage. Reynaud shrugged. 'Quatre vingt onze, quatre vingt douze, ça depend.' Depends on what, I wondered. Ambiguity clouded every utterance.

Not least of my perplexities was trying to understand the identities of his various wines.

A few facts were well established. I knew that the vineyards of Rayas itself (there is no Château) were situated in low hills to the north of the town of Châteauneuf; that the vines were grown on sandy, north-facing slopes, surrounded by pine trees; and that the famous *galets roulés* of Châteauneuf (large glacier-worn stones that elsewhere cover the vineyards, absorbing the heat of the day and radiating it back at night) were entirely absent from this cool, infertile terrain. All of which meant that the grapes took longer to ripen, building flavours of unusual purity and elegance.

I also knew that Reynaud owned a Côtes du Rhône estate, Fonsalette, but I learnt that there was another vineyard at Courthezon, not far from Château de Beaucastel but outside the Châteauneuf appellation. And then there was Pignan, ostensibly the second wine of Rayas, which sometimes tasted better than Rayas itself. There seemed no consistent logic to the labelling. I had to piece together the explanations, interpreting the secretive clues provided by Monsieur Reynaud, as we tasted from chipped glasses, briefly rinsed to remove some of the grime.

The red wine of Rayas was famous for being 100 per cent Grenache, from very old vines giving incredibly low yields. But I discovered that there was also a little Syrah, and a little Cinsault, the proportions of which might vary from year to year. I tasted the '93 Cinsault, unblended. It seemed the best wine of that vintage, juicy, elegant and alive. All three grapes were also planted at Fonsalette and normally combined together, though Reynaud sometimes made a pure Cuvée Syrah. That, too, I tasted – it was wonderful but unobtainable.

Both Rayas and Fonsalette were essentially single-vineyard wines (though Fonsalette might occasionally include rejected components of Rayas) but Pignan was a puzzle. 'What goes into it?' There was a pause. 'Oh, the less good wines of Rayas and some other things, it's a secret.' When I pressed him for a clue, he whispered in my ear – that his vineyard at Courthezon produced wonderful Grenache.

As for the whites, I was told that the 1991 Rayas was made from Grenache Blanc and Clairette; the Fonsalette from Grenache Blanc, Clairette, Chardonnay and Marsanne. Whether that was true and whether it applied in other vintages, heaven knows.

By all the rules most of these wines should have been undrinkable – I have never seen scruffier cellars – and rumour had it that mistakes were made and that a great deal of the production had to be discarded. But the best wines were magnificent – beautifully fine-textured reds with an unmatched autumnal splendour, and deep-coloured, old-fashioned whites with startling complexity, aromas of straw and quinces.

Rare, wonderful – and a mystery, like the man himself.

Muttering a private shorthand to his sister, gazing mournfully at his dogs, exercising some unspoken control over his labourers and smiling diffidently at visitors, Jacques Reynaud was unfathomable. I had the impression of an ancient child, sleepwalking through a hostile world and somehow surviving – and that at the heart of all his peculiarities there was an innocence, untouched.

It is said that he died while buying a new pair of shoes.

GLOSSARY

Barrique. Small wooden barrel, usually made of oak, with a typical volume of either 225 litres or 228 litres (usually the latter in the Rhône).

Bâttonage. Stirring of the lees that settle at the bottom of the barrel or tank during élevage.

Brettanomyces (**or brett**). Type of yeast found most commonly in wines that have undergone cask or barrel ageing. Generally considered a fault due to the flavours it contributes, often akin to horse, band-aid or banana skin. Considered by some to add complexity to a wine in small doses.

Cap. Mass of grape skins, pips and other matter that rises to the top of a container during fermentation.

Conservatory. Vineyard dedicated to the conservation and propagation of specific plant material, often old, pre-clonal vinestock.

Cordon de Royat. Horizontal system of training grapevines on wires.

Cuvée spéciale. In Châteauneuf-du-Pape this denotes a 'special blend' or 'special bottling' that in a producer's range is generally placed above the *tradition* bottling in quality and price.

Demi-muid. Medium-sized wooden barrel, usually made of oak, with a typical volume of 600 litres.

Échalas. Tall wooden stakes used to support single grapevines, commonly used in the Northern Rhône for Syrah.

Élevage. Literally the 'raising' or 'upbringing' of the wine, in other words the maturation or ageing of the wine, usually in wooden barrels.

En vrac. Wine that is ready to drink that is stored in large volumes, rather than in bottle.

Foudre. Generic term for a large wooden barrel, usually made of oak, that can vary in size between 10 and 120 hectolitres.

Fût. Generic term for a wooden barrel.

Galet roulé (**plural:** *galets roulés*). Large rounded pebble.

Gobelet. Single self-supporting vine, not trained on wires. A bush vine.

Grappes entières. Whole bunches of grapes, including the stalks.

Grès. Hard sandstone, from yellow ochre to crimson in colour.

Hectolitre. Unit of 100 litres.

INAO. The Institut National de l'Origine et de la Qualité, a French organization charged with the regulation of agricultural products with protected designation of origin.

Indigenous yeasts (or natural yeasts). Strains of wild yeasts that live on grape skins or in cellars.

Lees. A sediment left after fermentation, consisting of dead yeast cells and fragments of grape matter.

Lieu-dit (**plural:** *lieux-dits*). Named vineyard site.

Malolactic fermentation (malo). A second fermentation that converts harder malic acid into milder lactic acid. Standard practice in red wines, optional in white wines.

Natural wine. A wine made with minimal intervention, typically organic or biodynamic, made without recourse to additions such as tartaric acid, and sometimes without adding sulphites.

Négociant. A producer that buys in grapes, must or wine, rather than using grapes grown in owned vineyards.

Oenologue. A trained winemaker.

Safre. Soft, friable sandstone, usually yellow ochre coloured.

Sélection parcellaire. Single-vineyard wine.

Stage. Short-contract employment or work experience at a winery.

Syndicat. A union of growers from a particular commune or appellation.

Tradition. In Châteauneuf-du-Pape this denotes the most representative bottling in a producer's range, usually the cheapest and most classic in style. Some producers only make a *tradition*, and no *cuvées spéciales*.

Training styles. Methods of shaping the growing vine by using specific pruning methods, and usually involving the use of a supporting structure such as wooden stakes or wires.

Volatile acidity (VA). Acetic acid, whose presence in a wine in noticeable amounts can have a negative effect on aroma and flavour.

Whole bunch. Bunches of grapes that have not been destemmed.

BIBLIOGRAPHY

Bailly, Robert, *Histoire De La Vigne et Des Grands Vins Des Côtes Du Rhône*, Avignon: Orta, 1978

Bischel, Rolf, *Tavel: The people and the wines*, Bordeaux: Féret, 2011

Campbell, Christy, *Phylloxera*, London: HarperCollins, 2004

Charnay, Pierre, *Vignobles et Vins des Côtes du Rhône*, Aubanel, 1985

Chauvel, Paul, *Sites et Vins des Côtes du Rhône: Zone septentrionale*, Challes les Eaux: Curandera, 1988

Comiskey, Patrick J., *American Rhône: How maverick winemakers changed the way Americans drink*, Oakland, CA: University of California Press, 2016

Coulon, Paul and Philippe Abbal, *Pourquoi un Vin est-il Bon? L'Analyse d'un vigneron et d'un scientifique*, Paris: Editions France Agricole, 2013

Dangréaux, Bernard, *Le Rhône et le Vin: Du vin des cimes au vin des sables*, Grenoble: Glénat, 2002

Dion, Roger, *Histoire de la Vigne et du Vin en France des Origines au XIXe Siècle*, Paris: CNRS Editions, 2010

Dovaz, Michel, *Châteauneuf-du-Pape*, Boulogne: Jacques Legrand, 1992

Fanet, Jacques, *Les Terroirs du Vin*, Hachette, 2001

Johnson, Hugh and Jancis Robinson, *The World Atlas of Wine*, 6th edition, London: Mitchell Beazley, 2007

Karis, Harry, *The Châteauneuf-du-Pape Wine Book*, Roermond: Kavino, 2009

Larousse Encyclopaedia, Paris: Librarie Larousse, 1933

Livingstone-Learmonth, John, *Gigondas: Its wines, its land, its people*, Les Editions du Bottin Gourmand, 2012

Livingstone-Learmonth, John, *The Wines of the Rhône*, 3rd edition, London: Faber & Faber, 1992

Lorch, Wink, *Wines of the French Alps*, London: Wine Travel Media, 2019

MacDonogh, Giles, *Syrah, Grenache & Mourvèdre*, London: Penguin, 1992

Maltman, Alex, *Vineyards, Rocks, & Soils: The Wine Lover's Guide to Geology*, New York, NY: Oxford University Press, 2018

Mayberry, Robert W., *Wines of the Rhône Valley: A guide to origins*, Totowa, NJ: Rowman & Littlefield, 1987

Parker, Robert M., Jr, *Wines of the Rhône Valley*, New York, NY: Simon & Schuster, 1997

Pomerol, Charles, *Terroirs et Vins de France: Itinéraires oenologiques et géologiques*, 3rd edition, Orléans: BRGM, 1990

Portes, Jean-Claude, *Châteauneuf-du-Pape: Première AOC de France*, Châteauneuf-du-Pape: Organisme de Défense et de Gestion de l'AOC Châteauneuf-du-Pape, 2016

Robinson, Jancis, Julia Harding and José Vouillamoz, *Wine Grapes*, London: Allen Lane, 2012

Robinson, Jancis, *The Oxford Companion to Wine*, 4th edition, Oxford: Oxford University Press, 2015

Serroy, Jean, *The Rhône Wines: Côtes and Valley*, Grenoble: Glénat, 2013

The Encyclopedia of Côtes-du-Rhône and Rhône Valley AOC Wines, Avignon: Inter Rhône, 2019

INDEX

Note: 'Cave', 'Château', 'Domaine', 'Maison', forenames and initials are ignored when alphabetizing producers.

4 Vents, Domaine les 324
7ième Clos, Au 167

Abbé Dîne, Domaine l' 97
Achard-Vincent, Domaine 246–7
acid adjustments 24
Ad Fines 64
Adhémar family 180
ageing wines 335–49
Agneray, Frédéric 202
agriculture raisonnée 115, 208, 219, 264, 303
Alary, Denis 11, 111, 115
Alary, Domaine 11, 36, 46, 111, 112
Alary, François/Frédéric 112
Alary, Jean-Etienne 111
Alazard, Loïc 141
Albigensian Crusade 16
Aléofane, Domaine 294, 324–5
Alicante Bouschet 73
Aligoté 47, 242–3, 247
Allemand, Theo 300
Allemand, Thierry/Domaine Thierry 299–300
Allobroges 16
Alloïs, Domaine 152
Alpilles, IGP 65
Amadieu, Domaine des 111
Amadieu, Jean-Baptiste 120
Amadieu, Pierre 35, 113, 127
Amandine, Domaine de l' 146
Amauve, Domaine de l' 143, 144–5

Ameillaud, Domaine l' 113
Amido, Domaine 228, 232
Amouriers, Domaine les 133
Amphores, Domaine des 48, 294
Amsellem, Emma/Paul 279
Ancienne École, Domaine l' 161
André, Domaine Pierre 46, 96
Andrines, Domaine des 234
Anges, Domaine des 150
Anglès, Vincent 99
Anglès, Xavier 97–8, 99
Anglore, Domaine l' 23–4, 226, 229, 230
Antonin, Domaine d' 202
Aphillanthes, Domaine les 23, 108, 195
appellation system 49–50
    Côtes-du-Rhône 51–3
    Côtes-du-Rhône Villages 53–4
    Côtes-du-Rhône Villages with geographic
        name 54–5
    crus 55–6
    demotion 58
    IGPs 60–5
    Northern Rhône sections 58–60
    opting out 66
    Other Rhône Valley 50–1
    Southern Rhône sections 56–7
Aqueduc, Domaine de l' 220
Aqueria, Château d' 226, 229, 231
Aqueria, Louis Joseph/Robert d' 231
Aramon 71

Ardèche, IGP 61–2
Ardhuy, Gabriel d' 185–6
Ardhuy, Marie-Pierre d' 186
ARENI 150
Armenier, Catherine/Philippe/Sophie 88
Arnaud, Fredéric 201–2
Arnaud, Joséphine 200, 202
Arnesque, Domaine de l' 197
Arnoux 133
Arsac, Domaine 62
Artémis Domaines 281, 282
Aubert, Domaines André 182
Aubery-Laurent, Michèle 25, 168, 169
Aubun 39
Aureto 152
Avril, Vincent 86–7
Avril, Paul 86
Avril, Paul-Eugène 87
Ay, Anne-Sophie/Christophe/Dominique 125

Bailly, Robert 306
Bakke, Even 148, 151
Balazu des Vaussières 232
Balme, Domaine Elodie 105, 116
Balme, Elodie 58, 105, 115
Balthazar, Casimir/Franck/René/Domaine
    Franck 300
Banate, Domaine la 171, 173–4
Banneret, Domaine du 80–1
Barge, Domaine 257, 280
Barge, Gilles/Julien 257
Barral, Philippe 172
Barret, Matthieu/Matthieu Barret Sélections
    302
Barroche, Domaine la 75, 96
Barrot, Julien 75
Barruol, Louis 21–4, 122, 125–6, 127, 159,
    161, 185
Bastide, Domaine de la 167, 192
Bastide du Claux, La 156
Bastide Saint Dominique, La 46, 96, 113
Baume, Louis de La 190
Baumet, Vincent 14, 21, 187–9, 192
Baux, Antoinette/Marguerite des 190
Bayon de Noyer, Luc and Rémi 191
Beau Mistral, Domaine 108
Beaubois, Château 235, 238–9
Beaucastel, Château de 19, 32, 44, 76, 79,
    81–3, 152, 159
Beaucastel, Pierre de 82

Beauchêne, Château 97
Beauharnais, Empress Joséphine de 281
Beaumes de Venise 119, 133–9, 335, 336
Beaurenard, Domaine de 47, 83, 108
Belle, Domaine 320, 322, 329
Bellion, Laurent 145
Benetière, Domaine 269
Bernard, Jacky 128, 130
Bernardins, Domaine des 40, 134, 135, 137
Bertrand, Thomas 192
Besnardeau, Marc and Mireille 193
Besson, Domaine Serre 161
Betton, Domaine 321, 329
Bez, Bruno Le 231
Bez, Raphaël de 229
Biguet, Domaine du 309
Billon, Domaine 269, 272
biodynamic viticulture 19–20
    Ardèche, IGP 62
    Brézème 333
    Cairanne 111, 112
    Château-Grillet 283
    Châteauneuf-du-Pape 82–3, 85, 88, 93–4
    Condrieu 279
    Cornas 302, 305
    Costières de Nîmes 235, 239, 240
    Côte-Rôtie 268, 268
    Crozes-Hermitage 328, 329
    Diois 246, 247
    Gadagne 100
    Gigondas 124, 126
    Hermitage 315, 318, 319
    Lirac 224
    Luberon 155
    Massif d'Uchaux 185, 186, 187
    Rasteau 106, 108
    Sablet 140
    Saint-Andéol 211
    Saint-Joseph 290, 292
    Saint-Maurice 163
    Suze-la-Rousse 191
    Tavel 232
    Vacqueyras 132
    Vaison-la-Romaine 117
    Valréas 169
    Vinsobres 159, 160, 161
    Visan 166, 167
Biscarelle, Domaine de la 96
Bischel, Rolf 230
Bizard, Château 13, 179, 180–1

black rot 19
Blanc, Cave Christophe 280
Blanchard, Baron 334
blending 42–3
Bois de Boursan, Domaine de 96
Bois de Meges, Domaine 197
Bois de Saint-Jean, Domaine de 97, 99
Bois des Dames, Domaine 197
Bois Pointu, Le 97
Boissière, Domaine de 240
Boisson, Bruno 109
Boisson, Domaine 109, 113
Bon Remède, Domaine du 152
Bonfils, Christian 140
Bonneau, Domaine Henri 83–4
Bonneau, Henri 80, 84, 106
Bonnefond, Christophe/Patrick/Domaine
    P&C 257–8
Bonserine, Domaine de 260, 280
Bordeaux hermitagé 310–11
Borie, Domaine la 190, 192
Borty, M. 17, 221
Bosquets, Domaine des 121, 122, 123, 127,
    226
Bosquets des Papes, Domaine des 97
botrytis 28, 31, 36–8, 40–1, 43, 276
Bott, Domaine 269
Boucarut, Château 223
Bouchard, Emmanuel 168
Bouchard brothers 170
Bouchassy, Château de 226
Bouïssière, Domaine la 126
Bouletin, Eric 131–2
Boulle, Daniel/ Hélène 195
Bour, Henri Jr 178–9, 180, 181
Bour, Henri Sr 179
Bourboulenc 42, 45–6, 48
    Châteauneuf-du-Pape 73, 81, 85, 87
    Gigondas 127
    Visan 167
Bourg, Domaine Mikael 306, 309
Boussier, Sylvain 100
Boutin, Mikaël/Domaine Mikaël 106
Bouvade, Domaine la 171, 174
Bouyer, Vincent 179, 181
Boyer, Benjamin 206
Boyer, Vincent 13
Bramadou, Domaine du 115–16, 198
Brechet, Julien 121, 123, 127
Brechet, Laurent 48

Brès, Nicolas 107
Bressy, Jérôme 64, 106–7, 186
Brettanomyces (brett) 24
Brézème 62, 330–4, 344
Brisset, Damien 35, 318
Brissot, Daniel 320
Brotte 202
Brun Argenté see Vaccarèse
Brunel, Fabien 77, 78
Brunel, René 215
Brunier, Daniel 79, 95–6
Brunier, Edouard/Frédéric/Henri/Hippolyte/
    Nicolas 95
Brusset, André/Daniel 111
Brusset, Domaine 108, 111–12, 126
Brusset, Laurent 111–12
Bruyères, Domaine les 329
Burgaud, Domaine Bernard 269
bush vines (gobelets) 20–1, 28

Cabasse, Domaine de 142, 145, 146
Cabernet 292
Cabernet Sauvignon 35, 48, 122, 247
Cabotte, Domaine la 183, 185–6
Caillet, Frédéric 258
Cailloux, Domaine les 76, 77, 78, 96, 151
Cairanne 55, 103, 108–13, 115, 199, 200–1,
    336
    grape varieties 31, 36, 44, 46
Cairanne, Cave de 26
Caladoc 37, 39
Calitor 39
Callet, Bernard 224
Camarèse see Vaccarèse
Cambie, Philippe 76–7, 219
Camp Galhan, Domaine 198, 218–19
Campbell, Christy 17
Campuget, Château de 240
Cannonau see Grenache
Canorgue, Château la 155
Carabiniers, Domaine des 224, 232
carbonic maceration 23–4
Carignan (Carignan Noir) 20, 23, 31–2, 47,
    197
    Beaumes de Venise 136
    Cairanne 109
    Costières de Nîmes 236
    Grignan-les-Adhémar 179
    Lirac 224
    Luberon 155

Massif d'Uchaux 187
Rasteau 103, 106, 107
Saint-Andéol 210
Signargues 233
Valréas 168
Vinsobres 160
Carignan Blanc 31, 47
Carignan Gris 31
Carignan Noir *see* Carignan
Carle, Mr 17
Carod, Cave 248
Cartier, Florence/Jean-Pierre 141
Castaud, Louis 137
Castel Oualou 223
Cavale, La 156
cave cooperatives 18, 25–6, 58
Cayron, Domaine du 126
Cécilia, Cave 19, 25–6, 193
Cécillon, Cave Julien 48, 288–9, 329
Cécillon, Julien 288–9
Cellier, Nancy 324
Cellier des Dauphins, Le 26, 161
Cellier des Princes 87
Celliers de Chartreux, Les 206–7, 208
Cévennes, IGP 65
Chabrier, Christophe 219
Chabrier, Patrick/Domaine 217, 219
Chambeyron, Christophe 264
Chambeyron, Domaine 269, 280
Chamfort, Thibaut 140, 142
Champ Morel 329
Champagne Louis Roederer 317
Champet, Domaine 269
Chante Cigale, Domaine 92
Chantecôtes *see* Cécilia, Cave
Chanzy, Maison 206
Chapelle, Domaine de la 100
Chapitre, Domaine du 210, 211
Chapoutier, M. 34, 44
    Châteauneuf-du-Pape 97
    Condrieu 280
    Cornas 304
    Côte-Rôtie 269
    Crozes-Hermitage 329
    Gigondas 127
    Hermitage 311, 313, 314–15
    Lirac 226
    Saint-Joseph 294
    Saint-Péray 309
Chapoutier, Marius 314

Chapoutier, Mathilde/Maxime 315
Chapoutier, Michel 19, 312, 313, 314–15, 318
Charavin, Domaine Rabasse 108, 113
Charavin, Robert 102, 103, 197
Charavin family 185
Charbonnière, Domaine de la 96, 133
Chardonnay 47
    Côte-Rôtie 258
    Diois 242–3, 247
    Rayas, Château 352, 353
Charité, Domaine de la 234
Charles II 16
Charnay, Pierre 46, 266
Charvin, Domaine 84–5
Charvin, Gerard/Laurent 84–5
Chasselas 48
Chastan, Carole/Dani 123–4
Chatagnier, Domaine Aurélien 280, 294
Château-Grillet 60, 273, 274, 281–4, 344
Châteauneuf-du-Pape 56, 69–98, 183
    acid adjustments 24
    ageing wines 335, 336, 339, 341
    blending 42
    bush vines 20–1
    climate change 11–12, 79, 148
    clones 21
    comparison with other appellations 99, 121,
        226–7, 230
    cuvée speciale 76–8
    destemming 22
    grape varieties 28–9, 31–2, 36–8, 40–1,
        43–4, 46–8, 73–4
    history 16, 17, 69–73, 80
    irrigation 14
    key producers 80–97
    Lirac vineyards 222–3
    négociants 34–5
    organic viticulture 20, 75, 82, 85, 87, 89,
        93, 95
    Rayas, Château 351–4
    situation and soils 74–5
    white 74
Châtillon-en-Diois 242–3, 246, 247, 248, 338
    grape varieties 37, 38, 47
Chatus 48
Chaudière, Alex 151
Chaudière, Frédéric 11, 151
Chaume, Thibaud 13–14, 162
Chaume-Arnaud, Domaine 13–14, 52, 159–
        60, 162, 164

Chaume-Arnaud, Philippe/Valérie 159–60
Chaussy, Daniel 21
Chauvet, Céline 124
Chave, Bernard 316
Chave, Damien 115
Chave, Domaine J.L. 288, 300, 311–13,
    315–16, 348–9
Chave, Domaine Yann 316–17, 329
Chave, Erin/Gérard 315
Chave, Florent 150
Chave, Jean-Louis 11, 285–7, 311–13, 315–16
Chave, Natacha 324–5
Chave, Yann 316–17, 324
Chave Sélections, J.L. 34, 316, 321
Chemins de Sève, Domaine les 110, 113
Chêne, Domaine du 280, 294
Chêne Bleu 64, 150–1
Chèze, Louis 13, 270
Chinieu, Gilles 204, 205
chlorosis 31
Chusclan 38, 46, 204–7, 337
Cigale, Domaine Chante 97
Cinsault 23, 28, 33–4, 38, 48
    Beaumes de Venise 136
    Châteauneuf-du-Pape 73, 84, 87, 91–3
    Lirac 224, 225
    Massif d'Uchaux 187
    Rasteau 103, 106
    Rayas, Château 353
    Saint-Julien-en-Saint-Alban 330
    Signargues 233
    Tavel 228
    Vinsobres 160
Citadelle, Domaine de la 155
Clairette (Clairette Blanche) 41–2, 46, 48, 336
    Brézème 331
    Cairanne 112
    Châteauneuf-du-Pape 73, 81, 87, 90–1, 93,
        95–6
    Clairette de Bellegarde 237–8
    Costières de Nîmes 237
    Diois 241, 242, 243–4, 246, 247
    Gigondas 125, 127
    Lirac 226
    Massif d'Uchaux 187
    Rayas, Château 353
    Saint-Julien-en-Saint-Alban 330
    Séguret 145
    Vacqueyras 133
    Vinsobres 160

Clairette Blanche see Clairette
Clairette de Bellegarde 41, 238–40, 336
Clairette de Die 242–5, 247–8, 338
    grape varieties 36, 37, 40, 42, 46
Clairette Rose 42, 46, 85, 93, 226
Clairmont 26
Clape, Auguste 295, 301
Clape, Domaine 52, 295, 297, 300, 301–2,
    309
Clape, Olivier 295, 297, 301–2
Clape, Pierre 295, 301–2
Clavel, Claire 207–8
Clavel, Denis 208
Clavel, Domaine 206, 207–8
Clefs d'Or, Domaine les 97, 260
Clément, Sébastien 98, 100
Clement V, Pope 16, 69–70, 134
Clerc, Domaine Martin 269
climate 10–11
climate change 11–14
    acid adjustments 24
    Châteauneuf-du-Pape 11–12, 79, 148
    Condrieu 13, 276
    Cornas 298
    Côte-Rôtie 253, 256, 268
    Diois 244
    Plan de Dieu 148, 195
    Rousset-les-Vignes 172
    Saint-Cécile 192–3
    Saint-Maurice 163
    Saint-Pantaléon-les-Vignes 172
    Syrah 197
    Ventoux 148
    Vinsobres 159
    whole bunches vs destemming 22
clones 21
Clos Bellane 169, 197
Clos de l'Abbé Dubois 215
Clos de Trias 148, 151
Clos Derrière Vieille 126
Clos des Boutes 238
Clos des Cazaux, Domaine le 127, 133
Clos des Centenaires 240
Clos des Papes 48, 76, 86–7
Clos des Saumanes, Le 100
Clos des Serènes 226
Clos du Caillou, Le 85
Clos du Caveau, Le 133
Clos du Joncuas 122, 123–4, 133
Clos du Mont-Olivet 73, 76, 86, 92

Clos du Palay, Domaine 146

Clos du Tourelles, Domaine de 83

Clos Saint Jean 78, 97, 219

Clusel-Roch, Domaine 255, 258

Cohola, Château 140, 142

Collard, Anne/François 240

Collière, Domaine la 106

Collines du Bourdic, Les 220

Collines Rhodaniennes, IGP 64–5

Colombier, Domaine du 320, 329

Colombo, Jean-Luc 14, 297, 307, 309, 333

Colombo, Laure 307

Combe, Xavier 167

Combe Julière, Domaine 103, 108, 197

Combebelle, Domaine de 177

Combier, David/Julien/Laurent/Domaine 325

Combin, Daniel 84

Comité des Vignerons de Vinsobres 161

Comité Interprofessionel des Vins des Côtes-
   du-Rhône 72

Comtadine, Cave la 177

Comtés Rhodaniens, IGP 61

Condorcet, Domaine 70

Condrieu 262, 269, 272–80, 287, 313, 344
   and Château-Grillet 281, 282
   climate change 13, 276
   Collines Rhodaniennes, IGP 65
   comparison with other appellations 253, 271
   grape varieties 40–1, 44, 60
   history 16

Constant-Duquesnoy, Domaine 161

Cooperative de Cairanne, Cave 113

Cooperative de Roaix Séguret, Cave 115

cooperatives 18, 25–6, 58

cordon de Royat 20, 28

Cornas 60, 286, 296–306, 314
   ageing wines 344, 345
   Ardèche, IGP 62
   grape varieties 29

Coste Chaude, Château 167

Costières de Nîmes 10, 20, 26, 65, 234–40, 337
   grape varieties 45, 47

Côte-Rôtie 24, 60, 251–69
   ageing wines 343–4, 345, 347, 348, 349
   Collines Rhodaniennes, IGP 65
   comparison with other appellations 271,
      286, 298, 299, 314
   grape varieties 28, 29, 31, 40
   négociants 34

Coteau-Brûlé 70

Coteaux, Cave les 167

Coteaux de Die 41, 242, 246, 247, 338

Coteaux des Baronnies, IGP 65

Coteaux des Travers, Domaine des 102–3, 108,
      185, 187, 197

Coteaux du Pont du Gard, IGP 65

Coteaux Saint-Maurice, Cave des 26, 162, 164

Côtes-du-Rhône appellation 51–3

Côtes-du-Rhône Villages 53–4
   with geographic name 54–5, 58

Côtes du Vivarais 64, 212–15, 337

Coudoulis, Domaine 224–5

Coulange, Domaine 212

Coulet, Domaine du 294, 302

Coulon, Daniel 47–8, 83

Coulon, Frédéric/Paul/Régine/Victor 83

coulure 12, 224
   grape varieties 28, 36, 37, 39, 275
   vintage guide 338, 341, 342

Counoise 28, 34, 36, 37
   Châteauneuf-du-Pape 73, 82, 87, 92

Courac, Château 200, 201–2

Courbis, Domaine 286, 294, 306

Courbis, Domaine Gérard 294

Couron, Domaine de 209, 212

Couroulou, Domaine de 130–1

Coursodon, Jérôme/Domaine 289

Couston 38–9

Couston, Julien 39

Coyeux, Domaine de 135–6, 137–8

Cramette, Jaeok 283, 284

Crémant de Die 242, 244–8, 338
   grape varieties 36, 40, 42, 46, 47

Crève Coeur, Domaine de 140, 142

Cri de l'Araignée, Le 193

Cristia, Domaine de 14, 78, 96

Croix des Pins, Château la 127

Cros de la Mure, Domaine 52, 186

Croze Granier, Domaine 97

Crozes-Hermitage 60, 286, 321–30, 344, 345
   cooperatives 26
   Drôme, IGP 62
   grape varieties 29

crus 55–6

Cugnette 48

Cuilleron, Cave Yves 48, 272, 277

Cuilleron, Claude 277

Cuilleron, Yves 29, 270–2, 277, 279–80, 291

Cuvée du Vatican 97

cuvée speciale 76–8

Dal, François 268
Dantec, Dominique Le 228
Dard, René-Jean 325–6
Dard & Ribo 294, 320, 322, 323, 325–6
Darnaud, Claire 317
Darnaud, Emmanuel 318, 329
Daumas, Elodie 177
Daumen, Jean-Paul 79, 94–5
Dauvergne-Ranvier 35, 127
David, Jean/Jean-Luc/Domaine 145
Delas Frères 34
    Condrieu 275, 280
    Cornas 306
    Côte-Rôtie 259, 269
    Crozes-Hermitage 329
    Grignan-les-Adhémar 182
    Hermitage 312, 313, 317
    Saint-Joseph 295
    Ventoux 152
Delobre, Jean 290
Delorme, Ambre/Christophe/Francis/
        Madeleine 231
Delorme, Domaine 212
Demazet 98
Demoiselle Suzette 133
Derenoncourt, Stéphane 107
Dervieux, Albert/Yvonne 267
Dervieux, Jean 267, 295
Dervieux-Thaize, Albert 267, 295
Dervieux-Thaize, Domaine 295
Descours, Jean-Louis and Christopher 156
destemming 13, 21, 22–3
Devoy Martine, Château le 223, 226
Dieu-le-Fit, Domaine 166
Diffre, Château la 146
Diois 62, 241–8, 338
    grape varieties 41, 42, 47
Dionysos, Domaine de 187
Domitian, emperor 15
Dorthe, Frédéric 210, 211
Dorthe, Jean-Luc 209
downy mildew 28, 32, 215, 224
Drôme, IGP 62, 65
Duché d'Uzès 29, 45, 179, 215–20, 337
Duclaux, Benjamin/David 258–9
Duclaux, Domaine B&D 258–9, 280
Ducos, Joseph 71, 72, 89
Duèse, Jacques 16
Dumaine, Cave Olivier 329
Dumien-Serrette, Domaine 306

Durand, Domaine 300, 306
Duras 30
Durban, Domaine de 139
Dureza 29, 48, 292
Durfort, La Cave 220
Durieu, Domaine 97
Durif 30, 48
Duseigneur, Bernard 223
Duseigneur, Domaine 96, 202, 223, 226
Dussaud, Elie 85

Eames, Charles 27
east bank vs west bank 203
échalas 31, 255, 257, 282
Echevin, Domaine de l' 166
Engerer, Frédéric 281
Entrefaux, Domaine des 322, 329
Ermitage, Château l' 240
esca 28, 33, 45
Escaravailles, Domaine des 108, 116, 219
Espigouette, Domaine de l' 108, 133, 195, 196
Estevenin, Vincent 88
Etienne, Sébastien 215
exports
    Cairanne 112
    Châteauneuf-du-Pape 70, 78, 89
    Diois 248
    history 16–17
    négociants 34
    Vinsobres 159
Eyguestre, Domaine 145

Fabre, Adrien 13, 162, 163, 165, 166
Fabre, Claire 77, 95
Fabre, Francis 233, 234
Fabre, François 166
Fabre, Jean-Henri 184
Fagotière, Domaine la 97
Famille Brechet 226
Famille de Boel France 187
Famille Perrin 34–5, 127
Farge, Domaine Guy 289, 306, 309
Farge, Guy/Thomas 289
Faucon Doré, Domaine 177
Faure, Maison 307
Faure, Philippe 209, 210
Faurie, Bernard/Domaine Bernard 311,
        317–18
Faury, Domaine Lionel 269, 280, 287, 290
Faury, Lionel 24, 275, 290

Fayolle, Domaine JC & N 320–1
Fayolle, Laurent 326–7
Fayolle Fils & Fille, Domaine 326–7, 309
Félibrige 98
Fenouillet, Domaine de 138
Fer Servadou 30
Feraud, Domaine Eddie 97
Feraud, Laurence/Paul 89–90
Feraudy, Hugues de 137–8
Férigoule, Serge and Frédéri 132
Ferme des Arnaud 117, 118, 133
Ferme des Sept Lunes, La 290
Ferme du Mont, La 35, 97, 127, 152
Ferme Saint Martin, Domaine de la 138, 152
Ferrand, Domaine de 96
Ferrando, Isabel 46, 92–3
Ferraton, Jean Orëns/Michel/Samuel 318
Ferraton Père et Fils 34, 35
    Condrieu 276
    Cornas 306
    Crozes-Hermitage 329
    Hermitage 312, 318
    Saint-Joseph 294–5
Ferrotin, Domaine 182
Fesselet, Valentine 14
Fines Roches, Château de 38
flavescence dorée 19–20
Fleurieu, Jean-René de 240
Florane, Domaine la 14, 162, 164–6, 197
Foillard, Jean 229
Fond-Croze, Domaine 117, 118
Fondrèche, Domaine de 151, 198
Fonsalette, Château de 34, 52, 90–1, 123, 132,
    187, 353
Font Barrièle, Château 240
Font de Michelle, Domaine 96
Font du Loup, Château de la 97
Font du Papier, La 124
Font-Sane, Domaine 126
Fontaine des Fées, Domaine 140, 142
Fontaine du Clos, Domaine 133
Fontavin, Domaine de 127
Fontenille, Domaine de 155–6
Fontségugne, Château de 98, 100
Fortia, Château 72
Fourel, Lucie 324
Fourmone, Domaine la 133
Fraissinet, Monique/Domaine 230
François et Fils, Domaine 269
François I 287

Frey, Caroline 319
Frouin, Xavier 320

Gadagne 97–100, 336
Gaillard, Domaine Pierre 269, 272, 280, 291
Gaillard, Pierre 14, 270, 271–2, 277, 279, 291
Gallety, Domaine 214
Gallucci, Jean-Louis 150
Gamay 30, 38, 48
    Côte-Rôtie 258
    Diois 243
    Saint-Joseph 293
Gamay Noir 37
Gangloff, Domaine Yves 259, 280, 294
Gangloff, Pierre/Yves 259
Garancière, Domaine la 124
Garcin, Ralph 42, 77
Gard, IGP 64, 65
Gardine, Château de la 97
Garrigue, Domaine la 133
Garriguettes, Domaine des 98, 100
Gaspard, Bruno 85
Gasq, Gilles 196–7
Gasqui, Domaine de la 152
Gassier, Michel/Domaine Michel 239
Gatimel, Comte Henri de Régis de 221
Gaulle, Charles de 328
Gentaz, Marius 267, 295
Gentaz-Dervieux, Domaine 267, 295, 296
geography 3–5
geology 6–10
George IV 281
Georges-Lombrière, Domaine 97
Gérard, Domaine Xavier 259–60, 280, 287,
    294
Gérard, François 260
Gérard, Xavier 24, 259–60, 274, 275
Gigondan, Bruno 172
Gigondan, Domaine 171, 172, 174
Gigondas 110, 119–27
    acid adjustments 24
    ageing wines 335, 336, 338, 341, 342
    clones 21
    grape varieties 31, 39, 41
    négociants 35
    old-vine conservatory 21
    white wines 127
Gigondas La Cave 26
Gilles, Guillaume/Domaine Guillaume 302–3
Gimel, Philippe 13, 148, 152

Girasols, Domaine les 108
Giraud, Domaine 97
gobelets (bush vines) 20–1, 28
Gonnet, Guillaume 96
Gonon, Domaine 48, 288, 291–2, 296
Gonon, Jean 263, 266, 287, 291–2, 296
Gonon, Pierre Jr 291–2
Gonon, Pierre Sr 291
Good Year, A 155
Goubert, Domaine les 127, 141
Gourget, Domaine du 189
Gourt de Mautens, Domaine 47, 64, 106–7
Graciano 30
Gradassi, Domaine Jérôme 97
Graillot, Alain 156, 327
Graillot, Domaine Alain 323, 327
Graillot, Maxime 327
Gramenon, Domaine 19, 52, 161, 168, 169, 198
Gramiller, Domaine 108
Granaccia *see* Grenache
Grand Montmirail, Domaine du 127
Grand Veneur, Domaine 44, 96, 226
Grande Bellane, Domaine 170
Grands Bois, Domaine les 108, 193
Grands Chais de France, Les 248
grands crus 262–3
Grands Devers, Domaine des 170
Grange, Jacques 317
Grangeneuve, Domaine de 41, 178–9, 181
Grangeon, Baptiste 78
Granier, Jean-Marie 233
Grapillon d'Or, Domaine du 124
Gras, Benjamin 126
Gras, Yves 21, 126, 197
Gravennes, Domaine des 191
Gray, Terrence 315
Grenache (Grenache Noir) 27–9, 31–3, 35–7, 39, 46–7
  ageing 79, 335, 338, 342, 343
  Beaumes de Venise 136, 138
  blending 42
  bush vines vs trellising 20, 21, 28
  Cairanne 109, 111
  carbonic maceration 23
  Châteauneuf-du-Pape 73, 80, 82, 84–9, 91–4, 96
  climate change 12, 13
  clones 21
  Costières de Nîmes 236

Côtes du Vivarais 213, 214
Diois 244
Duché d'Uzès 217
Gadagne 99
Gigondas 121–6
Grignan-les-Adhémar 179, 181, 182
irrigation 14
Lirac 224, 225
Luberon 155
Massif d'Uchaux 186, 187
Nyons 174
Plan de Dieu 195, 197
Plant de Brunel 215
Puyméras 176, 177
Rasteau 101, 103, 106, 107, 108
Rayas, Château 353
Roaix 116
Rousset-les Vignes 172, 173
Saint-Andéol 210, 211, 212
Saint-Cécile 190, 193
Saint-Julien-en-Saint-Alban 330
Saint-Pantaléon-les Vignes 172
Séguret 143
Signargues 233
Suze-la-Rousse 190
Tavel 228, 231
Vacqueyras 131, 132
Valréas 168, 169, 170
Vinsobres 158, 160
Grenache Blanc 39–40, 41, 43, 46, 48
  Beaumes de Venise 136
  blending 42
  Cairanne 112
  Châteauneuf-du-Pape 73, 81, 87, 90–1, 96
  Costières de Nîmes 237
  Duché d'Uzès 217, 218
  Grignan-les-Adhémar 179
  Massif d'Uchaux 187
  Rayas, Château 353
  Saint-Maurice 164
  Séguret 145
  Vacqueyras 133
  Vaison-la-Romaine 118
Grenache Gris 46, 73
Grenache Noir *see* Grenache
Grignan-les-Adhémar 171, 178–82, 185, 337
  climate change 13
  Drôme, IGP 62
  grape varieties 29, 33, 41
  history 18

Gripa, Bernard 308
Gripa, Domaine Bernard 294, 308–9
Gripa, Fabrice 308–9
Grippat, Jean-Louis 58, 288, 296, 305, 311
Gros, Guillaume 154, 156
Gros Pata, Domaine 118
Grüner Veltliner 30
Guigal, E. 34, 40
    Condrieu 275, 280
    Cornas 304
    Côte-Rôtie 256, 260–1, 269
    Hermitage 321
    Saint-Andéol 211
    Saint-Joseph 295, 296
Guigal, Etienne/Marcel 260
Guigal, Philippe 260, 261
Guillaume-Corbin, Cédric 20, 158, 160–1
Guiot, Château 240
Guthmuller, Denis 19, 20, 25–6
guyot 28

Habrard, Domaine Laurent 294, 321, 327–8
Habrard, Laurent 322, 327–8
Haeni, Nicolas 145
Hall, Romain 134, 137
Hallereau, Cédric 11
Harding, Julia 40
Haute Valeur Environnementale (HVE)
    certification 181, 211, 248, 305, 328
Hautes Cances, Domaine les 113
Hauts Châssis, Domaine des 329
Helfenbein, Charles 330, 331, 332, 333
Helfenbein, Domaine 333
Henry IV 200
Hermitage 60, 309–21
    ageing wines 343, 344, 345, 346, 347, 348,
        349
    comparison with other appellations 253,
        256, 286, 297, 298
    destemming 22
    Drôme, IGP 62
    grape varieties 29, 31, 43, 44
    négociants 34
Hermite, Domaine de l' 315, 316
history
    Châteauneuf-du-Pape 69–73, 80
    geological 6–10
    winemaking 15–19
Houillon, Adeline/Aurélien/Emmanuel 177
Houillon, Domaine 176, 177

Houser, Yves Jean 111
Hue, Jérôme 187
Hugo, Victor, Les Misérables 287

Indication Géographique Protégée (IGP) 60–5
Innocent III, Pope 16
Institut National de l'Origine et de la Qualité
        (INAO)
    founding 72
    Gadagne 98
    Gigondas 120, 127
    Grignan-les-Adhémar 180
    Marselan 36
    Sablet 139
    Saint-Andéol 209–10
    Signargues 233
    syndicats 54
    Ventoux 148
irrigation 14
    climate change 13

Jaboulet, Antoine/Gérard/Paul 319
Jaboulet, Domaine P&V 329
Jaboulet Aîné, Paul 34, 348
    Crozes-Hermitage 323
    Hermitage 311, 317, 318–19
Jacouton, Domaine Jean-François 294
Jacquère 48
Jaillance 244, 248
Jamet, Catherine/Pascal 292
Jamet, Domaine 48, 52, 254, 261–2, 280
Jamet, Domaine Catherine & Pascal 48, 292
Jamet, Jean-Luc/Joseph/Loïc 262
Jamet, Jean-Paul 13, 22, 254–5, 261–3
Janasse, Domaine de la 87–8, 152
Jas, Domaine du 192
Jasmin, Robert/Domaine 263–4
Jaume, Alain 35, 295
Jaume, Pascal/Richard/Domaine 160
Jausset, Marie/Romain 86
Jean XXII, Pope 70
Jefferson, Thomas 188, 281, 310
Jefford, Andrew 235
Joanis, Château Val 156
John XXII, Pope 16
Jolie, Angelina 83
Jolivet, Domaine 294
Joly, Pierre 177
Joncier, Domaine du 33, 226
Jouffret, Roudil 232

Juge, Michel 295
Jullien, Thomas 138
Jurançon Noir 215
Juvenal, Château 152

Kerschen, Nancy 288
King, James 14, 148
King, Joanna 148
Kint, Jean T' 173
Knapp, Rafaël 190

Lafond, Pascal 231
Lafond Roc-Epine, Domaine 226, 228, 231
Lancelot, Jean-Luc 87
Larousse Encyclopaedia 230
Latour, Bernard 195, 196
Latour, Emilien/Julien 196
Lattard, Domaine 248
Laudun 26, 46, 199–202, 337
    comparison with other appellations 195,
        204, 205
Laudun Chusclan Vignerons 201
Laurent, Camille 325
Laurent, Maxime-François/Philippe 169
Le Roy de Boiseaumarié, Baron Pierre 18,
        72–3, 75, 120, 230, 287
Lemenicier, Jacques 309
Leperchois, Christian and Fabien 224
LePlan-Vermeersch 190
Levet, Agnès 21, 264, 266
Levet, Domaine 21, 264
Ligière, Domaine la 128, 130, 133, 139
Lignane, Château de 189
Lionnet, Domaine 306
Lirac 18, 26, 221–6, 227
    ageing wines 335–6, 337
    comparison with other appellations 130, 200
    grape varieties 33, 43, 44, 46
Lises, Domaine des 327
Livingstone-Learmonth, John 282, 295, 310
Loche, Louis Gambert de 320
Loftus, Simon 90, 351–4
Lombard, Christelle/Fabien 247
Lombard, Domaine 331, 332, 333
Lombard, Fabien 244, 245
Lombard, Jean-Marie 331, 333
Lombard, Pascal 272
Lombard, Sylvette/Maison 333
Longue Toque, Domaine de 133
Lorch, Wink 242

Lorient, Domaine de 307, 309
Louis XII 200
Louis XIII 281, 310
Louis XIV 16, 82
Lôyane, Domaine la 226
Luberon 26, 147, 152–6, 237, 337
    grape varieties 45
    Vaucluse, IGP 62, 64
Lucie, Domaine de 324
Luminaille, Domaine la 20, 32, 52, 103, 107

Maby, Domaine 225, 228
Maby, Richard 225
Macabeu 47
Machon, Domaine Gaylord 328–9
Machon, Gaylord 323, 328–9
Magni, Domaine Patrice 97
Magnouac, Sébastien 144, 146
Malbec 37
Malijay, Château 197
Malmont, Domaine 145
Manarine, Domaine la 196–7
Manissy, Château de 226, 232
Manzone, Bruno 236, 237
Manzone, Domaine 237, 238
maps
    Côtes-du-Rhône and Côtes-du-Rhône
        Villages 53
    Northern Rhône AOCs 59
    Other Rhône Valley appellations 51
    Rhône Valley 2
    Rhône Valley IGPs 63
    Southern Rhône AOCs 57
Maravilhas, Domaine des 202
Marcoux, Domaine de 76, 88, 106, 226
Marès, Cyril 235, 238, 239
Marès, Henri 239
Margan, Nathalie 155
Marrenon 26, 152, 154, 156
Marres, Damien 170
Marroquin *see* Cinsault
Marsanne 29, 43, 44, 48, 60
    Beaumes de Venise 136
    Brézème 331, 334
    Cairanne 112
    Crozes-Hermitage 324, 326, 327, 328, 329
    Duché d'Uzès 217
    Hermitage 313
    Massif d'Uchaux 187
    Rayas, Château 353

Saint-Joseph 253, 289, 292
Saint-Julien-en-Saint-Alban 330, 334
Saint-Maurice 164
Saint-Péray 307, 308
Marsanne, Domaine 294
Marselan 35–6
Martial 15, 310
Martin, Domaine 197
Martin, Paul Clair 17
Martinelle, Domaine 139, 152
Martinelles, Domaine des 329
Mas Carlot 235, 238, 239
Mas de Boislauzon 21, 96
Mas de Casalas, Le 187
Mas de Libian 211
Mas de Restanques 133
Mas de Sainte Croix 170
Mas des Bressades 239
Mas des Volques 217, 219
Mas du Notaire 240
Mas Isabelle 226
Mas Oncle Ernest 152
Mas Saint-Louis, Domaine 96
massal selection 21
Massart, Loïc 110, 113
Massif d'Uchaux 183–7, 232, 337
Mathieu, Domaine André 96
Maupas, Domaine de 248
Maurel, Vincent 78
Mayberry, Robert W. 203
Mazone, Domaine 240
McKinlay, Walter 146
mechanization 21
Méditerranée, IGP 61
Meffre, Gabriel 35, 127, 133
Melody, Domaine 322, 329
Mengin, Yves 331, 333–4
Merlin, Domaine François 269
Merlot 27, 48, 292
Meunier, Jean Baptiste 124–5
Michel, Domaine Johann 303
Michel, Eric 186
Michel, François 95
Michel, Johann 295, 303
Michel, Joseph 299
Michel, Robert 295, 299, 303
Michelas St Jemms, Domaine 329
Miquettes, Domaine des 294
Miraval 83
mistral 12, 233

Mistral, Frédéric 98
mites 36, 43
Moine, Lucien Le 93
Molénat, Franck 58, 115
Molinié-Boyer, Fanny 235, 240
Molinié-Boyer, François 240
Monardière, Domaine la 130, 131
Monastrell see Mourvèdre
Mondeuse 30
Mondeuse Blanche 29
Monge, Franck 244
Monge Granon, Cave 244, 247
Monier, Domaine 292–3
Monier, Domaine Gabriel 192
Monier, Jean-Pierre 292
Monier-Perréol, Domaine 292–3
Mont-Redon, Château 112, 144, 226
Mont-Thabor, Château 97
Montagnon, Julien 332
Monteillet, Claudy/Jean-Luc/Mélina 181
Monteillet, Domaine de 48, 181, 264–5, 280, 287, 294
Montez, Stéphane 181, 264–5
Montfaucon, Château de 223, 224, 225–6
Montfrin, Château de 240
Montine, Domaine de 161, 181
Montirius, Domaine 133
MontPlaisir, Château 161
Montvac, Domaine de 126, 133
Montvin, Aliot de 150
Mordorée, Domaine de la 97, 226, 231–2
More, Pierre-Michel 174
moths 32
Moulin, Domaine du 161
Moulin de la Gardette 124–5
Moulin la Viguerie, Domaine 230, 232
Moun Pantaï, Domaine 193
Mourchon, Domaine de 144, 146
Mourgues du Grès, Château 65, 240
Mourre du Tendre, Château du 23
Mourvèdre 21, 31, 32–3, 197, 335
  Beaumes de Venise 136
  Cairanne 109, 112
  Châteauneuf-du-Pape 73, 80, 82, 84–9, 92–3, 96
  Diois 244
  Gigondas 121, 123, 125, 126
  Grignan-les-Adhémar 179
  Laudun 202
  Lirac 225

Massif d'Uchaux 186
Nyons 174
Plan de Dieu 195
Rasteau 103, 106, 107
Roaix 116
Rousset-les Vignes 172
Sablet 140
Saint-Andéol 210
Saint-Gervais 208
Saint-Pantaléon-les Vignes 172
Séguret 143
Signargues 233
Tavel 231
Vacqueyras 131
Valréas 168
Vinsobres 160
Mouton, Domaine 280
Mur-mur-ium, Domaine 152
Muscardin 37, 87, 197
Muscat 134, 136, 137, 247, 248
Muscat à Petits Grains 241, 242
Muscat à Petits Grains Blancs 36, 40, 134
Muscat à Petits Grains Noirs 36–7, 40, 134
Muscat de Beaumes de Venise 36, 40, 103,
    133–9, 336
mutage 104, 105, 134

Nacker & Fils 310
Nages, Château des 239
Nalys, Château de 97, 260
Named Villages 54–5, 58
Nativelle, Yves 137
Natura, Domaine 220
natural wine
    appellation system 66
    Ardèche, IGP 62
    Cairanne 112
    Cornas 302
    Côte-Rôtie 267–8
    Crozes-Hermitage 326
    Massif d'Uchaux 187
    Puyméras 176, 177
    Saint-Joseph 290, 293
    Saint-Maurice 163, 164
    Saint-Péray 309
    Signargues 234
    Tavel 229
Nebbiolo 40, 122
négociants 34–5
Négrette 30

Negron, Didier 92
Nerthe, Château la 42, 70–1, 77, 88–9, 144,
    187
Nicholas I, Tsar 310
Nicolas (wine merchant) 310
Niero, Domaine Rémi 275, 277–8
Niero, Rémi 272, 276, 277–8
Niero, Robert 277
Nodin, Domaine Rémy 309
Notre Dame de Cousignac, Domaine de 212,
    213, 214–15
Nyons 174–5

Ogier, Domaine Stéphane 34, 65
    Châteauneuf-du-Pape 97
    Condrieu 280
    Côte-Rôtie 265–6
    Côtes du Vivarais 215
    Gigondas 127
    Lirac 226
    Saint-Joseph 294
    Seyssuel 272
Ogier, Michel 265
Ogier, Stéphane 265–6, 270
Olivier, Nicolas 220
Olivier, Vincent 231
Ondines, Domaine les 133
Or de Line, Domaine l' 48, 97
Or et de Gueules, Château d' 240
Oratoire St Martin, Domaine 112
organic viticulture 18–20
    Ardèche, IGP 62
    Beaumes de Venise 138
    Brézème 334
    Cairanne 111, 112
    Château-Grillet 283
    Châteauneuf-du-Pape 20, 75, 82, 85, 87,
        89, 93, 95
    Chusclan 205
    Clairette de Bellegarde 238
    Condrieu 277, 278, 279, 280
    Cornas 300, 303, 305
    Costières de Nîmes 235, 239, 240
    Côte-Rôtie 255–6, 257, 258, 267, 268
    Côtes du Vivarais 214
    Crozes-Hermitage 324, 325, 328, 329
    Diois 244, 246, 247
    Duché d'Uzès 217, 220
    Gadagne 100
    Gigondas 123–4, 126

Grignan-les-Adhémar 181
Hermitage 316, 317, 318, 319, 320
Laudun 201
Lirac 224
Luberon 155, 156
Massif d'Uchaux 185, 186
Muscat de Beaumes de Venise 138
négociants 34
Plan de Dieu 195, 197
Puyméras 176–7
Rasteau 106, 107
Rochegude 189
Rousset-les-Vignes 173
Sablet 140, 142
Saint-Andéol 211, 212
Saint-Cécile 193
Saint-Joseph 291, 292, 293
Saint-Julien-en-Saint-Alban 334
Saint-Maurice 163
Séguret 144, 145
Signargues 234
Suze-la-Rousse 191, 192
Tavel 231
Vacqueyras 131, 132
Valréas 169, 170
Ventoux 151, 152
Vinsobres 159, 160
Visan 165, 167
Organisation Internationale de la Vigne et du
      Vin (OIV) 72
Ortas Cave de Rasteau 108
Orviel, Domaine de l' 220
Other Rhône Valley appellations 50–2
Ouréa, Domaine d' 126, 133
Overnoy, Pierre 177, 229

Paillère & Pied-Gû, Domaine 141
Pallières, Domaine les 127
Paolucci, Julie 20, 103, 107
Paris, Domaine Vincent 294, 303–4
Paris, Vincent 303–4
Parker, Robert 78, 261, 307, 310
Pays des Bouches du Rhône, IGP 65
Pégau, Château 89
Pégau, Domaine du 89–90
Pélaquié, Domaine 199, 202, 223, 232
Pélaquié, Luc 199, 201, 202, 228
Pellaton, Philippe 201
Péquélette, Domaine la 20, 42, 158, 160–1
Pergaud, Domaine de 334

Perréol, Domaine 292–3
Perréol, Philippe 292
Perret, André 278
Perret, Domaine André 278, 294
Perrin, Cécile/César/Jacques/Jean-Pierre/Marc/
      Matthieu/Pierre/Thomas 82
Perrin, Domaine Roger 48, 97
Perrin, François 38, 79, 80, 81
Perrin, Nicolas 34
Perrin family 82, 159
Perrot, Georges 106
Persan 48
Pesquié, Château 11, 151–2, 198
Petit, Gaël 232
Petite Verdière, La 192
Peuchet, Jacques 200
Peylong, Domaine 244, 247
Pfifferling, Eric 23–4, 229, 232
phylloxera 17–18, 42
      Brézème 331
      Châteauneuf-du-Pape 70–1, 82, 89
      Condrieu 274, 280
      Cornas 296
      Côte-Rôtie 252
      Diois 243
      Grignan-les-Adhémar 180
      Hermitage 311, 315
      Lirac 221
      Saint-Andéol 209
      Saint-Joseph 315
      Seyssuel 270
      Tavel 227
      Vacqueyras 128
Piaugier, Domaine de 36, 142
Picardan 48, 81, 87
Pichon, Domaine Christophe 280, 294
Picpoul 87
Picpoul Noir 87
Piéblanc, Domaine de 152
Pieds-Noirs 18, 179, 222
Piegeade, Domaine de la 133
Pierre-Laine, Domaine la 212
Pierres Sèches, Domaine des 294
Pigeade, Domaine de 139
Pinault, François 281
Pinchon, Jean 277
Pineau d'Aunis 30
Pinot Noir 37, 38, 43
      Châteauneuf-du-Pape 70
      Diois 243

and Grenache, kinship between 93
    rotundone 30
Pins, Rodolphe des 224, 225
Pique-Basse, Domaine 108, 116
Piquepoul Blanc 37–8, 46–7, 48, 111
Piquepoul Gris 37, 47–8, 111
Piquepoul Noir 21, 37–8, 106, 111
Pitt, Brad 83
Plan de Dieu 55, 193–7, 232
    climate change 148, 195
    comparison with other appellations 110,
        185, 337
Plant de Brunel 215
Plantevin, Domaine Philippe 193
Plantevin, Maison 116
Pliny the Elder 16, 134, 243, 252, 310
Plumet, Eric 183, 185, 186
Pommier, Rafaël 214–15
popes 16, 69–70, 80, 98, 227
Porte Rouge, Domaine 97
Portes, Jean-Claude 70
Pouchoulin family 331
Pouizin family 85, 170
Poulet, Emmanuel 248
Poulet & Fils, Cave 247–8
Pourquier, Alain/Lionel 219
Pourra, Domaine du 127
Pouzin, Rémi 166
powdery mildew 239
    grape varieties 32, 36, 37, 41, 43, 45, 215
premiers crus 262–3
Prieuré de Montézargues 232
Probus, emperor 15
Prunelard 30
Puy de Maupas, Domaine le 177
Puyméras 14, 171, 172, 175–7, 337
Puzelat, Thierry 229

Quatre Cerises, Domaine des 331, 333–4

Rabusas, Domaine de 202, 206
Raoux, Domaine Jocelyn 226
Raspail-Ay, Domaine 125
Raspail et Fils, Jean-Claude 248
Rasteau 58, 64, 101–8, 197, 336
    comparison with other appellations 109,
        110, 113–15
    grape varieties 29, 31, 32, 46
    Vaucluse, IGP 64
    Vin Doux Naturel (VDN) 46, 101–7, 134

Rayas, Château 90–1, 132, 133, 187, 351–4
Redortier, Château 139
Réméjeanne, Domaine la 52
Renard, Domaine le 113, 197
Renjarde, Domaine de la 187
Renouard, Domaine 240
Reynaud, Albert/Bertrand 90
Reynaud, David 323, 329
Reynaud, Domaine 220
Reynaud, Emmanuel 90–1, 132, 187
Reynaud, Jacques 90, 132, 351, 352–4
Reynaud, Louis 90, 132, 351–2
Reynaud, Marceline 329
Ribo, François 325–6
Ricard, Guy 129, 130–1
Ricard, Jean 131, 132
Ricard, Pierre 131
Richard family 89, 187
Richaud, Domaine 109, 112–13
Richaud, Marcel 109, 112–13, 115
Riesling 30
Roaix 58, 113–16, 336
Robert, Laurent 103, 197
Robert, Stéphane 304–5
Robin, Domaine Gilles 329
Robinson, Jancis 10, 40
Rocalière, Domaine la 232
Rocca Maura 26, 202, 226
Roche, Domaine 110, 113
Roche, Romain 110
Roche-Audran, Domaine 117–18, 167
Roche Buissière, La 177
Rochecolombe, Château 212
Rochegude 14, 183, 185, 188–9, 337
Roches Fortes, Domaine des 118
Rochette, Vincent 117–18
Rolet, Danielle/Nicole/Xavier 150
Rolle see Vermentino
Romak, Mark 322
Romance, Domaine la 204, 205
Romaneaux-Destezet, Domaine 48, 293
Romanée Conti, Domaine de la 230
Romans 15–16
    Châteauneuf-du-Pape 69
    Chusclan 204
    Condrieu 274
    Cornas 296
    Côte-Rôtie 252
    Duché d'Uzès 216
    Gigondas 119–20, 125

Hermitage 310
Laudun 200
Luberon 153
Saint-Péray 306
Romarins, Domaine des 233, 234
Roméro, André 106, 107
Roméro, Frédéric 107
Roquevignan, Domaine de 189
Roseau, Benoît 293, 309
Roseau, Domaine Benoît 269, 280, 293
Rosiers, Domaine de 269
Rostaing, Domaine 254, 266–7, 275, 280, 295
Rostaing, Pierre 267
Rostaing, René 254, 263, 266–7, 295
rotundone 30
Rouanne, Château de 126, 159, 161
Roubine, Domaine la 127
Roucas Toumba 130, 131–2
Rouchier, Domaine 294
Rouette, Domaine de la 234
Rouge Bleu, Domaine 192, 193
Rougeot, Magali/Nicolas 189
Roussanne 29, 43–4, 46, 48, 60
    Beaumes de Venise 136
    Brézème 331, 334
    Cairanne 112
    Châteauneuf-du-Pape 73–4, 81–2, 87,
        89–90, 95–6
    Costières de Nîmes 237
    Crozes-Hermitage 326, 327, 328, 329
    Duché d'Uzès 217
    Gigondas 127
    Hermitage 313
    Saint-Joseph 253, 289, 292, 293
    Saint-Julien-en-Saint-Alban 330, 334
    Saint-Maurice 164
    Saint-Péray 307, 308
Rousset, Domaine 322, 329
Rousset-les-Vignes 58, 171–4, 337
Rousset-Rouard, Yves 155
Ruth, Château de 193

Sablayrolles, Frédéric 207
Sablet 36, 103, 119, 139–42, 336
Sabon, Aimé/Christophe/Isabelle 87
Sabon, Céline/David/Marie 86
Sabon, Denis/Gilbert/Jean-Jacques/Noël/
    Roger 92
Sabon, Domaine Roger 92, 226
Sabon, Joseph/Séraphin 86, 92

Sabon, Thierry 73, 86
Saint, Edmée Bernard Le 72
Saint Amant, Domaine 138–9
Saint-Andéol 64, 209–12, 337
Saint-Andéol, Domaine 113
Saint-Apollinaire, Domaine 177
Saint-Cécile 185, 188, 190, 192–3
Saint-Cosme 35, 269
Saint-Cosme, Château de 21–2, 24, 35, 120,
    124–7, 159
Saint-Désirat, Cave 292
Saint-Estève d'Uchaux, Château 187
Saint Firmin, Domaine 220
Saint Gayan, Domaine 127, 142
Saint-Gervais 58, 206–8, 337
Saint Jean du Barroux 13, 148, 152, 198
Saint-Joseph 60, 261, 263, 285–8
    ageing wines 344
    carbonic maceration 24
    climate change 13
    comparison with other appellations 253,
        262, 271, 274, 298, 299, 307, 321
    grape varieties 29
    key producers 288–95, 316
Saint-Julien-en-Saint-Alban 330, 332–4, 344
Saint-Maurice 58, 157, 161–4, 337
Saint-Pantaléon-les-Vignes 26, 171–4, 337
Saint-Pantaléon-les-Vignes, Cave 171, 174
Saint-Péray 44, 60, 306–9, 344
Saint-Pierre, Domaine 133
Saint-Préfert, Domaine 46, 92–3
Saint-Roch, Château 223, 226
Saint Siffrein, Domaine de 97
Sainte-Anne, Domaine 207, 208
Sainte-Cécile 26, 109, 337
Saladin, Domaine 19, 23, 210, 212
Saladin, Elisabeth 23, 211, 212
Saladin, Henri/Marie-Laurence 211, 212
Salel & Renaud, Domaine 62
Sang des Cailloux, Domaine le 130, 132
Santa Duc, Domaine 20, 21, 42, 126, 197
Saouma, Mounir 93
Saouma, Rotem 93–4
Saouma, Rotem & Mounir 93–4
Sarbèche, Domaine de la 309
Sauzon, M. 287
Schioppettino 30
Ségriès, Château de 221, 226, 232
Séguret 119, 142–6, 336
Semelles du Vent, Domaine les 127

Séminaire, Domaine du 170
Sénéchaux, Domaine des 97
Serine
    Brézème 334
    Côte-Rôtie 21, 253, 258–9, 264, 266, 268
    Crozes-Hermitage 325
    Saint-Julien-en-Saint-Alban 334
Serre, M. 92
Serre des Vignes, Domaine du 182, 198
Serres, Olivier de 33, 200, 270
Seyssuel 269–72, 291, 332, 344
Shiraz *see* Syrah
Short, Graham 148
Sibu, Domaine les 127, 141
Signac, Château 204, 206
Signargues 26, 29, 232–4, 337
Simian, Château 187
Sinnae, Maison 26, 201, 202, 206
soils 5, 56, 203
Solitude, Domaine de la 17, 70, 96
Sollier, Domaine le 34, 65, 198, 220
Sorrel, Domaine Marc 319–20, 329
Sorrel, Guillaume 319, 320
Sorrel, Marc 319
Souchon, Nicolas 217–18, 219
Souhaut, Hervé 293
Soumade, Domaine la 107–8, 127
Stehelin, Bertrand 141
Stehelin, Domaine Bertrand 127, 141
Steinmaier, Anne/Guy 208
Steinmaier, Jean 207, 208
Stéphan, Jean-Michel 24, 268
Stéphan, Maison 267–8
Stéphan, Romain 268
Stérimberg, Henri Gaspard de 16, 310
Sud-Est Vin Bio 19
Supparo, Isabelle 187
Suze-la-Rousse 185, 188, 189–92, 337
Swan, Malcolm 150
syndicats 54–5
    Châteauneuf-du-Pape 72–3, 75
    Condrieu 274
    Costières de Nîmes 235
    Côte-Rôtie 267
    Diois 247
    Gadagne 97, 99
    Gigondas 122, 126, 127
    Sablet 139
    Saint-Andéol 209
    Saint-Gervais 207

Signargues 233
Tavel 230
Valréas 167
Syrah 27–32, 34, 38, 40, 43, 48, 60, 197–8,
    275
    ageing wines 335, 343
    Beaumes de Venise 136, 138
    Brézème 331, 333, 334
    Cairanne 109, 111
    Châteauneuf-du-Pape 70, 73, 80, 82, 86–89,
        91–2
    Cornas 296, 303
    Costières de Nîmes 236, 240
    Côte-Rôtie 252–5, 258, 260–1, 265, 267–8
    Côtes du Vivarais 213, 214
    Crozes-Hermitage 323, 325, 326, 328, 329
    Diois 243
    Duché d'Uzès 217, 220
    Gigondas 123, 124, 125
    Grignan-les-Adhémar 179, 180, 181
    Hermitage 311, 313, 316, 318
    irrigation 14
    Laudun 202
    Lirac 224, 225
    Luberon 155
    Massif d'Uchaux 186, 187
    mistral 12
    Nyons 174
    Puyméras 176, 177
    Rasteau 103, 106, 107
    Rayas, Château 353
    Roaix 116
    rotundone 30
    Rousset-les Vignes 172, 173
    Saint-Andéol 210, 211
    Saint-Cécile 193
    Saint-Joseph 286, 288, 289, 291, 292, 293
    Saint-Julien-en-Saint-Alban 330, 334
    Saint-Maurice 162
    Saint-Pantaléon-les Vignes 172
    Séguret 143
    Seyssuel 270, 272
    Signargues 233
    synonyms and sub-types 266
    Tavel 231
    Vacqueyras 131
    Valréas 168, 169, 170
    Ventoux 148
    Vinsobres 158, 160
Syrah decline 31, 197

Tain, Cave de 26
  Crozes-Hermitage 323, 329–30
  Hermitage 311, 313, 320
  Saint-Joseph 295
  Saint-Péray 309
Tardieu, Bastien/Michel 304
Tardieu-Laurent 35
  Condrieu 280
  Cornas 304, 306
  Hermitage 321
  Seyssuel 269
Tardieu-Vitelli, Valentine 156
tartaric acid 24
Tavel 226–9
  ageing wines 336, 337
  carbonic maceration 23–4
  climate change 12
  comparison with other appellations 223, 245
  grape varieties 33, 38–9, 41, 44, 46–7
  history 18
  key producers 229, 231–2
Tempier, Domaine 32
Tempranillo 13
Terme, Domaine du 127
Terra Vitis certification 208
Terrasses d'Eole, Les 152
TerraVentoux 152
Terre des Amoureuses 62
Terre des Chardrons 238, 240
Terret Noir 21, 38, 87
Terriers, Domaine les 215
Texier, Eric 334
Thébaïde, Château la 142
Thibot family 211
Tix, Domaine du 152
Tolleret, Philippe 154
Tours, Château des 64, 90, 132–3
Tours, Domaine des 52, 64
Tramier, Pierre 82
Tramier, Vincent 167
Trapadis, Domaine 108
Trebbiano Toscano see Ugni Blanc
trellising 13, 20–1, 28, 40
Trinquevedel, Château de 232
Trollat, Raymond 291–2, 296
Truc, Georges 6–10, 25, 26, 28, 165
Truel, Paul 35, 37
Tulle de Villefranche family 70, 71, 89
Tunnel, Domaine du 294, 304–5, 309

Ugni Blanc 44–5, 46, 47, 145
Unang, Château 14, 148, 152
Usseglio, Domaine Pierre 97, 226
Usseglio, Domaine Raymond 44, 96
Uzès, Dukes of 216–17

Vaccarèse 38, 73, 87, 92, 106
Vache, Christian 131–2
Vache, Damien/Martine 131
Vacheron, Jean-Dennis/Sylvie 85
Vacqueyras 43, 44, 128–33, 223, 336
Vaison-la-Romaine 116–18, 336
Val des Rois, Domaine du 168, 170
Vallet, Domaine 294
Vallot, Anaïs/François 161
Vallot – Le Coriançon, Domaine 52, 159, 161
Valréas 164, 165, 167–70, 337
Vaucluse, IGP 62–3
Vaudieu, Château de 22, 40, 48, 97
Ventoux 119, 147–52
  ageing wines 335–6, 337, 338
  climate change 13, 14
  comparison with other appellations 153,
    154, 217, 237
  grape varieties 30, 45, 46
  Vaucluse, IGP 62, 64
Verde, Domaine de la 133
Vedeau, Stéphane 169
Verdie 247
Vermeersch, Ann/Dirk 190
Vermentino 45, 154, 217, 237
Vernay, Christine 256, 262–3, 275, 279
Vernay, Domaine Georges 65, 255–6, 269,
    275, 278–9, 282, 294
Vernay, François 278
Vernay, Georges 41, 269, 274, 278–9, 290
Verquière, Domaine de 108, 140, 142
Verrerie, Château la 153, 156
Verrière, Domaine de la 150
Verset, Alain 295
Verset, Domaine Alain 306
Verset, Noël 295, 300
Vespolina 30
Vessière, Château 240
Viaud, Jean-Claude 227
Vidal, Audrey/Jean-Claude 80–1
Vidal-Fleury 260
Vieille Julienne, Domaine de la 42, 79, 94–5
Vieux Donjon, Le 76, 77, 95

Vieux Télégraphe, Domaine du 79, 95–6
Vigier, Domaine 215
Vigne des Pères, La 294
Vignerons Ardéchois 213
Vignerons Créateurs 26, 238
Vignerons d'Estézargues, Les 26, 233, 234
Vignerons de Roaix Séguret, Les 58, 144
Vignerons de Valléon, Les 26, 174
Vignerons des 4 Chemins, Les 26, 201, 202, 206
Vignes de l'Arque, Les 220
Vignoble Alain Ignace 133, 139
Vignoble Art Mas 167
Vignobles Assemat 226
Vignobles Chirat 269
Vignobles de Seyssuel, Les 272
Vignobles Mayard 96
Vignobles Verzier 269
Villa, Domaine Pierre-Jean 255, 268, 272, 280, 294, 329
Villa, Pierre-Jean 13, 263, 266, 268, 270–1, 275–6
Villa Safranier 108
Villard, François 35, 270–2, 277, 279–80, 291, 309
Ville Rouge, Domaine de la 11
Villeneuve, Domaine de 96
Vin de France 66
Vin de Pays see Indication Géographique Protégée
Vin Doux Naturel (VDN) 103, 134
  Rasteau 46, 101–7, 134
Vincenti, Sébastien 151
Vindemio 152
Vins de Vienne, Les 34, 268–9, 271, 277, 279
Vinsobraise, La 26, 161
Vinsobres 157–61
  ageing wines 337
  climate change 14
  comparison with other appellations 110, 163, 165

cooperatives 26
Drôme, IGP 62
grape varieties 29
vintage guide 335–6
  Northern Rhône 344–9
  Southern Rhône 338–43
Vintur, Domaine 148, 152
Viognier 29, 40–1, 44, 48, 60
  Beaumes de Venise 136, 139
  Brézème 331
  bush vines vs trellising 21
  Château-Grillet 281
  Condrieu 272, 275, 276
  Costières de Nîmes 237
  Côte-Rôtie 253–4, 258, 265, 267–8
  Duché d'Uzès 217, 218
  Gadagne 99
  Gigondas 127
  Grignan-les-Adhémar 179, 180, 181
  mistral 12
  Saint-Gervais 208
  Saint-Joseph 293
  Saint-Julien-en-Saint-Alban 330
  Saint-Maurice 164
  Séguret 145
  Seyssuel 270, 272
Viret, Alain/Philippe 163–4
Viret, Domaine 162, 163–4
Visan 14, 157, 162, 164–7, 337
Visan, Cave de 26
Vistre, Domaine du 240
Voeux, Christian 143, 144–5
Voge, Alain/Louis 305
Voge, Domaine Alain 52, 294, 305, 309
Vouillamoz, José 40, 44

Wallut, Jacques 139
west bank finesse 203–4
whole bunches vs destemming 22–3
Wilfried, Domaine 108